MANNERHEIM

MANNERHEIM
THE FINNISH YEARS

by
J.E.O. SCREEN

HURST & COMPANY, LONDON

First published in the United Kingdom in 2000 by
C. Hurst & Co. (Publishers) Ltd.,
41 Great Russell Street, London, WC1B 3PL

This revised paperback edition published 2014.

© J. E. O. Screen, 2014
All rights reserved.
Printed in India

Distributed in the United States, Canada and Latin America by
Oxford University Press, 198 Madison Avenue, New York, NY 10016,
United States of America.

The right of J. E. O. Screen to be identified as the author of this publication is asserted by him in accordance with the Copyright, Designs and Patents Act, 1988.

ISBN 9781849043625

A Cataloguing-in-Publication data record for this book
is available from the British Library.

www.hurstpublishers.com

This book is printed on paper from registered sustainable
and managed sources.

CONTENTS

PREFACE AND ACKNOWLEDGEMENTS *page* ix
PREFACE TO THE SECOND EDITION xii

CHAPTERS

I. THE WHITE GENERAL 1

Finland in 1917 – Mannerheim's career in Russia – From 'exile' to command – From planning to action – War begins – Organizing an army – Mannerheim's strategy and German intervention – Towards victory – Triumph – Resignation

II. REGENT 43

In Sweden – From unofficial diplomat to regent – Military and foreign policy problems – Elections and a new government – The constitution – Intervention in Russia? – Stylish regent but rejected presidential candidate – Departure abroad

III. CIVILIAN 74

Advocate of intervention – Private life – Travel – Humanitarian work – Passed over for public service

IV. CHAIRMAN OF THE DEFENCE COUNCIL 104

Lapua and Mäntsälä – Work in the Defence Council – Seventieth birthday celebrations – The language problem – Foreign relations – Resignation? – Negotiations with the Soviet Union continued – From resignation to commander-in-chief

V. THE WINTER WAR 137

At war – War or peace? – The exercise of supreme command

VI. THE 'ARMISTICE' 160

Peacetime commander-in-chief – In the 'War Cabinet' – Finland and German plans – Towards war

CONTENTS

VII. THE CONTINUATION WAR 177
Successful Finnish offensives but no German victory – Wartime GHQ – Health – Attempts to leave the war – Near disaster

VIII. PRESIDENT 206
President for peace – Under the Control Commission – Power slips away – Health deteriorates – The war responsibility case – Resignation

IX. TESTAMENT 240
Retirement – The Memoirs – Death – The man – The legacy

BIBLIOGRAPHY 268

INDEX 278

ILLUSTRATIONS

between pages 40 and 41

1. Mannerheim during the Civil War on a tour of inspection in Karelia, April 1918
2. Mannerheim towards the end of the Civil War
3. At the victory parade in Helsinki, 16 May 1918, to mark the end of the war
4. Mannerheim in Helsinki, 16 May 1918
5. Mannerheim in 1919
6. Arrival in Stockholm on a state visit, February 1919
7. K.J. Ståhlberg
8. P.E. Svinhufvud

between pages 134 and 135

9 & 10. Mannerheim's seventieth birthday celebrations, 4 June 1937
11. Kyösti Kallio
12. Juho Niukkanen
13. Väinö Tanner
14. Risto Ryti
15. Erik Heinrichs
16. Rudolf Walden
17. At General Headquarters during the Winter War

between pages 188 and 189

18. The Continuation War: group at Lipola on the Karelian isthmus, 8 October 1943
19. Seventy-fifth birthday celebrations, 4 June 1942
20. Adolf Hitler as a self-invited guest at Mannerheim's seventy-fifth birthday
21. Mannerheim on a tour of inspection in Eastern Karelia, summer 1943

ILLUSTRATIONS

between pages 224 and 225

22. As President, speaking at the opening of parliament, 7 April 1945
23. As President, attending the installation of Archbishop Aleksi Lehtonen in Turku Cathedral, 10 June 1945
24. J.K. Paasikivi

between pages 254 and 255

25. At Montreux, Switzerland, towards the end of his life
26. The funeral, 4 February 1951
27. Mannerheim's death mask
28. Autograph letter from Mannerheim to an official at the British Foreign Office, 1936

MAPS

The Civil War in Finland, 1918	15
The Winter War	142
The Continuation War	180
The Soviet offensives, June 1944	202

PREFACE AND ACKNOWLEDGEMENTS

The life of Baron Gustaf Mannerheim (1867–1951) fell into two distinct parts. The first comprised his service as an officer in the imperial Russian army, a not unusual career for a nineteenth-century Finnish nobleman: it was ended by the Russian Revolution. The second comprised his service in Finland, beginning in 1918 as commander-in-chief of the White Army and ending as president of the republic in 1944–6. My book *Mannerheim: the Years of Preparation*, published in 1970, covered his life up to the end of 1917. I abandoned my intention to continue immediately with a work on the second part of his life. This was partly because of the unavailability of archive material and the consequent lack of scholarly studies on Finnish history between 1918 and Mannerheim's death. The passage of time has remedied these drawbacks and my retirement has afforded me the opportunity to return to the study of Mannerheim. The result is this book, *Mannerheim: the Finnish Years*.

Mannerheim has been the subject of hundreds of books and articles. Why should there be another book about him, and what can it possibly add to existing works? The latter question must be asked particularly in relation to the two-volume biography by General Erik Heinrichs, who was Mannerheim's closest colleague for much of the period of the Second World War, the eight volumes by Professor Stig Jägerskiöld, with their rich documentation, and the single volume by Veijo Meri with its perceptive grasp of Mannerheim's character. If my book lacks the personal knowledge and military experience of Heinrichs, the pious and extensive detail of Jägerskiöld and the human insight of Meri, perhaps it has a more solid basis in historical scholarship as well as some differences in interpretation. I emphasize Mannerheim's anti-Bolshevism and anti-socialism, and suggest they delayed for longer than is normally acknowledged his readiness for reconciliation with his defeated enemies from 1918. I also stress his role in drawing Finland into Germany's aggressive war against the Soviet Union in 1941. But I believe that Mannerheim's failings, even as commander-in-chief, can be acknowledged without detracting from his essential greatness. I hope that this book will convey

PREFACE AND ACKNOWLEDGEMENTS

to the reader the fascination I have long felt for Mannerheim's achievements and his character.

The English translation of Mannerheim's *Memoirs* is an abridgement, so I have at times quoted from the Swedish-language original. Where Mannerheim's correspondence has been published I have referred to the published sources; in other cases references are to the relevant archival collections. There is an emphasis in the book on archival sources and scholarly monographs from Finland and Britain. However, Finnish and British monographs not only reflect the study of Finnish and British archival sources but also Swedish and German and, to a lesser extent, French and Russian (Soviet) archival sources. Jägerskiöld's biography is invaluable for its quotations from numerous manuscript sources. Translations are my own unless otherwise stated.

I am indebted to the Mannerheim Foundation and the National Archives of Finland for permission to use all parts of the Mannerheim Archive, including the Grensholm Collection. It is a pleasure to record my thanks to the staff of the National Archives of Finland, and in particular Mr Jussi Kuusanmäki, for their assistance. The Library of the School of Slavonic and East European Studies has been an invaluable resource in London, and its staff – my former colleagues – have been most kind. Mr Markku Palokangas and Mr Lauri Honkala of the Military Museum of Finland helped greatly over the illustrations.

I wish to thank the Mannerheim Foundation for granting me permission to quote from Mannerheim's letters and his *Memoirs*. Crown Copyright is reproduced with the permission of the Controller of Her Majesty's Stationery Office. Extracts from the Churchill Papers are quoted by kind permission of The Master, Fellows and Scholars of Churchill College in the University of Cambridge. Baroness Isa Gripenberg kindly gave me permission to see the papers of Bertel Gripenberg at Åbo Akademi Library and talked to me about his friendship with Mannerheim.

For comments on the manuscript I am grateful to my wife Leena Screen, my daughter Dr Elina Screen, Professor David Kirby and Mr T. H. Bowyer. Dr Ruth Greenham provided valuable advice about Mannerheim's medical history. The publishers, C. Hurst & Co., have waited patiently for this book – a gap of thirty years between two volumes of a single biography must be exceptional.

PREFACE AND ACKNOWLEDGEMENTS

The picture acknowledgements are as follows: Military Museum of Finland, 1–6, 9–10, 21–3, 25–7; Ministry of Foreign Affairs, Helsinki, 7–8, 11–16, 24; Finnish Defence Forces Photographic Centre (SA-Kuva), 18–20; Hulton Getty Picture Collection, 17; Public Record Office, 28.

London J. E. O. SCREEN
November 1999

PREFACE TO THE SECOND EDITION

After the publication of *Mannerheim: The Finnish Years* in 2000, Dr J. E. O. Screen continued to follow scholarship in Mannerheim actively, though his research now concentrated on the eighteenth-century Finnish army. He annotated his own copy of *The Finnish Years* with details of minor typographical and other corrections, as well as noting works by Jussi Kuusanmäki and Markku Jokisipilä that offered new perspectives on Mannerheim's divorce and the Ryti-Ribbentrop agreement respectively. My father died suddenly on 24 September 2009. He was keenly aware that research always moves on, and had he lived, he would doubtless have integrated aspects of subsequent scholarship into this paperback edition. In the circumstances, his text is unaltered, but we are very grateful to Hurst & Co. for the opportunity to incorporate his minor amendments in this corrected paperback edition.

Berkhamsted ELINA SCREEN
September 2013

CHAPTER I

THE WHITE GENERAL

'At the head of Finland's young, victorious army I stand here today and greet in its name the government which has gone through such chequered fortunes ...'[1]

FINLAND IN 1917

The Russian Revolutions of 1917, which ended the successful career in the imperial army of Lieutenant-General Baron Gustaf Mannerheim, did not leave Finland unscathed. Part of the Russian Empire since 1809, Finland had suffered since the end of the nineteenth century from Russian attempts to diminish its autonomous constitutional status and augment Russian control over its government. Its increasing strategic significance as a border zone of the Russian capital, St Petersburg (Petrograd), was a key motive behind Russian policy in Finland and the outbreak of the First World War with Germany in August 1914 led to a tightening of the Russian grip. Russification turned the Finns, who until the end of the nineteenth century had been loyal subjects of the Emperor, into bitter opponents of the imperial regime and created the popular ideological basis for independence.

The Russian February Revolution, which overthrew the Emperor, led to the restoration of constitutional government in Finland. The parliament elected in 1916, with an overall socialist majority, was convened and a coalition government of socialists and non-socialists was formed. The collapse of the imperial government in Russia, however, resulted in friction between the Russian Provisional Government, which claimed supreme authority in Finland, and the Finnish government (known as the senate) and parliament. The internal stability of Finland was threatened by the continuing presence in the country of a large Russian garrison. This was needed for the

[1] Speech, 16 May 1918. Mannerheim, *Minnen*, I, p. 292.

defence of the Empire, but its soldiers and sailors became increasingly revolutionary and undisciplined.

Political and social divisions in Finland were exacerbated by economic factors. Fear of unemployment, food shortages and inflation helped to radicalize the Finnish working class as 1917 wore on. The non-socialists were also afraid that society, law and order and the protection of property might break down. The government lacked an effective police force and there was no Finnish army.

In the spring and summer of 1917 the Finnish socialists advocated a greater degree of independence but the attempt which they led in July 1917 to have parliament declared the supreme authority in Finland (except for foreign policy and military matters) was defeated by a combination of the Russian Provisional Government and the Finnish non-socialists. Parliament was dissolved, the socialists left the government, and in the elections in October the non-socialist parties gained a majority of sixteen. With the Bolsheviks' seizure of power in Petrograd in November, and the increased chaos it brought about, the non-socialists became anxious for complete separation from Russia.

The Finnish socialists wavered between parliamentary action and revolution on the Bolshevik model, and in mid-November 1917 they called a general strike in support of their political and social demands. Most of southern Finland then fell under the control of revolutionary socialist committees. There was an outburst of violence by armed socialist Red Guards that terrified the bourgeoisie and irrevocably sharpened the divisions in Finnish society. Parliament passed some of the legislation demanded by the strikers, and the moderate socialists called off the strike. The non-socialist parties now came together and formed a new government on 27 November 1917 under Pehr Evind Svinhufvud, a champion of constitutional legality. This government aimed to secure Finland's independence, economic stability and recovery, and to maintain order. In an atmosphere of tension and suspicion, with militant and many moderate socialists fearing a counter-revolution, parliament voted on 6 December 1917 to declare Finland an independent republic. However, Germany and Sweden refused to grant recognition without Russian approval of Finnish independence. This forced the Svinhufvud government to ask the Soviet government for recognition, which it obtained on 31 December 1917. Recognition was granted by Sweden, France and Germany early in January 1918.

The Finland to which Mannerheim returned on 18 December 1917 was thus in the throes of political, social and economic upheaval. However, as he recorded in his *Memoirs*, in contrast to the 'passive hopelessness' he found in Russia, in Finland there was 'an unbroken determination to fight for our country's liberation'.[2] Those who were determined to resist a slide towards revolutionary socialist rule were to find in Mannerheim a powerful reinforcement.

MANNERHEIM'S CAREER IN RUSSIA

Gustaf Mannerheim was fifty when he returned to Finland. Born into a Swedish-speaking Finnish noble family on 4 June 1867, his initially happy childhood was shattered by his father's bankruptcy and his mother's death. He was sent to the Finnish Cadet Corps to train to become an officer, but was expelled in 1886 for bad conduct. However, the military life appealed to him and, like many Finns of his social background (particularly earlier in the century), he decided to seek a career in the imperial Russian army. He entered the Nicholas Cavalry School in St Petersburg in 1887 and in 1889 was commissioned not, as he hoped, in the guard, but in a line cavalry regiment in Poland. Energetic use of his slender connections secured his transfer to the prestigious Chevalier Guards regiment in 1891. He moved back to St Petersburg where his regimental service was followed by an attachment from 1897 to 1903 to the Imperial Stables Administration where his knowledge of horses and skill with them were put to good use.

His financial difficulties as a poor man in an expensive milieu were resolved in 1892 by an arranged marriage to a rich Russian, Anastasia Arapova, whose father had been a Chevalier Guard. But the Mannerheims were not a happy couple and in 1903 Anastasia left him, taking their daughters Anastasie (1893–1978) and Sophie (1895–1963) to France. Political difficulties occurred as well as marital ones. The Russian assault on the Finnish constitution placed Mannerheim, as a Finn in Russian service, in a difficult position. He continued to serve, acknowledging a duty to the Russian imperial state that was unacceptable to many Finns, including his own elder brother Carl, who was expelled from Finland for his constitutionalist, anti-Russian stand.

[2] Mannerheim, *Memoirs*, p. 131.

Mannerheim returned to soldiering in 1903 as commander of the demonstration squadron of the Officers' Cavalry School at which future cavalry regimental commanders were trained. The outbreak of the Russo-Japanese War offered the opportunity for active service, and Mannerheim volunteered. In Manchuria he gained valuable combat experience and an understanding also of what not to do in war. He was promoted colonel for bravery on the battlefield. In 1906–8 he undertook a military reconnaissance across Sinkiang and northern China at the request of the Russian general staff. He reported personally to the Emperor Nicholas II on the results of this expedition in October 1908.

After commanding a line cavalry regiment in Poland from 1909 to 1911, Mannerheim was appointed to command a guards cavalry regiment in Warsaw in 1911, in which capacity he was promoted to the rank of major-general. In August 1914 he went to war as commander of the Independent Guards Cavalry Brigade, an appointment he had received earlier in the year. Proving himself a capable general, he became commander of a cavalry division in 1915 and of a cavalry corps (one of only ten such formations in the Russian army) in June 1917. He was awarded the Order of St George, 4th class, for gallantry, an honour which afforded him intense satisfaction. In May he was promoted lieutenant-general.

Although for a time in late 1916 and early 1917 Mannerheim had commanded a force of some 40,000 Russian and Rumanian troops on the Rumanian front, he never served in a major headquarters or was involved in strategic decision-making. He was not a general staff officer and lacked higher professional military education: like most applicants, he had failed the examination for entry to the General Staff Academy. His loss may not have been great in that the Academy's course was criticized as insufficiently relevant to the conduct of operations. In any case, by the time of the Russian Revolution, Mannerheim was a thoroughly experienced front-line general who combined professional diligence and considerable intelligence with his basic military knowledge. He not only knew the business of war intimately but also recognized its human cost.

The Revolution represented a disaster to Mannerheim as an officer personally loyal to the Emperor. He was utterly repelled by the 'democratization' of the army and the destruction of its discipline and fighting capacity. It came as a relief to be transferred to the reserve in

September 1917 'on grounds of opposition to the present conditions'.[3] A new career in Finland was now his only option and, after some delay, he made the dangerous journey across revolutionary Russia from Odessa to Petrograd and on to Helsinki. As a citizen of newly-independent Finland he could leave the Russian army with a clear conscience.

Mannerheim's service in Russia had profound consequences both for him personally and for Finland. He had gained in Russia the professional military experience which was to be the foundation for his place in Finnish history. He was a mature leader. As a young man he had learned self-discipline, and the passage of time had developed his strength of will, readiness to assume responsibility, and commanding personality – to which was allied an imposing presence. He had acquired a sympathy for Russia, in whose cosmopolitan upper-class society he had felt at home. He had gained an understanding of Russia's strategic interests and an appreciation of great power politics. Having fought for the Entente throughout the First World War, he was convinced of the rightness of its cause and was sharply critical of German policy and conduct of war. Politically he was not a reactionary and had criticized policies of that nature in Russia after the Revolution of 1905. He did, however, recognize the need for strong government and was a convinced monarchist, favouring a constitutional monarchy in Russia. The Revolutions of 1917 undoubtedly strengthened his antipathy to party politics and his social conservatism. Above all, he became an implacable opponent of Bolshevism.

FROM 'EXILE' TO COMMAND

On arriving in Helsinki on 18 December 1917 Mannerheim stayed first with his eldest sister Sophie who was the well-connected matron of the Surgical Hospital. Shortly afterwards he moved to the vacant apartment of his half-sister Marguerite and her husband Michael Gripenberg. He paid a brief visit to Petrograd between Christmas and New Year to see friends: this was to prove his final visit to the city where he had spent so many years.

In Helsinki he quickly became involved with those who were planning the formation of a new Finnish army. This involvement was facilitated by his background and his political awareness as well as by his

---
[3] Telegram cited in Jägerskiöld, *Gustaf Mannerheim 1906–1917*, p. 329.

military experience. Two main languages are spoken in Finland, Finnish and Swedish. At the time of Mannerheim's return Swedish was spoken by some 11 per cent of the population. The Swedish-speaking upper class to which he belonged was losing its place as the ruling élite in Finland not only because of the parliamentary reform of 1906 (and Mannerheim had represented the baronial branch of his family in the Estate of Nobles in that final historic Diet) but also because of economic and social change and the rapid rise of both a politically-conscious Finnish-speaking middle class and a powerful socialist party. Nevertheless, the old, tightly-knit Swedish-speaking families remained important. With this background, it was natural that Mannerheim had tried to follow events in Finland while in Russian service, and had often had strong opinions about them. Bundles of the Helsinki Swedish-language newspaper *Hufjvudstadsbladet* were always welcome and he was a diligent correspondent with members of his family in Finland and Sweden. Thus Mannerheim was not completely out of touch with events and opinions in Finland when he returned.

Nevertheless, fear that Mannerheim had become russified caused him to be treated with some initial caution by the military planners in Helsinki, some of whom knew him from the Finnish Cadet Corps. Despite this caution, the 'old boys' network' of the Corps was useful in securing Mannerheim's prompt acceptance and participation in Finnish military planning. It was clear that in the new situation caused by the Russian Revolution and Finnish independence he was firmly in the Finnish patriotic camp.

The caution of the military planners towards Mannerheim was undoubtedly caused not only by his 'Russian' past but also by concern over his reactions to their close involvement with Germany. While he had been eager for Finland to demonstrate its loyalty to the Russian Empire by raising troops to serve in its army during the First World War, a Finnish 'Activist Committee' had persuaded the Germans to accept Finns for military training with the object of fighting against Russia for Finland's independence. Activism was led by mostly Swedish-speaking university men and supported by a number of Finnish political exiles. Its supporters looked to Germany as the source of arms and of an intervention force which would back up a Finnish national rising to drive the Russians out of Finland. The clandestine recruitment and despatch to Germany of nearly 2,000 young Finns to receive military training indicated the recruits' patriotic idealism and represented a considerable organizational achievement by the Activist Committee. The Finnish recruits were formed into the 27th Royal Prussian Jäger Battalion in May 1916 and sent to the Baltic front where they gained combat experience against the Russians between June 1916 and February 1917. The Jägers were to constitute the main hope of organizing an effective Finnish army in mid and late 1917 provided they could be brought home, a decision dependent on German policy towards Finland.

From May 1917 the Activist Committee, which attracted support from all the non-socialist parties, was developing its formerly clandestine district organization, which had smuggled the Jägers out of Finland, into a paramilitary one. The Committee intended to coordinate and control the local home guards that grew up in Finland, under various guises, from the summer of 1917 in response to the threat to law and order posed by the Russian soldiery and by disturbances in the countryside. These home guards were particularly strong in Ostrobothnia but they were also well recruited in Karelia. They developed more slowly in urban areas. By October 1917 the home guards of different types and origins were drawing together under the guidance of the activists. The socialists saw these 'White Guards' as 'slaughterers' and a threat to their own people and policies. There was a parallel growth of Red Guards among the working class although their numbers declined somewhat after the general strike.

A 'Military Committee' was formed during the First World War by a few former officers of the Finnish army which had been disbanded in 1901. Some of its membership overlapped with that of the Activist Committee. After the Russian Revolution the Military Committee developed various plans – based on German support – for the creation of a new Finnish army. The Committee acquired a semi-official advisory status in November 1917 and became a fully-fledged official body on 7 January 1918 when the government charged it with the task of establishing an armed force in Finland. By 7 January 1918 Mannerheim had become a member of the Military Committee. It has been claimed that members had considered him as a possible future commander-in-chief in November 1917 although the matter could not be pursued because he was far away in Russia.[4]

[4] *Finlands frihetskrig skildrat av deltagare*, II, p. 155.

Perhaps this facilitated his prompt involvement with the Committee in 1918, but his experience was surely the crucial factor.

He attended three meetings, held in different places because of the risk to members' security in the dangerously disorderly capital. The last was on 13 January, by which time Mannerheim had seen enough of the Military Committee to realise that it was incapable of action. Its members were accustomed to lengthy discussion and its chairman, Lieutenant-General Claes Charpentier, though a distinguished soldier, lacked the quality of decisive leadership which the circumstances of the time demanded. After the formal end of the 13 January meeting, Mannerheim announced that he could no longer collaborate with the members of the Committee. 'They had wasted time and effort over unimportant matters, and when something of real importance arose, it was shelved … Any day we might be surprised and arrested, and what would become of our movement if its organizing centre no longer existed?' Asked what he proposed, Mannerheim said that they should move to Ostrobothnia that night or the following morning and set up an army headquarters. The members of the Committee asked both him and the chairman to write a report for the next day about what should be done. 'I had already given my opinion, and I lit my cigar and departed. I did not write a report. It was high time for action and not writing.'[5]

Mannerheim made a speciality of the dramatic intervention and he seldom used it to greater effect. The chairman was uncomfortable, no doubt sensing his own inadequacy; the members recognized in Mannerheim the man they needed as their leader. Captain (subsequently Major-General) Hannes Ignatius, one of the principal members of the Committee and in due course a confidant of Mannerheim, wrote afterwards that in the few meetings he had attended Mannerheim had made a deep impression on the Committee as 'a commanding, energetic and self-confident soldier – just what we lacked'.[6] Next day Charpentier agreed to stand down as chairman. Before accepting the post, Mannerheim wanted to see Svinhufvud to find out the government's attitude both to his taking the chairmanship and to the general situation.

Mannerheim, with Charpentier, met Svinhufvud on 15 January. He met him again the following day in the presence of Ignatius and

---

[5] Mannerheim, *Memoirs*, p. 133.
[6] Ignatius, *Från ofärdsår till självständighet*, p. 209.

of Arthur Castrén, a member of the government. Svinhufvud gave Mannerheim – orally – the task of organizing the forces for maintaining order which, on 12 January, parliament had voted to raise. The two discussed the likely need to expel the Russian troops in Finland if they refused to agree to leave voluntarily. Mannerheim had learned officially on joining the Military Committee of the existence of the Jäger Battalion, and wanted its immediate recall.[7] But he was anxious to avoid intervention by Sweden or Germany and believed he had obtained from Svinhufvud an assurance to that effect. Svinhufvud subsequently claimed that he had made no such promise. A result of this misunderstanding was a sharp conflict between Mannerheim and the government in early March when he learned that Germany had agreed to send an intervention force to Finland at the request of the Finnish government. Believing that he had made acceptance of his appointment conditional on no foreign intervention, he felt betrayed.

The absence of any discussion between Mannerheim and the government about how his forces were to be financed gave an indication of the administrative confusion then prevailing in Finland. Private finance had already funded the work of the Military Committee, and Mannerheim fixed up a considerable credit through the good offices of a prominent banker with whom he had been at school. Shortly afterwards – and equally informally – the government agreed to guarantee an enlarged credit of 9 million marks.

The Military Committee agreed on 17 January to move to Vaasa, the provincial capital of Ostrobothnia, and set up a headquarters under Mannerheim's command. They travelled north by night train on 18 January. Mannerheim was provided with false papers, since passengers' documents were inspected by Russian soldiers, and as a former Russian general he was an obviously suspicious person. At Tampere station, where Russian soldiers checked his identity documents, his knowledge of Russian aroused their suspicion and only his appeal to a young Finnish railwayman, who declared his papers to be in order, prevented a nasty situation. It was therefore as the result of singularly good fortune that Mannerheim arrived in Vaasa on 19 January 1918. Here he set up his headquarters and his residence in the offices of the provincial administration. He began immediately to organize his staff, take stock and make plans.

---

[7] There are reports that in 1916 he had heard to his displeasure of what he regarded as

MANNERHEIM: THE FINNISH YEARS

FROM PLANNING TO ACTION

Mannerheim opened his headquarters on 21 January, immediately signing himself as commander-in-chief. Headquarters was initially composed of members of the Military Committee. Hannes Ignatius became quartermaster-general, through whom operational matters were handled. He had completed the course at the Russian General Staff Academy but had not been selected to join the general staff itself. Lacking any recent military experience, he proved more useful to Mannerheim in political than military matters. Colonel Martin Wetzer, who had recent front-line experience in the Russian army, became chief of staff. Colonel Adolf von Rehausen, an officer of the 'old' Finnish army, became first inspector of artillery and then of small arms. Captain Aimo Hallberg, whose career in the old army had been very brief, served as head of the quartermaster's department. There were also two civilians, one a railway official, and later Mannerheim made the wise comment in his *Memoirs* that successful civilian work 'was in some cases a better preparation for the kind of jobs the war called for' than past military experience.[8] Although he appealed successfully for officers of the old army and ones who had served in Russia to join the government forces, it was often difficult to find them suitable appointments. Fortunately, Mannerheim possessed the tact and charm to ease them into places where they could do most good, or at any rate least harm, while protecting his own position from potential disloyalty.

Apart from two small police training units, the home guards, or defence corps as it would now be more appropriate to call them, were the principal forces at Mannerheim's disposal. They were organized on a local basis, and it was difficult for headquarters to discover their numbers, weapons and state of training, although the district commander in Ostrobothnia, Colonel (self-styled Major-General) Paul von Gerich, a capable former officer in the Russian army, had a better grip on his area than most district commanders. By late January 1918 the defence corps outside southern Finland numbered some 24,500 men. This compared with some 30,000 Red Guards throughout Finland. The Russian soldiers and sailors in the country numbered around 70,000; they were mostly in the south. The problem for the

---

the treasonable enlistment of Finns in the German army. Paasikivi, *J. K. Paasikiven päiväkirjat 1944–1956* (hereafter Paasikivi, *Päiväkirjat 1944–1956*), II, cols 829–30.

[8] Mannerheim, *Memoirs*, p. 150.

defence corps was their acute lack of weapons. Some had been purchased and brought in from Germany by the activists in October 1917 and a few more in November and December, and as a result of these shipments and black market purchases in Petrograd they possessed in January 1918 some 9,000 army rifles, a small number of pistols and a few machine-guns. The bulk of the weapons were in Ostrobothnia.

Fifty-one Jägers had reached Finland as instructors, some coming with the shipments of weapons, others by different routes. Of these twenty-five went to Ostrobothnia and ten to Karelia. Training was chiefly in the hands of civilians although a few officers and NCOs of the old army also acted as instructors. The energetic and determined leadership of the Jäger Captain Woldemar Hägglund in Karelia was recognized on 24 January when Mannerheim confirmed his appointment as district commander in Viipuri. The next day Hägglund was instrumental in causing the outbreak of hostilities between his defence corps and the Russians and Finnish Red Guards. Another Jäger who became important in Karelia was Captain Aarne Sihvo, whom Mannerheim had met in Helsinki on 17 January, and impressed powerfully despite Sihvo's inherent distrust of Swedish-speaking Russian officers and amazement that Mannerheim retained his Russian military servant. Sihvo proved a capable subordinate though relations between them were never more than formally correct.[9]

Mannerheim's first plans for the formation of a force for the restoration of order were excessively modest. He aimed to raise a cadre of 400 men in each of ten defence corps districts, which would form a paramilitary police. In a more detailed plan sent to Svinhufvud on 24 January, he had begun to think of an augmented and genuinely military force for dealing with the disorderly Russian troops and the country's 'bandit element'.[10] He wanted to use the Jägers as the basis for a regiment of 4,000 men who would form a mobile troubleshooting formation. Significantly, he acknowledged the effectiveness of rapid and decisive intervention by small numbers of troops. The defence corps would support the paramilitary police. The importation of weapons for his men and the early recall of the Jägers were essential, as were measures to stop additional Russian troops and their weapons entering the country. Mannerheim was clearly not at this

[9] Saarikoski, *Keskustajääkäri Aarne Sihvo*, pp. 76–80.
[10] Mannerheim's letter is quoted in full in Jägerskiöld, *Gustaf Mannerheim 1918*, pp. 36–8.

time thinking of fighting a war but hoping for time to prepare his modest forces to deal with localized trouble. His hopes proved vain as events sped towards a crisis. His plan of 24 January was immediately overtaken and more extensive measures were soon needed to create a proper army – although his appreciation of the value of decisive action by small forces was to be thoroughly vindicated. In any case, the plan reached Svinhufvud only after hostilities had ended: its despatch by post suggested either a striking lack of urgency or carelessness at headquarters.

These were difficult days for Mannerheim in Vaasa because the defence corps in Ostrobothnia were as eager to take action against the Russians as their fellows in Karelia. Mannerheim had to balance this enthusiasm against his own desire for more time to organize and prepare for action and the conflicting messages coming from the government in Helsinki about the desirability of disarming the Russians or leaving them alone, depending upon the likelihood of their remaining neutral in any internal conflict in Finland. That conflict was now fast approaching. After 24 January the Finnish socialists moved rapidly towards revolutionary action, and on 25 January the government responded to the deteriorating situation by ordering provincial governors to give the defence corps, as government troops, every assistance. On 27 January the government appointed Mannerheim 'commander-in-chief for the maintenance of order in northern Finland' – this decision and that declaring the defence corps to be government troops were made public the following day. The government succeeded in getting the neutrality of the Russian troops in Finland confirmed by the Bolshevik government in Petrograd, but the increasing possibility of their being disarmed by the defence corps, together with ideological affinity, moved the Russians to cooperate with the Red Guards. During the night of 27/28 January 1918 the Finnish radical socialists used the Red Guards, mobilized for the purpose, to carry out a *coup d'état*. They seized control of Helsinki and of the industrial centres of southern Finland. Members of the government, with the exception of four who got away to Ostrobothnia at the last moment, went into hiding. On 31 January the Red Guards in Helsinki ordered Mannerheim's arrest, but they were too late. The Bolshevik government in Russia supported the Finnish revolution and cooperation between Russian troops and the Red Guards over the supply of arms and volunteers intensified.

Mannerheim had already decided on 22 January to use the local defence corps to disarm Russian garrisons in southern Ostrobothnia the next day. He put off this operation on orders from the government, to the frustration of the defence corps men, one of whose leaders he nevertheless won over with a characteristically deft appeal from one old soldier to another. When Mannerheim assembled his staff on 25 January to discuss the situation, all but one favoured action against the Russian troops. The exception was Major-General Ernst Löfström, an experienced front-line officer from the Russian army. Mannerheim had been anxious to employ him, but was unconvinced by his arguments about the dangers posed by the superior numbers of the Russians and the weakness of the defence corps. He counted on surprise, the demoralization of the Russians and the likely non-intervention of their officers to outweigh the apparent disparity of numbers, weapons and training. He decided to act, and Svinhufvud, with whom he was in telephone contact, agreed. Orders were issued to the defence corps to concentrate on 27 January and to disarm the Russian garrisons in Vaasa, Ylistaro, Lapua, Seinäjoki and Ilmajoki during the early hours of the next day. Late on 27 January Mannerheim received a message from Svinhufvud asking for the operation to be postponed because of negotiations with the Russians, but to have deferred action again would have demoralized the defence corps and compromised his own authority, which was not strong in relation to his independent-minded volunteer forces. Mannerheim therefore put the message in his pocket, got into his sleigh and left for nearby Ylihärmä to await news of the night's events.

This historic decision was made more fortunate by its coincidence with the Red *coup d'état*. It won for Mannerheim the initiative in the north of Finland, and began the clearance of a firm base in a region crucial for communications with the outside world through Sweden. It backed up the fighting already in progress in Karelia and which had threatened to disrupt Mannerheim's plans. But because of the Red *coup*, the government forces, which had moved against the Russians, also became engaged in the suppression of a rebellion. For White Finland the ensuing war was a War of Liberation or Independence fought to free the country from Russian influence both direct, in the form of the Russian troops who were backed by the Bolshevik government, and indirect, in the shape of the Finnish 'People's Commissariat' with its dangerous links to the Russian Bolsheviks.

The war also became a civil war, of 'White' Finn against 'Red' Finn, with all the cruelty and bitterness of such a struggle. For Mannerheim the war was clearly one of liberation, but it was also a crusade against Bolshevism.

WAR BEGINS

The planned disarmament of the Russian garrisons was accomplished successfully and with little fighting. The favourable local publicity gained for Mannerheim by these events has been justifiably described as a 'media breakthrough':[11] he was quick to inform the outside world, through Stockholm, of his success. He also sought to assure the Russian soldiers in Finland that he was obliged to disarm them in order to secure their neutrality in his struggle against the bandits and traitors who opposed his forces. His appeal to them to spill no more blood had limited success. There was some hard fighting before the northern coastal towns of Kokkola, Oulu and Tornio were freed from the Russians and the Finnish Red Guards, but by 6 February the Whites' rear and land communications with Sweden were secure.

Important as these operations had been, Mannerheim had to pay continual attention to the threat to his base from the south and to the need to control the vital lateral railway from Haapamäki via Jyväskylä to Pieksämäki and on to Savonlinna and Elisenvaara – the link between the Whites in Ostrobothnia and those in Karelia. Energetic local leadership had secured most of north-eastern Finland for the Whites by 8 February, while in Karelia the Vuoksi river divided Whites to the north from Reds to the south. The White seizure of Vilppula on the railway from the Red stronghold of Tampere to Haapamäki checked Red efforts to advance north in early February. In any case the Reds were slow to gather forces for a determined advance north, partly because they concentrated on neutralizing the defence corps in southern Finland. They had done this by the end of February but not before Mannerheim had been given a vital breathing space. From early March a 'front' ran across Finland comprising blocking positions on various railways and roads. Railways were vital for the transport of men, arms and supplies, while tactical movements, except over short distances, had to be by sleigh in the winter conditions which also forced the untrained troops to shelter in buildings at night.

[11] Westerlund, *Polle*, I, p. 57.

The Civil War in Finland, 1918

On 28 January Mannerheim was asked by Senator Heikki Renvall, who became the leader of the so-called Vaasa Senate (the rump of the lawful government that had escaped from Helsinki), how long he thought the action would take. He thought for a moment before replying: three-and-a-half months, 'a prediction which was to prove right almost to the day'.[12] This reply was undoubtedly based on careful earlier consideration of the time needed to create an army to crush the rebellion. Creation of an army – with its headquarters staffs, officers, men, arms and equipment – was one of Mannerheim's major preoccupations, parallel with planning and directing the fighting of the war already in progress. The senators in Vaasa had publicly declared on 1 February not only that they were the lawful government but also that he had been appointed commander-in-chief, and his authority to act in that capacity was extremely broad. 'His orders and directions are to be obeyed by all officials and citizens absolutely and without delay, as long as military activity continues.'[13] The weakness of the government and in particular the absence of a war ministry (although Senator Alexander Frey assumed responsibility for military matters) gave Mannerheim powers that in a normally-functioning state would be divided between the commander-in-chief and the war ministry. He was not one to shrink from the exercise of power, and in fact opposed the Vaasa Senate's desire to form a war ministry on the grounds that it would cause friction and impede decision-making. Mannerheim was determined to fight the war in his own way, which in itself provided ample occasion for friction and even conflict.

In a postscript to a letter of 17 February to his brother Johan, who had settled in Sweden, Mannerheim wrote of the government: 'On the whole I have the impression that R[envall], now that he thinks the situation is less dangerous, is becoming capricious and making himself important. However, they are at present obeying my wishes without arguing, although I feel that at times he would like to do so.'[14] This exemplified Mannerheim's attitude to the government whom he unjustly looked on as more of a hindrance than a help in his running of the war. 'Handling domestic politicians remained Mannerheim's

---

[12] Mannerheim, *Minnen*, I, p. 226. A slightly different version, with a prediction of three months, is given in *Finlands frihetskrig skildrat av deltagare*, IV, p. 15.
[13] The proclamation is cited in *Itsenäistymisen vuodet 1917–1920*, II, pp. 497–8.
[14] To Johan Mannerheim, 17 February 1918. Mannerheim, *Brev*, pp. 183–4.

blind spot; when he had to deal with them, his usual flair for coming to terms with distasteful realities seems to have deserted him.'[15] He resented as interference the government's assertion of its own interests and its representation to him of the complaints it received about the army.

There were, of course, points of unity between the commander-in-chief and the government. Both strongly opposed a Swedish offer to mediate in the war; there could be no mediation with rebels. They also agreed in opposing the Swedish intervention in the Åland islands in February which deeply offended the patriotic Finns. A force of Finnish defence corps had reached the islands on 10 February and begun to disarm the Russians there, and ostensibly to protect the inhabitants from a possible conflict, but probably to pursue annexationist ambitions, the Swedish government sent a force to the islands. Mannerheim's communications with Åland ran through Stockholm and by the duplicitous expedient of suppressing or altering his telegrams to the Finnish commander there, the Swedes induced the Finnish Whites to evacuate the islands on 24 February. Mannerheim was furious and the incident wrecked Finno-Swedish relations for some time. Finland regained control over Åland only in March after the arrival of a German expeditionary force compelled the Swedes to leave. The Germans' arrival in Åland also roused Mannerheim to fury, but he was quick to take advantage of the situation to appoint a military governor to uphold Finnish interests in the islands.

Although foreign relations were clearly a matter for the government – and agreed as such at a meeting with the senators on 17 February – Mannerheim continued to take a keen interest in them. In March he set up a political department at headquarters, headed by his brother-in-law Michael Gripenberg, to handle his foreign contacts as well as his political correspondence. This prompted criticism that he was seeking to interfere in the work of the government. Inevitably the separation of some military and foreign policy matters was scarcely possible in wartime, and as commander-in-chief Mannerheim held discussions with foreign diplomats. However, his attitude did not make for easy cooperation. Over the matter of German intervention he also felt that the government had reneged on its promise to him not to seek foreign intervention.

---

[15] Upton, *The Finnish Revolution*, 1917–1918, p. 311.

In mid-February the Senate broached with Mannerheim the delicate questions of the Swedishness (as opposed to linguistic Finnishness) of headquarters and the employment of Finns who had served as officers in the Russian army, matters which upset many members of the defence corps. These men wanted a representative body at headquarters through which they could express their grievances. The idea of a soldiers' council was understandably anathema to Mannerheim after his experiences in Russia but he was sufficiently flexible in his approach to the unusual situation in Finland to accept the creation on 20 February of an Advisory Committee to the Commander-in-Chief to improve the atmosphere. He used this Committee to keep in touch with the morale of the defence corps troops, to instil in them better discipline, and finally in April to help turn the various defence corps companies into infantry regiments organized like the rest of the army. That reorganization made the Committee redundant. Its formation did not put an end to the complaints against Mannerheim, the causes of which were too deep-seated to be so easily removed.

The defence corps had their grievances but they also had a strong motivation to fight based on hatred of the Russians and of the Finnish Reds who fraternized with them. Red atrocities – real and imagined – were magnified to increase the Whites' fighting zeal. Mannerheim played his part in this, for example by publicizing the murder of seventeen White prisoners at Mäntyharju. Given the feelings of hatred that prevailed, the White army's conduct towards the enemy was frequently ruthless; armed Russians who were captured were usually shot immediately. This was also the fate of many Red Finns. Mannerheim's conduct towards the Red prisoners has been the subject of controversy.[16] Accustomed to war being conducted according to commonly-accepted principles, he was plainly unhappy with indiscriminate blood-letting, but stopping it was hampered both by the peculiar legal situation with regard to the rebellion and by the practical limits of his own authority over soldiers who were eager for vengeance.

The Vaasa Senate had proclaimed on 1 February that those taking up arms against the government would be regarded as traitors. This ruled out the possibility that captured Reds could be regarded as prisoners of war: there was no clear state of war with Russia and Finnish law did not recognize a state of civil war, hence it was not

[16] Analysed by Manninen, 'Mannerheim ja punavangit', *Historiallinen aikakauskirja*, 79, 1981, pp. 195–206.

possible in law to try captured Reds by courts-martial. The ordinary process of the criminal law had to be followed. This situation was only partly modified as the war proceeded.

In mid February Mannerheim told a correspondent for the Swedish newspaper *Dagens Nyheter*. 'The revolutionaries have made themselves guilty of treason and rebellion and the punishment for that is death. I do not determine that punishment. The law does that and it must be obeyed.' He also stated that he believed it impossible to build bridges between the lawful government and the anarchists and social democrats responsible for causing the civil war. A little later he claimed to have been misrepresented and said that it would be necessary to build bridges after the conflict had ended. This was undoubtedly an afterthought, albeit a prudent one, because from the context of the interview his original remarks were clearly intended to apply to the post-war situation and not, as he claimed, to the current one.[17]

Already on 8 February Mannerheim had ordered that murderers and arsonists captured in the act during fighting should be shot, and later orders authorized the execution of saboteurs. The government accepted the use of 'instant courts' to judge these cases. However, the capture of prisoners at the front remained a problem and Mannerheim asked for the comments of his new Advisory Committee. He issued a revised version of their proposals in orders of 25 February; courts-martial were prohibited and those accused of offences had to be held for trial by civilian courts. Those committing sabotage or resistance in rear areas were to be shot 'on the spot'. Rebels who surrendered in battle might be taken prisoner at the discretion of the commander. Although Mannerheim's orders of 25 February were not free from ambiguity, it was clear that prisoners taken in battle were not to be shot.[18] Before the battle for Tampere, on 26 March, Mannerheim reminded the army that Reds who surrendered should be treated as prisoners of war, and 'no actions should stain the honour of White Finland'. He also expressed his concern over what the many foreigners in Tampere would report about Finland's conduct as a civilized nation.

It is easy to take a cynical view of this remark and suggest that Mannerheim might not have been so concerned about the fate of the

---

[17] *Dagens Nyheter*, 14 Feb. 1918, no. 43; 26 Feb. 1918, no 55; Paavolainen, *Poliittiset väkivaltaisuudet Suomessa 1918*, I, p. 310; Manninen, 'Mannerheim ja punavangit', p. 195.

[18] Paavolainen, *Poliittiset väkivaltaisuudet Suomessa 1918*, II, p. 68.

Reds in Tampere had foreign observers not been present, just as it is possible to suggest that he was ambivalent about the treatment of the Reds.[19] This is unfair to Mannerheim. It is clear from his orders between March and May 1918 that he tried to stop the execution of captured Reds. The constant repetition of these orders showed the resistance of the army to humanitarian ideals. Almost all units contained individuals prepared to kill prisoners.[20] Executions continued – some 500 immediately after the capture of Tampere – although, when the war ended, some 80,000 Reds were treated in effect as prisoners of war. Mannerheim clearly wanted the Red leaders and those guilty of crimes to be tried promptly by court-martial and punished, but he was prepared to let the majority of the Red prisoners go free. The law and the government were against this approach and he failed to change the situation. Mannerheim's attitude to the Red prisoners almost certainly moderated as the Whites' victory became more certain. His likely attitude in April 1918 was reflected in a private interview in 1930 when he said: 'Enough blood has been spilled. I do not want to get the name of the executioner of Finland.'[21] In this hope he was disappointed; the Finnish communists and their sympathisers abroad did indeed regard him in that light because of his role in the suppression of the 'Finnish revolution'.

The ultimate fate of many Red prisoners was hard. Gathered into camps in poor conditions to await trial, some 10,000 of them died of hunger and disease between June and September 1918. This figure may be compared with the 7,000 killed (on both sides) during the fighting and about another 10,000 killed (also on both sides) in reprisals and various acts of terror. The Finnish working class was embittered and alienated by what it regarded as savage bourgeois repression. It was no help to Mannerheim's reputation that his policy towards the prisoners would have kept many thousands out of the notorious camps, or that he was not even in Finland when most of the deaths occurred. He was the subject of demonstrative working-class loathing and ridicule in the 1920s and into the 1930s.[22]

---

[19] Upton, *The Finnish Revolution 1917–1918*, pp. 316–17.
[20] Paavolainen, *Poliittiset väkivaltaisuudet Suomessa 1918*, II, p. 96.
[21] Interview with Kai Donner, cited in Manninen, 'Mannerheim ja punavangit', p. 204.
[22] For examples see Peltonen, 'The Return of the Narrator', pp. 127–30.

THE WHITE GENERAL

ORGANIZING AN ARMY

It was an article of faith for Mannerheim that Finland had to fight the war in 1918 without foreign intervention. Not only did he fear the international complications that might ensue (and about which he was proved right when German intervention actually occurred) but he also believed that Finland's independence would be set on a firmer basis if it were secured by the efforts of the Finns themselves. This attitude did not mean that he was averse to foreign support. He wanted arms and ammunition and other supplies as well as capable volunteers to help train and lead the army he had to form. He turned immediately to Sweden and Germany. Fearful for its neutrality and scared of the reaction of the Swedish socialists, the Swedish government refused to release arms from its depots and sought to prevent serving soldiers from volunteering for service in Finland. Nevertheless, Mannerheim's appeal for general staff and artillery officers evoked a prompt response and numerous officers and NCOs, both serving and reserve, also left for Finland. His brother Johan in Sweden became a leader of the organization Friends of Finland which provided much aid, including the recruitment of a 'Swedish Brigade' of volunteers. However, it was Germany which first provided the vital supplies of arms and munitions, as well as an advance contingent of eighty Finnish Jägers, and then released and sent the Jäger Battalion itself.

Mannerheim moved his headquarters to Seinäjoki soon after the clearance of southern Ostrobothnia so as to be nearer operations to the south, and it remained there, housed in a train, until the end of March when it followed operations towards Tampere, moving on to Mikkeli (and into buildings) in April. The headquarters at Seinäjoki were surrounded by a wire fence for well-founded security reasons (there was an attempt to assassinate Mannerheim towards the end of February), and became known sarcastically as the chicken coop.[23] However, location in a train was practical and convenient, not least for communications. The telegraph and telephone lines alongside the railway were eventually supplemented by more secure teleprinter links to the front headquarters. The arrival of four Swedish general staff officers on 10–11 February permitted the reorganization of headquarters along more rational and decentralized lines. The Swedish officers served principally in the operations section under Ignatius,

[23] On the assassination attempt see Westerlund, *Polle*, I, p. 78–82.

the quartermaster-general. Their contribution was outstanding, as was that of the Swedish artillery officer who took charge at Pietarsaari of the formation of the Finnish artillery. They brought the professionalism that was lacking among some of the older Finnish officers. The chief of staff, after Colonel Wetzer was moved to command the Vilppula front, was first Colonel K. E. Berg and, from 3 March Colonel Gösta Theslöf. All were Finns. The chief of staff attended to the receipt and allocation of incoming reports. He was not the head of the various sections of headquarters and in many respects Mannerheim acted as his own chief of staff and attended to a vast amount of detail. Fortunately, he possessed the vigour, physical fitness an mental stability to carry the burden that fell to him and to survive on only four or five hours' sleep most nights.

The quality with which Mannerheim most impressed the Swedish officers was his calmness. Colonel Ernst Linder who received command of the front in Satakunta, remarked on his cordial reception by Mannerheim and was surprised by the commander-in-chief's youthful appearance and by the fact that he did not seem at all strained or weighed down by the enormous burden which rested on his shoulders.[24] Captain Gösta Törngren noted: 'The towering and elegant figure, the graceful movements, but above all the calm and searching gaze of the eye of the military commander captivated and attracted'. Mannerheim gave him the impression of being in total command over his surroundings.[25] He possessed the admirable quality in a commander of resistance to distraction from his main aim; he was impervious to cries for help from fronts (usually Karelia) other than those where he was concentrating his operations. This required strong nerves. However, he was not always calm: he could fly into a rage but never totally lost control.

Another Swedish officer, Captain Count Wilhelm Archibald Douglas, commented on other aspects of Mannerheim's character in the face of the difficulties confronting him. 'It required during those first weeks all the tact and firmness of the commander-in-chief, all the strength of his engaging personality, to get such loosely-joined machinery, which was so ill fitted for the circumstances, to work and to do so in the desired direction.' And again, when writing of the White offensive in March, 'General Mannerheim was himself the primary

---

[24] Linder, *Från Finlands Frihetskrig*, p. 15.
[25] *Finlands frihetskrig skildrat av deltagare*, VIII, p. 9.

driving force. He was a masterly exponent of the delicate art of asking for the absurd in order to attain the possible.'[26] He was also prompt with words of congratulation, encouragement or condolence.

Many difficulties confronted Mannerheim. The defence corps volunteers were recruited on a local basis and were not always amenable to serving away from their home regions. Discipline was foreign to them and they were liable to go home if and when they wanted. It was hard to discover which troops were where and how well they were armed. Numerous weapons had been seized from the Russian army in Ostrobothnia but they were kept by the defence corps who took them, preventing their distribution to units elsewhere which needed them more. Only with the arrival of 44,000 rifles and other arms and ammunition from Germany on 17 February could the systematic arming of the White troops begin. Ammunition for the Whites' modest artillery (seized from the Russians or sent from Germany) remained insufficient long after the supply of small arms ammunition became satisfactory. Until an enormous programme for the production of uniforms and equipment bore fruit, most soldiers wore their own clothes, with the addition of a white armband to denote their allegiance. Until the end of the war, when the food situation became bad, rations were adequate and the army benefited from many gifts of provisions and clothing from patriotic citizens, although there was no shortage of money to pay for whatever was needed. Lack of locomotives and rolling stock hampered use of the vital railways until more were captured at Tampere.

Nevertheless, by 19 February when Mannerheim divided his forces into four groups – Satakunta, Häme, Savo and Karelia – his headquarters was functioning reasonably efficiently and he had a good idea of the general situation. The rear areas were also better organized. He had been devoting time and energy to the creation of an army with which to take possession of the south. His original plans for an army of 4,000 men raised by enlistment had grown by mid-February to a scheme for a field army of twenty battalions totalling some 10,000. In addition there was to be an enlisted cavalry regiment (based on the earlier mounted police detachment) and 600 gunners. Enlistment in fact proceeded slowly. Many men who might have enlisted were already serving as volunteers in the defence corps. There was also a feeling, especially strong in Karelia, that serving for pay

[26] Douglas, *Kriget i Finland 1918*, pp. 44,103.

was inappropriate in the circumstances and would check the willingness of men to volunteer.

During the first half of February some districts (particularly in Ostrobothnia) successfully introduced local conscription. On 11 February Mannerheim received a delegation from Kristiina which proposed the introduction of conscription nationally. He doubted the need for this but promised to bring the proposal to the attention of the Senate. He did so later that day, asking the Senate to introduce conscription on the basis of the Military Service Law of 1878, which had fallen out of use but never been repealed. His sudden change of mind, which may have been influenced by headquarters, was prompted not so much by the desire to recruit men in large numbers, which conscription made possible, as to make it supplementary to enlistment, which he intended to continue, and bring under military discipline the volunteers of the defence corps who would thus become subject to the Law. The Senate, which had already considered conscription, now moved quickly and issued the necessary proclamation, after securing Mannerheim's approval of its terms, on 18 February.

Hesitation about conscription was partly due to doubts about the likely response of the population and also partly to the fear of bringing in men who were politically unreliable. In fact only a small percentage of men failed to register and many undesirables were weeded out by the local conscription boards although some Red sympathisers did get through into the army. In practice most conscripts fought as well as the other White troops. The first were inducted at the end of February and by the end of April some 28,000 conscripts were serving, which went a long way to solving the army's manpower problem. To these conscripts had to be added the 13,000 defence corps volunteers serving at the front at the beginning of March and some 4,500 enlisted men. By the end of the war Mannerheim commanded an army of 80–90,000, when the local defence corps units were added to the regular army of 55–60,000. Until the end of February he still hoped to obtain more men by enlistment but he bowed to the inevitable and discontinued it in March, accepting that his field army would be composed of conscripts. The enlisted units were limited to the Uusimaa Dragoons, six grenadier battalions (two regiments) and some artillery. At first the soldiers of the White Army were mostly farmers, and the term 'farmers' army' came into common use but by May the army comprised a representative cross-section of the population.

Providing officers and NCOs for the army was far from easy. Some of the Swedish volunteers (84 officers and 200 NCOs) did helpful work but their incorporation into Finnish-speaking units caused language problems. The use of Swedish was not normally a difficulty at headquarters since it was the usual language of senior Finnish officers, although some who had served in the Russian army were rusty as to Swedish military terminology. After protests from Finnish-speaking units about orders being in Swedish, Mannerheim's headquarters laid down on 26 February that they should be written in Finnish, which meant that they had to be translated from Swedish, and sometimes back again – this was not always done accurately. The Jägers who returned in mid-February – and earlier – formed a useful body of instructors. A school was set up at Vöyri to train NCOs, but most of the men being trained there had to be committed to battle as a unit because of the shortage of troops. The military knowledge possessed by the officers and NCOs of the former Finnish army was out of date and the officers were rather old for tactical command at unit and subunit level. They were also resented as Swedish-speakers although some knew Finnish well. Finnish officers with service in the Russian army – and thus perceived as siding with the oppressor of Finland – were the object of acute suspicion and hostility on the part of many Finnish soldiers and especially the Jägers. It was to the Jägers that Mannerheim naturally looked as junior leaders of the new army – of the twenty-one battalions of conscripts he intended to form according to the scheme he approved on 25 February.

The main body of the Jäger Battalion – over 1,000 men – reached Vaasa on 25 February and were inspected and warmly welcomed by Mannerheim and Senator Renvall at a parade the following day. The Germans had allowed them to bring their arms and equipment as well as shipping a large quantity of other munitions. The Jägers were led by the Finnish Lieutenant-Colonel Wilhelm Thesleff, a disaffected general staff officer in the Russian army who had been captured – or allowed himself to be captured – by the Germans and gone over to their side, an action which aroused Mannerheim's revulsion. Thesleff had appointed the Jägers to ranks appropriate to the plan they had produced for their employment in Finland, arrangements all made without reference to Mannerheim, their commander-in-chief.

The Jägers saw themselves as the nucleus of a rapidly-formed striking force of three regiments (totalling some 6,000 men, drawn from the defence corps) which would crush the rebellion at a single blow. This idea was rejected by Mannerheim who had no wish to squander his best-trained cadres in an impractical assault on what he knew to be a numerous, determined and effectively-armed enemy. Thesleff was equally determined not to have the Jägers dispersed and, worse still, put under the command of 'Russian' officers. Predictably the two men failed to agree at acrimonious meetings on 27 and 28 February and 1 March. Matters were not helped when members of the government travelled to headquarters at Seinäjoki on 2 March to inform Mannerheim of the forthcoming intervention in Finland by a German expeditionary force. His rage at this betrayal – as he saw it – was compounded when Renvall, having been lobbied by the irate Jägers, put their case to him. They had even threatened 'to march off to the nearest front and there take the war into their own hands' if they did not get their way.[27] Mannerheim threatened resignation but agreed to see a delegation of Jäger officers.

Mannerheim saw them on 3 March, reminded them that he too was a 'Russian' officer, and put to them – not without effect – his case for their employment as the only possible trainers of the conscript army with which he intended to win the war. He sent them away to look at a new organizational scheme. He was wise enough to recognize the need to pacify the Jägers for the good of the White cause, and climbed down. With reluctance, he set up a Jäger brigade of three large regiments, each commanded by one of the German officers who had previously served with the Jäger Battalion and had volunteered to serve in Finland. However, having dispersed the Jägers to train the conscripts who were to form the Jäger regiments, Mannerheim quickly began reorganizing them along standard lines. In this he had the support of the most senior of the German officers, Eduard Ausfeld, who was appointed a colonel in the Finnish army. By the beginning of April Mannerheim had more or less achieved the organization he originally intended, only in the form of three Jäger brigades, and with the German officers employed as brigade commanders. In the so-called 'Jäger conflict', which caused him so much irritation at the time, Mannerheim conceded the initial battle but won the war.

---

[27] Thesleff, *Upplevelser under krigsåren 1914–1918*, p. 113.

MANNERHEIM'S STRATEGY AND GERMAN INTERVENTION

Mannerheim intended to crush the rebellion by recapturing southern Finland, and his plans for the creation of an army were directed to that end. At first he had considered an offensive in Karelia designed to seize Viipuri and cut the Reds off from their allies and munitions in Petrograd. However, this strategically attractive plan involved considerable risks. The bulk of the White forces would have to operate on a distant flank, with which communications (via one railway route) would be vulnerable to counterattack along the length of the front. It was also uncertain whether the Bolsheviks would intervene in operations so close to Petrograd, and an offensive a little further west, from Savo towards Kouvola, presented similar difficulties. Headquarters therefore turned to a plan to encircle the Red forces around Tampere, a scheme which would eliminate a major concentration of the enemy, seize an important town, and above all remove the threat to the railway to Karelia. The plan was thus a preparatory stage for the decisive offensive in Karelia. Mannerheim decided on 27 February to proceed with the Tampere operation. He wanted to strike quickly before the thaw turned the lakes into obstacles to movement and gave improved opportunities to the defence. The operation would also show the government's supporters in the south that their liberation was approaching. He outlined the plan for the first phase, the encirclement and destruction of the Red forces north of Orivesi, on 2 March, and followed this up with detailed orders on 5 March, although the date for the operation was not yet given.

An offensive strategy was also essential for the Reds. Their army and government encountered similar organizational problems to those confronting Mannerheim and the Vaasa Senate but were less efficient and determined in tackling them. The Red Guard, which reached a maximum strength of some 90,000 men and women, lacked capable leaders and never became a properly disciplined military force although its members at times fought with great bravery. For a long time the Reds had the edge on the Whites in weapons and munitions, receiving much Russian material. Their forces were also augmented, particularly in the early stages of the war, and in Karelia, by some 10,000 Russians who fought sometimes as units and sometimes as individuals, including gunners and a number of professional staff officers who assisted the Red Guard commanders. One of these, Colonel M. S. Svechnikov, directed three assaults on the Whites at Vilppula in February, and in effect acted as Red commander first on the northern front and then more widely. He organized a fresh Red offensive beginning on 9 March, but in spite of tough fighting it made no progress either towards Haapamäki or in Savo and Karelia. One reason for the Red failure in central Finland was the concentration of White troops for their own forthcoming offensive. The Red war effort was also hampered when the Bolsheviks signed the Peace of Brest-Litovsk with Germany on 3 March and agreed to the immediate withdrawal of Russian forces from Finland. Although this did not completely stop involvement of Russians with the Finnish Reds, their role was greatly curtailed.

Mannerheim's plan to capture Tampere became more urgent when he learned from the government on 2 March that German troops were expected in Finland. German intervention was the product of the intensive lobbying by the Finnish diplomatic representative in Berlin, Edvard Hjelt, which he had begun on 9 February after the breakdown of peace negotiations between Germany and Russia. This appeal for help fitted in with the Germans' plans to create a swathe of client states along Russia's western frontier in order to prevent any possible resumption of hostilities on their eastern front. Hjelt's action went far beyond the appeal for munitions and the return of the Jäger Battalion which Mannerheim wanted. By the time the government in Vaasa learned of the coming of the German expedition, its first troops were on their way to the Åland islands and the operation could not be stopped. A further expedition was to be sent to the Finnish mainland.

Mannerheim argued with the senators against German intervention on the grounds that it would endanger Finnish independence and cause internal problems. He assured them that he would be able to win the war without it. The senators seemed to accept his view but on the next day were persuaded by Thesleff to change their minds and accept German intervention. Thesleff made it plain that he was willing to serve as commander-in-chief if Mannerheim carried out his threat to resign. The senators, whose sympathy towards Germany was as instinctive as Mannerheim's towards the Entente, preferred the certainty of the rapid end to the war which German intervention offered to the slower and more risky alternative propounded by Mannerheim, even if that intervention involved international complications. The severity of those complications became clear later when there was widespread criticism in Scandinavia for bringing one of the belligerents into the region, the possibility of British and United States recognition disappeared, and France eventually broke off diplomatic relations with Finland. Moreover, the treaties which Hjelt signed with Germany on behalf of Finland on 7 March reduced the country to a German client state.

Mannerheim was informed on 4 March of the government's decision not to refuse German intervention, and Gösta Törngren, who was present, recorded Mannerheim's reaction in his diary: 'Germany's decision to land on Åland and "crush the rebellion" in Finland roused Mannerheim almost to rage … The general, who always wanted the whole time an orientation towards Scandinavia and Sweden, was in despair.'[28] His first reaction was to consider resignation, but after reflection and an appeal by Ignatius (himself a supporter of German intervention) to his sense of duty to carry out his life's greatest undertaking, he decided to stay and try to salvage all he could from what seemed to him a political disaster and a betrayal of Svinhufvud's promise to him – as he considered it – not to ask for foreign troops. It was a case where 'duty and personal ambition coincided' but nonetheless a personal defeat.[29] He asked the government to insist that the expeditionary force should come under his command and state in a proclamation that its task was to cleanse Finland from Russian troops, not to intervene in the rebellion. He also took care to express these wishes directly to General Erich Ludendorff, the German quartermaster-general, in a telegram on 5 March, at the same time thanking Emperor Wilhelm II for the help Finland had already received. The German high command acceded to Mannerheim's requests in a telegram from Field-Marshal Paul von Hindenburg, the chief of the general staff, on 10 March. The main German force, the Baltic Division of some 9,500 men commanded by Major-General Count Rüdiger von der Goltz, sailed from Danzig on 1 April – later than planned because of ice conditions and the need for minesweeping – and landed at Hanko two days later.

Mannerheim accepted that German intervention shortened the war but not that it was necessary or even desirable. He wrote to his aunt

[28] Cited in Jägerskiöld, *Gustaf Mannerheim 1918*, p. 184.
[29] Upton, *The Finnish Revolution 1917–1918*, p. 350.

Hanna Lovén in Stockholm on 11 March: 'We have a bit of hard organization behind us and I think the day is not so far distant when we can finally bring help to the south. I believe we could have cleaned up the country with our own forces but naturally it will go more rapidly with the Germans' help and thus save many lives. However, the feeling of having fought and won in an unequal struggle without the help of others would have been of the greatest importance and value for the future of the nation. What is easily obtained does not exactly contribute to steeling a nation, and steel is what would be needed if one wants to stand on one's own feet and compel the respect of others for one's newly-won independence.'[30] Given this attitude, it is not surprising that Mannerheim wanted to press on with the Tampere operation as quickly as possible so as to gain a decisive victory before the Germans landed.

On 7 March, in a gesture of appreciation and goodwill, the government appointed Mannerheim general of cavalry, with seniority from 28 January. He was rather amused at the title, considering how little cavalry came under his command, but knew that the government was correctly following the practice of qualifying the rank of full general by the arm in which its holder had served. The promotion had the value of ensuring that Mannerheim outranked any general the Germans were likely to send to Finland.

Before starting the Tampere operation the new general of cavalry had to overcome serious doubts about the plan on the part of his most senior commanders. On 8–9 March he met them at Kauhajoki and listened to their views. The arguments for delay, notably the limitations imposed on mobile offensive operations by the army's poor state of training, seemed compelling; not only was there no common system of training (the Swedish volunteers followed Swedish regulations, officers from the old Finnish and Russian armies used Russian practice, and the Jägers followed German regulations) but many soldiers in the White army received only two weeks' very basic training and few more than six weeks; many went into battle having previously fired no more than three or four practice shots with live ammunition. This low level of training affected the army's tactical capability, and inexperienced junior leaders had difficulty in handling units and sub-units in battle. More senior officers found the maintenance of control over their troops exceedingly hard, while their orders

---

[30] To Hanna Lovén, 11 March 1918. Mannerheim, *Brev*, pp. 184–5.

from headquarters did not always correspond with the situation at the front because of the difficulty in keeping in touch.

Mannerheim listened to his commanders' objections and won over most of the proponents of delay in private conversation. His biographer, Erik Heinrichs, who was one of the Jäger majors who met him at Seinäjoki on 3 March and who became his chief of staff in 1942, thought that at the meeting at Kauhajoki Mannerheim grew into a military commander,[31] recognizing the difficulties but deciding to go ahead with the defence corps troops at his disposal. He wanted a victory for political reasons before the Germans arrived and was determined to take risks to achieve it. He allowed a little more time for the troops to concentrate before ordering the offensive to begin on 15 March.

TOWARDS VICTORY

The Tampere plan was basically simple but needed the coordination of several commanders moving independently. Mannerheim intended first to trap the Red troops in North Häme by encircling Orivesi. Despite Colonel Wilkman's victory at Länkipohja on 16 March, the other White commanders failed to move fast enough to prevent the enemy from slipping away from Orivesi to Tampere on 20 March although much ground had been gained and the threat to the railway at Haapamäki eliminated. The next phase of the operation involved encircling Tampere by cutting the railways from there to Pori and Hämeenlinna. By 25 March this had been accomplished but at such heavy cost in casualties that Mannerheim decided to commit to the battle for Tampere some of the Jäger troops whom he had intended to save for the operation in Karelia. The Swedish Brigade (less than a weak battalion) was also sent into battle on 28 March, Maundy Thursday, which because of the heavy casualties became known as 'Bloody Maundy Thursday'. Red resistance was fierce, and the exhausted Whites, after suffering very heavy losses gained only the fortified high ground to the east of the town. Meanwhile heavy Red counterattacks towards Tampere from the south at Lempäälä were repulsed between 25 and 30 March. Having first directed operations against Tampere himself, Mannerheim handed over responsibility for the final assault to Colonel Wetzer on 28 March. Wetzer did not attack again until 3

---

[31] Heinrichs, *Mannerheim Suomen kohtaloissa*, I, p. 155.

April and resistance continued until 6 April when the Reds in Tampere finally surrendered.

With forces inferior in numbers, Mannerheim had eliminated an army of 25,000. At Tampere some 1,800 Reds had been killed and 11,000 captured. The Whites lost over 600 killed. A modern Finnish military historian has written appositely: 'From the viewpoint of tactics and the operational art, the Tampere operation was a successful battle of annihilation ... The Whites' war machine was able to carry out a quite complex operation, in which severe friction appeared at all levels. Not even Mannerheim was without a share in generating it but on the other hand he was capable of such a degree of flexibility, adaptation and improvisation that at a cursory glance it seemed as if events had proceeded according to plan.'[32]

Mannerheim had underestimated the Reds' defensive capacity and probably expected too much of his commanders, who did not always respond with sufficient energy to his directions. Even after he moved his headquarters forward and took personal control he was not always able to keep them moving. Three times he went a long way forward to watch the assaults on Tampere and each time was disappointed by the outcome. On 25 March, at Vehmainen, he came under fire, with one shell bursting only 30 metres away from him. He was subsequently awarded the Cross of Liberty 4th class for his personal bravery on that occasion; it was a decoration he especially valued and was to wear regularly. But he had not just shown personal courage; he had the inner strength to see the operation through to success. On 20 March, when the situation in Karelia was bad and Orivesi had not yet been taken, he telegraphed to Thesleff, his potential rival whom he had sent back to Germany to act as liaison officer with the forthcoming German expeditionary force, to hasten its despatch. He added, to Thesleff's considerable satisfaction: 'Delay fatal'.[33] If it was a moment of doubt, it was quickly overcome. Ernst Linder, who met Mannerheim on 6 April, remarked that he showed no outward sign of all the exertion, tension and strain to which he had been subjected during the month since their last meeting.[34]

Mannerheim's victory at Tampere was decisive in that the Reds never recovered from the blow although they were to fight on,

---

[32] Ahto, 'Sotaretkillä', in *Itsenäistymisen vuodet 1917–1920*, II, p. 353.
[33] Thesleff, *Upplevelser under krigsåren 1914–1918*, p. 132.
[34] Linder, *Från Finlands Frihetskrig*, p. 136.

sometimes stubbornly but hopelessly, for another month. He held a well-deserved victory parade in Tampere on 7 April and congratulated his troops in an order of the day. 'This victory means not only the freedom and independence of Finland, this victory is also a cultural victory of the whole world over the Russian Bolsheviks and their subversive and culturally destructive doctrines.'[35] This was surely not just rhetoric, although there was rhetoric in plenty in Mannerheim's orders of the day in this as in later wars. He had not forgotten the crusade against Bolshevism even if the enemy at Tampere had mostly consisted of Finns. He had also achieved his victory before the German expeditionary force had made its presence felt.

Encountering little or no opposition, the German Baltic Division advanced rapidly towards Helsinki, which it liberated after some fighting on 14 April, the Red leaders fleeing to Viipuri. A second German force of about 3,000 men under Colonel Otto von Brandenstein sailed from Tallinn and seized Loviisa on 7 April. On 19 April, with the capture of Lahti, it cut the railway between Viipuri and Helsinki. The Red forces were now divided. Western Finland was cleared by the Whites by 20 April and the Red guards retreated eastwards, killing and destroying property as they went. There was severe fighting before these Reds were neutralized by Germans moving north and Wetzer's men moving south; this operation was the first in which the Germans acted not independently but in accordance with Mannerheim's wishes. By 2 May the Germans had eliminated the Reds throughout the south except in the Kymi valley. This major contribution to the White victory was recognized as such by Mannerheim despite his disappointment that Helsinki had been freed by von der Goltz rather than himself.

In April Mannerheim was occupied not only with the direction of the war as a whole but also with the long-awaited offensive in Karelia. On 7 April, in a move which left his headquarters free to concentrate on supreme command rather than on the detail of operations, he divided his forces into a Western Army under Major-General Wetzer and an Eastern Army under Major-General Ernst Löfström. Mannerheim, who considered Löfström the most suitable general to command the Viipuri operation, had met him while returning from a visit to

---

[35] Order of the day no. 38, 11 April 1918. *Puhtain asein. Suomen Marsalkan päiväkäskyjä vuosilta 1918–44*, p. 34.

Karelia between 4 and 6 April – even before the fall of Tampere – and outlined his intentions, though expecting the army commander to work out the details. The Jäger troops were gradually transferred to Karelia, and by the time the Viipuri operation began on 20 April twelve of the White Army's eighteen infantry regiments had been concentrated there. Mannerheim moved his headquarters on 10 April to Mikkeli, a good location from which to direct operations in Eastern Finland by an army which he now considered capable of manoeuvre.

Before the new offensive began Mannerheim received an unwelcome letter from Senators Svinhufvud and Frey. Svinhufvud had resumed his position as head of the government on reaching Vaasa via Germany and Sweden after a daring escape with Senator Jalmar Castrén from Helsinki to Tallinn on a hijacked icebreaker. Löfström's appointment aroused strong criticism, especially in Karelia, as another proof that 'Russians' were being favoured over Finnish-speaking Finns. Complaints had been made to the government, particularly by some Karelians, which ventured to suggest to Mannerheim that Wilkman would be more popular in place of Löfström, and that Ausfeld could replace Wilkman, enabling Sihvo to serve only under a German.[36] An irony of the proposal was that Wilkman was also a 'Russian' officer although, in the eyes of the Finnish nationalists, he had the merit of being a Finnish-speaker. This interference outraged Mannerheim, who kept a tight personal control over appointments and promotions. He asked Svinhufvud, Renvall and Frey to headquarters on 14 April and explained to them that Löfström was the only practicable choice, pointing out that in any case he himself would be in command of operations in Karelia. As commander-in-chief he, of course, had the overall responsibility; the senators appeared not to notice this sleight of hand. Löfström remained in charge of the Viipuri operation. Mannerheim knew the value of the services of the 'Russian' officers. The episode showed that, despite the government's professed confidence in Mannerheim, and its view that he was irreplaceable while hostilities continued, it heeded the considerable and influential opposition to him as a 'Swedish-Russian' general whose Finnish patriotism was suspect.

[36] The letter is reproduced in full in Jägerskiöld, *Gustaf Mannerheim 1918*, pp. 198–9. The original is in Kansallisarkisto (National Archives of Finland). C.G.E. Mannerheimin arkisto (Mannerheim Archive), Box 602.

The Viipuri operation began with a successful drive by Ausfeld to cut the railway to Petrograd near the Russian frontier. The Russians no longer intervened; they had taken heavy casualties in the course of a White victory at Rautu near the frontier on 5 April. Wilkman's group moved to cut off Viipuri from the north but failed to take the town by surprise. Sihvo's force was to cut communications to the west of Viipuri. There was severe fighting before the final assaults on the town on 28 and 29 April which led to the surrender of the garrison of some 15,000 Reds. Victory had been won even if not in a way that was quite according to plan. Mannerheim held a victory parade in Viipuri on 1 May.

He quickly ordered the clearance of the remaining area in Red hands, the Kymi valley, and Linder completed this operation on 5 May. The Russians evacuated their last outpost in Finland, the fort at Ino, opposite Kronstadt, on 15 May. The lawful government had been reestablished throughout Finland. The war had ended.

Mannerheim possessed exactly the qualities of leadership, initiative, generalship, determination and flexibility that were needed in the commander-in-chief at that time. Deeply imbued with a sense of personal mission to crush Bolshevism, aware of the wider significance and implications of the war and yet acutely conscious of the dignity and honour of Finland as a newly-independent state, touchy about his status, Mannerheim proved a difficult partner for the government. Understandably, he looked back on the war 'not without emotion'. 'Seldom can a war have been carried through to victory with such small resources, seldom such exacting operations executed with improvised troops.'[37] The victory had not been won, as he had wished, with Finnish forces alone but to create an army so swiftly and to bring the war to a successful conclusion in such a short time was a remarkable achievement.

TRIUMPH

Already on 4 May headquarters had issued orders to concentrate troops in Helsinki for a victory parade on 16 May. Mannerheim was determined to show the capital the Finnish army that had won the war and thus reduce the propaganda value of the German liberation of Helsinki. He also had a second and covert aim for the parade – by

[37] Mannerheim, *Memoirs*, p. 183.

drawing much of the Western Army into Helsinki, to move troops nearer to the eastern frontier. The troops already in Karelia sent only representative units to the parade.

The events of 16 May were carefully staged. Mannerheim had a fine sense of display and appreciated the value of ceremonial. Mounted on the handsome Neptune, sent over from Sweden by his brother Johan the previous month, Mannerheim looked every inch the victorious commander-in-chief. At 10 a.m. he inspected the troops in Töölö in north-west Helsinki. Then, at 11.45, he rode into the city centre at the head of a numerous suite and followed by his army. Arrived in the Senate Square, he entered the Senate building, again accompanied by his suite, to address a session of the government. Further speeches outside in the Square were followed by a Te Deum in the cathedral at 1.30 p.m. Young women dressed in white scattered flowers in his path as he went up the steps. At 2.30 he took the salute as the 12,000 troops marched past him along the North Esplanade, the column taking an hour and a half to go by.

'It was', as General Linder subsequently wrote, 'a day which will always remain indelibly engraved in the memory of everyone who took part. The sun shone from the clear May sky, the earth stood half in blossom and hopeful. Where we marched shouts of welcome met us from poor and rich, from old and young, from people in bright array or deep mourning, from thousands of throats. Already from far away one saw a swell of hundreds of white handkerchiefs which waved at us.'[38]

This veritable triumph was one of the greatest days of Mannerheim's life, perhaps the greatest. It was certainly a fitting conclusion to the only war in which he fought on the winning side. It established in the Finnish public mind his role as the leader of the White army, the White General, and ensured that his name, which had been virtually unknown in January, became familiar throughout the country. But Mannerheim carefully used the occasion to make both political and military points. His speech to the government, whom he greeted in the name of Finland's 'young, victorious army', reminded the senators of how they had been stripped of authority by the rebellion. 'Determined that such a state of things shall never recur, the army regards it as its right to express openly its firm hope that safeguards will be given, through the creation of a social order and an executive

[38] Linder, *Från Finlands Frihetskrig*, p. 206.

power of the state, which for ever will protect us against new months of terror such as those through which our country has passed. The army regards it as the only possible guarantee of this, that the helm of the ship of the Finnish state is placed in a strong hand, which is not reached by party strife, and not forced, through compromises, to whittle down the power of the government... the dead demand that their sacrifice shall not have been in vain.'[39]

This was a command for a strong government, for unity, for a fresh start. 'They were hard words that I said to the Senate,' Mannerheim recalled.[40] He had in effect fired a shot in the campaign about the future constitution of Finland although next day he authorized Georg Schauman, a liberal politician with whom he had been at school, to deny that this had been his intention. His words – which were taken as supporting a monarchy – had to be understood in their literal sense and nothing more.[41] That was quite enough. In any case, J. K. Paasikivi, who became prime minister a few days later, believed that Mannerheim intended 'that a king should have been obtained for Finland already in May'.[42] Mannerheim was not alone in favouring a monarchy as a defence against revolution; this was also, after all, the constitutional norm in Europe.

To the members of parliament Mannerheim made another point. 'Finland's future as an independent state depends on its army, and its army in turn on the support which you, the representatives of Finland, give to it. I am convinced that this army, which has saved the country, will obtain from you all the support it needs to remain the defence of the country and the people.'[43] Headquarters had already started planning the army's postwar organization in mid-April when Mannerheim approved a scheme whereby it would consist of nine divisions, each with three infantry regiments, but only one battalion in each regiment serving in peacetime. By 16 May the future of Finland's army was already contentious and was to be a major contributory factor to Mannerheim's early resignation as commander-in-chief. The conflicts that had been apparent during the war now surfaced powerfully.

[39] The full text is given in Ignatius, *Carl Gustaf Mannerheim*, pp. 63–4; this translation is from Borenius, *Field-Marshal Mannerheim*, p. 176.
[40] Jägerskiöld, *Gustaf Mannerheim 1918*, p. 244.
[41] Schauman, *Valtiomuototaistelu Suomessa 1918*, p. 30.
[42] Ikonen, *J. K. Paasikiven poliittinen toiminta*, p. 181.
[43] Ignatius, *Carl Gustaf Mannerheim*, p. 66.

RESIGNATION

It has been rightly said that 'With regard to politics, it was fashionable in the White Army to be an activist, Fennophile and Finnish-speaking, supportive of the Finnish-speaking peoples as an ideal, and pro-German. On the other hand it was unfashionable to be Swedish-speaking, Swedophile and believing in cooperation with Russia.'[44] These contrasting attitudes were not necessarily mutually exclusive; for example, some of the leading Jägers were Swedish-speaking although in other ways they fell into the 'fashionable' category. What weakened Mannerheim's political position was that he was overwhelmingly 'unfashionable'. Edvard Hjelt expressed not untypical fears that the autocratic Mannerheim would become the political focus for pro-Entente conservatives and jeopardize a pro-German and anti-Russian policy.[45]

However, Mannerheim did support the Finnish nationalists' annexationist ambitions in Eastern Karelia which, if realized, would have resulted in Finland acquiring a strategically more favourable frontier with Russia. As a counterpoise to Red Finnish propaganda, he even issued a proclamation to the Karelians on 23 February in which he promised 'not to sheathe my sword ... until Lenin's last soldier and hooligan is driven out of Finland and Russian Karelia as well'.[46] Small Finnish forces were sent across the frontier into Eastern Karelia during the war but could not be maintained there because of the risk of conflict with British troops protecting the Murmansk railway.

Mannerheim was much more interested in advancing to Petrograd than in operations in Eastern Karelia, although he believed that helping the establishment of a new, White, Russian government in Petrograd – alongside which Finland had to live – could lead to the cession of Eastern Karelia to Finland as a reward for its aid in crushing Bolshevism in Russia. He needed German support for a Finnish expedition to Petrograd but it was not forthcoming, despite the Germans' ready agreement to retain troops in Finland and help train the

[44] Manninen, 'Taistelevat osapuolet' in *Itsenäistymisen vuodet 1917–1920*, II, p. 153.
[45] See Hjelt's letter to Svinhufvud, 25 April 1918, in Jägerskiöld, *Gustaf Mannerheim 1918*, pp. 254–5.
[46] Ignatius, *Carl Gustaf Mannerheim*, p. 41. Was this form of words an echo – conscious or unconscious – of Alexander I's famous declaration at the time of the French invasion of 1812 that 'I will not sheathe my sword until not a single enemy soldier remains in my empire'? Shilder, *Imperator Aleksandr Pervyi*, III, p. 83.

Finnish army, and the belief of Emperor Wilhelm II in April that 'Mannerheim perhaps is suitable to restore order in Petersburg'.[47] Nor was the idea of cooperation with the Russian Whites received favourably by the Finnish government. In any case the Finnish army, whose soldiers now wanted to go home, was in no condition to conduct an offensive against Petrograd. So Mannerheim's ambition to be its liberator, about which he had written to his brother Johan as early as 21 February ('we ought to get there'), had to be deferred.[48]

Mannerheim's 'Swedishness' was as undeniable as it was contentious in White Finland during and after the war. In 1918 his knowledge of Finnish, the language of the overwhelming majority of the population, was virtually non-existent. He had learned some Finnish at the Finnish Cadet Corps (where his last mark in the subject had been nine out of twelve) but he had to resort to private lessons when preparing for his matriculation examination. He had written to his uncle and guardian, Albert von Julin, on 15 October 1886: 'Finnish will not be an easy nut for me to crack.'[49] However, he attained a satisfactory mark of eight. Thereafter he had no need of Finnish and the speeches he made in it during and after the war were prepared for him. When the headmaster of the Finnish grammar school in Tampere tried to converse with him in Finnish in April 1918, he got nowhere because Mannerheim simply could not speak it.[50] He stumbled over the delivery of a speech in Finnish to the Finnish Church in London in November 1918 and the text of a speech in Finnish from 1921 has the years and numbers written out in full to avoid errors.[51]

Mannerheim was a capable linguist, proficient in French and Russian and later speaking good English and German. His Finnish eventually became good but in 1918 and for some years afterwards his lack of it was a stick which politicians, particularly the Agrarians and the Progressive Party, used to beat him. In an obvious but vain attempt to appear more Finnish he even went through a brief period of signing himself Kustaa instead of Gustaf Mannerheim. The politi-

---

[47] Cited in Nurmio, *Suomen itsenäistyminen ja Saksa*, p. 216.
[48] To Johan Mannerheim, 21 February 1918. Mannerheim, *Brev*, p. 184.
[49] Cited in Jägerskiöld, *Den unge Mannerheim*, p. 93.
[50] Ylikangas, *Tie Tampereelle*, p. 499.
[51] Michael Gripenberg's diary, 17 November 1918. Mannerheim Archive, Box 123; Speech to Helsinki Defence Corps, 28 January 1921. National Archives of Finland, C.G.E. Mannerheim. Grensholm Collection, VAY 5634.

cians' complaints about him found a ready popular echo because the Finnish-language press was already stoking up resentment against the 'Swedes' for their dominance in the higher ranks of the army.

Opponents of Mannerheim during the war had accused him of interference in Finnish foreign policy over Eastern Karelia, favouritism over appointments, hostility to activists, anti-Finnishness and installing a Russian system at headquarters. Dr V. O. Sivén, the acting head of the Board of Medicine, an activist and prime opponent of the 'Russian' Mannerheim, believed that Svinhufvud had agreed in mid-April to dismiss him at the end of the war. Mannerheim himself was doubtful if he would continue in office to organize the new army. He wrote to his brother Johan on 29 April: 'I will do so only in the event that I really feel that I enjoy the full confidence of the country and can carry out this task with the full authority necessary for its success.'[52] Demands for the 'fennicization' of the army intensified in mid May.

On 20 May Mannerheim sent his resignation to the government on the grounds that he had accomplished the task for which he had been appointed. The reasons for this timing are unclear. Perhaps he wanted to know if the government supported him fully or not; perhaps he knew that it was asking the Germans' advice about the future Finnish army. On 22 May the government decided to ask Mannerheim to organize the army on German lines and using German advisers and instructors; if he did not agree he was to be asked to stay on until a new commander-in-chief had been appointed. There followed several days of negotiations, between Mannerheim and the government on 23 May, and between the government and other parties. Matters were not helped by his resignation becoming known to the press. He was prepared to go a long way to meet the government's wishes: he accepted a German pattern of training while insisting on keeping some Swedish officers in service. However, he refused to give up the right to promote officers and wanted a future war minister's role restricted to administration. As for the use of the army, he favoured assistance to the Russian monarchists to recover Petrograd rather than a campaign to liberate Eastern Karelia.

The government's discussions behind Mannerheim's back with von der Goltz – who wanted the Germans to run the army, limited to three divisions – and their proposal to make Thesleff war minister

[52] To Johan Mannerheim, 29 April 1918. Mannerheim, *Brev*, p. 186.

(*Above*) 1. Mannerheim on an inspection tour in Karelia, April 1918. (*Below*) 2. Towards the end of the Civil War with Major General Ernst Linder's daughter (*centre*) and Major Michael Gripenberg (*right*). (Both: Military Museum of Finland)

(*Left above*) 3. Mannerheim at the victory parade in Helsinki on 16 May 1918 to mark the end of the war. (*Left below*) 4. Scene during the same occasion. (*Right above*) 5. Mannerheim in 1919. (*Below*) 6. Mannerheim greeted in Stockholm by King Gustav V of Sweden at the beginning of a state visit, 12 February 1919. (All these photos: Military Museum of Finland)

(*Right*) 7. K.J. Ståhlberg (1865–1952), progressive party politician, jurist, first president of Finland 1919–25. (*Below*) 8. P.E. Svinhufvud (1861–1944), conservative politician, lawyer, prime minister 1917–18, regent 1918, president 1931–7. (Both photos: Ministry of Foreign Affairs, Helsinki)

deeply offended him. On 27 May, having had his fill of intrigues and what he saw as the government's disloyalty, he wrote his final letter of resignation. He believed 'that the government did not want to create the preconditions for the supreme military command which would allow me to carry responsibility for the solution of the great questions which are ahead'.[53] It was clear that he had no wish to see German control over the army and over Finnish foreign policy, or an end to the prospect of an advance on Petrograd. He recognized that neither the commander-in-chief nor the government had any freedom of action given the willing subservience of the latter to Germany. He remained convinced that the government was compromising Finland's neutrality and that Finland ought to be neutral in the World War. On 29 May the government accepted his resignation, and it was made public in the press on 30 May. To the right-wing political élite Mannerheim, though a meritorious soldier, was a political parvenu and expendable.[54]

In recounting in his *Memoirs* the events leading up to his resignation, Mannerheim conflated several of the official and unofficial meetings he attended with members of the government. Since by 30 May his written resignation had already been accepted, he clearly misdated his bitter and dramatic description of how he resigned at a meeting with the government on 30 May after Senator Frey told him of the intention to entrust the organization of the army to the Germans. 'I lay down my command this evening and go abroad tomorrow … Only two weeks before, the President of the Senate had warmly welcomed me in the same chamber, thanking me for what I had done for the salvation of my country. On May 30th, 1918, the members of the government had not a word to say to me when I left the chamber, and no one rose to offer me his hand.'[55] Whatever the exact circumstances of the personal parting between government and commander-in-chief, Mannerheim's departure was so abrupt that plans for an official dinner in his honour had to be abandoned.

His decision to go abroad after resigning was a demonstration of the distance he wanted to put between himself and the Finnish government. The words in his *Memoirs* reflected accurately his thoughts at the time: 'I realized that under existing conditions I could not

[53] Cited in Manninen, 'Mannerheimin ero toukokuussa 1918', p. 37.
[54] Vares, *"Kansakunnan kaapin päällä"*, pp. 8–13.
[55] Mannerheim, *Memoirs*, pp. 182–3.

influence the course of events, whereas outside ... my own country I would have greater possibilities of informing myself of the world situation, thereby serving the interests of my country. I had no doubt that for Finland to continue the course she had set herself would lead to disaster.'[56]

At the personal level there was little to keep Mannerheim in Finland. 'My departure ... presented me with no difficulties, since I possessed neither a home nor goods ... It was more difficult to leave the army I had created and lose the sense of community which I felt so strongly.'[57] He was assured of the sympathy and good wishes of his closest and personally devoted colleagues, several of whom resigned with him, and who dined him out on 30 May. He was not to leave Finland entirely destitute. On accepting his resignation, the Finnish government had decided to pay him an annual pension of 30,000 marks which corresponded to the salary of the prime minister (and was equal to £880 at the average rate of exchange for June 1918).

Sweden, where he had relations, was Mannerheim's obvious destination. He left Helsinki for Turku on 1 June 1918 after first calling on Svinhufvud and saying some 'hard words' to the man who, since 18 May, had been Finland's regent or head of state.[58] From Turku he took the boat to Stockholm. He was gone, but not forgotten, either in Finland or abroad. His resignation and voluntary exile were to prove fortunate for Finland and for himself.

---

[56] Mannerheim, *Memoirs*, p. 184.
[57] *Ibid.*
[58] Manninen, 'Mannerheimin ero toukokuussa 1918', *Sotahistoriallinen Seura ja Sotamuseo. Vuosikirja*, IX, 1976, p. 39.

CHAPTER II

REGENT

'Europe and the whole world have had to pay a heavy price for allowing Bolshevism free play in 1919.'[1]

IN SWEDEN

In Stockholm Mannerheim was warmly received by Swedes who had recently fought alongside him in Finland or helped the Finnish cause. King Gustav V invested him with the Grand Cross of the Order of the Sword, an honour which — as in other instances — Mannerheim interpreted as recognition of the Finnish army as a whole. He spent part of the summer visiting his brother Johan and sister-in-law Palaemona on their estate at Grensholm (near Norsholm, roughly between Linköping and Norrköping) and in seeing various relations and acquaintances. His younger daughter Sophie (known as Sophy), then aged twenty-three, arrived from England to join him.

One of the general advantages Mannerheim brought back with him on returning to Finland was his complete freedom from family ties. His two daughters had a peripatetic upbringing after leaving Russia with their mother, and attended boarding schools in Switzerland, Belgium and Paris. Anastasie, the elder, went to England to attend a college in Manchester in 1912. She had become a Roman Catholic and in 1914 entered a Carmelite convent in London, taking the veil as Sister Theresa of the Infant Jesus in February 1917. These decisions upset Mannerheim's sister Sophie but he understood and accepted them. In 1918 Sophy began to train as a nurse at St Thomas's Hospital in London, where Sophie Mannerheim herself had trained. Mannerheim and his wife were no longer in contact, and it had been difficult to keep in touch with his daughters during the war; in any case, he had not wished to have them with him in Poland before 1914. However, before leaving Helsinki he had asked the British consul

[1] Mannerheim, *Memoirs*, p. 236.

there if Sophy could have permission to join him since 'she is quite alone', by which he meant without any members of the family. The British, who controlled passenger traffic across the North Sea because of the war, acceded to his request 'for political reasons'.[2] In consequence he now had to mobilize his sister-in-law and his sister Eva, who also lived in Sweden, to keep an eye on Sophy. He was undoubtedly concerned about his daughters' wellbeing, as this episode with Sophy and his financial support for them showed, but their relationship was inevitably rather distant, given the many years they had spent apart. Although Sophy was often with him from mid 1918 to early 1920, his correspondence shows repeated efforts to arrange for her to spend time with other people. He never allowed his family to distract him from anything he wanted to do.

The serious business of Mannerheim's stay in Sweden was his contacts with the diplomatic corps in Stockholm, particularly the Allied ministers there. He also kept in close touch with events in Finland and went there for a short visit towards the end of June. In his conversations with Sir Esmé Howard, Ira Morris and Eugène Thiébaut, respectively the British, United States and French ministers in Stockholm, Mannerheim developed several arguments. First he attempted to justify the acceptance by the Finns of German arms during the Civil War. Secondly he stressed the extent to which the present Finnish government had come under German influence, making his own position in Finland untenable. These points helped to establish him as a sympathizer of the Allies and dissociate himself from the pro-German policy in Finland. Thirdly he endeavoured to convince the ministers of the need to encourage pro-Allied elements in Finland by sending food supplies there and acknowledging Finnish claims to a northern port (Petsamo) and to Eastern Karelia. If the removal of German troops were made a condition of such Allied support, so much the better. Lastly he tried to encourage the Allies to intervene against the Bolsheviks in Petrograd, a matter still of great concern to him, although it was principally Finnish policy that figured in his discussions with the Allied representatives.

Mannerheim proved a capable unofficial diplomat. He was able to express Finland's national interests independently of the position of the Finnish government and in some respects gain a sympathetic

---

[2] Mannerheim to Lindley, 25 May 1918 and Foreign Office minutes. Public Record Office [PRO], F.O.371/3211, 92418/92418/56; 96469/92418/56.

hearing for them. After visiting Helsinki at the end of June and beginning of July 1918 he discussed with the Allied ministers in Stockholm his idea of going to London and Paris as a special representative of the Finnish government in order to improve Finland's relations with the Allies. This plan won Allied approval but not that of the Finnish government which asked him instead to go to Vienna as Finnish minister, an offer he felt obliged to refuse since his acceptance of it would have compromised his position with the Allies. Howard's recommendation on 13 July that it might be useful for Mannerheim to visit London and Paris was minuted in the Foreign Office with the comment: 'It is fairly clear that he is our friend, and his influence in Finland will probably revive in time.'[3] The goodwill Mannerheim built up with the Allies during the summer and autumn of 1918 was to prove of immense value both for Finland and himself when his influence did revive.

The Germans were interested in Mannerheim's activities in Stockholm and even got a report from an agent of a conversation between him and Howard on 9 July. His understandable desire in the summer to go to Warsaw to recover his possessions there – they had survived the war in store – necessitated getting the Germans' permission. The German foreign ministry and high command seized the opportunity to arrange in August an invitation for him to visit the front and be received by the Emperor in the course of the journey. Mannerheim was too wary to allow a private visit to be converted into a political trap, particularly since Howard advised that to go would prejudice his position with the Allies.

A bout of Spanish influenza in mid August enabled him to prevaricate and after recovering he left for Norway to join a friend, Hjalmar Linder, to shoot deer in the mountains above Lyse Fjord near Stavanger. The occasion gave proof of Mannerheim's physical fitness in that he completed a climb of 1,500 metres (nearly 5,000 ft) over a distance of 27 kilometres (nearly 17 miles) in twelve hours. The party included Linder's beautiful half-sister Catharina (Kitty) with whom he fell in love and clearly, from their correspondence, hoped to marry when he had obtained a divorce. He secured the divorce in 1919 but marriage to Kitty Linder eluded him.[4] After returning to Stockholm from

---

[3] Howard to Foreign Office, 13 July 1918. F.O.371/3206, 123376/144/56.
[4] Mannerheim's letters to Kitty Linder. Mannerheim Archive, Box 952.

Norway he used private business as the excuse for further delay in accepting the Germans' invitation. He was occupied in the autumn with taking an apartment in Stockholm, moving out of the Grand Hotel which had hitherto been his base there. By then his pension arrangements had been sorted out. It was a curious coincidence that the Finnish government's payments office only received the instruction to pay his pension on 25 June when he was in Finland.

Confidence in a German victory and belief in German protection against a possible attack by Russia influenced the Finnish government's policies well into the autumn. The rump parliament, from which almost all the Social Democrat representatives had been excluded, was divided over the future constitution between the monarchists (the conservatives and most of the Swedish Party) and the republicans (the liberals and the Agrarians). The government, with the support of a slender monarchist majority in parliament, declared the country a monarchy and on 9 October 1918 parliament elected Prince Friedrich Karl of Hesse as king of Finland; a German prince was considered essential to ensure strong ties with Germany. This decision caused a sharp deterioration in relations with the Allies.

Mannerheim took care to convey the opinions of the Allies to Helsinki, and although his reports were disregarded during the summer, the situation gradually changed. The weakening of Germany following Allied victories in France from August 1918 necessitated a revision of Finnish policy. On 10 October 1918 Mannerheim wrote to his cousin Erland Nordenskiöld: 'The government, hitherto hypnotized by Germany's greatness, seems gradually beginning to open its eyes and realize the importance of the Western powers. May it not be too late. The situation, both external and internal, is very disturbing and demands the purposeful work of a strong government to correct the mistakes perpetrated by the lack of judgement and laxity of the present senate.'[5] The collapse of Germany in November 1918 left Finland in a crisis. The victorious Allies would determine territorial questions at the peace conference and they alone controlled the food supplies urgently needed in Finland. Finland had to restore good relations with the Allies as a matter of urgency. Already in October the government had been wise enough to turn to Mannerheim.

[5] To Erland Nordenskiöld, 10 October 1918. Mannerheim, *Brev*, p. 190.

FROM UNOFFICIAL DIPLOMAT TO REGENT[6]

The Finnish foreign minister, Otto Stenroth, proposed to the government on 1 October 1918 that Mannerheim be asked to go to England and France to work for the recognition of Finland's independence by Britain and the United States. Despite some opposition, an emissary was sent to Stockholm to seek his assent and to ask him to come to Helsinki for discussions. Mannerheim came. He was prepared to accept the mission, which was as vital to Finland as it was delicate and difficult – but, as so often with him, only on his own terms. He believed that a private visit to learn about the political situation would constitute a more effective approach to the Allies than to go as the envoy of a government he regarded as compromised. Only if circumstances in London and Paris were right would he be willing to consider undertaking a special mission for the government. Not without satisfaction, he remarked to Svinhufvud, 'Now you want to play this trump card.'[7]

During this stay in Helsinki in October a former Russian prime minister, A. F. Trepov, suggested to Mannerheim that he might command a Russian and German intervention force moving from Finland to crush the Bolsheviks in Petrograd.[8] He was interested in the idea, though using Allied rather than German troops to assist the Russians. He recognized that a visit to London and Paris would also give him the opportunity to discuss intervention plans with the Allies.

The British expressed willingness to receive Mannerheim and by the end of October had arranged his passage; they noted his denial that his journey was official. He left Stockholm for Bergen on 31 October, accompanied by Michael Gripenberg as his secretary. His sailing was delayed by storms but after a rough passage he reached Aberdeen on 11 November and arrived next day in London where celebrations of the armistice were in progress.

Among the rumours surrounding his journey was one that he was to replace Rudolf Holsti as official Finnish representative in London. However, the British, who had noted the changed political

---

[6] The term regent was a constitutional device to designate Finland's interim head of state until a new constitution could be adopted. It was not a consequence of the election of a king.
[7] Cited in Heinrichs, *Mannerheim Suomen kohtaloissa*, I, p. 270.
[8] Jägerskiöld, *Gustaf Mannerheim 1918*, pp. 315–16.

situation in Finland, recognized that Mannerheim was 'too big a man' for that: 'He is clearly marked out as Svinhufvud's successor.'[9] Throughout October and November a major redirection of Finnish policy was in progress which was to lead to that outcome.

A broad non-socialist coalition was considered essential because of the threatening situation. After difficult negotiations, a new government was formed on 27 November under Lauri Ingman, with a bare monarchist majority. Its programme included early parliamentary elections in February or March 1919, the deferment of consideration of the constitution until after those elections, and the replacement of Svinhufvud as regent by Mannerheim. Some conservative pro-Germans disliked the idea of his recall, remembering his attitude in May 1918 and being uncertain of his ability to lead the country.[10] Others on the right believed he would be a unifying force and that the military situation made his return as a soldier desirable. Crucially, he was seen as the one man the Allies trusted. The republicans, particularly the Agrarians, had their doubts about him; he was perceived as a monarchist with ideas of intervention in Russia although Georg Schauman praised him as possessing 'the tact and sureness of conduct which are now required both in our internal affairs and especially in our foreign policy: he is besides an honest and wise patriot'.[11]

On 10 December Svinhufvud announced his resignation so that Mannerheim could be elected regent by parliament. Not without a sharp debate, he was elected, by 73 votes to 27 (mostly Agrarians) on 12 December 1918. Thus Mannerheim assumed not merely an official role during his negotiations with the Allies but the position of Finland's head of state.

Mannerheim's discussions in London and Paris were conducted against the background of his increasing involvement with Finnish politics. Although not in fact certain what appointment he was to be offered, he gave at the outset the impression that he expected to become regent but wanted to be sure of the Allies attitude before accepting the appointment. To Lord Robert Cecil, the parliamentary under-secretary at the Foreign Office, whom he saw with Holsti on 15 November, he stressed the need for food supplies even before raising the question of British recognition of Finnish independence.

[9] Minute on Clive to Foreign Office, 1 November 1918. F.O.371/3207, 182460.
[10] Vares, *Kuninkaan tekijät*, p. 286.
[11] Cited in Vares, *ibid.*, p. 287.

On that, as on territorial questions, Cecil wanted to await the decision of the peace conference. Mannerheim had also to put the Finnish government's case for Prince Friedrich Karl. 'Evidently himself a strong monarchist', and fearing that republican sentiments made the election of another candidate as king unlikely, Mannerheim asked if negotiations with Prince Friedrich Karl should be broken off, and was advised that they should.[12]

Mannerheim made similar points to Sir Esmé Howard, who had been transferred to London. He convinced Howard of the urgent need for grain deliveries, but made no headway on recognition or on Allied acceptance of a Finnish occupation of Petrograd, should a Bolshevik attack on Finland be defeated and the Russians be pursued across the frontier. Howard noted, correctly, that Mannerheim 'would like to play the role of the saviour, not only of Finland, but also of Russia, for which country he undoubtedly has considerable sympathies, so long as it does not interfere with Finnish independence'.[13] Mannerheim told the Finnish government to abandon Prince Friedrich Karl; by 12 December it had done so.

Already by 20 November Mannerheim had stated his willingness to assume the regency once he had completed his mission in London. Ingman, the prime minister designate, consulted him about the suitability of Colonel Rudolf Walden to be war minister, and he approved. In other ways the government was formed without reference to him, and this caused him some difficulties with the Allies who doubted that it represented the complete change of policy they required. At first it was thought in Helsinki that Mannerheim could not be elected regent until his return but he forced the government's hand by pointing out that London required a more rapid change of course.

Towards the end of November Mannerheim went to Paris to find out the French position over recognition. Stephen Pichon, the foreign minister, demanded as the price of restored relations a new, Entente-oriented government, the abandonment of Prince Friedrich Karl, early elections and the removal of all German troops and advisers. To Mannerheim this seemed acceptable and hopeful but it was not the breakthrough he really wanted. Back in London he saw A. J. Balfour, the foreign secretary, on 10 December, and came away in

---

[12] Memorandum by Lord Robert Cecil, 15 November 1918. F.O.371/3207, 190067/144.

[13] Memorandum by Howard, 19 November 1918. F.O.371/3207,191086/144.

the mistaken belief that Balfour had promised Britain would join France in recognizing Finland's independence. In fact Mannerheim had again failed to make progress on British recognition, being assured only of British goodwill and a promise to act in consultation with its Allies.[14]

Despite his skilful diplomacy (helped by his excellent French; his English was less fluent), Mannerheim had not managed to avoid returning '*avec les mains vides*' and in a position where it could be said that '*il n'a rien fait*', as he had expressed his fears to a member of the Foreign Office Political Intelligence Department on arrival in London.[15] He had not obtained the hoped for Allied recognition, but only the terms that Finland had to fulfil before recognition could be granted. That was something, but he had learned that Finland was still not fully trusted, and very much on probation as far as the Allies were concerned.

He returned to Finland via Copenhagen and Stockholm, where the Swedes had recently demanded a plebiscite to determine the future of the Åland islands, a plan which Mannerheim obviously opposed. From Stockholm he requested the despatch of an ADC to meet him in Turku and asked for suitable accommodation to be prepared for him in Helsinki. He reached Turku on 22 December, to be met by the city fathers and guards of honour from the army and the Defence Corps (Civil Guards) which were in process of reorganization.

Fortunately he did not return entirely empty-handed. The discussions he had set in motion about grain deliveries bore fruit and by a happy coincidence the first shipment arrived in Turku on the day of his return. He mentioned the Allied promise of allowing grain imports in the proclamation he issued to the Finnish people. The principal theme of this proclamation was unity. He had accepted the regency 'convinced that my sincere intention will be understood by the entire people of Finland and that this people will now finally unite with one accord to uphold Finland's independence and liberty.'[16] On 23 December he reached Helsinki where an enthusiastic

[14] Memorandum by Balfour, 16 December 1918. F.O.371/3207, 206323/144, Memorandum, 23 December 1918. 210220/144. To Michael Gripenberg, 22 September 1934. Mannerheim Archive, Box 906.
[15] Minute by Simpson, 21 November 1918. F.O.371/3207, 189920.
[16] Mannerheim, *Minnen*, I, pp. 325–6.

reception and the responsibility of office awaited him. He returned to the theme of unity in his speech to the government on 28 December; he hoped that the whole people would unite around the government 'when it honestly strives to treat all classes justly and as far as possible to even out injustices where they occur'.[17]

MILITARY AND FOREIGN POLICY PROBLEMS

An atmosphere of uncertainty, fear, intrigue and bellicosity prevailed in Finland throughout 1919. The last contingent of German troops had left on 16 December 1918 and a few remaining officers departed in early January 1919. An undeclared state of war existed with Bolshevik Russia and there was fear of what might happen after the Germans' withdrawal. How could the Royal Navy's presence in the Baltic compensate for the departure of the German army? Would the Russian Whites defeat the Bolsheviks and, if so, how would they regard Finland? How threatening were the numerous Russian exiles in Finland? Would the Finnish activists realize their aims of helping the Estonians to independence, the Ingrians to autonomy and the Eastern Karelians to union with Finland? Could Swedish designs on the Åland islands be resisted? When would Allied recognition be forthcoming?

The key domestic issue was the nature of the constitution and the powers of the head of state. The constitution was considered against the background of the sore divisions of the Civil War. The left was smarting from defeat and its consequences, including the casualties of the post-war prison camps. The right was alarmed by the rapid recovery of the Finnish Social Democrats and by the agitation directed by the Finnish Communists from Russia and particularly directed at the army, many of whose conscripts were unsympathetic to the government. Internal stability and peaceful democratic development could not be taken for granted. Intrigues flourished, as did espionage. Would there be a left-wing *coup* – or a right-wing one? Mannerheim was not above this unstable and threatening situation. He was very much part of it, a figure of hope to the conservatives, of opportunity to the activists, of fear and hatred to the left and, often, of suspicion to the centre.

[17] *Ibid.*, p. 327.

Mannerheim never expected his regency to last more than a short time: the office was by its nature provisional and would end when he confirmed a new constitution. Until then, however, he possessed certain monarchical powers derived from the Swedish constitution of 1772 and 1789, which was held to remain in force in Finland. He had to sanction and promulgate laws passed by parliament; he nominated the prime minister and ministers and the most senior members of the judiciary, and appointed envoys; and he had the right to grant pardons. He could declare war, conclude peace and enter into alliances. He commanded the armed forces, which was no formality: on 30 December 1918 he issued an order personally assuming the supreme command. Military problems were prominent among those with which he had to deal.

Mannerheim left unchanged the army organization created by the Germans (three divisions and one brigade), but called back to office his Finnish collaborators from the War of Independence, notably Ignatius as chief of the general staff. The prominence of the 'Russians' did not go down well with the Jägers and their supporters. Relations between the commander-in-chief's staff and the chief of the general staff were defined in a somewhat complicated way in March 1919. French officers arrived by invitation to provide advice, for example on weapons procurement. Mannerheim had no wish for unnecessarily high defence expenditure, nor did he want a long period of compulsory military service. He confirmed the new provisional military service law in February 1919 which provided for eighteen months' conscription. Also in February he confirmed a decree on the organization of the Defence Corps, which he strongly supported as a guarantor of social stability and as a reinforcement of the army. The Defence Corps were now allowed to nominate their own commander-in-chief, who was subordinate to the war minister but appointed by the head of state; this was designed to give the Defence Corps an independent position which was to prove controversial, since considerable reliance was placed on them for internal security in the event of mobilization.

The army's peacetime deployment placed some troops on the Russian frontier, defensive positions were planned on the Karelian isthmus, and mobilization plans were revised in April 1919. These provided mainly for defence, but there was also a defensive-offensive scheme involving a counter-attack and a very general scheme for an offensive against Petrograd. The army was to double in size on mobilization to six divisions and two brigades, but adequate equipment was lacking even for the peacetime army. Poor material conditions and a low level of training made the peacetime army's 20,000–30,000 men a less effective force than was desirable. Mannerheim tried hard to overcome these problems. He was a keen supporter of the new Cadet School which was founded in January 1919 to train future officers. This sought to revive the traditions of the old Finnish Cadet Corps, from which Mannerheim had been expelled and whose old boys' club had made him an honorary member in October 1918 – a source of some amusement to him as well as satisfaction.

The prime minister, who had been appointed not by Mannerheim but by Svinhufvud, was Lauri Ingman, a professor of practical theology who eventually became archbishop. An experienced politician from the Old Finnish conservative party, Ingman was a pro-German monarchist but his conservatism was above all pragmatic and he was able to recognize and respond in an undogmatic way to the realities of political developments. Mannerheim got on well with him, seeking – and valuing – his advice at difficult moments, and successfully resisting the demands of the Allies in January 1919 for Ingman's dismissal as pro-German. He regarded the government as competent and generally worked with it without friction, taking his decisions both in the council of state (the formal executive meeting of the government and the head of state) and outside it. A minor disagreement concerned what flags might be carried at the funeral of a socialist leader in April 1919. Ingman was prepared to allow trades union red flags while Mannerheim was against the display of red flags of any description – an indication of his total hostility to socialism and its symbols. On this issue the regent had to give way.

The principal issues confronting Mannerheim and the government related to foreign policy, above all the question of Allied recognition. As early as 23 December 1918 he confirmed that new parliamentary elections would be held on 1 March 1919. He was disappointed that Allied recognition did not quickly follow, and attempted through France to obtain it in January 1919. The Allies decided not to act, ostensibly because they linked the recognition of Finland's independence to the future of Russia, but probably also because the United States mistrusted Mannerheim as undemocratic and did not want to strengthen his position in advance of the promised parliamentary elections. Britain stated in March that recognition would be granted only to the new government formed after the elections. The presence of Finnish volunteer troops in Eastern Karelia complicated relations with Britain since its troops from Murmansk were operating in the region, and the British were keen to return the so-called Murmansk Legion to Finland under an amnesty. This consisted of Red Finns whom they had enlisted during 1918 to help resist German and Finnish expansion in Eastern Karelia. Neither Mannerheim nor Ingman favoured an amnesty for these rebels.

Mannerheim always took the view that the question of Finnish territorial gains in Eastern Karelia would be decided by operations against Petrograd. However, he was prepared to accept an invasion of the Olonets region by Finnish volunteers in April in support of a local rising. Despite discussions with White Russian representatives in early 1919, the Finns resisted attempts to persuade them to join in an attack on Petrograd because the Russians refused even to consider the recognition of Finnish independence, while the backing of the Allies, which was regarded as essential, was also unclear. The Allies did back Finnish support for the Estonians during their War of Independence at the beginning of 1919; Mannerheim facilitated the despatch of Finnish volunteers on humanitarian grounds, but their commander was given strict orders not to move any distance into Russia. In the absence of White Russian recognition of Finland, Mannerheim was not prepared to risk Finnish lives in the pursuit of Russian interests, particularly in an operation not under Finnish control. The last Finnish volunteers returned from Estonia in April 1919.

The Åland islands question remained a stumbling-block to the good relations with Sweden which Mannerheim was keen to establish as part of a general policy of cooperation with the Scandinavian countries, to which he recognized Finland was bound by historic, political and cultural ties, he also wanted Finland to emulate the Swedish policy of neutrality. He was delighted to receive an invitation from the King of Sweden to undertake a state visit to Stockholm in February, and took the initiative in securing invitations for similar visits to Copenhagen and Oslo as extensions of the same tour. Apart from dissident voices on the left, where Mannerheim was hated for his victory over Finland's socialists, the visits to Stockholm on 12–13 February and Copenhagen on 17–18 February were successful in that he was generally well received and Finland's status as an independent country was publicly recognized. Threats from the Norwegian socialists made him cancel plans to continue to Oslo; he was able to plead illness as the reason. In his determination to show off the ribbon of the Order of the Sword conferred on him by King Gustav V in June 1918, Mannerheim had not worn a greatcoat on his arrival in Stockholm despite the chilly weather. Towards the end of the visit he developed a cold with a high temperature and had to delay his departure for Copenhagen. He was still not fully fit when he left Stockholm on 20 February to return to Finland.

The purpose of the royal invitation to Stockholm was to discuss the Åland islands, and Mannerheim and the Finnish foreign minister, Carl Enckell, were involved in various meetings with the King and members of the Swedish government. Mannerheim shared the Finnish view that Åland was an inalienable part of Finland. Intending to present the King with the Grand Cross with Chain of the Order of the White Rose of Finland which he had recently instituted, he gave expression to his strong sense of symbolism and belief in its importance by adding a ninth rose to the chain to represent Åland as one of the historic provinces of Finland. He was prepared to allow the Swedes to share in the fortification of a few of the islands – he recognized their strategic importance to Sweden as well as to Finland – but this was unacceptable to the Swedes as compromising their neutrality. The Swedish government held to its view that the people of Åland should have the right of self-determination, and in April tried to refer this aim to the Peace Conference in Paris. The move failed, but Finno-Swedish relations remained overcast as the result.

ELECTIONS AND A NEW GOVERNMENT

Although foreign policy concerns continued after the parliamentary elections of 1 March 1919, the results of those elections completely changed the face of domestic politics and marked a watershed in Mannerheim's regency. The Social Democrats had done well in the local elections in December 1918 but it came as a surprise when they won 80 seats in March, becoming once more the largest party in the 200-seat parliament. The Agrarians won 42 seats (a notable increase), the conservative Coalition Party 29 (a considerable defeat), the Progressive Party (liberals) 26, the Swedish People's Party 22 and the Christian Labour Party 2 seats. There was thus a non-socialist majority, with sufficient conservatives and Swedes to impose a delay on constitutional legislation, but the monarchism generally supported by those parties had suffered a total defeat: the liberals, Agrarians and, of course, the Social Democrats all supported a republican constitution. Moreover, the balance of opinion had also shifted decisively against intervention against Petrograd, while the Social Democrats remained implacably opposed to the existence of the Defence Corps. The 'White Finland' forged in the War of Independence seemed threatened.

Mannerheim suffered personally from the new circumstances. As he told the Swedish Archbishop Nathan Söderblom in April 1919, 'It was difficult to be head of state with eighty Social Democrat votes against you.'[18] The Agrarians were also critical of him. Although their leader, Santeri Alkio, acknowledged Mannerheim's charm, his inability to speak Finnish weighed heavily against him and there were fears of his intentions regarding Russia. Alkio even suspected the monarchists of plans to make Mannerheim dictator. Mannerheim's position as regent became less secure and his chances of a continuing role in the government of Finland through election as president of the inevitable republic disappeared. He nevertheless did what he could to mitigate the problems that arose as the result of the March elections.

It was a measure of how serious the conservatives' defeat had been that Ingman was not reelected. He and his government continued in office while the formation of a new government was under negotiation, and this took time. The Agrarians declined to go into coalition with the Social Democrats but the latter promised outright opposition if, as Mannerheim wanted, a comprehensive non-socialist coalition government was formed. The liberals would not go into a government with the conservatives, thus defeating Mannerheim's hopes. Discussions then centred on a liberal-Agrarian coalition. Mannerheim first asked K. J. Ståhlberg, an eminent lawyer and leading member of the Progressive Party, to form a government but he declined. An attempt was made to impose on Mannerheim a liberal-Agrarian coalition led by Mikael Soininen but this he rejected, regarding Soininen as too weak to be prime minister and likely to end up cooperating with the socialists. He also objected to his own

---

[18] Cited in Jägerskiöld, *Riksföreståndaren*, p. 16.

exclusion from the process of appointing a prime minister. He regarded it as his prerogative to invite a politician to form a government and carried the point.

On 9 April Mannerheim asked Kaarlo Castrén, a liberal monarchist who had served under Ingman and in whom he had confidence, to form a government. Castrén succeeded in assembling a minority government of six liberals, four Agrarians (among them Alkiolan) and four Swedes, together with two independent ministers, one of whom was his friend Rudolf Walden who continued as war minister. Rudolf Holsti, then Finnish envoy in Paris, was to become foreign minister in place of Enckell, whom Mannerheim would have liked to retain. Holsti was strongly against Finnish intervention in Russia and favoured a pro-Allied rather than a Scandinavian, neutral policy. The new government was appointed on 17 April 1919. The British regarded it as more satisfactory than its predecessor but to Mannerheim it was less so.

THE CONSTITUTION

The determination of the monarchists in 1918 to have a German prince as king of Finland had precluded the possibility of securing a Scandinavian prince instead. The monarchists believed that only a German king would provide Finland with adequate security and internal authority. A member of the Swedish royal house was in any case out of the question given the conflict over the Åland islands and fears that he would be biased towards Swedish in the question of the relative status of the Finnish and Swedish languages. A Danish prince might have been considered, and Mannerheim had thought of Prince Aage, a cousin of King Christian X. However, he had to make the best of political circumstances that pointed to a republican constitution: 'In principle I was a Monarchist, but I was by no means blind to the fact that a Republican form of government, provided it offered a firm basis for an ordered civil and social structure, could quite well secure the continuance and recovery of the State.'[19] In his speech opening the new parliament on 4 April 1919 Mannerheim reflected the principal aim of the non-socialists, which was to avoid a repetition of the catastrophe of civil war: 'In such times as we now live in, only that constitution which gives the government adequate author-

---

[19] Mannerheim, *Memoirs*, p. 222.

ity and power is able to guarantee the preservation and peaceful development of the state'.[20]

A constitutional committee chaired by Ståhlberg had already worked on a draft constitution and a revised version of this – with a president elected for six years instead of a king – was considered by the Castrén government in May. Differences arose over the powers of the president to veto legislation and dissolve parliament and whether he should be elected by parliament or by electors chosen by the people. Mannerheim was against giving the president only a suspensive veto and against his election by parliament, wanting him to have greater power in relation to parliament and to be independently elected. He had his opinion recorded in the minutes of the Council of State on 13 May but let the draft go forward to parliament. There it was decided to adopt the election of the president by electors chosen by the people, but to have the first president elected by parliament. When parliament voted on 14 June to introduce the constitution as a matter of urgency, the right, whose opposition had been strengthened by Mannerheim's lobbying, mustered enough votes to block its passage. This caused a furore on the centre and left who did not want the regency to continue while the constitution 'lay over' for consideration by the next parliament, which would not be elected until 1922.

Although the procedure was legally questionable, a new constitutional proposal was brought forward by Heikki Ritavuori, a radical member of the Progressive Party. Bargaining with the right made the new proposal more acceptable to them, while some concessions were also made to the left. The new draft strengthened the position of the president although his veto remained suspensive. It became impossible for parliament to dismiss him, but he could dissolve parliament; he could not, however, declare war and make peace without its consent. He was commander-in-chief of the armed forces but in time of war could transfer his command to another person. The former draft even prohibited the conferring of decorations; this was overturned – to Mannerheim's satisfaction, since he regarded decorations as a feature of international courtesy. Enough conservatives were prepared to accept the new constitution for parliament to vote on 21 June 1919 for its immediate adoption: Mannerheim failed to persuade the conservatives as a whole to continue to oppose the constitution.

[20] *Mannerheim Suomen vapauttaja ja valtionhoitaja*, p. 123.

REGENT

The constitution now needed only Mannerheim's assent to become law. The Social Democrats and Agrarians had agreed that they would vote to end his regency if he refused his assent, a danger to the stability of the regency under the 1772 constitution of which Ståhlberg had already warned him in April.[21] Mannerheim demanded time in which to consider his decision, but after much hesitation and further discussions with politicians, particularly on the right, he signed the constitution into law on 17 July 1919. His hesitation had been prompted more by foreign policy considerations – the possibility of intervention against Petrograd – than by the nature of the constitution itself.

INTERVENTION IN RUSSIA?

The Russian Whites, both the generals fighting the Bolsheviks within Russia and the politicians and diplomats abroad, were almost unanimously opposed to any changes to the frontiers of the old Russian Empire without the approval of a Russian constituent assembly. They were thus angered by the Allies' decision in May 1919 to recognize the independence of Finland. British recognition was dated 6 May, that of the United States 7 May, while France informed the Finns on 12 May of the ratification of its earlier recognition. For Mannerheim the delay in Allied recognition had become increasingly irritating, particularly since Finland had fulfilled the conditions for recognition outlined to him in December 1918, and he was therefore well satisfied with its final attainment. It was especially valuable in strengthening Finland's position in relation to the Russian Whites: for example, the Allies included recognition of the independence of Finland and Poland among their conditions for recognizing the Russian government of Admiral A. V. Kolchak in late May 1919.

Mannerheim's attitude towards intervention by Finland in Russia was unshakeable. He believed that the Bolsheviks should and would be defeated, that Finland would have to establish good relations with a new 'White' Russia, and that by capturing Petrograd and quickly handing it over to the Russian Whites Finland would secure their lasting gratitude and goodwill and thus guarantee its own security. The basis for his belief in the Russians' prospective gratitude to Finland may have been his own positive experiences in Russia, from

[21] From Ståhlberg, 9 April 1919. Mannerheim Archive, Box 603.

which he knew that not all influential Russians were rabid nationalists, as most Finns, with their bitter experiences of russification, believed. There was little support for his opinion in the statements of the Russian Whites. Mannerheim's view of the Russian Whites' gratitude to Finland was just as much a matter of faith as was his belief in early 1918 that Finland should fight for its freedom without foreign intervention. However, these attitudes were inconsistent. If it was so vital for Finland's national dignity to fight alone for its freedom, why should Russia not take a similar line? And would not a successful Finnish attack on Petrograd reinforce long-standing Russian concerns about the security of the city and arouse lasting feelings of anxiety rather than gratitude? If Mannerheim considered these points he also dismissed them.

A vital element in Mannerheim's approach to Finnish intervention against Petrograd was his insistence on the precondition that the Russian Whites should recognize Finland's independence. He also sought territorial concessions from the Russians in Eastern Karelia and Petsamo. He thought it was in the Russians' interests to gain Finnish support in creating around Petrograd a base for a broad anti-Bolshevik operation. However, 'Instead of offering us e.g. East Karelia and 500 millions [francs] together with autonomy in Ingria they let the opportunities slip by and quarrel about whether Finland's independence should be recognized or not.'[22] As regent, his sympathy for Russia did not blind him to Russian obstinacy or to Finnish national interests. Much as he wanted to defeat Bolshevism and play a leading part in the Petrograd operation, he was not a Russian White general, though some Russian Whites thought of him as such. Nor was he the 'vulgar military adventurer in disguise for Western consumption under a smooth and pleasing exterior', as perceived by Captain Harold Grenfell, R.N., who served in British intelligence in Helsinki in the spring of 1919 before the Finns obtained his recall because of his left-wing sympathies.[23] His responsibilities as Finnish head of state were always in Mannerheim's mind as he attempted to drive through his intervention plan. In so doing, however, he encountered difficulties from all three parties concerned – the Finns, the Russian Whites and the Allies, whose diplomatic, military and financial support was desirable if not essential.

[22] To Carl Enckell, 15 April 1919. Mannerheim Archive, Box 911.
[23] Grenfell to Director of Naval Intelligence, 26 April 1919. F.O. 371/3736, 65297.

Finnish efforts towards the end of April 1919 to interest the Allies and the Russian Whites in a Finnish attack on Petrograd got nowhere and Holsti, who was then in Paris, worked against the idea. In May the Finnish general staff prepared plans for an offensive against Petrograd, an operation broadly supported by the army as a means of eliminating the Bolshevik threat to Finland's security and applying pressure on Russia to cede Eastern Karelia to Finland. The activists, a group of ardent anti-socialist nationalists who had been important in the Jäger movement during the World War and in the formation of the Defence Corps, were also strongly opposed to Bolshevism and in favour of incorporating Eastern Karelia in Finland. Unlike Mannerheim, they had no wish to transfer a captured Petrograd to the Russian Whites, whom they disliked and mistrusted. Instead they aimed at its neutralization as an international free city; some even wanted its total destruction. Mannerheim's backing for the Olonets expedition won the activists' support and they recognized in him the only prominent Finn likely to carry out a successful attack on Petrograd. The activists were few in number and addicted to conspiracy but they held influential positions of leadership in the Defence Corps.

Some Finnish conservatives were prepared to back intervention to pre-empt a possible Red attack on Finland – tension on the frontier was high in early June 1919 – and others were even supportive of an alliance with a White Russia. The centre was more hostile to the Russian Whites while the Social Democrats were totally opposed to any intervention in Russia, either in Olonets or against Petrograd. Thus neither the government – with the exception of Castrén, the prime minister, Walden and Leo Ehrnrooth, the acting foreign minister – nor parliament was likely to back Mannerheim's Petrograd plan although he could count on the backing of the army officers, including the Jägers, and the Defence Corps.

The Allies had sent to the Baltic in May a military mission led by Lieutenant-General Sir Hubert Gough. Mannerheim had particularly wanted a British military mission to come to Finland to counteract the effects of German influence. Gough met Mannerheim on 26 and 27 May, and pointed out that intervention in Karelia would be possible only when Admiral Kolchak agreed. An advance by Finnish troops alone on Petrograd would be regarded by the British government as highly undesirable; there should be a joint Russo-Finnish operation. This would be favoured by the British government and was thought likely to produce good relations between Finland and Russia.[24]

Gough rejected the regent's conditions for Finnish participation in the capture of Petrograd: the neutralization of the Baltic, the razing of the fortress of Kronstadt and nearby Finnish fortresses, the creation of a demilitarized zone between Russia and Finland, the transfer of the Petsamo district to Finland and a referendum on the union of Eastern Karelia with Finland. Mannerheim also asked for war materials, food supplies for Petrograd and financial aid. He was both disappointed and annoyed when Gough explained that the Allies had taken no decision about intervention. In fact the French were keen on intervention and by mid June the British had come round to thinking that Finland might attack Petrograd if both the Finnish parliament and Admiral Kolchak agreed. However, no firm promises of Allied support for Finland were given. Gough had expressed to Winston Churchill, the secretary of state for war, in mid June the essence of Mannerheim's position and his problem: 'Mannerheim is dying to attack Petrograd ... But on the other hand, Mannerheim's own position in Finland is not too firm and he is certainly risking it by any such action.'[25]

Mannerheim also discussed intervention plans with Russian generals, notably in June with General N. N. Yudenich, who commanded the Russian forces in Estonia, and whose personality and capability made an unfavourable impression on him. As a result of these discussions, he agreed with Yudenich on 18 June a draft treaty which provided for Russian recognition of Finland and for the Peace Conference or the League of Nations to decide such matters as self-determination for the Eastern Karelians and the neutralization of the Baltic and the Gulf of Finland. Mannerheim was to command the entire operation against Petrograd and Russian troops were to be permitted to concentrate in Finland and advance from there on their own sector of the front. This draft treaty needed the agreement of Kolchak and the Finnish government to come into effect, but it was sent for comment to the British and French before the government was informed. The Allies raised no objections although they declined to accept responsibility for the intervention or to 'interfere between Mannerheim and

[24] Gough to Mannerheim, 26 May 1919. Mannerheim Archive, Box 603.
[25] Churchill Archives Centre. Churchill Papers, Char 16/8, Gough to Churchill, 14 June 1919.

his government in the event of differences of opinion arising'.[26] Holsti, on learning of the existence of the draft, proceeded in early July to kill any prospect of Finnish action by stating to an indignant government that a treaty had been concluded with the Russians without their knowledge and without any safeguards for Finland from the Allies.

Meanwhile Yudenich tried in vain to get Kolchak's agreement to the draft. The general pointed out its necessity to obtain the cooperation of the Finns. 'Mannerheim, thoroughly Russian, can intervene only with assistance of political circles and popular masses on whom he is entirely dependent.'[27] But the admiral would make no concessions. Nevertheless, Kolchak turned to Mannerheim personally on 23 June to induce the Finnish government to start 'active military operations in the direction of Petrograd ... this is not the time for doubts and waverings, connected with any political questions. Not allowing thoughts of the possibility of any unresolved difficulties in the future between liberated Russia and the Finnish nation, I ask you, General, to accept my appeal as a sign of the Russian army's unchanging memory of your glorious past in its ranks and of Russia's sincere esteem for the national freedom of the Finnish people'.[28] These fine words were to no avail. Mannerheim replied on 14 July that the Finnish parliament would not agree to intervention without definite guarantees of Finland's existence as a national state. A favourable moment for Finnish intervention therefore seemed to have been lost.

However, Mannerheim was considering another option. In mid June he had contemplated refusing to confirm the constitution and instead dissolving parliament in the hope of obtaining election results more favourable to the conservatives than those in March. In mid July he returned to the possibility of dissolving parliament as part of a scheme to attack Petrograd. The initiative for this plan came from the activists who were concerned about the defeats recently suffered by the Finnish expedition to Olonets and fearful that he might not win the presidential election. Mannerheim met Kai Donner, an activist leader (and a future biographer), on 7 July and, according to Donner, favoured a *coup* before the presidential election in order to overcome the government's unwillingness to attack Petrograd. On

[26] Gough to Mannerheim, 2 July 1919. Mannerheim Archive, Box 603.
[27] Yudenich to Kolchak, 8 July 1919, sent by O'Reilly (Vladivostok) to Foreign Office. *Documents on British Foreign Policy 1919–1939*. First series, III, p. 435.
[28] 'Kolchak i Finliandiai', *Krasnyi arkhiv*, 33, p. 128.

10 July the activists formulated a plan in which Mannerheim would defer confirmation of the constitution. He would then dissolve parliament on the grounds that new elections were required. Next he would confirm the constitution and declare a state of war, which would begin a few days later with an attack on Petrograd. Mannerheim was extremely nervous about the plan, and accepted it in outline only provided that he could persuade the conservative Coalition Party to form a government.

Mannerheim broached the scheme to Ingman, as a trusted adviser, on 14 July and asked if the conservatives would support it and form a government. Ingman pointed out that after confirming the constitution Mannerheim would lose the power to declare war and parliament would have to be called in order to do so. A meeting of conservative politicians on 16 July decided against a modified activist proposal, supported by Mannerheim, which took account of this objection by deferring the declaration of war until after the capture of Petrograd. The conservatives would not act without broad support from the other non-socialist parties, and no support was likely from the centre. Other conservatives took the same line and Mannerheim was informed of the Coalition Party's negative attitude on 17 July. In consequence, he decided to confirm the constitution that afternoon, remarking 'A soldier cannot act in politics without the support of any political party.'[29] There was no way forward.

The activists' plan, which would have plunged Finland into a severe political crisis if it had been implemented, was not really defeated by 'the lawyers, to whom the letter of the law and the republican constitution ... seemed in themselves more important than endeavours which did not have in every case guarantees and assurances against possible failure'.[30] It was in fact blocked by Mannerheim's recognition of political reality which proved stronger even than his longing to intervene in Russia.

STYLISH REGENT BUT REJECTED PRESIDENTIAL CANDIDATE

The constitution, which Mannerheim confirmed after so much heart searching, received a justifiably favourable verdict in his *Memoirs*

[29] Ingman's diary, cited in Jägerskiöld, *Riksföreståndaren*, pp. 204–5.
[30] Donner, *Sotamarsalkka vapaaherra Mannerheim*, p. 238.

though he made a number of significant criticisms. He objected to the prime minister acting for the president when the latter was unable to carry out his duties because this conflicted with 'the principle that the head of state should be independent of parliament'.[31] He thought there should be a vice president. He favoured a clear separation of powers between parliament and government, objecting to members of parliament serving as ministers because of their dependence on political parties. It was undeniable that 'His views on the relationship between government and parliament were fairly far from the fundamental principle of the parliamentary system of government.'[32] Yet Mannerheim recognized the 'value and efficiency' of the Finnish constitution which he attributed largely to 'the fact that the power of the President under the Finnish constitution is greater than that of the heads of other European States which introduced new constitutions at about the same time'.[33] The constitution has proved to be remarkably durable, with the first significant changes taking place only in the late 1980s and 1990s, notably with the election of the president directly by the people instead of through an electoral college.

Mannerheim had consistently opposed any weakening of the president's powers during the discussion of the constitution in 1919. Although not entirely satisfied with the outcome, he nevertheless considered that the president's authority, as eventually enacted, was sufficiently great for him to allow himself to be persuaded to stand for election to that office in 1919. Persuasion was needed because the regency had been for him a period of intensive and demanding activity and he felt tired and was suffering from a recurrence of rheumatism.

Throughout the regency Mannerheim lived and worked not in the former imperial (now the presidential) palace but in the more modest residence of the former governor-general in the South Esplanade, where 'everything is rather dilapidated and dirty' but which he lacked the time to attend to.[34] The palace was used for occasions such as the formal closing and opening of parliament. He had a military and a civil chancery to handle business. Among his aides-de-camp was the

[31] Mannerheim, *Minnen*, I, p. 356.
[32] Lindman, 'Vuoden 1919 hallitusmuodon synty' in *Suomen kansanedustuslaitoksen historia*, VI, p. 425.
[33] Mannerheim, *Memoirs*, p. 224.
[34] To Kitty Linder, 6 January 1919. Mannerheim Archive, Box 952.

artist Akseli Gallen-Kallela, who was also active in designing decorations and uniforms for the new Finnish state and who became a friend. In January 1919 he told Kitty Linder of his routine: 'I get up at 7–8 according to the time at which I went to bed. At 9 I am brought papers to go through. At 10 I receive the representatives of the military. From 12 to 1 I receive the people who are not content to submit their business through ... the head of my military chancery ... From 1 to 2 lunch and at 2 begins the turn of the civilians. From 7 to 8 dinner and from 8 work continues, receptions, meetings, etc. which go on indefinitely. Between 11 and 1 I go to bed ... I hope to succeed in eliminating some things and to receive fewer people but in the meantime I am the slave of my too broadly conceived duties.'[35]

Mannerheim entertained extensively, his daughter Sophy acting as his hostess. He had long been separated from his Russian wife and now wanted a divorce. This might well be considered advantageous to his ambitions in Finland. However, the real reason was so that he could be free to marry Kitty Linder although he was constantly concerned to keep his and Kitty's intentions secret. An attempt to obtain a divorce early in 1919 ran into problems because his wife wanted to contest it,[36] but it eventually went through, discreetly and speedily, in the court at Hanko but seemingly not until September 1919[37] (this may have been the date of the decree absolute issued by the church authorities, with the civil court judgement occuring earlier in the year).

Mannerheim was a charming and attentive host and as such won even the approval of Santeri Alkio, who regarded himself as a plain man of the people. The conservative politician Tekla Hultin was one of many women who fell under his spell despite her initial criticism of the 'effusive rapture' with which his personal qualities were often described. 'Now I myself was overcome by his absolute personal nobility and charm. And this during a five-minute political conversation. What power of enchantment would he not then exert if he allowed the full battery of his handsome smile and his beautiful eyes to bring someone under his fire.'[38]

[35] To Kitty Linder, 21 January 1919. Mannerheim Archive, Box 952.
[36] To Kitty Linder, 30 December [1918], 27 January, 4 February and 4 March 1919. Mannerheim Archive, Box 952.
[37] Eeva, *Vaiettu ja vaiennettu avioliitto*, pp. 100–01. Eeva could find no court records of Mannerheim's divorce case and dated the divorce to 25 September 1919 on the basis of Mannerheim's entry in the church records of his Helsinki parish.
[38] Cited in Jägerskiöld, *Riksföreståndaren*, p. 246.

Mannerheim excelled especially in the representational role of the head of state. To his charm he added an imposing physical presence and elegant demeanour. The commander of the British squadron in the Baltic, Rear-Admiral Walter Cowan, who called on Mannerheim on 9 May 1919 in connection with British recognition of Finland's independence, commented on 'the handsomest foreigner I have ever met, very tall, gracefully built with beautifully made clothes'.[39] At formal occasions such as the inauguration of the Finnish Opera on 19 January 1919, the ceremonies on 31 May at which the University of Helsinki conferred on him the degree of doctor of philosophy *honoris causa*, and the commemorative parade in Helsinki on 16 May, he was a striking and dignified focus of attention, whether in civilian dress or in uniform.

Extensive tours around the country, particularly in connection with anniversaries of the War of 1918, brought Mannerheim to the notice of a wide public, of whom considerable numbers were impressed and enthusiastic. He travelled to Ostrobothnia, Tampere and Hämeenlinna in January 1919, to Karelia and Savo in February, to Tampere and Viipuri on the anniversaries of their liberation in April, and to Turku in May. There were parades by the army and the Defence Corps, civic dinners, numerous speeches of welcome and gratitude, and cheering crowds of adults and schoolchildren. When children greeted him he was particularly delighted, and he had the happy knack of sweeping them along with him and patting these nearest to him. He was able to combine formality with informality; in modem parlance he could 'work a crowd'. He claimed to be as 'nervous as a beginner' about his speeches,[40] which he delivered in Finnish as well as Swedish. Those which he made during these tours emphasized the achievements and sacrifices of the War of Independence as well as the need for vigilance, unity, fulfilment of duty and love of country in building for the future. The adulation he received on these tours contrasted with the harsh reality of political life in Helsinki. However, the style of his regency left its mark, and it was said by his admirers in the words of the Swedish poet Esaias Tegnér – not without reason – that 'There lay a glamour over Gustaf's days'.[41] The

---

[39] Bennett, *Cowan's War*, p. 109.
[40] To Kitty Linder, 27 January [1919]. Mannerheim Archive, Box 952.
[41] Edelfelt, *Sophie Mannerheim*, p. 232.

great receptions that he introduced were continued under the republic and President Ståhlberg was anxious to know how Mannerheim had done things as regent.

That he should continue as head of state by being elected as president was important to the political right (the conservatives and the Swedes), who regarded him as the last effective obstacle to political control passing into the hands of the centre and left acting together. He was not the only possible candidate for the right, but was considered the best qualified because of his competence in foreign and defence policy. Towards the end of June he decided to stand, well aware that the election of the first president by parliament would greatly diminish his chance of success.

The Social Democrats were, of course, totally opposed to Mannerheim being president. They decided not to put up their own candidate in order that the successful candidate should be a non-socialist whom they regarded with less revulsion than Mannerheim and who would not pursue an interventionist foreign policy. The centre moved against him too. He had the sympathy of some in the Progressive Party because of his experience but even they had doubts because they feared an increase in domestic political tensions if he were elected. The Agrarians, however, were hostile to Mannerheim. Alkio, their leader, had long regarded him as 'really too royal'. The president must be 'a Finnish man. An unassuming civilian. A man of the people'. Mannerheim 'is not a Finn and unfortunately never will be. He is a political actor. His policy is coordinated with the Russian monarchists in Finland. If he becomes president, this would signify such a commotion on the part of the socialists that I fear a new insurrection. His position would represent a strengthening of the positions of the Swedes.'[42] As in 1918, Mannerheim was damned for his Swedishness and his Russianness, while even his military background and personal style were held against him.

K. J. Ståhlberg emerged as Mannerheim's opponent, backed by the Progressives and the Agrarians, and despite considerable pressure from the right, including a delegation of Jägers, he refused to stand down. The commander-in-chief of the Defence Corps expressed to the speaker of parliament the hope of his organization that Mannerheim would be elected. The election took place on 25 July 1919. Ståhlberg

[42] Alkio's diary, cited in Alanen, *Santeri Alkio*, p. 546 and Jägerskiöld, *Riksföreståndaren*, pp. 227–8.

received 143 votes to Mannerheim's 50 (the conservatives and most Swedes), and on 26 July was sworn in as Finland's first president.

Mannerheim did not stay in Helsinki for the election. Following the recommendation of his sister Sophie, he left to join her in taking the waters at the spa of Runni near Iisalmi in Eastern Finland. He informed the council of state of his departure and during his absence the prime minister, in accordance with the constitution, assumed responsibility for one major foreign policy decision about the Murmansk Legion, to Mannerheim's eventual annoyance. At Runni Mannerheim continued to receive official telegrams, one of which contained the news of the election. On 26 July he issued a farewell order of the day on laying down the supreme command of the army and navy. The president sent him an open letter of appreciation of his services on 30 July. Runni became 'a place of pilgrimage' with numerous people wanting to see him.[43] He was deluged with telegrams and letters expressing regret at the result of the election and appealing to him not to leave the country.

His election defeat was naturally a severe disappointment to Mannerheim, but he put a brave face on it. His sister wrote on 30 July to their aunt: 'Gustaf himself takes the matter so splendidly ... But one's heart absolutely bleeds when one thinks of how he entered into conditions here and of the great social programme he intended to carry out.'[44] Later he was more reconciled to the situation. He wrote on 12 September to his Polish friend Princess Marie Lubomirska, with whom he had conducted a touching correspondence during the World War: 'I am again free, delighted to have no responsibility any more. My only disappointment is that I could not settle up with the Bolsheviks on our frontiers before I returned to private life. The whole world would find things very much calmer if at least in Petersburg this centre for Bolshevism were destroyed.'[45]

Mannerheim's reference to his regret at not being able to intervene in Russia against the Bolsheviks was unsurprising. More remarkable was his sister's reference to his social programme since this had not yet publicly emerged. However, in a speech to a delegation from the Coalition (conservative) Party on 15 September, and published next day, he outlined how he thought that Finland should unite to resist

[43] To Kitty Linder, 4 August [1919]. Mannerheim Archive, Box 952.
[44] Cited in Edelfelt, *Sophie Mannerheim*, p. 234.
[45] To Marie Lubomirska, 12 September 1919. Mannerheim, *Brev*, p. 199.

the threat from the extreme left, to which concessions were out of the question. Cooperation with the extreme left, he said, could begin only when they had understood that 'we are firmly determined not to relinquish a hair's breadth of our rights' and that the threats of the masses would have no effect. Respect for the law and the rights of others was essential. 'This means also that society cannot avoid some sacrifices to even out real injustices and, to the extent that the hard-pressed economic situation permits, make itself ready to carry out those social reforms which in a perceptible and lasting way will promote the aspiration of the working class for a materially untroubled existence, and powerfully underline its need for cultural improvement in all its different forms.'[46] As a private citizen he was to put his words into practice through initiatives in social work designed to improve the lot of the people and help draw the nation together. In the run-up to the presidential election Castrén, the prime minister, believed that Mannerheim would be no obstacle to democratic reforms. He may have been right.

However, the determined character of Mannerheim's conservatism could never be doubted. It was well expressed in a letter to Marie Lubomirska in 1921 in which he stated his difficulty in comprehending those who could only give up before 'the excessive demands of the masses, who lend assistance to their endeavours to shatter the historic foundations of the life of our society. I have difficulty in understanding beauty in the existence which people are preparing after they have pushed aside such values as religion, country, history, in a word everything that civilization and culture have given us.'[47]

Mannerheim did not hurry to leave Runni – his rheumatism was not much better – and he set out for Helsinki only on 11 August, travelling by road and arriving on the 16th. Enthusiastic crowds came out to greet him along the route and he was received in Helsinki not only by cheering civilians but also by a parade of 7,500 Defence Corps men from different parts of the country. He had hinted at the possibility of being declared the honorary commander-in-chief of the Defence Corps and the organization had been happy to oblige. The parade and the crowds demonstrated the extent of popular support he enjoyed but the centre was deeply offended by the speech of

---

[46] Mannerheim, *Minnen*, I, pp. 362–3.
[47] To Marie Lubomirska, 9 November 1921. Cited in Jägerskiöld, *Mannerheim mellan världskrigen*, p. 25.

the commander of the Helsinki Defence Corps, referring to a president whose heart did not beat in time with theirs and to the White General as the only one whose will could be law to them. There were fears, not for the first or last time, that Mannerheim might use the Defence Corps to stage a *coup d'état*.

Ståhlberg at first wanted to keep the Castrén government in office and make Mannerheim commander-in-chief of the army. Mannerheim's initial reaction, expressed to Ingman on 30 July, was that the aim of this plan was to 'lull the country into a false sense of security and thus make it easier for public opinion to resign itself to the new situation'.[48] Ståhlberg was to fail in both of his aims. Castrén could not continue as prime minister when the Swedish Party members resigned from the government. Walden also resigned as war minister when it became clear that Mannerheim was not going to accept appointment as commander-in-chief. The new government of the centre parties, formed by J. H. Vennola on 15 August 1919, was less in favour of intervention in Russia than its predecessor.

Mannerheim had no intention of becoming commander-in-chief unless he received wide-ranging authority and was assured that the government would follow policies of which he approved. He wanted to be commander both of the army and the Defence Corps, to appoint all officers and have responsibility for political surveillance returned to the general staff. He also demanded the declaration of a state of war and preparations for an attack on Petrograd. He was probably prepared to bargain on some of these points, and later claimed that he had asked questions rather than set conditions.[49] Vennola's government would not accept his terms although not all the ministers were against intervention if the Allies would support and finance it. However, Alkio in particular believed that acceptance of Mannerheim's conditions would create two rulers in the country and threaten the president and parliament. It became clear to Mannerheim that no progress was being made. He had already turned down the post of Finnish minister in Paris which Ståhlberg had offered him as an alternative on 11 August; no doubt he regarded it as a kind of exile. On 30 August he informed Ståhlberg that he declined the offer of appointment as commander-in-chief because his differences of opinion with both the president and the government meant that he

[48] Cited in Jägerskiöld, *Riksföreståndaren*, pp. 249–50.
[49] To Michael Gripenberg, 24 September 1934. Mannerheim Archive, Box 906.

could not carry the responsibility involved. However, he was ready to serve the country if the threat of war became imminent.

Mannerheim considered it 'a sacrifice to relinquish command of an army in whose creation I had .... taken part'.[50] However, as in May 1918, he wanted more authority as commander-in-chief than the government was prepared to concede and he would not give way. From his point of view, he had made a wise decision in rejecting the offer in 1919. A purely and restricted military role, subordinate to a government of the centre, which he feared was moving towards collaboration with the socialists, would only cause friction and give him the frustrating sense of lost opportunities. Mannerheim's decision, like that of the government, came from an awareness that he was no ordinary soldier but a deeply politically-minded general with clear ideas of his own on Finnish foreign and defence policy. His concept of the role of commander-in-chief was scarcely consonant with that civilian control over the military which characterizes democracies. His refusal to accept office in the new political circumstances was followed by changes to senior appointments in the army and the diplomatic corps which replaced some of those most sympathetic to his plans. This underlined the extent to which Finland had taken a new course.

A further irritant for Mannerheim during August was learning of the agreement concluded by Holsti with the British on 19 July for the repatriation of the Red Finns who had served in the Murmansk Legion. Mannerheim had opposed any amnesty for these rebels and believed that the agreement had been reached unlawfully without his knowledge as head of state. It was eventually concluded that Castrén had been empowered to decide the matter since on 19 July Mannerheim was no longer exercising his duties as head of state. The fact that Mannerheim raised the matter was indicative of his annoyance with Holsti and his continuing hostility to any softening of policy towards the Red Finns.

DEPARTURE ABROAD

By the end of August, with no public employment in Finland and increasingly disillusioned with the course of politics there, Mannerheim had decided to go abroad, where he expected to enjoy his freedom

[50] To Karin Ramsay, 8 August 1919. Mannerheim, *Brev*, p. 198.

REGENT

twice as much 'as soon as I leave, with my native soil, its internal politics far behind me'.[51] He intended to go with his daughter via Stockholm and London to Paris and perhaps the south of France and in late autumn to return to Finland for the winter. He left Helsinki for Sweden on 17 September 1919, seen off by numerous well-wishers. He had begun a period as a private citizen but his public profile remained high and he was no ordinary observer of events.

---

[51] To Julio Reuter, 28 August 1919. Cited in Jägerskiöld, *Riksföreståndaren*, p. 260.

CHAPTER III

CIVILIAN

'To live and work in small conditions has never particularly attracted me but the course of events has more or less made it a necessity and I hope that the merit of spending my time in my quarrelsome fatherland *"me fera pardonner mes pechés* [sic] *de jeunesse"*.'[1]

ADVOCATE OF INTERVENTION

Mannerheim's earlier contacts with diplomats and politicians, his position as an anti-Bolshevik Finnish general and his status as a former head of state – a status which he guarded jealously – ensured him a ready hearing from men of influence throughout his travels during the latter part of 1919 and early 1920. Although he always made clear that he travelled as a private individual, it was well known that he remained a figure of importance in Finland. He was preoccupied with the situation in Russia, anxious to support the restoration of a White government there, and concerned to influence the British and French into the pursuit of a consistent interventionist policy which would also safeguard Finland's position. He had not abandoned hope of Finnish intervention against Petrograd as part of the general anti-Bolshevik Russian policy which he advocated.

He arrived in London on 25 September 1919, having travelled via Sweden and Denmark. On 6 September, before leaving Helsinki, he had told the British chargé d'affaires, Sir Coleridge Kennard, 'that he had but to start a campaign in the Press and work up public feeling in order to win over the Centre and Right here in support of a military campaign against Petrograd'.[2] Kennard was unconvinced that popular support would be forthcoming, and after Holsti had poured poison in his ear about Mannerheim's supposed links with pro-German

---
[1] To Emanuel Nobel, 4 May 1925. Mannerheim, *Brev*, p. 226.
[2] Kennard to Curzon, 8 September 1919. *Documents on British Foreign Policy 1919–1939*. First Series, III, p. 539.

elements in Finland he even reported on 14 September that 'in any dealings which we may have with General Mannerheim, honest though I believe him to be, we should proceed with extreme caution and reserve'.[3] Mannerheim certainly found the Foreign Office reserved in its attitude to intervention. It was also non-committal when he urged the British to advise the Finnish government not to make peace with the Bolsheviks. Lord Hardinge of Penshurst wrote to the foreign secretary, Lord Curzon: 'Gen. Mannerheim was very persistent in pressing for action on our part'.[4] Mannerheim found Winston Churchill, the secretary of state for war, sympathetic to his anti-Bolshevik views but although Churchill was a member of the cabinet, his influence on foreign policy was limited. Mannerheim had one success: after a meeting with him, Lord Northcliffe and his newspaper, *The Times*, became supportive of Finnish intervention in Russia.

The Times published on 7 October 1919 a statement by Mannerheim in which he summarized his foreign policy: 'I have worked for a free and independent Finland, in close relationship with the great Western Powers, seeking agreement also with Scandinavian countries, and striving to create secure foundations for good and fertile relations with the Russia of the future, between whom and Finland geographical laws demand that there should be close economic intercourse.' He believed that military action to liberate Petrograd and the surrounding territory would 'permit the establishment of a stable and healthy-minded Russian Government, and thus ... remove from our frontiers the peril of Bolshevism and its inevitable infiltration'. He perceived in this policy a humanitarian and patriotic mission which destiny had bestowed on Finland. He emphasized that peace between Finland and the Bolsheviks would endanger Finland and deprive it of the moral support of Western countries. A sign from those countries would suffice to encourage the clear-sighted elements in Finland to render to this country, to civilization, and to the Russia of the future the signal services which Finland alone can render at this hour.[5] But, despite Mannerheim's efforts, neither the sign from the Western powers nor action by the 'clear-sighted elements' in Finland proved forthcoming.

---

[3] Kennard to Curzon, 14 September 1919. *Documents on British Foreign Policy 1919–1939*. First Series, III, p. 110.

[4] Hardinge to Curzon, 2 October 1919. F.O.371/3740, 137097.

[5] *The Times,* 7 October 1919.

The outbreak of a railway strike while Mannerheim was in London prompted him, in a letter to his sister Sophie from Claridge's Hotel, to remark on the threatening appearance of workers' processions with their red flags. He praised the British government for its firmness and its use of volunteers to keep the trains running, and hoped that it had not allowed itself to be intimidated when the strike, which he regarded as having been provoked by the Bolsheviks, came to an end. A deep mistrust of organized labour pervaded his comments.[6]

On 8 October he travelled to Paris. There he had discussions with the prime minister Clemenceau, Marshal Foch, senior foreign ministry officials, politicians and journalists. He was sent to see the destruction caused by the war in north-eastern France and was moved by what he saw. His plans to go to Warsaw to see friends and retrieve his possessions stored there during the war were delayed by his decision to remain in Paris because of his wish to keep in touch with the decisive developments that were taking place in Russia towards the end of October.

In Paris he also had discussions with White Russian diplomats and members of the Russian Political Conference, which attempted to represent the interests of counter-revolutionary Russia to the Allies. The Russians favoured Finnish intervention against Petrograd but remained cautious about the recognition of Finnish independence. Finnish intervention again appeared timely in October 1919. The White Russian armies seemed once more to offer a serious threat to the Bolsheviks. Admittedly Kolchak had been forced back into Siberia, but the army of General A. I. Denikin, operating from the south of Russia, had seized Orel, less than 200 miles south of Moscow and approached Tula in mid October. General Yudenich advanced towards Petrograd from Estonia early in October and by 20 October was at Pulkovo, just outside the city. Mannerheim believed the White Russians were stronger than ever before and that the moment for Finnish intervention to tip the balance against the Bolsheviks had come. He forwarded to the Finnish government a report that the French government was prepared to lend Finland £30 million in return for immediate intervention, but this offer was never confirmed.

Mannerheim believed that he ought to make a personal appeal for Finnish intervention. He did so in the form of an open letter to President Ståhlberg, which he sent from Paris on 28 October to Lauri

[6] To Sophie Mannerheim, 5 October 1919. Mannerheim, *Brev*, pp. 200–1.

Ingman with the request that he should publish it as he thought appropriate. In the letter, which appeared in the press on 2 November, Mannerheim argued that the fall of the Soviet regime was only a matter of time and that Finland had, perhaps for the last time, the opportunity to share in that regime's destruction and in so doing guarantee its own security. If Finland did not seize this opportunity and Petrograd were captured without Finnish help, there would be boundless difficulties in future Finno-Russian relations, and if the Russian Whites outside Petrograd were defeated, Europe as well as Russia would hold Finland responsible.

In his *Memoirs* Mannerheim wrote: 'The reception accorded this letter in Finland was mixed.'[7] In fact it received very little support and much criticism. Even conservatives such as Lauri Ingman had serious reservations about an interventionist policy because of the risks involved. It was correctly judged that the right 'wanted to preserve the image they had created of [Mannerheim] … as Finland's "White General"' and 'shunned as alien' his image as the '"general of intervention"'.[8] Although Mannerheim was defended by the right-wing press, politicians and newspapers of the centre and left were savagely critical of him as an undemocratic, intriguing, reactionary warmonger. The letter completely failed to arouse public support for intervention; the government was unmoved, and on 4 November it rejected a White Russian appeal for military cooperation.

The open letter proved a serious miscalculation and it was not long before Mannerheim recognized it as such. It also proved wrong in its assessments, and caused the right to lose faith in him as an authority on foreign policy.[9] Not only was Finnish public opinion unmoved, but Allied backing for Finland never materialized and the Russian Whites proved incapable of defeating a more ruthlessly-led enemy operating with the advantage of interior lines. By 27 October Yudenich was in retreat and by mid November the remnants of his army were back in Estonia and on the point of dissolution. Denikin and Kolchak were also driven back.

Mannerheim realized what a controversial figure the open letter had made him. He wrote to Hannes Ignatius in December 1919 that he had thought of coming home but considered that 'my presence

---

[7] Mannerheim, *Memoirs*, p. 235.
[8] Paasivirta, *The Victors in World War I and Finland*, p. 176.
[9] Vares, "*Kansakunnan kaapin päällä*", pp. 48–9.

in Finland would not be of use but only contribute to inflaming feelings on one side and the other without any practical result.'[10] The open letter had emphasized the difference between Mannerheim's way of thinking and that of the majority of Finns, and contributed strongly to his rejection as a political figure throughout the 1920s.

In early November Mannerheim continued his discussions with the Russians in Paris and kept the British Military Mission there informed of his ideas, which were based on the assumption that he would command an attack on Petrograd from Finland. He told the British on 7 November rather cautiously: 'I might be willing to take Petrograd and thus strike what might prove to be a decisive blow at Bolshevism, but I am not going to occupy the liberated territory indefinitely and have my men do nothing but constitute a cordon sanitaire and risk getting them bolshevised by the influence of inaction.' He added in a self-satisfied reference to his role in the Finnish war: 'I organised the whole of Finland in six weeks while fighting on two fronts, and I think that if I liberated Petrograd, the Russians ought to be able to organise that territory in three months.'[11]

However, by mid November he had recognized the changed situation with regard to Russia and had accepted that there was no longer any hope of Finnish intervention at that time. He felt that he had done what he could in London and Paris and deeply regretted that Finland had not exploited the situation offered by Yudenich's offensive. His judgement that the Bolsheviks' situation would have been different if Finland had intervened is probably correct. Lenin told the Seventh All-Russian Congress of Soviets on 5 December 1919: 'Finland did not go to war and Yudenich met defeat', which may be taken to mean that Yudenich was defeated because Finland did not join in the war.[12] However, for all his anti-Bolshevism and sympathy with the cause of the Russian Whites, Mannerheim recognized that 'the Russians prosecuted this enterprise with an outrageous thoughtlessness'.[13] Even when the Russian Whites most wanted Finnish assistance, S. D. Sazonov, their foreign minister, was only prepared

[10] To Hannes Ignatius, 23 December 1919. Mannerheim, *Brev*, p. 206.
[11] Churchill Papers. Char 16/41, Brigadier-General E. L. Spears to Churchill, 8 November 1919.
[12] Heinrichs, *Mannerheim Suomen Kohtaloissa*, I, p. 382; B. E. Shtein, *Russkii vopros na Parizhskoi mirnoi konferentsii*, pp. 253–4; Lenin, *Polnoe sobranie sochinenii*, 39, p. 394.
[13] To Sophie Mannerheim, 20 November 1919. Mannerheim, *Brev*, p. 204.

to recognize Finland's independence subject to eventual confirmation by a constituent assembly and 'on the condition that the Finns recognize the necessity of safeguarding the interests of Russia in the Baltic'.[14]

With some exaggeration, Mannerheim poured out his bitter feelings on 8 November to Brigadier-General Spears of the British Military Mission to the French government. Spears reported that Mannerheim said: 'I was stopped from taking Petrograd in the Spring of 1918 by the Germans. I was stopped from taking Petrograd in the Spring of this year, largely by the Russians. On both of these occasions I had almost absolute power in Finland, and the expedition would have been a relatively easy matter. When a short time ago, the Russians sent Shebeko[15] to Finland to try and induce a weak, pacifist and socialist government to do what I was stopped from doing, instead of meeting the Finns half-way with concessions they devoted practically all their energies to the discussion of the guarantees which Finland should give Russia, with the result that even those who were hesitating and perhaps even inclined to favour intervention became definitely opposed to any military action on the part of Finland.'[16]

On 24 November 1919 Mannerheim left Paris for Warsaw. The trip was by no means only to meet friends from his time in Warsaw before the war and to claim his possessions, although he greatly enjoyed renewing so many old friendships in spite of the uncomfortable living conditions there. The purpose of his journey was primarily political – it was 'a clear example of the appearance of both the national and the international interest in the general's activity'.[17] The British knew of his plans and Churchill asked Brigadier-General A. Carton de Wiart, head of the British Military Mission in Warsaw, to keep him informed of Mannerheim's activities and how he was received by the Poles. Carton de Wiart noted that he had come to find out if the Poles meant business in their fight with the Bolshevics [sic], – and if there was a chance of a combined offensive in the spring'.[18]

---

[14] Memorandum from the Russian *chargé d'affaires* in London. Documents on British Foreign Policy 1919–1939. First Series, III, p. 620.

[15] N. N. Shebeko, a former member of the Russian Council of State and a diplomat.

[16] Churchill Papers. Char 16/41, Spears to Churchill, 9 November 1919.

[17] Hovi, 'Mitä Mannerheim teki Varsovassa syksyllä 1919?', p. 142.

[18] Churchill Papers. Char 16/14, Carton de Wiart to Sir Archibald Sinclair, 13 December 1919.

Mannerheim had two meetings with General Piłsudski, the Polish head of state, on 4 and 12 December, and discussions with members of the diplomatic corps in Warsaw. Russia remained his preoccupation and he developed the idea of a Polish-Finnish offensive against the Bolsheviks. Although both countries mistrusted the views of Yudenich and Denikin, the inability of those generals to defeat the Bolsheviks on their own gave Poland and Finland the opportunity to obtain White Russian recognition of their independence in return for their military collaboration.

Piłsudski told Mannerheim, who reported his views to the French foreign ministry and to the British, that he was prepared to cooperate with the Russian Whites in a spring offensive provided they recognized Poland's independence. Mannerheim doubted if the Russians would do so unless strongly pressed by the Allies. Poland was prepared to support Latvia against the Bolsheviks if Finland would support Estonia. A preliminary scheme was thus afoot for a joint anti-Bolshevik alliance by Poland, Latvia, Estonia and Finland in collaboration with Denikin; Piłsudski hoped that Mannerheim would ensure Finland's participation. Mannerheim was very pessimistic about Denikin's chances of success unless he was supported by a broad alliance of border states.

Mannerheim's chances of obtaining Finland's participation in any action against Russia were non existent. However, Finnish activists were still hopeful that he might lead Finnish expeditions in Eastern Karelia and against Petrograd and seize power in Finland by means of a right-wing *coup*. A White Russian general met Finnish activists in Helsinki at the end of November and hoped to secure Mannerheim's immediate return to Finland so that he could command a Russo-Finnish force for the relief of Petrograd. The activists' ideas were actually discussed with Mannerheim on 12 December while he was in Warsaw. He was unwilling to carry out a *coup* himself, but would return to Finland if asked. But there was to be no *coup* in Finland.

On 13 December Mannerheim left Warsaw for Paris. There, and in London in mid December, he made a final and unsuccessful attempt to persuade the Allies to pursue a consistent anti-Bolshevik policy and support the alliance he proposed. He was disappointed that Lord Curzon, the foreign secretary, would not see him and interpreted this as evidence of a total lack of British interest in intervention and in the fate of Denikin. He spent Christmas in Switzerland with his daughter

CIVILIAN

Sophy but was back in Paris in early January 1920. On 5 February he returned to Finland, being fêted on arrival in Turku and again on reaching Helsinki on 7 February. White Finland had not forgotten the White General or lost its enthusiasm for him, even if it disregarded his views on Finland's Russian policy.

Any hope of a restored White Russia rapidly disappeared in the course of 1920. The Allied blockade of Soviet Russia was lifted in January. Poland itself was threatened by a Soviet invasion which was only turned back outside Warsaw in August. On 16 November the last Russian White soldiers were evacuated from the Crimea: the Bolsheviks had won the Civil War. Already in June the Finnish government had opened peace negotiations with the Soviet government and on 14 October the Peace of Tartu was signed, regularizing relations between Finland and the Bolshevik government. Mannerheim told Tekla Hultin: 'It is a bad peace.'[19] He did not trust the Bolsheviks to keep their word. Bolshevik agitation in Finland would continue. He blamed the non-socialists for their feebleness. He also blamed the Russian Whites for their failure to recognize the reality of the national states that had sprung up along the borders of the old Russian Empire. Despite his efforts, his hopes of crushing Bolshevism had been dashed. As the only successful ex-Russian White general, Mannerheim greatly feared for the future of Finland and of Europe.

PRIVATE LIFE

Despite his activity during the latter part of 1919, Mannerheim felt acutely that he had been sidelined. This was clearly apparent in his *Memoirs* where he wrote: 'Throughout the twelve years which followed upon the first Presidential election … my part in Finland's political life was that of an observer.'[20] His attitude towards those years was summed up in the title of the relevant chapter his *Memoirs* – 'Our gains dissipated' – and in his characterization of them as 'the period of decay in the 1920s'.[21] He was also worried about his own future. Carl Enckell, then Finnish minister in Paris, recorded that he had never seen Mannerheim so pessimistic as one time in November

---

[19] Cited in Jägerskiöld, *Mannerheim mellan världskrigen*, p. 21.
[20] Mannerheim, *Memoirs*, p. 245.
[21] *Ibid.*, p. 228, 244.

1919 when he visited him at the legation. 'I tried to console him and said that banks and industrial concerns in Finland would appeal to his authority by offering directorships etc.'[22] Mannerheim went away depressed.

In fact in 1920 he was offered and, after consulting his brother Johan, accepted appointment as chairman of the board of management of the Union Bank. He continued in the same capacity with Helsingfors Aktiebank after the depression had forced the Union Bank into difficulties and led the two banks to merge in 1931. He resigned as chairman only in 1935 to devote his time to other work. He carried out his duties conscientiously but not without irritation. After sorting out some problems with the Union Bank in 1924 he complained to Johan: 'It has been a hard labour and I am utterly bored by these negotiations and this everlasting talk with indecisive men without the capacity to take action.'[23] He commented, after chairing the board for the last time: 'I had both shade and light, perhaps more shade than light.'[24]

Fortunately for Mannerheim's freedom of activity, he was not to be dependent on directorships to supplement his Finnish pension. That pension would in any case have spared him the poverty that befell so many former Russian generals who had emigrated but he also acquired financial independence thanks to the generosity of his fellow countrymen. Although there were richer men in Finland, Mannerheim now possessed the means to follow an elegant life style, to travel, and to associate with the influential and the wealthy without apparent concern for his finances. This was a welcome transformation for a man who had usually been poor and never wealthy, except perhaps in the early years of his marriage. Mannerheim was not good at economizing – for example, he always wanted the best in clothes, guns and golf clubs. Of course good clothes are economical in the long run and he even instructed his shirtmakers in London's Jermyn Street: 'To avoid shrinkage please cut sleeves of woolen [sic] shirts with more material than usually.'[25]

Mannerheim may have given an outward impression of not under-

[22] Enckell, 'Några minnen från mitt samarbete med Gustaf Mannerheim', in *Marskalken av Finland friherre Gustaf Mannerheim*, p. 42.
[23] To Johan Mannerheim, 30 May 1924. Grensholm Collection, VAY 5627.
[24] Speech in Mannerheim Archive, Box 604.
[25] Draft in Mannerheim Archive, Box 814.

standing or caring about money, but the reality was entirely different. Numerous notes and letters among his papers show how carefully he watched his financial affairs although much was handled by professional advisers. His correspondence with his brother Johan frequently concerned financial matters. Mannerheim followed the fluctuations of the Finnish mark attentively and sought to invest – in Finland and abroad – so as to reduce the risks of currency depreciation, inflation and war. He was concerned to borrow money as cheaply as possible – understandably because at times his borrowing was extensive.

On 9 February 1920, shortly after his return to Finland, Mannerheim received a national gift from the Finnish people. This was nothing to do with the government. At the end of May 1918 the non-socialist parties had discussed the possibility of a national gift to him and Svinhufvud had said that the government considered the gift of a country estate appropriate, although Alkio thought that his pension was an adequate acknowledgement of his services. However, nothing was done because of Mannerheim's resignation. The national gift was the result of a private initiative taken on the day of the presidential election, which resulted in an appeal in the press on 26 July 1919 by twenty-four prominent citizens for a gift for the liberator of the fatherland. The sum collected in General Gustaf Mannerheim's National Fund was 7,600,000 marks (some £72,000 – then a massive sum – at the average exchange rate for 1920). Several hundred thousand Finns who contributed signed the address – dated 25 July 1919 – and their signatures, collected into twelve leather-bound volumes, were to occupy a place of honour in his home. The address itself, in addition to setting out the nation's gratitude for his achievements, specified the terms of the gift, 'the interest on which is at your free, personal disposal during your lifetime, and which is later to be used in accordance with instructions given by you'.[26]

For several years Mannerheim had no permanent home in Finland. He had lived during his regency in the residence of the former governors-general in central Helsinki, also using the villa Kesäranta (on the north-western outskirts of Helsinki) which had been their summer residence. Later in 1919 he rented an apartment at 14 Aleksanterinkatu, Helsinki, and in the spring of 1920 took a three-year lease on another apartment in Helsinki at 5 Mariankatu (near the

---

[26] Mannerheim, *Memoirs*, p. 238.

House of the Nobility). It was to Mariankatu that he took his possessions when they arrived from Warsaw, although sadly some had been broken or pilfered in transit.

Only in 1924 did Mannerheim finally settle when he leased a splendid wooden house, 22 (now 14) Kalliolinnantie, in Helsinki's elegant Kaivopuisto district. The house was owned by the industrialist Karl Fazer and his terms allowed Mannerheim to renovate it at his own expense, and to rebuild the interior according to his own ideas. He ensured the separation of the reception rooms, the bedrooms and the domestic services and, with an eye to entertaining, secured good circulation between the reception rooms, easy access from the domestic offices to the rest of the house, and an adequate number of guest rooms. The rebuilding and the care he took over its furnishing and decoration, in which he was advised by Akseli Gallen-Kallela, created a worthy home which in its essentials may still be seen: after his death it was opened as the Mannerheim Museum.

Mannerheim stamped his personality on his house. The furniture and mementos from his service in the Russian army and earlier years in Helsinki were supplemented by suitable purchases for the large house and by numerous gifts, including some outstanding pictures. His interest in the orient was reflected in various furnishings and ornaments, such as a group of buddhas in his study. Hunting trophies, including eventually a magnificent tiger skin testified to his enthusiasm for sport, and weapons and banners proclaimed his military background. Carefully arranged photographs included not only family and friends but heads of state and members of the Russian imperial family, a reminder of his past service as a Russian guards officer. The windows at the back of the house gave a fine view over the entrance to the South Harbour. The house combined elegance and suitability for entertaining with comfort. Visitors were impressed. Lady Diana Cooper, whom Mannerheim entertained there in August 1938 with her husband Duff Cooper, then First Lord of the Admiralty, wrote: 'Wonderful house, marvellous food and wines, all of which he arranges, the right flowers, china objects and the right lighting and after dinner a first-class budding she-pianist.'[27]

In her references to the food and wines and to 'Mannerheim's epicureanism'[28] Lady Diana had touched upon one of his special interests

---

[27] Cooper, *The Light of Common Day*, p. 233.
[28] *Ibid.*, p. 234.

dating from childhood – his father had been an enthusiastic epicure. Mannerheim combined a delicate palate with very definite ideas about individual recipes and the structure of menus. He was expert on both Russian and French cuisine, and exchanged recipes and ideas with various friends but above all with his sister Countess Eva Mannerheim Sparre, whom he helped in 1935 with the publication of her excellent cookery book.

Mannerheim followed the Finnish custom of leaving town in summer for a country cottage or seaside villa. He enjoyed the bracing air of Hanko on the south coast and first rented and then purchased an island with a villa there, devoting much attention to its extension and furnishing and to the planting of flowers, which he loved, in the rocky garden. The noise from a nearby café disturbed him and so he leased it, renaming it 'The House of the Four Winds' and ensuring that it attracted a more dignified and quiet clientele; he remained its proprietor for seven years. Possibly he thought at first that his principal residence might be in Hanko because he became registered with the Lutheran parish there in 1919 and only transferred his registration to the Swedish-language parish of South Helsinki in 1935.[29] At Hanko, as in Helsinki, he was able to entertain: his summers there were punctuated by a succession of house guests, and he also enjoyed the company of friends attracted to Hanko as a yachting centre, such as Henrik Ramsay, the managing director of the Finnish Steamship Company (FÅA-SHO), and Virginie Hériot, the noted French yachtswoman. Mannerheim's villa at Hanko was destroyed during the Second World War.

For Mannerheim the 1920s and 1930s were a period when a number of friendships – with Hannes Ignatius, Ernst Linder, Rudolf Walden and others – flourished. By the end of the 1920s, and even more in the 1930s, death was beginning to diminish the circle around him, not least among his own family. His sister Sophie died in 1928, and this was a great blow; their relationship had been close, and with her contacts in the caring professions she had played a significant part in setting up the child welfare organization to which Mannerheim devoted much time. His brother Johan died in 1934, breaking what Mannerheim regarded as the closest of his relationships with his brothers and sisters though not his link with Johan's estate at Grensholm since he remained on friendly terms with his sister-in-law, Palaemona.

[29] Labart, 'Kahvilanpitäjänä Hankoniemellä', in *Mannerheim: tuttu ja tuntematon*, p. 132.

She visited him from time to time and elicited from him the compliment: 'I am always pleased to have someone to stay with me with whom I get on and who is also sensible enough not to make any demands on me.'[30]

Mannerheim arranged in 1920 to pay his ex-wife Anastasia an annual allowance of 36,000 francs, 'which should suffice for living in France. Besides I will try to pay her debts. I have difficulty m doing more.'[31] However, she complained in 1933 to Carl Enckell, with whom she had previously corresponded when he was Finnish minister in Paris, that Mannerheim had halved her allowance without warning and remained deaf to pleas to restore it. She referred to is hard heart while acknowledging that 'the general is in essence neither miserly nor wicked'.[32] The letter – of which the outcome is unknown – may be connected with the fact that in the years before her death in Paris in December 1936 a reconciliation took place which clearly pleased and comforted both of them. Mannerheim visited her and helped with her medical care. When she died he was concerned that a requiem mass should be said for her and that she should have a fitting gravestone. He maintained friendly relations with his sister-in-law, Countess Sofia (Sonia) Mengden, in France and helped her financially in 1943 and 1944, to her joy and gratitude.[33]

His daughter Sophy settled in Paris where she had a place in the Russian community but no occupation. She paid occasional summer visits to her father in Finland but they got on each other's nerves. He thought her life disorganized although he was to praise her efforts to promote Finland's cause during the Winter War. In 1949 he was critical of her failure to keep him informed about an accident in which she broke her leg; and expressed the hope to a correspondent that she would avoid another accident in future 'and save me the great expense' it involved.[34] His other daughter Anastasie left convent life, though without the loss of her faith, and by 1939 was living in Harrow, near London.

[30] To Palaemona Mannerheim, 11 March 1934. Grensholm Collection, VAY 5630.
[31] To Sophie Mannerheim, 16 May 1920. Mannerheim Archive, Box 905.
[32] Anastasia Mannerheim to [Carl Enckell], 11 January 1933. Mannerheim Archive, Box 911.
[33] From Sonia Mengden, 20 February 1943. Mannerheim Archive, Box 504.
[34] To Sophy Mannerheim, 16 January 1949; to Consul General Kaarlo Brusin, 24 January 1949. Mannerheim Archive, Box 53.

Mannerheim remained untrammelled by family life. He never remarried. From late 1918 until well into 1919 he was undoubtedly eager to marry Kitty Linder; in December 1918 he hoped that the new year 'will bring the fulfilment of our wishes and happiness'.[35] His letters to '*Chère et charmante Kitty*' or '*Ma bonne et chère petite Kitty*' were written with obvious affection.[36] She came from the same Finnish noble background as he did. The fact that she was twenty years younger may have put her off marriage to him; other factors may have been the need – for which he blamed himself – to withdraw his first attempt to obtain a divorce before it came to court, and his desire for secrecy about their friendship while his divorce remained unsettled. Against his wishes she returned to Munich where her mother and sister lived, and although they continued to correspond during 1920 the tone of his letters became less ardent. By 1921 it was clear that they were no more than friends. Marriage to such a prominent – and peripatetic – public figure as Mannerheim must have been a daunting prospect, and perhaps they both recognized this.

Mannerheim solved the problem of finding a companion to escort to concerts or to give the help he needed when entertaining by conscripting the wives of friends as what he described as his 'two lady assistants'.[37] Mary Procopé, wife of Hjalmar J. Procopé, diplomat and politician, and Karin Ramsay, wife of Henrik Ramsay (mentioned above), were called upon to assist with his arrangements in the 1920s and 1930s, even at some inconvenience to themselves. They were exactly the type of attractive and intelligent women whose company Mannerheim most enjoyed.

Rumours abounded about his friendships with beautiful women, such as the singer Hanna Granfelt, Countess Jeanne de Salverte, and the eminent and wealthy French yachtswoman Virginie Hériot. Henrik Ramsay commented on Virginie Hériot's pleasant appearance, discreet and unassuming character, her charm which he thought appreciably exceeded the high standard of French women, and her logical and lucid conversation.[38] Mannerheim corresponded frequently with her during 1927. She was then thirty-seven. She wrote to him

---

[35] To Kitty Linder, 30 December [1918]. Mannerheim Archive, Box 952.
[36] Mannerheim Archive, Box 952.
[37] To Palaemona Mannerheim, 11 March 1934. Grensholm Collection, VAY 5630.
[38] Henrik Ramsay, *Sommar och segel*, pp. 174, 176.

as '*Mon cher grand chef*', signing herself in tones of increasing affection as '*votre petit Pirate*'. Her yachting commitments and his travelling plans made meeting difficult, while her health and that of her mother prevented her from accompanying him on a planned trip to East Africa and the Sudan or to Palestine. She noted in May 1927: '*Tout ce qui arrive est toujours pour nous séparer.*' However, they met on the Riviera and also in Bordeaux, about which she wrote: '*Je ne puis oublier nos tous moments de Bordeaux.*' She was sad that he had to go to India without her. Her letters became less ardent in tone, yet in 1929 she could write, '*Jamais je n'ai oublie l'ami sincère que vous êtes.*'[39] She died in 1932.

Mannerheim's long friendship with Princess Marie Lubomirska, dating back to his time in Warsaw, was important. They had conducted a warm correspondence during the First World War and remained in regular contact through meetings and by letter until the friendship was ended by her death in 1934. Admiration was not just on his side. She clearly adored him, confiding to her diary in June 1918: 'Contact with him was as invigorating as the mountain air. Even in a ballroom his steadfastness as a gallant knight was well evident. Our general was a little rigid with some wooden manners of speech and none of the deadly, facile and glittering Slav charm. I keep his letters preciously, and the very possession of them is a comfort to me. My friendship has brought him happiness during the war. I shall regret that I am no longer young when shaking his hand on his return.'[40]

In his last years – after the Second World War – he enjoyed the company of Countess Gertrud Arco-Valley, a sister of the Swedish bankers Jacob and Marcus Wallenberg. Her cheerful vitality and good taste brightened his visits to the Riviera and to Switzerland as well as to the country house he then had in Finland.

Mannerheim's attractiveness to women was evident. Ester Ståhlberg, the wife of the first president, was an exception to female adulation. She was long his determined opponent, regarding him as a dangerous intriguer, and impolite to her and her husband. Her diary is full of snide remarks about him: 'He is handsome but rather haughty looking'[41] and 'Mannerheim leaves me completely cold, whatever sort

---

[39] From Virginie Hériot, 20 December 1926, 5 January, 26 February, 26 May, 6 July, 11 November 1927, 28 October 1929. Grensholm Collection, VAY 5346–47.
[40] Lubomirska, *Pamiętnik księżnej Marii Zdisławowej Lubomirskiej 1914–1918*, p. 645.
[41] *Ester Ståhlbergin kauniit, katkerat vuodet*, p. 68.

of a charmer others may see him as.'[42] More typically, Lady Diana Cooper came under his spell in 1938. 'He looks fifty and is said to dye his hair (and Brendan [Bracken] swore that he had rouged lips) and he is only seventy-two. He's old Russian Imperialist (that I find irresistible) and says in French "*Pardon*".'[43] Marie Lubomirska's pen portrait of him is refreshingly frank although he possessed charm in plenty even if it were not of the Slav variety. But perhaps there was something deadly about his charm which caused society ladies and secretaries to succumb willingly to his requests for help, however demanding. He was used to getting his way and at the same time his thanks were greatly cherished.

Mannerheim did not hesitate to ask the Finnish legations in a number of European capitals to undertake various services for him. These ranged from storing or forwarding his luggage or various purchases to the provision of documentation for his motor-cars, travel tickets, currency transactions and the posting of letters. During the Continuation War he asked if the legation in Madrid could find him a supply of good Havana cigars, which it did. Some of the ministers to whom he turned, like Carl Enckell and G. A. Gripenberg, were friends but in any case Mannerheim was not a man whose requests could be refused.

The daily running of Mannerheim's home was entrusted to two very capable housekeepers. He also had a valet. He had replaced the Russian soldier who accompanied him to Finland with a Swedish soldier who had served as a volunteer in the White Army. From 1926 to 1939 his valet was a young Austrian who had waited on him in Austria and impressed him with his efficiency. During the period of the Second World War Mannerheim had a succession of military servants. In the 1930s the Uusimaa Dragoon Regiment always provided him with a dragoon to look after his horse. He had been appointed honorary colonel[44] of this regiment, at the request of its officers, in 1928. Exercise was important to Mannerheim and he usually rode daily when in Helsinki.

---

[42] *Ester Ståhlbergin voittojen ja tappioiden vuodet*, p. 291.
[43] Cooper, *The Light of Common Day*, p. 232. Mannerheim was seventy-one in 1938.
[44] *Kunniapäällikkö* (Finnish); *hederschef* (Swedish).

TRAVEL

Mannerheim travelled often in the 1920s and 1930s. Partly this was for the enjoyment, eventual rest or warmer climates that travel afforded, together with the opportunity to see friends, but another reason was that he found Finland constricting and quarrelsome and its politics – particularly in the 1920s – a source of anxiety and frustration. In the 1930s he also undertook a number of official visits abroad following his appointment as chairman of the Defence Council.

Mannerheim was a devotee of hunting, which took him regularly abroad although he also joined hunting and shooting parties at home, mixing as a convival guest with a number of Finnish industrialists and estate owners including Karl Fazer, Petter Forsström and the poet Bertel Gripenberg. Mannerheim was a good shot with a rifle but less so with a shot-gun. Although he willingly shot partridge, pheasant, duck and hares, it was bigger game that especially attracted him. In Finland that meant elk; in the Tyrol, where he hunted regularly in the autumn from 1922 to 1938, it included mountain-goats and in Sweden, where he shot on his brother's estate, deer. The mountains of the Tyrol provided physical and mental as well as sporting refreshment: Mannerheim had succumbed to the lure of mountain scenery during his expedition to Central Asia and northern China in 1906–8. In 1935 he joined a hunt in East Prussia and another in 1937 near Berlin, each time at the invitation of Hermann Göring, whom he had met through official visits to Germany, and who combined control of the hunting grounds of the Reich with his other duties. The antlers of a magnificent elk Mannerheim shot in East Prussia in September 1935 joined the many other hunting trophies that adorned his home.

The call of big game hunting, particularly the desire to shoot a tiger, took Mannerheim twice to India. The first time was in 1928 when he had the additional motive of wanting to be out of Finland during the commemoration of the outbreak of the War of 1918 and thus avoid compromising his position by participating in ceremonies sponsored by a government of which he disapproved. The impulse for the journey was provided by the British Major-General Walter Kirke, who had met him in 1924 while in Finland to advise on the country's defence. Mannerheim sailed from Marseilles on S.S. *Rawalpindi* in December 1927. The three months he spent in India and Burma proved too little 'to get even a "bird's eye view" of India, but just enough to give one an idea of how to plan a possible new journey'.[45] From Bombay he travelled to Lucknow, where he was the guest of the District Commissioner. A hunting trip in the foothills of the Himalayas was followed by a visit to Delhi, where he saw Kirke. A second period of hunting followed at Seoni in the Central Provinces. A third took place in Sikkim, where he became friends with the Political Officer there, Colonel F. M. Bailey. His visit to Burma (sailing from Calcutta) proved unsatisfactory for hunting. Mannerheim's return journey to Europe was by sea from Bombay to Basra, by air – uncomfortably, because of air pockets – to Cairo and then by sea again from Alexandria to Venice. Countess de Salverte travelled on the same liner. The trip to India had been a rich experience; he had shot seventeen animals but, most disappointingly, no tigers. One hunt, using nine elephants to hem in the prey, had come close, but 'The tiger was too clever for us'.[46]

On Mannerheim's second visit to India in 1937 he was luckier and shot four tigers. This time the reason for the journey was an invitation from Colonel Bailey, who had visited him in Finland in 1934, and was currently British Minister in Nepal. As in 1928, there was an element of escape in Mannerheim's decision to leave Finland for a longer period; he was glad to be away during the 1937 presidential election and to have a break from the frustrations of Finnish defence planning, although as chairman of the Defence Council he always carefully arranged his foreign travel so that he would not be away from Finland while vital discussions about the government's budget proposals were taking place. He travelled to India by way of London – where he bought a Purdey double-barrelled hunting rifle to add to his arsenal – sailing from Tilbury on S.S. *Mooltan* on 10 December 1936. The 'roughness of the arrangements and poor cuisine' on the ship displeased him.[47]

With his earlier contacts in India and those in London derived from his official position in Finland, Mannerheim was treated by the governing establishment in India as a distinguished visitor. He got on well with the English whose 'broad vision of facts and situations'

[45] To Hannes Ignatius, 7 March 1928. Mannerheim, *Brev*, p. 232.
[46] To Hannes Ignatius, 1 February 1928. Mannerheim, *Brev*, p. 229.
[47] Snow to Eden, 10 April 1937. F.O. 371/21077, N2301/965/56.

he found interesting[48] and whose easy sense of racial superiority he shared. (In his letter of condolence to the widow of a British official killed by a tiger when going to the aid of a beater, Mannerheim wrote: 'I learned to know in your husband that fine type of an englishman [sic], brave, determined and with his heart always open to help even if the one needing it was only a native beater'.)[49] In Bombay he was invited to stay with the governor, Lord Brabourne, whose 'court' impressed him with its regulated formality. On 3 January 1937 he travelled north to Bailey's hunting camp near Banabassa just inside Nepal. There he shot his first tiger and on 13 January a second one. After an interval shooting in southern India – and a stay with the governor of Madras – Mannerheim returned to Nepal on 2 February as guest of the Maharajah at a grand tiger hunt near Belauri in which no fewer than 180 elephants were employed. On 6 February he shot a man-eating tiger, one of the largest to be killed in Nepal, with a length of 10 feet and 7 inches (3.23 metres). On 13 February he shot his fourth, hitting the animal in the heart, modesty but no doubt correctly acknowledging this as 'due rather to good luck than skill'.[50] Before returning to India he called on the Maharajah in Katmandu.

He travelled back to Europe by sea from Ceylon, returning to Helsinki from London in April 1937. The trip had been intensely rewarding – in addition to the tigers he had shot a python and a crocodile as well as other game. For a man nearing his seventieth birthday, contending with a hot climate was a considerable physical feat. The camping was well organized, but there was exertion in plenty during long days in rough country with thick vegetation. Moreover, elephants – from the howdahs of which tigers were shot – gave a hard ride.

Not all Mannerheim's foreign travel proved so successful. In 1923, attracted by descriptions of North Africa by his sister Eva and her husband, the artist Count Louis Sparre, he had decided to go to Algeria and Morocco, but soon after arriving in Algeria he had a serious accident. His car crashed into a stone wall, throwing him into a field five metres below the level of the road and the car hung menacingly above him as he lay helplessly with a broken leg, broken collar-bone and several broken ribs. Help did not arrive for four and a half hours.

[48] To Elsie Mannerheim, 23 May 1934. Mannerheim Archive, Box 903.
[49] Draft to Mrs E. M. Bourne, [1932]. Grensholm Collection, VAY 5644.
[50] Cited in Soikkanen, *C. G. E. Mannerheim: suurriistan metsästäjä*, p. 114.

His driver suffered a cut to the head, but his companions escaped with no more than bruises. Mannerheim spent a month in Algiers in hospital and convalescing. Because of insufficient traction, the broken leg healed 2 cm. shorter than the other, a deficiency he corrected by the use of inner soles in his shoes and stirrups of different lengths when riding.

He was always careful about his health; rheumatism troubled him most. He underwent an operation in 1931. In 1936 he suffered from painful kidney stones. Gout attacked him occasionally. He worried about his diet and his weight, writing to Emanuel Nobel in May 1925 that he was about to go to Karlsbad (Karlovy Vary in Czechoslovakia), 'in order through assiduous drinking of the water to try to paralyse the effects of the heavy diet one puts up with in our Nordic countries'.[51] He told his brother-in-law: 'Carlsbad is thronged with people, but the number of Christians is not great. What types and what impudence!'[52] Mannerheim shared the anti-Jewish sentiments typical of the Russian officer corps to which he had belonged.

In 1926 he went to Vichy, where 'the treatment seems to me both agreeable and effective', but Karlsbad called him back:[53] it was an attractive place where he saw friends and acquaintances and played golf, but at times he also found it noisy, not least with jazz music. He liked golf because it provided the exercise he could not get in Helsinki. In 1935, 1936 and 1937 he took the waters at Bad Wildungen, near Kassel, but in 1938 he patronised Montecatini near Lucca to avoid the political complications of a visit to Germany in the prevailing international situation; he told the British minister in Helsinki 'that conditions in Germany were not such that he would be likely to enjoy a visit there this time'.[54] These medically-supervised cures, in the course of which he lost weight, did him good, as did his regular holidays in Switzerland, particularly at Lausanne where he also visited his dentist.

Through travel Mannerheim also sought to keep abreast of political and military developments in Europe – for this his visits to London, Paris and Stockholm were particularly valuable. He wrote to Ernst Linder on 24 February 1936 of his recent stay in Stockholm: 'Thanks

[51] To Emanuel Nobel, 4 May 1925. Mannerheim, *Brev*, p. 226.
[52] To Michael Gripenberg, 15 May 1925. Mannerheim Archive, Box 906.
[53] To Sophie Mannerheim, 4 April 1926. Grensholm Collection, VAY 5628.
[54] Snow to Collier, 21 October 1938. F.O. 371/22270, N5198/3609/56.

to you and your friends I had the opportunity for a good deal of really thorough conversations with people whose opinion and writings are truly of importance.'[55] In a letter to the Finnish minister in London in 1932 he regretted not having been there for three years: 'It would have interested me very much to get to meet leading politicians and soldiers and be able to form my own opinion for myself, even if it were superficial, of the situation in the world.'[56] Mannerheim was always open to ideas and information and eager to profit from what he had learned. After his travels in 1934 he wrote: 'I have ... seen so much abroad that certain ideas have crystallized in my mind and I want to come home as quickly as possible to carry them out without unnecessary delay.'[57]

Sometimes the timetable of his journeys did not allow for the courtesies he regarded as important. The Finnish minister in Copenhagen was requested in autumn 1924 to inform the Dowager Empress Maria Fedorovna of Russia that Mannerheim had been too short a time in Copenhagen 'to permit a journey to Klampenborg', her home after having been evacuated from revolutionary Russia.[58] The Empress had been his colonel-in-chief in the Chevalier Guards and, as he recorded in his *Memoirs*, 'On several occasions in the nineteen-twenties when I passed through Copenhagen ... I had the opportunity to offer my former Colonel-in-Chief my homage.'[59] He also called on the Grand Duke Nikolai Nikolaevich, the former Russian commander-in-chief, in his place of exile outside Paris. Mannerheim maintained contacts with Russian former comrades as well as members of the imperial family. His correspondence with friends and acquaintances was extensive and multi-lingual. Many strangers wrote to express their admiration for him or to solicit his aid. In two letters that survive from 1925 the writers urged him to reform his alleged habit of excessive drinking. He annotated one: 'The result of political opponents' campaign of lies.'[60] It was no wonder he wanted to travel abroad.

[55] To Ernst Linder, 24 February 1936. Mannerheim, *Brev*, p. 257.
[56] To Armas Saastamoinen, 19 January 1932. Mannerheim, *Brev*, p. 239.
[57] To Eva Sparre, 23 December 1934. Mannerheim, *Brev*, p. 249.
[58] Cited in Virkkunen, *Mannerheimin kääntöpuoli*, p. 111.
[59] Mannerheim, *Memoirs*, p. 9.
[60] From Irja Lehmussaari, 31 January 1925. Grensholm Collection, VAY 5649.

CIVILIAN
HUMANITARIAN WORK

Travel provided diversion, but Mannerheim possessed a great capacity for work. With no official employment in the 1920s, he found some outlet for his energy in organizing social and humanitarian work. His sister Sophie had a strong concern for child welfare and encouraged him to call a meeting in October 1920 to consider the foundation of an association for the care and protection of children. Key figures in the scheme were Sophie's friend Erik Mandelin, who had already produced plans for improving child welfare, and the young paediatrician Arvo Ylppö. The result of their collaboration was the establishment of General Mannerheim's Child Welfare Association, of which Mannerheim became honorary president and his sister chairman. The aim was to provide a central committee to give uniform direction to local organizations throughout the country. Mannerheim supported the Association financially and by providing office space in his apartment for the first two years of its activity.

Having seen how many men had been rejected for military service as medically unfit, Mannerheim had a military interest in the creation of a healthy nation. However, it would be wrong to see his concern for child welfare as a cynical attempt to provide fitter cannon fodder. Of course the improvement of children's health and the care of the many orphans of the Civil War would help to form healthy young people who he hoped would become useful and patriotic citizens. But Mannerheim also thought of child welfare as a means of healing a divided society – and said so in his appeal to the nation to support the new Association. His paternalistic aims fitted in with the concern for social reform he had expressed in September 1919. Yet some sections of society were not prepared for any process of social healing that involved so much as his name, and although his Association flourished it was boycotted by the socialists and many politicians of the centre rejected it.

Mannerheim's Association never became the sole national coordinating organization that he hoped it would be. In 1922 another national association was formed, closely linked to his adversary Ester Ståhlberg, the wife of the president. Mannerheim wrote to his brother Johan on 18 February 1925. 'My Child Welfare Association, which has grown enormously and has slowly grown to nearly 300 local sections, is also now the object of a skilfully started and well-aimed intrigue on the part of Mrs Ståhlberg and her followers.'[61] In 1936 the Mannerheim Association admitted that it was only one of several child welfare associations and became a member of a new central organization of these bodies. The Association's work, in which Mannerheim at first took a close interest, was nevertheless pioneering and important, creating a training centre for care workers, providing numerous clinics and health visitors, and contributing to a significant drop in infant mortality. He was also concerned with the Association's formation of young farmers' clubs.

Mannerheim had a further contact with young people through scouting. He had been made an honorary scout in August 1919 and as such he instituted a badge – the Mannerheim Badge – 'to try to increase the interest of young people in the scouting movement' and 'to create a new generation, independent of narrow party and political frontiers, in which real comradeship and brotherhood join with physical and moral national virtues'.[62] Mannerheim frequently presented it personally and attended various other scouting activities. He became honorary chairman of the Finnish Scouting Association and in 1933 entertained Lord and Lady Baden-Powell during their visit to Finland. In a letter to Baden-Powell he wrote of his 'firm belief that the Scout-movement is the best form of education for the young'.[63]

Apart from his Child Welfare Association, Mannerheim's other major humanitarian activity was with the Finnish Red Cross. He accepted an invitation from Professor Richard Faltin, an eminent surgeon with experience of military surgery, to become its chairman and was duly elected on 8 February 1922, holding the post until his death. Mannerheim had experienced personally the work of the Finnish Red Cross when being treated by Faltin, with whom he had been at school, at a field ambulance in Manchuria during the Russo-Japanese War. This no doubt added to the appeal of the invitation. Through the Red Cross, to which he devoted much time during the 1920s and – rather less – the 1930s, he was able to combine work for the needy with preparations to assist the army in the event of war. Participation in the meetings of the International Red Cross also

---

[61] To Johan Mannerheim, 18 February 1925. Mannerheim, *Brev*, p. 225.
[62] Cited in Vesikansa, *Suomen partioliike 1910–1960*, p. 7.
[63] To Lord Baden-Powell, 6 December 1933. Grensholm Collection, VAY 5644.

broadened his international contacts. He became a keen supporter of Red Cross ideals.

He began by reorganizing the structure of the organization and promoting fundraising. He rapidly raised its profile, installed it in better premises, developed its stock of emergency stores and arranged a link with his Child Welfare Association. Under his chairmanship cottage hospitals were founded in frontier districts, equipment was provided by 1939 for ten field hospitals (with a total of 1,500 beds), and funds were raised to build a Red Cross Hospital in Helsinki. This hospital – to which he made a sizeable donation – opened in 1932 and provided training in military surgery. The Red Cross also gave much-needed help to the unemployed during the depression of 1931–3. His secretary in the organization from 1928 to 1938, Elsa Könönen rightly pointed out that humanitarian work was not just an interest for him, and that those who worked with him 'saw how whole heartedly he devoted his time, thoughts and influence to this work'.[64] And Mannerheim himself recorded in his *Memoirs:* 'This work has given me satisfaction, and I am thankful to have been able to serve my country in this manner at a time when the authorities did not require my services.[65]

PASSED OVER FOR PUBLIC SERVICE

The bitterness of Mannerheim's remark about the requiring his services reflected the fact that he held no official appointment until 1931. He remained an outsider throughout the 1970s and refused invitations to the palace during the Ståhlberg presidency. However, his name was mentioned several times in connection with senior posts in the army and the Defence Corps. The first was during the crisis over the command of the Defence Corps in 1921. Criticism in a newspaper article of Finnish foreign policy and of some of Finland's allies by the commander of the Helsinki Defence Corps, Major-General Paul von Gerich, prompted diplomatic protests, and the government asked the commander-in-chief of the Defence Corps, Colonel Georg Didrik von Essen to dismiss von Gerich. He refused on the grounds of the Defence Corps's autonomy and was himself dismissed. The new commander-in-chief,

[64] Könönen, *Vuosikymmen Mannerheimin sihteerinä,* p. 106.
[65] Mannerheim, *Memoirs,* p. 251.

Major-General K. E. Berg, did dismiss von Gerich but was severely criticized for so doing and committed suicide.

In September 1921, having failed to get von Essen back as commander-in-chief, the representatives of the Defence Corps proposed Mannerheim instead. He agreed to their proposal, but President Ståhlberg refused to appoint him for undisclosed 'relevant reasons'.[66] These probably included an unwillingness to provide Mannerheim with his own army which, the president believed, would have given great influence to what he regarded as the conspiratorial and provocative circles who supported him and diminished that of those who were prepared to cooperate with the new republic. Ståhlberg also feared that the appointment would provoke an adverse reaction from Soviet Russia. He appointed as commander-in-chief a young Jäger lieutenant-colonel, Lauri Malmberg, who held the post until the Defence Corps was disbanded in 1944. This, of course, was a disappointment to Mannerheim who had been willing to serve as substantive commander-in-chief of the Defence Corps and not just as their honorary commander; he was also indignant that Svinhufvud had induced Malmberg to put himself forward as a candidate.

Under Malmberg the Defence Corps concentrated increasingly on military training while its development as heir to the Defence Corps of the War of Independence became less important. However, this was not to Mannerheim's liking. In the draft of a letter in 1926 he explained that the role of the Defence Corps should not be 'a link in the defence against an external enemy. In the event of war we must reckon on two enemies, the external and the internal, which as circumstances permit will surely raise its head. To free the army from all concern about its rear, communications, internal order, etc. is a task of extraordinary importance which must be solved by the ... Defence Corps.'[67] Because of these views Mannerheim's relations with the Defence Corps became more distant until the mid 1930s.

The next time Mannerheim was considered for a military appointment was in the spring of 1924 at the time of the notorious so-called 'officers' strike'. This was when the majority of the army's junior officers (notably the Jägers) submitted their resignations *en masse* in an attempt to force the removal of officers regarded as 'Russian', particularly Lieutenant-General Wilkama (formerly Wilkman), the army

---

[66] Blomstedt, *K.J. Ståhlberg*, p. 420.
[67] Draft to Lauri A. Yrjö-Koskinen, 22 December 1926. Mannerheim Archive, Box 302.

CIVILIAN

commander, and Major-General Oskar Enckell, chief of the general staff, who were thought to be blocking the army's development. Some of the Jägers wanted Mannerheim as Wilkama's successor – rather curiously in view of his own 'Russian' background, but they regarded him as a powerful figure who would raise the army from what they considered to be its state of decay. Their hopes were disappointed because Ståhlberg supported Wilkama and most resignations were withdrawn. Mannerheim knew himself that his appointment was impossible because a parliamentary majority opposed it. He stayed away from the parade on 16 May 1924, thus preventing any possible demonstration in his favour by the Defence Corps.[68] There was a possibility that Mannerheim might have become chairman of the Defence Council set up by Ståhlberg in 1924 to advise on defence planning and needs, but he was not even made a member. The president knew how much the Agrarians were against Mannerheim receiving any appointment.

However, the aims of the 'striking' officers were soon met and a purge of the 'Russians' took place. Enckell resigned in 1924, and Wilkama was forced out in 1926 after Lauri K. Relander, an Agrarian, had succeeded Ståhlberg as president the preceding year. Before his departure Wilkama had recommended either Mannerheim or Löfström for the post of Chief Inspector of the Army but Relander thought them too old. Mannerheim's name was again mentioned in 1925 and 1926 for the post of army commander but it was made clear to Relander that there would be difficulties in parliament if he were appointed. Too many politicians distrusted him. It can have been little consolation that in 1925 Major-General Kirke, the head of the British Military Mission to Finland, sent Mannerheim a copy of his report on the future of the Finnish defence forces and asked if they could discuss it.[69] When the president appointed Sihvo as acting army commander in May 1926 and confirmed him in the post in 1928, the door had closed on Mannerheim once again.

Distrust between the politicians and Mannerheim was mutual and extended to detail. On learning that Kallio, when prime minister in 1929, had enquired about the possibility of buying Gallen-Kallela's portrait of him in evening dress, obviously to be placed in the cham-

[68] Rennie [British minister in Helsinki] to Ramsay MacDonald, 19 May 1924. F.O.371/10423, N4756/220/56.
[69] From Kirke, 19 January 1925. Mannerheim Archive, Box 602.

ber of the Council of State where there was already a portrait of him in uniform, Mannerheim commented: 'I myself suspect that my portrait in uniform with the sword on the table by Järnefelt is a thorn in the flesh for the gentlemen in the Council of State and they would rather have wanted me in evening dress like the other heads of state.'[70]

The political sensitivity surrounding Mannerheim was revealed again in 1928 in connection with the commemoration of the tenth anniversary of the War of Independence. The foreign minister, Hjalmar Procopé, proposed to the government that Mannerheim should be honoured with the title of field marshal, but his colleagues rejected this as 'too warlike'.[71] The prime minister Juho Sunila, an Agrarian, even feared adverse socialist reactions if he countersigned an open letter from the president to Mannerheim acknowledging his achievements. Mannerheim, who was well aware of his controversial position, wanted to be abroad when the main celebrations took place on 16 May 1928, but Ignatius dissuaded him: he could not disappoint the thousands of veterans who planned to come to Helsinki and for whom he remained a popular hero.

Mannerheim did not receive the title of field marshal but the officer corps presented him with a field marshal's baton as a manifestation of their opinion. Relander paid a ten-minute formal call on Mannerheim and found that 'although ... he could not be given the title of marshal, he was in every way friendly and cheerful and contented looking. This is an excellent proof of what a gentleman and a good man he is.'[72] Courtesy was Mannerheim's forte and Relander was, after all, the head of state. The president, no doubt to his relief, was spared a display of what Mannerheim himself described as the 'Mannerheim temperament' which could produce outbursts of bad temper when he failed to get his own way.[73] Relander in fact used the state visit of King Christian X of Denmark, which coincided with the celebrations of 16 May 1928, to be particularly attentive to Mannerheim in the cause of promoting national unity. In the opinion of the British minister, Mannerheim 'responded with tact and discretion to the hand of amity thus extended to him'.[74]

[70] To Johan Mannerheim, 10 November 1929. Grensholm Collection, VAY 5629.
[71] Relander, *Presidentin päiväkirja*, II, pp. 16–17.
[72] Ibid., pp. 83–84.
[73] Cf. Könönen, *Vuosikymmen Mannerheimin sihteerinä*, p. 121.
[74] Rennie to Austen Chamberlain, 18 May 1928. F.O.371/13291, N2860/44/15.

CIVILIAN

Mannerheim's initial opinion of Relander had not been flattering. 'He is no striking personality and his election is above all an expression of the incapacity of the parliamentary system at the present time, weakened by party strife and envy, to bring forward the country's best leaders, but elected as he is with the votes of the so-called right he frees us from the grip of the socialists and the reckless progressives.'[75]

However much Mannerheim wanted to create a united country, the socialists remained anathema to him and his reference to the 'so-called right' showed his dissatisfaction with the conservatives who had accepted the politics of compromise of the republic. Both right and centre regretted his speech in April 1920 at a Defence Corps festival in Tampere in which he opposed in practice the government's policy of granting an amnesty to convicted Red prisoners from the War of 1918.[76] The rapid rehabilitation of traitors and their participation in the political process was unpalatable to Mannerheim, and he continued to be critical of what he saw as the failure of the republic to recognize the danger of Bolshevik Russia and the growing strength of communism and its fellow-travellers within Finland. He feared a new insurrection. In Tampere in April 1920 he was himself nearly the victim of a planned assassination attempt by one of a group of communist infiltrators.[77] In 1923 he was one of the first signatories of an appeal to all citizens to support the Safeguard Finland Association (*Suomen Suojelusliitto*) – secretly founded in 1921 – in acting against the internal threat of cooperation between communists and social democrats.

Yet Mannerheim kept out of politics, although he followed developments carefully. The Swedish People's Party invited him to be its candidate in the 1924 presidential election but he declined on the grounds that as such he would not contribute to the national unity he regarded as essential. He recommended the party to support one of the Finnish non-socialist candidates. He clearly did not want to be identified with the Swedish-speaking minority in Finland, despite Swedish being his own mother tongue, and saw himself as above the language divide.

[75] To Johan Mannerheim, 18 February 1925. Mannerheim, *Brev*, pp. 225–6.
[76] Speech, 4 April 1920. Mannerheim Archive, Box 624; Vares, "*Kansakunnan kaapin päällä*", p. 52.
[77] Manninen, 'Murhayritys Mannerheimia vastaan ja muita uutisia', p. 68; Rumpunen, 'Erään isoisän ansioluettelosta', p. 70.

It is impossible to disagree with the French minister in Helsinki who reported in 1924 that Mannerheim was not content with honours or pleasures; he wanted power – and not just formal power but real power.[78] This determination to have real power and not be a mere figurehead was a major obstacle to his employment in the 1920s, quite apart from his unacceptability to most politicians. He would not have had great power as army commander and would probably have found the post as frustrating as he later found aspects of his work as Chairman of the Defence Council in the 1930s. His period in the wilderness in the 1920s spared him the responsibility for a fractious officer corps, difficulties with parliament and conflicts over defence policy such as the naval building programme. Perhaps also the long break from responsibility contributed to his later ability to hold office at an advanced age; Churchill, de Gaulle and Adenauer all experienced a similar long phase of unemployment before being recalled to public service at ages when their contemporaries were retiring or had already retired.

Nevertheless, Mannerheim's craving for activity, particularly in the military sphere, became so acute that in 1925 he even contemplated leaving Finland and joining the French Foreign Legion. He enquired about this possibility in September 1925 through the secretary of the French legation in Norway. He acknowledged that his proposal might be thought inappropriate for a man of his status but noted that Prince Aage of Denmark had not thought this in his case. Mannerheim wanted to serve under Marshal Lyautey in Morocco. However the French army considered his request impossible. They could not have given him a lower rank than lieutenant-colonel, for which he already exceeded the retirement age. Their refusal of his request at the end of November 1925 not only referred to the problem of giving him a suitable rank, but also pointed out that the pacification of Morocco had caused a reduction of their forces there. By then the delay had caused Mannerheim to lose interest in the idea.

Had Mannerheim joined the French Foreign Legion it would have caused a sensation in Finland: he had more support among the people than among the politicians. Perhaps he intended a protest so that his absence from the country would be noticed.[79] However,

---

[78] Cited in Nevakivi, 'Mannerheim ja muukalaislegioona', *Suomen Kuvalehti*, 13/1989, p. 11.

[79] Nevakivi, 'Mannerheim ja muukalaislegioona', p. 13.

given the political situation in Finland in the mid 1920s, the relief on the left, and centre and even among some conservatives at his departure would have outweighed the popular shame that no place could be found for him at home. Only a shift in the political balance together with a return to a situation of serious internal and foreign policy problems could make Mannerheim once more employable in Finland. That shift occurred at the beginning of the 1930s.

CHAPTER IV

CHAIRMAN OF THE DEFENCE COUNCIL

'A patriotic spirit ... is all we require and then we need not ask where a man stood fifteen years ago.'[1]

LAPUA AND MÄNTSÄLÄ

Mannerheim's appointment as Chairman of the Defence Council in was an indirect consequence of a fundamental move to the right in Finnish politics during the preceding year. In his *Memoirs* Mannerheim described how the reaction against communism 'became an overwhelming popular movement, known under the name of the Lapua Movement. A Communist-engineered disturbance at Lapua [in Ostrobothnia] at the end of November 1929 provided the signal for a local manifestation of popular anger, which was followed by numerous local meetings and expressions of opinion all over the country.'[2] The provocative communist meeting in Lapua – which included the singing of an anti-Mannerheim song – did indeed spark off a sharp local reaction, which was rapidly expanded and coordinated by supporters of 'White Finland'. Mannerheim did not himself believe the Ostrobothnians were anti-democratic, and he criticized the bourgeois press and politicians who in his view were 'extraordinarily unsympathetic' to the movement.[3] However, many of those attracted to the Lapua Movement had little or no sympathy for the parliamentary system with its weak governments and leftist tendencies. The emergence of a national anti-communist movement was, of course, welcome to Mannerheim, and when he stayed in Helsinki for longer than usual during the summer, to follow the exciting course of events, this variation to his routine prompted rumours that the movement planned to make him dictator.

Mannerheim's relationship to the Lapua Movement remains controversial and obscure. He had many personal connections with its leaders and supporters, for example through the industrialists Petter

---

[1] Speech on 16 May 1933. Mannerheim, *Minnen*, II, p. 41.
[2] Mannerheim, *Memoirs*, p. 243.
[3] To Johan Mannerheim, 16 June 1930. Mannerheim, *Brev*, p. 235.

CHAIRMAN OF THE DEFENCE COUNCIL

Forsström and Rudolf Walden and through Kai Donner, the activist who had been involved in the interventionist plans in July 1919 and who did indeed favour a Mannerheim dictatorship. The government and president tried to appease the Lapuans' demands for tougher anti-communist legislation, but parliament would not pass the proposed new press law. The Lapuans threatened to use force, President Relander capitulated, the government resigned and in July Svinhufvud formed a new government committed to anti-communist legislation. Not all of it passed through parliament, which was then dissolved.

For the activists of the Lapua Movement Svinhufvud was an unpopular choice as prime minister because of his devotion to the principles of legality and opposition to the violence which the Movement engendered. When refusing to accept all the activists' demands he had told their leaders: 'Then take Mannerheim as leader, but what do you think he can do? No government in this country can act without the support of parliament.'[4] This was a lesson Mannerheim had learned in 1919, but were circumstances different in 1930?

The Lapuans exerted further pressure on the politicians by means of a Farmers' March in Helsinki on 7 July 1930, when 12,000 men from all over the country demonstrated against communism. Mannerheim was one of the dignitaries present at the march and lending it his backing. He considered the marchers' declaration 'far sighted and dignified' and described the movement as 'a notable historical event and I should like to hope that the consequences of this disinterested popular patriotic movement, built on a sound basis, will be favourable.'[5] He thought it 'incredible that so many influential forces, which ought to be directly interested in bringing about guarantees so that communism cannot once more raise its head in our country and so that society will not slide further down the downward path, now fight as if for life in order to curtail the chances of the Lapua folk.'[6]

On 30 September 1930, before the elections, Mannerheim issued a statement in which he expressed the hope that 'everyone who remembers the year 1918 will give their support to the selfless patriotic aspirations which through the influence of the Lapua Movement have

---

[4] Cited in Siltala, *Lapuan liike ja kyyditykset 1930*, p. 115.
[5] To Palaemona Mannerheim, 7 July 1930. Grensholm Collection, VAY 5630.
[6] To Johan Mannerheim, 28 August 1930. Grensholm Collection, VAY 5630.

come to influence our public life'.⁷ This, like his presence at the Farmers' March, was a potent reminder that he was a possible focus for right-wing aspirations. However, in the situation brought about by the Lapua Movement he kept out of direct involvement with politicians, remaining in the background, in a typical Mannerheim 'wait and see' position. But the parliamentary system endured, and no call came to lead the nation. The elections produced a non-socialist majority in parliament, enabling the anti-communist laws, which effectively crushed the party, to be passed in October 1930.

The election of P. E. Svinhufvud as president on 16 February 1931, narrowly defeating Ståhlberg, completed the victory of the right although the activists in the Lapua Movement felt cheated of a total triumph. Nevertheless, the strong government which had been the aim of Mannerheim and his associates seemed to have been attained by the autumn of 1931. The country appeared set on a more favourable course, and he had once more received an official position. However, not all the supporters of the Lapua Movement were satisfied with the suppression of the communists, and in late 1931 they began agitation against the social democrats.

On 27 February 1932 a lawful social democrat meeting at Mäntsälä in southern Finland was attacked by a large number of rightists, many of them members of the Defence Corps, armed and in uniform. They demanded an end to Red Marxist social democracy and appealed to the Defence Corps and the leaders of the Lapua Movement for support, but allowed the socialists in Mäntsälä to disperse. The Lapuan leaders seized the opportunity to direct the revolt and demand the resignation of the government. The Mäntsälä revolt attracted some support from other local Defence Corps, but the organization as a whole remained loyal to the established order. The army's most senior officers were also loyal although some others were sympathetic to the rebels' demands. Sihvo, the army commander, wanted firm action against the rebels while Malmberg, the commander of the Defence Corps, advocated caution. Svinhufvud, who took personal charge of the situation, wanted to avoid bloodshed between the army and the Defence Corps men at Mäntsälä, but he also proved a determined upholder of law and order and invoked against the Lapuan leadership the security law enacted to deal with the communists. The government did not resign.

⁷ Cited in Heinrichs, *Mannerheim Suomen kohtaloissa*, II, p. 19.

CHAIRMAN OF THE DEFENCE COUNCIL

Mannerheim by this time held an official appointment as Chairman of the Defence Council – and remained honorary commander-in-chief of the Defence Corps. However, in spite of these positions he kept out of involvement in the affair. He sympathized with the rebels' aims and was certainly opposed to the use of force against them. The contacts between his friend Hannes Ignatius and K. M. Wallenius, the former chief of the general staff who was one of the leaders of the rebellion, gave rise to the belief that Ignatius was acting, perhaps indirectly, as Mannerheim's representative. Yet Mannerheim did not either openly support the rebels or deny rumours that he supported them. He also resisted attempts to get him to back the president, and refused to join the special council Svinhufvud set up to act with him during the crisis. Mannerheim wanted the revolt to be ended by the resignation of what, having seen it in action, he now regarded as a weak government: he hoped that Walden would form a new government.

Svinhufvud's radio address on 2 March marked the turning point in the crisis. He demanded that the rebels return home and promised that only those who had incited the revolt would be punished. He also promised that after peace had been restored 'the defects in public life would be removed by lawful means'.[8] The rebels wavered, the army blockaded Mäntsälä, and the rebellion ended peacefully on 6 March. The leaders were arrested and the Lapua Movement was at an end although an extreme right-wing party, the IKL (Patriotic People's Movement), soon arose in its place. Bourgeois legality and democracy, with wide support, had triumphed. At the end of 1932 a new government was formed under T. M. Kivimäki to handle the economic crisis caused by the depression. Economic recovery contributed to the decline of Finnish fascism. Kivimäki's government won Mannerheim's respect.

Like some supporters of the Mäntsälä revolt, Mannerheim had hoped – following Svinhufvud's promise – for changes to the electoral system which would have benefited the right. However, nothing was done. His calculated distance from the government in March 1932 showed his continued dedication to the ideals of 'White Finland'. He remained convinced that the time would come when all patriotic Finns would 'see the surest support of the country in a united White front'.[9] Despite his genuine desire for national harmony,

[8] Cited in Juva, *P. E. Svinhufvud*, II, p. 471.
[9] Cited in Ahti, *Kaappaus?*, p. 305.

demonstrated through his humanitarian work, a nation that included the socialists on equal terms with the rest remained outside the field of Mannerheim's vision.

WORK IN THE DEFENCE COUNCIL

The idea that Mannerheim might become chairman of the Defence Council seems to have originated with Colonel Paavo Talvela in the course of discussions among leaders of the Lapua Movement in 1930. The proposal was raised with President Relander, who had no objection, and with the assistant minister of defence, Major-General Hugo Österman, who had had the same idea but gone further, linking it with the appointment of Mannerheim as commander-in-chief in the event of war. This combined proposal gained the backing of Svinhufvud, the prime minister. Österman then discussed it several times with Mannerheim, whose attitude was cautious. He was concerned not only about the powers of the Defence Council and the authority of its chairman but also about the political leadership to whom he would be responsible. Progress was impossible because of the forthcoming presidential election. Mannerheim would not have served – or been given the chance to serve – had Ståhlberg been elected, but the election of Svinhufvud clarified the situation and opened the way for his return to public service at the age of sixty-three, three years over the retirement age for Finnish generals.

On 3 March 1931, the day after taking office as president, Svinhufvud offered the chairmanship of the Defence Council to Mannerheim, who asked for time to consider but accepted on condition that Walden was appointed a member. Discussions, involving Mannerheim, on the role of the Defence Council had continued for some time. A decree issued on 11 March 1931 reshaped the powers of the Council and its chairman to meet many – but not all – of Mannerheim's requirements. One of the last acts of Svinhufvud's government (then led by J. H. Vennola) was to appoint him a member and chairman of the Defence Council on 20 March 1931, and he had an unofficial understanding with Svinhufvud that in the event of war he would be appointed commander-in-chief. This important arrangement – which greatly increased his authority – was made known, at the request of the Defence Council, to a limited number of key personnel during 1932.

CHAIRMAN OF THE DEFENCE COUNCIL

The Defence Council as constituted in 1931 remained an advisory body but acquired a proactive role. It was empowered to meet when summoned by its chairman and to take the initiative in making proposals to the president on major questions of principle concerning defence. These included planning – for example the mobilization and concentration of the army; arms and equipment; the bases of defence expenditure; the strength of the defence forces; and general questions of defence preparedness. The Council became a military body. Its members were the commanders of the armed forces and the Defence Corps, the chief of the general staff and two generals proposed by the defence minister and appointed by the president. The minister himself lost the chairmanship and even ceased to be a member, although he was entitled to attend. The general staff provided a colonel or lieutenant-colonel as secretary. Meetings were held irregularly according to need, varying from four to thirteen times a year. The chairmanship was not intended to be a full-time appointment and Mannerheim was able to fit his foreign travelling – and initially his bank chairmanship as well – around his new duties.

Despite the extensive changes to the remit of the Defence Council, the duties of its chairman were remote from the extensive executive powers which Mannerheim had sought in vain in 1919. Acceptance of the post, even linked to holding supreme command in war, represented a considerable compromise on his part; it was a measure of his readiness to serve the country and his expectation of a favourable attitude on defence questions during the Svinhufvud presidency. But the absence of executive responsibility, which freed him from routine duties, was in many ways an advantage to him, as was the separation of the Defence Council from the ministry of defence, of whose competence in military matters he had a low opinion. His position, under the president, was independent. He gained more than an office in the general staff headquarters; he also obtained a base from which he could put forward his views on matters extending beyond defence in its narrow sense as he endeavoured to improve defence preparedness and raise the will of the nation to defend itself in what he saw as an increasingly dangerous Europe.

Nevertheless, Mannerheim quickly felt the need to strengthen his position as chairman and seized opportunities to do so as time passed. He wrote to the Finnish minister in London in 1932; 'My work as chairman of the Defence Council is unfortunately so very unclear that the good one believed one could do seems in fact doubtful, opposed as the Defence Council is by the political minister, who clearly scents a danger in this institution which is independent of him ... The highest military command should be freed from political influence and interference...'.[10] The political reality of a minister of defence could never be overcome although Mannerheim successfully resisted an attempt to strengthen the ministry in 1932. However, his position in relation to the army improved in that year when the inspectors of the different arms were placed under him. It was further strengthened in August 1933 when the president ordered the commander of the armed forces to follow Mannerheim's directions relating to wartime operational preparations, planning and organization as long as he remained chairman of the Defence Council. This was the result of an initiative by Österman, Sihvo's replacement as commander. Mannerheim also gained in authority when he was appointed field marshal on 19 May 1933.

The attempt to make Mannerheim a field marshal in 1928 had failed, but the political climate in 1933 was more favourable and senior military men tried again, linking the proposal with the fifteenth anniversary of the War of Independence. The government agreed although political considerations caused the actual conferment of this exceptional honour to be deferred from 16 May, the obvious date because it coincided with the defence forces' anniversary parade, to 19 May. News of the honour was brought to Mannerheim by the minister of defence – the proposal and the decision had been kept secret from him and came as a surprise. He was pleased because he regarded it as a recognition of the European significance of the War of Independence in stopping the advance of Bolshevism although he acknowledged that it would take him time to get used to his new rank. He thought that 'In a little ultra-democratic country it could seem quite pretentious to indulge in the luxury of a field marshal', but it was 'not so frightful when the marshal costs the state nothing'.[11]

In fact the decision of the Council of State to confer the 'title' of field marshal on Mannerheim – although the president agreed to the 'title and rank' – led to the exaction of a stamp duty fee of 4,000 marks, equivalent to one month's pay as chairman of the Defence

---

[10] To Armas Saastamoinen, 19 January 1932. Mannerheim, *Brev*, p. 240.
[11] To Johan Mannerheim, 28 May 1933, cited in Jägerskiöld, *Mannerheim mellan världskrigen*, p. 136. To Ernst Linder, 25 May 1933. Mannerheim, *Brev*, p. 244.

CHAIRMAN OF THE DEFENCE COUNCIL

Council. Mannerheim's rate of pay – approximately that of a major – was clearly based on the part-time nature of his appointment. As he remarked to Lieutenant-Colonel Airo, the secretary of the Defence Council, when he took the money out of his wallet to pay the fee, 'It's a good job they haven't made me a more important man.'[12] The extraordinary petty-mindedness – or thoughtlessness – shown in the exaction of the fee was compounded by the refusal of the minister of defence to acknowledge that field marshal was a military rank. In practice, however, the appointment was recorded in an army order and regarded as a rank, with its own insignia. Mannerheim received a second, official field marshal's baton, but often used the older, unofficial one given to him in 1928 because it was lighter.

With his appointment as chairman of the Defence Council Mannerheim once again became a public figure. As such he was asked by the government, albeit reluctantly, to represent Finland at the ceremonies to mark the tercentenary of the death of King Gustavus Adolphus of Sweden in 1632 at the battle of Lützen in Germany, a battle in which Finnish cavalry had played a distinguished part. He joined the Crown Prince of Sweden in the commemorations, making a powerful and much-praised speech in recognition of the king's greatness. He went on to meet President Hindenburg in Berlin, looking, despite his sixty-five years, 'like a young cavalry officer'.[13] The Finnish minister in Berlin, the social democrat Wäinö Wuolijoki, had been reluctant to meet Mannerheim but was compelled to act as his host, and was forced to admit the success with which he had carried out his representational functions. He thought that Mannerheim was not at all an extreme rightist, and that the social democrat press should desist from its violent attacks on him.[14]

One aspect of his becoming a field marshal which particularly gratified Mannerheim was its generally good reception in Finland; it was not attacked by the non-right-wing press as he might have expected. The title emphasized his unique position in relation to the armed forces and in the country; Field Marshal Mannerheim became less of a 'White' figure and more of a national one, and he contributed to this gradual transformation by a speech to veterans of the War of Independence on 16 May 1933 when he said that, given a willing-

---

[12] Cited in Selén, *C. G. E. Mannerheim ja hänen puolustusneuvostonsa*, p. 93.
[13] Heinrichs, *Mannerheim Suomen kohtaloissa*, II, p. 42.
[14] Selén, *C. G. E. Mannerheim ja hänen puolustusneuvostonsa*, p. 202.

ness to defend the country, 'we need not ask where a man stood fifteen years ago'.[15] This was a notable concession to the former Reds, and over the next few years a cautious rapprochement developed between Mannerheim and the social democrats, particularly as they came to recognize that he was not responsible for the deaths in the postwar detention camps.

Mannerheim was particularly heartened by the public mood in May 1933. 'There is certainly much that moves in the depth of the people, much that one can scarcely suspect until at some patriotic celebration one is once more powerfully reminded of it.'[16] However, the Lützen commemoration in 1932 and the anniversary celebrations of 1933 were high points for Mannerheim in a period of intensive work. As chairman of the Defence Council he set about familiarizing himself with the armed forces, their organization, training and the areas in which they were likely to fight in a war with the Soviet Union. That country, with its hostile ideology and rapidly-developing industrial and military resources, was obviously Finland's likely enemy. The possibility of Finland being able to resist a Soviet surprise attack was greatly enhanced with the introduction of a new territorial system of mobilization in 1934. This freed the peacetime army, hitherto used as the cadre for expansion on mobilization, to act as covering troops on the frontier while the nine divisions of the field army were mobilized in different parts of the country and then concentrated for action. The Defence Corps, with its local districts, acquired an essential role in the new mobilization system, which had Mannerheim's full support and produced an army of similar size to what he had advocated unsuccessfully in 1918. However, the change to the mobilization system was straightforward compared with the long struggle over defence appropriations, particularly for procuring equipment.

Mannerheim's efforts to increase defence spending ran into difficulties at first because of the need to reduce public expenditure at a time of world depression. There were political problems too. Liberal politicians, like Risto Ryti, were unconvinced of the existence of a military threat to Finland, while Mannerheim wrote of 'a hostile Soviet Russia armed to the teeth'.[17] The social democrats had a negative attitude to defence, which Mannerheim described it as 'defence

[15] Mannerheim, *Minnen*, II, p. 41.
[16] To Johan Mannerheim, 28 May 1933. Grensholm Collection, VAY 5630.
[17] To Palaemona Mannerheim, 4 July 1931. Grensholm Collection, VAY 5630.

nihilism';[18] they were totally hostile to the Defence Corps. However, by the end of the 1930s their opposition to defence was concentrated more on the amount of defence expenditure than on the principle of national defence, since they recognized the dangers of an increasingly unstable Europe. Despite these problems, Mannerheim helped to ensure that the reductions in the defence budget during the recession were relatively modest, and from 1934, as the Finnish economy recovered, he succeeded in securing additional funds for defence. Nevertheless, it was unsatisfactory that some savings were made by reducing the periods of training and others by not calling up the entire class of conscripts each year. This meant that by the time war broke out in 1939 some 110,000 men had not been trained.

An emergency procurement programme had been proposed in 1930 to meet some of the basic equipment needs on mobilization, but its implementation was considerably reduced as the result of the recession. The introduction of the territorial mobilization system showed up the army's deficiencies in equipment. There was a shortage particularly of anti-aircraft artillery and tanks, while the production capacity for small arms ammunition was low. The air force lacked modern planes. There were also few fortifications on the Karelian isthmus, the best Soviet invasion route. In 1934 Mannerheim issued a statement to the press designed to counter the belief in parliament that peace would continue and to stress the need for well equipped and trained defence forces. He took up the question of their equipment at a press conference he held at home on 25 July 1934 for twenty-four editors from the non-socialist press. His readiness to use the press in this way was innovative and the results were encouraging. He also lobbied members of parliament. His activities contributed to a change in the Agrarians' attitude to defence.

Following an extensive review of government expenditure in 1935, there was a considerable addition to the budget for defence equipment in 1936 and 1937. However, better assessment of the quality of equipment in store showed its condition to be worse than had been believed, and more funds were needed in consequence. Mannerheim told the president in October 1938 that 'in short as far as modem equipment is concerned, the land, sea and air forces are at present unfit to fight'.[19] With international tension rising, an emergency

[18] Mannerheim, *Minnen*, II, p. 10.
[19] To President Kallio, 7 October 1938. Grensholm Collection, VAY 5671.

procurement programme, accompanied by additional taxation, was enacted in 1938, to be carried out over the period to 1943. Because of widespread rearmament it proved difficult at that time to obtain material quickly from abroad, and Finland had to fight in 1939 with numerous deficiencies in equipment, particularly in artillery and aircraft.

Mannerheim showed great interest in the air force, whose composition and role were by no means clear. With typical thoroughness he set about familiarizing himself with the strategy of the air arm and the availability of different types of aircraft. He attended the Hendon Air Show, which he admired, in June 1934, and at the end of that year visited France and Germany to see what aircraft were in production or planned. He was impressed by the German aircraft industry and was inclined to purchase German planes. This information was relayed to the British in terms unflattering to Mannerheim by Colonel Jarl Lundqvist, the air force commander, and prompted an unsuccessful British attempt to arrange a visit by Mannerheim to Britain in the autumn of 1935. However, in 1936 he visited Britain and also Sweden, and considered various aircraft options. His concern for technical detail and changes of mind about aircraft procurement upset Lundqvist, to whom he was typically not prepared to delegate responsibility, and caused a delay, for example, in the eventual order for Bristol Blenheim light bombers from Britain in 1936.

The provision of adequate manufacturing capacity for armaments within Finland and the precise location of the necessary factories also greatly concerned Mannerheim. Thus he would have preferred the State Aircraft Factory to be sited at Kokkola on the west coast rather than at Tampere, as parliament chose in 1934, because Tampere's location and status as an industrial centre made it more vulnerable to Soviet air attack. He supported the construction of armaments factories underground, as with part of the State Artillery Factory at Jyväskylä in 1937 – at the time this was an innovative idea. He was eventually successful in his particular concern for cooperation with Bofors, the Swedish armaments firm, in the manufacture of artillery in Finland. Perhaps in his care to provide arms and ammunition in adequate quantities – where he had only partial success – he underestimated the need to accelerate the construction of fortifications on the Karelian isthmus. Compared to the air force, Mannerheim took little interest in the navy. He deplored the sums voted for the naval building programme before the depression, rightly believing that the money would have been more wisely spent on eliminating the basic deficiencies in the army and air force.

The election of Kyösti Kallio, the Agrarian leader, as president in 1937 in place of Svinhufvud made Mannerheim consider whether to continue as chairman of the Defence Council. He had accepted the position during Svinhufvud's period in office but had been disappointed by what he regarded as the president's ineffective attitude to defence. If Svinhufvud had been reelected, Mannerheim would probably have withdrawn; the election of Ståhlberg, who was also a candidate, would certainly have made him do so. Mannerheim was asked by Kallio to stay as commander-in-chief designate and he agreed, while wondering whether mutual confidence would exist between him and the new government, a majority coalition led by A. K. Cajander of the Progressive Party and containing both Agrarians and Social Democrats. He had reservations about Holsti as foreign minister and Väinö Tanner, the Social Democrat leader, as finance minister.

Mannerheim, who was concerned to enhance the readiness of the defence forces, proposed to strengthen his authority by assuming powers of decision over matters of defence preparedness which lay outside the remit of the president, the council of state and the minister of defence. The new minister, the Agrarian Juho Niukkanen, opposed this as probably unlawful and certainly transforming the chairmanship of the defence council from an advisory into an executive post, which it was not intended to be. Mannerheim contemplated resignation and Niukkanen was prepared for him to go but President Kallio saw him on 5 May 1937 and persuaded him to stay, pointing out the unlawfulness of his proposal but agreeing that changes to his position were needed.

Changes were introduced later in 1937 which brought about a greater concentration of power in the ministry of defence by moving into it most of the hitherto separate general staff. However, Mannerheim gained too because the remainder of the general staff – the operations and intelligence departments – remained outside the ministry in order formally to constitute a staff for him as chairman of the Defence Council to facilitate planning for war. This arrangement was not ideal organizationally but it was a necessary compromise to keep Mannerheim in his post; there was no possibility that Mannerheim would have agreed to transfer to the ministry of defence, which he regarded as bureaucratic, slow and vulnerable to political influence, and in any case his position of direct responsibility to the president precluded such a change. His personal standing and the authority he commanded as wartime commander-in-chief-designate meant that the reorganization had to work round him. He was prepared to continue as chairman for two more years. A new decree on the Defence Council in 1938 added two more generals to its membership and, by mentioning the chairman separately from members of the Council, indirectly affirmed Mannerheim's unique status.

SEVENTIETH BIRTHDAY CELEBRATIONS

Mannerheim's seventieth birthday on 4 June 1937 assumed the character of a national festival, and his friends ensured that it was celebrated in style. An organizing committee was set up, comprising the ministers of defence and the interior, several generals and some friends. He wrote to his sister Eva on 18 April 1937: 'Between ourselves, I feel unworthy of all this celebration and would have preferred to go away as on previous so-called notable days, but this time I have had to give way to persuasion'.[20] As late as 26 May he still did not know the final programme for the great day but expected it to be strenuous. The day did indeed prove long and crowded but he came through it with style, vigour and evident enjoyment. Even the weather played its part. When rain threatened the big military parade at noon, Mannerheim said that he always had fine weather for his parades, (an echo, perhaps, of the 'tsar's sunshine', familiar from his service in St Petersburg), and so it proved. He received a tremendous ovation before and after the parade.

During the morning Mannerheim received numerous callers from various walks of life. Among them was the president, who later delivered the congratulatory speech at an evening celebration in Helsinki's Exhibition Hall from which Finnish Radio arranged a major outside broadcast. Mannerheim gave a buffet supper party to end the day. His guests had left by 1.30 a.m. but he continued chatting to his friend G. A. Gripenberg for another two hours. On 5 June he attended a dinner in his honour and gave a lunch party the following day. Only after that could he get down to acknowledging all the greetings he had received, employing a secretary and three

[20] To Eva Sparre, 18 April 1937. Mannerheim, *Brev*, p. 269.

typists to write between 1,500 and 2,000 letters. He spent almost 3,500 marks on postage (a commemorative stamp was issued to mark his birthday) and over 3,000 marks on telegrams.[21]

In a letter to his aunt Mannerheim had expressed the hope that the celebrations 'would be a powerful anti-bolshevik demonstration and this time a demonstration with less dissent than before'. He was not disappointed, going on to tell her of the remarkable things he experienced, 'such as the visit and speech by the speaker of parliament (a socialist, who directly demonstrated against me in 1928), one of the socialists and one of the agrarians who had earlier been against me conveyed the government's respects, the remarkably warm speech by Kivimäki, a former prime minister – earlier one of Ståhlberg's strongest supporters – and last but not least the Jägers' presentation to me of a full-sized replica of their colour.' He thought that not all of his work after the war had 'vanished without a trace'.[22]

In this opinion he was right, although that was not the only reason for the changed spirit surrounding the celebration of his birthday. By the mid- and late 1930s he himself had become more conciliatory. He was a reluctant convert to conciliation, writing in 1935: 'Without enthusiasm and without inner vigour, I too have begun in my public pronouncements to keep myself more and more within the boundaries of the innocents and it has been so peaceful and quiet around my person. My political opponents look at me with gentle eyes, my speeches are quoted *in extenso* in the Ståhlberg party's newspapers (!), and I should scarcely be surprised if the Social Democrat newspapers soon begin to enter the lists on my behalf!'[23]

Mannerheim's conviction that war was approaching caused him to intensify his efforts to attain national unity. He emphasized in his speech on 5 June 1937 that 'If I could now make a gift to our people, it would be unity, mutual trust and contentment.'[24] While remaining staunchly anti-communist, he was moving towards acceptance of the social democrats. In 1934 he had approached Vainö Tanner over the need to increase the defence budget and had even acknowledged the social democrats' argument that defence expenditure ought to be considered in relation to the country's standard of living. In the

---

[21] To Elsie Mannerheim, 27 June 1937. Mannerheim Archive, Box 903.
[22] To Hanna Lovén, 5 July 1937. Mannerheim, *Brev*, p. 272.
[23] To Palaemona Mannerheim, 13 May 1935. Grensholm Collection, VAY 5631.
[24] Cited in Jägerskiöld, *Mannerheim mellan världskrigen*, p. 144.

autumn of 1936 he thought that they could be included in the government. For the first time he invited social democrats – the ministers Tanner and Väinö Voionmaa – to a dinner he gave at his house on 30 May 1937 in honour of the visiting British minister, Lord Plymouth. The social democrats were also changing their attitude towards him, partly because the scars of the Civil War were healing, helped by their participation in the 'red earth' coalition government which took office in 1937.

The broadening of Mannerheim's reputation and standing in the country showed that he was a beneficiary as well as an advocate of national unity. Indeed, his original pleas for unity on the terms of 'White Finland' had failed, to be replaced by the more inclusive approach exemplified by his speech of 16 May 1933. As has been appositely written, 'National unity did not happen on the conditions of the political right … but by recognizing the position of the social democrat labour movement.'[25] The leading social democrat newspaper acknowledged, in writing of Mannerheim's seventieth birthday, that he had recently shown more open views, even on internal politics, than many bourgeois politicians.[26]

Mannerheim's birthday celebrations, together with his prominent role in the twentieth anniversary of the War of Independence on 16 May 1938, served to establish him more broadly in the popular mind both as a unifying national force and as a Finn of exceptional distinction. The social democrat leader Väinö Tanner stated in a speech in June 1938 that 'the working class was no longer bitter' towards him.[27] Mannerheim was personally disturbed by the 'cult' which accompanied his new standing and which was even manifested in an unwelcome eagerness to delve into aspects of his private life. However, he undoubtedly recognized that his status as a national hero, which replaced that of the openly partisan White General, usefully enhanced his influence with the politicians.

THE LANGUAGE PROBLEM

Mannerheim had always taken a keen interest in the development of international relations. That interest became more acute with his

---

[25] Jussila, Hentilä & Nevakivi, *Suomen poliittinen historia*, p. 157.
[26] *Suomen Sosialidemokraatti*, 4 June 1937, no. 147.
[27] Tanner, *Kahden maailmansodan välissä*, p. 227.

appointment as chairman of the Defence Council and as tension grew in Europe during the 1930s. He had long advocated a close association between Finland and Scandinavia, particularly Sweden, believing that this would strengthen the country's vulnerable position on the frontier of the Soviet Union. He regarded the Soviet Union as a dangerous, expansionist great power with a growing industrial and military potential. Finnish-Swedish relations were disturbed by the conflict over the sovereignty of the Åland islands. In 1919 Mannerheim had taken a firm line on Finland's possession of the islands and successfully influenced Clemenceau towards supporting the Finnish position.

The decision of the League of Nations in 1921 to confirm Finland's sovereignty over Åland did not end difficulties with Sweden, while the internationally-guaranteed demilitarization of the islands left a worrying gap in the defences of both countries. Sweden was upset by the strident nationalism of some Finnish politicians and by their hostility towards the status in Finland of the Swedish language, which was spoken by some 10 per cent of the population. Finnish nationalists resented Swedish interference in what they regarded as a purely internal Finnish matter. Thus the language conflict in Finland in the 1930s, which focused particularly on the position of Swedish within the University of Helsinki, had international as well as domestic implications.

To Mannerheim the language issue was a divisive factor which had the potential to affect national defence in that it weakened Finnish society and hampered the development of good relations with Sweden. Despite Swedish being his mother tongue – in which he was a master of literary style – he did not support the efforts of many Swedish-speakers to defend the status of their language against the attacks of the Finnish nationalists; for example, he did not sign their mass protest of 1934. Significantly, he was content to be called *finne* (a Finn) – a term reserved by many Swedish speakers to describe Finnish-speaking Finns. Some Swedish-speakers thought him too Finnish, but he deprecated extreme Finnish nationalism for the same reasons that he disapproved of Swedish-language extremism. He saw himself as being above the language conflict, which to such a cosmopolitan European seemed trivial compared with the serious problems facing the country. He was openly critical of Swedish interference in the language conflict; and shared the Finnish nationalists' view that it was a matter for Finland alone.

However, Mannerheim did try — with modest success — to foster a spirit of reconciliation between the two language groups. On 6 February 1935, with his friends Walden and Ignatius, he published in the press an appeal for tolerance and understanding — directed to the nation as a whole but particularly to veterans of the War of Independence. The writers believed that with goodwill both language groups would see the fulfilment of their legitimate rights, and all citizens would be able to work to improve their standard of living and national security. Mannerheim's concern for national defence was clear in the final sentences of the appeal: 'The moment when our nation must concentrate all its strength is still to come. May God grant that we then find in our country a united people.'[28] The enactment in 1937 of changes limiting teaching in Swedish at the University of Helsinki removed the language conflict from current politics. The Soviet invasion in November 1939 was indeed met by the united nation of Mannerheim's hopes.

Mannerheim's lack of Finnish had been a major problem for him in 1918–19, not least because it had been used against him by the Finnish-language nationalists, and he recognized the need to know it. Finnish was the army's language of command and in the 1930s he had acquired a sufficiently good knowledge of the spoken language to be able to insist on its use by Swedish-speakers in his presence when talking of service matters. He could not avoid speaking with a noticeable accent and sometimes he would stumble over the pronunciation. He had taken language and conversation lessons and made careful lists of vocabulary; his papers include lists of questions to ask soldiers in the course of inspections (e.g. 'Where do you come from?') and the forms of words he needed to conduct meetings of the Defence Council.[29] He urged his secretary in the Finnish Red Cross, Elsa Könönen, to correct his pronunciation and when he misplaced the stress on words. Understandably he made other mistakes, especially when he was tired. He did not draft documents in Finnish but knew the language well enough to ensure that his intentions, whether stated orally in Swedish or translated, had been clearly expressed by his secretaries or by those he turned to for help. Although at times he regretted not being able to speak Finnish really well, he was seldom lost for a word and a Finnish speaker who

[28] Mannerheim, *Minnen*, II, pp. 52–3.
[29] Mannerheim Archive, Box 814.

addressed him in poor Swedish might be told peremptorily 'Speak Finnish!'[30]

FOREIGN RELATIONS

The aim of Finnish foreign policy in the 1920s and 1930s was to find security against the perceived threat from the Soviet Union. In the early 1920s there had been an attempt to align Finland with the Baltic countries and Poland, but this failed because of disagreements among the Baltic states and German and Soviet hostility to such collaboration. Mannerheim had not supported an alliance with the Baltic states because he was not confident of their ability to maintain their independence. He also thought such an alliance incompatible with close relations with the country's western neighbours. He viewed cooperation with Poland more favourably.

Finland's relations with Sweden were cool and the countries had different diplomatic priorities. To Finland the Soviet Union was an immediate source of danger while Sweden instead gave attention to the situation in Central Europe. The government and public opinion in Sweden were totally unprepared to compromise the country's neutrality by any defensive alliance with Finland, even as part of collective security arrangements sponsored by the League of Nations, but some Swedish army officers were less rigid in their attitude. Finland hoped to secure assistance through the League of Nations if it were attacked by the Soviet Union but in the absence of guarantees from Britain or France it was in fact isolated. The ineffectiveness of the League became clear during the early 1930s with the failure of the disarmament conference and Germany's withdrawal from membership in 1933. Finland signed a non-aggression pact with the Soviets as proposed by them in 1932. However, Soviet efforts to build up a security system in Eastern Europe caused concern in Finland and led to renewed interest in Sweden as a possible ally.

For Mannerheim defence and foreign policy were intertwined. He was aware that the war materials Finland would need in a crisis could only come from or across Sweden, and he recognized the desirability of cooperation with Sweden over the defence of the Åland islands. Agreement with Sweden on these matters could form the prelude to

---

[30] As was the case with Kustaa Vilkuna in October 1945. Virkkunen, *Mannerheim. Marsalkka ja presidentti*, p. 486.

his long-term aim, a defensive alliance between their two countries which would guarantee Finland's security and independence. He did not look to the Germans for assistance since he recognized that the development of friendly relations with them would only increase Soviet mistrust of Finland. He had no faith in the collective security system of the League of Nations. The growing instability in Europe in the early and mid 1930s, together with Soviet diplomatic efforts to promote its own security, brought Mannerheim to the conclusion in the spring of 1935 that the time had come for Finland to align itself with the countries of Scandinavia, especially Sweden; this would help it to keep out of great power conflicts. Though remaining strongly anti-communist and anti-Soviet, and always anxious to give warning of the danger of bolshevism, Mannerheim had accepted the existence of the Soviet Union as a fact and recognized the danger to Finland of becoming drawn into a conflict in which it was involved. He had ceased to be an interventionist White general.

Mannerheim's Scandinavian policy had the support of the foreign minister, Antti Hackzell, who had already publicly expressed the importance of cooperation with the Scandinavian countries and accepted an invitation to attend the Scandinavian foreign ministers' meeting in Stockholm in 1934. The prime minister, T. M. Kivimäki, and the chairman of the budget reduction committee, J. K. Paasikivi, shared Mannerheim's and Hackzell's desire for a Scandinavian policy orientation, with the aim of a defence agreement with Sweden. This was also supported by Finland's senior military officers. Mannerheim was to play a crucial part in winning over non-socialist opinion in Finland to support the new policy.

At a briefing to some thirty editors from non-socialist newspapers in mid June 1935, Mannerheim explained the importance to Finland of alignment with Scandinavia. His statement to that briefing was his reworking of a draft written according to his instructions by Paavo Talvela, a former Jäger and colonel in the general staff who had resigned from the army in 1930 to embark on a business career. Mannerheim had developed an acquaintance with Talvela, whose ability, judgement and contacts he clearly valued, and who later proved a successful field commander. The briefing had a considerable impact in gaining the sympathy of the press. It helped to overcome Finnish nationalist objections to closer association with Sweden and prepared the way for the prime minister's declaration to parliament of the Scandinavian orientation on 5 December 1935. Kivimäki stated that Finland would defend its neutrality against threats from any direction but that one of the most important tasks of Finnish foreign policy was to bring about cooperation with the Scandinavian countries to protect the neutrality of Scandinavia.

Parliament approved this unilateral declaration, but making it a reality proved more difficult. Swedish neutrality was the obstacle. The possibility of obtaining war materials from Sweden had been raised by Tanner with its social democrat government in the spring of 1935; unknown to him, his visit resulted from Mannerheim's suggestion, since the field marshal believed contacts between social democrats would be fruitful. Hackzell raised the matter again at the end of 1935 although no firm support was given by the Swedish government. However, Finland concluded useful arms manufacturing agreements with Bofors in 1936, and unofficial military contacts with Sweden were developed at which the defence of Åland was discussed.

The centre-left government of Progressives, Agrarians and Social Democrats formed after the 1937 presidential election removed from government the conservative politicians who had initiated the Scandinavian policy, leaving Mannerheim as the sole conservative survivor in a position of influence. Rudolf Holsti, the new foreign minister, whom Mannerheim distrusted on the basis of earlier experience, was less enthusiastic about the Scandinavian policy, retained faith in the League of Nations and hoped for cooperation with Britain and France. Discussions with Sweden about defence matters continued during 1936–8, but Mannerheim was relieved when Holsti was replaced in 1938 by Eljas Erkko, whose Scandinavian sympathies he regarded as a great improvement.

Swedo-Finnish talks, at a rising military level and eventually between the foreign ministers, finally resulted in agreement on a plan for the defence of Åland. Mannerheim had not been personally involved in the detailed discussions but had been active in driving them forward. The so-called Stockholm Plan, approved in January 1939, provided for the fortification of the most southerly islands and for the stationing of troops on the Åland 'mainland'. Swedish participation, should this be requested by Finland, would depend on Sweden's decision. However, even this slender cooperation came to nothing; Sweden insisted on seeking Soviet consent to the agreement and withdrew from the plan in June when this was not forthcoming.

Mannerheim had advised against involving the Soviet Union since it was not a signatory to the Convention of 1921 on the demilitarization and neutralization of the Åland islands. His advice proved right. Now all that remained of Finland's Scandinavian policy was limited cooperation with Sweden over defence industries and general staff discussions on Swedish military assistance in the event of an attack on Finland. There was no Swedish government backing for such assistance even if senior Swedish army officers supported it. Finland was isolated in an increasingly dangerous international situation.

Mannerheim, who was in any case inclined to pessimism, watched international developments with growing concern. His travels and his contacts kept him well informed. He was chosen to represent Finland at the funeral of King George V in January 1936 – where his distinguished bearing attracted attention – and used his time in London for discussions with politicians and senior military officers. He also had an audience with King Edward VIII. He was distressed to find Anthony Eden, the foreign secretary, unconcerned about the growing strength of the Soviet Union coupled with a belief that it did not stand in the way of peace in Europe. Winston Churchill was more sympathetic to Mannerheim's views on the danger presented by the Soviet Union but he was out of office. Mannerheim returned to Britain in September 1936 at the invitation of the British government – an acknowledgement of his importance – and the emphasis of the visit was on military contacts. The British arranged a programme calculated to appeal to Mannerheim and he was suitably pleased and impressed. His visit was returned by the Earl of Plymouth, parliamentary under-secretary of state at the foreign office, at the time of the seventieth birthday celebrations. Greatly to Mannerheim's disappointment, Holsti, the foreign minister, was chosen in preference to him to head Finland's representatives at the coronation of King George VI in May 1937, depriving him of the opportunity for further discussions with British leaders.

One consequence of Lord Plymouth's visit was that in April 1938 the British decided to appoint Mannerheim an honorary Knight Grand Cross of the Order of the British Empire (Civil Division). Although this was nominally 'in recognition of the valuable services which he has rendered to British cultural and other interests', political considerations were uppermost in the Foreign Office's intentions because he did not really qualify under the regulations for the award of British

CHAIRMAN OF THE DEFENCE COUNCIL

honours to foreigners. Mannerheim received the insignia from the British minister on 3 May 1938 and 'expressed his extreme gratification at the honour which had been conferred upon him and desired, with submission, that the expression of his gratitude might be conveyed to The King'.[31]

The incorporation of Austria into the German Reich in the spring of 1938 deepened Mannerheim's alarm about the course of events. In May 1938 he cancelled a planned hunting trip to Alaska, mainly because of the uncertain situation in Europe. The crisis in September 1938, which led to the Munich Agreement permitting Germany to dismember Czechoslovakia, was more serious, not least because it caused threatening movements by the Soviet Baltic fleet. Mannerheim proposed the recall of certain reservists for 'special training' to improve the readiness of Finland's coastal defences; this was partly implemented, unlike his recommendation that the Åland islands be occupied. A positive outcome of the crisis was its use by Mannerheim to drive through the new and accelerated defence procurement programme, already mentioned.

He did manage a health cure in Italy in the autumn of 1938, travelling back via Paris, London and Stockholm, in all of which he discussed international affairs. It seemed to him that France had abandoned its great power status. Britain was rearming but had neither the means nor the intention to carry out any action in the Baltic. He expected further demands from Hitler and believed that there would be war. In this he differed from the Finnish government which retained a more optimistic view throughout the summer of 1939. Mannerheim had been scathing in his comments about Czechoslovakia's capitulation to German demands in March 1939 'without firing a shot', adding for good measure that he had despised the Czechs ever since they had sold the Russian White leader Admiral Kolchak to the Bolsheviks.[32] In April 1939 Mannerheim warned his daughter Sophy in Paris: 'Everything makes it probable that war is inevitable.'[33] She rejected his advice to come to Finland.

Attempts by the Soviet Union to safeguard its security against Nazi Germany began seriously to affect Finland in April 1938 when Boris

---

[31] F.O.372/3261, T2278/2278/372; Halifax to The King, 6 April 1938; Snow to Halifax, 3 May 1938.

[32] To Eva Sparre, March 1939. Mannerheim, *Brev*, p. 285.

[33] To Sophy Mannerheim, 16 April 1939. Mannerheim, *Brev*, p. 288.

Yartsev, second secretary of the Soviet legation in Helsinki, began a series of unofficial discussions with Holsti and other ministers. Yartsev sought guarantees that Finland would not assist Germany in a future war against the Soviet Union by letting its forces operate through Finland. The Soviet Union was willing to help Finland defend itself and, as discussions continued, even offered support over the fortification of the Åland islands but wanted to be able itself to fortify the Finnish island of Suursaari in the middle of the Gulf of Finland 27 miles (43 km.) south of Kotka. Despite the military implications of these discussions – which continued until December 1938 – neither Mannerheim nor any other military leaders were informed of them. This was a consequence of the Finnish government's determination to reject any Soviet proposals which would not only compromise Finland's neutrality but also be totally unacceptable politically.

The Soviets tried again to negotiate with the Finns – on an official basis – in March and April 1939. This time Mannerheim was informed of the discussions and gave his advice about them. He was anxious to make minor concessions to the Soviet Union, provided they were of no military significance, in order to gain time for the strengthening of Finland's defence forces. His policy has aptly been described as 'the armed concessions line'.[34] The Soviets now focused on the small Finnish islands in the Gulf of Finland closest to Leningrad. These they wanted to lease, and even offered territory in Eastern Karelia in return. Mannerheim was prepared to give up these islands, which were of no military value to Finland but clearly of importance for the security of Leningrad. However, the Finnish government, fearing the wrath of public opinion, would not agree. Mannerheim wrote in his *Memoirs* 'that if there were really no one who was willing to risk his popularity in a matter so vital to the country, I was prepared to place myself at the disposal of the government, convinced as I was that my honest opinion would be understood.'[35] But no concessions were made and in consequence the Soviet government became convinced of Finland's hostility. The rejection in May 1939 by Finland – together with Sweden and Norway – of non-aggression pacts proposed by Germany angered the Germans without mollifying the Soviets. Mannerheim had favoured accepting the German proposal.

[34] Soikkanen, *Kansallinen eheytyminen – myytti vai todellisuus?*, p. 275.
[35] Mannerheim, *Memoirs*, pp. 300–1.

As has been mentioned, the Soviet Union rejected at the end of May the Finno-Swedish plans to fortify the Åland islands.

Meanwhile negotiations between Britain and France and the Soviet Union about Soviet support for its neighbours against Germany foundered because the countries in question, including Finland and Mannerheim personally, were opposed to inclusion in a Soviet guarantee. He maintained that 'a guarantee would be likely to be followed by the immediate practical consequence that Soviet Russia would proceed ... to demand a say in Finland's defence schemes. This could not, of course, be tolerated by Finland.'[36] When the negotiations with Britain and France came to nothing, the Soviet Union concluded an agreement with Germany on 23 August 1939. This notorious Nazi-Soviet pact was accompanied by a secret protocol putting Estonia, Latvia and Finland into the Soviet sphere of influence. Already in June and July Mannerheim had feared the consequences of an understanding between Germany and the Soviet Union. Now he immediately recognized the danger this pact, as a probable guarantee of Soviet expansion, represented to Finland. Finland no longer benefited from the balance of power that had hitherto prevailed in the Baltic between Germany and the Soviet Union.

RESIGNATION?

In addition to the international crises, the summer of 1939 witnessed a Finnish local difficulty caused by Mannerheim himself. The immediate cause was the failure of the defence minister – expressly against Mannerheim's wishes – to inform the government of the opposition of the Defence Council to the reduced sum the minister proposed for the fortification of the Åland islands. For Mannerheim, who was feeling increasingly frustrated by the government's attitude to security questions, this came as the last straw. He wrote to President Kallio on 23 May 1939 seeking his support for the line that the opinions of the Defence Council or its chairman on vital defence matters should be put to the Council of State when they differed from those presented to that body. Mannerheim met Kallio on 5 June to explain his opinion. Kallio, whose health was poor, then went on sick leave, and Cajander, the prime minister, was left to exercise his presidential powers.

---

[36] T. M. Snow, British minister in Helsinki, 20 June 1939. *Documents on British Foreign Policy 1919–1939*. Third Series, VI, p. 121.

On 16 June 1939 Mannerheim wrote to the president – the letter naturally going to Cajander – asking to resign as chairman of the Defence Council. He referred to deficiencies in the defence forces, and pointed out that his remaining as chairman would give the public the impression that he supported the inadequate measures taken over defence preparedness, and would thus 'lull many into an unjustified sense of security'.[37] The conservative newspaper *Uusi Suomi* learned of his resignation and published a special issue about it on 19 June, adding that the prime minister was unwilling to comment. An official statement later the same day denied that Mannerheim had resigned but accepted that he had expressed various wishes of a 'military technical character'.[38]

Mannerheim's timing of his resignation was well chosen since parliamentary elections were due on 1–2 July. The conservative press made the most of the opportunity. *Uusi Suomi* stated that if Mannerheim did not consider he could bear responsibility for the country's defence, the government had lost its authority. 'The defence minister can go and the government can go – provided the field marshal is at his place then confidence will be preserved. He is irreplaceable to every government and he is irreplaceable to the country.'[39] Mannerheim kept up the pressure by denying the official statement that his letter had not contained a request to resign.

Cajander did not share Mannerheim's view of his indispensability and was quite prepared for him to go. However, Kallio read of the matter in the press and was horrified: he intervened to keep Mannerheim at his post, sharply blaming Cajander for letting such a delicate matter become public, and also blaming Mannerheim for not consulting him. Mannerheim accepted the rebuke from the president, whom he greatly admired. After the government agreed to deal with the problems he had raised, he withdrew his resignation just five days before the elections. On 27 June the Council of State introduced a new procedure for its consideration of defence business, and this met most of Mannerheim's objectives by ensuring that it was informed of his opinions on defence preparedness where they differed from those of the defence ministry. His authority was considerably strengthened.

[37] Mannerheim, *Minnen*, II, p. 90.
[38] *Uusi Suomi*, 20 June 1939, no. 163.
[39] *Ibid.*

CHAIRMAN OF THE DEFENCE COUNCIL

The prime minister was not alone in being prepared to dispense with Mannerheim. Tanner, the finance minister, wrote to Kallio on 23 July 1939: 'Mannerheim has been extremely capricious and new proposals spurt out from him quite at random. Every time something happens abroad he loses his nerve.... This has already begun to irritate even his closest colleagues in the defence forces. Is he already too old for this important post, or what reason could there be? Sometimes I incline to Ryti's view that "M. as an old Russian general has copied the habits from there and, fearing possible future defeats, wants to procure scapegoats in advance." Be that as it may, in any event his recent conduct, and especially in connection with the midsummer crisis, was quite reckless. Possibly one must be prepared for the thought that such a difference with him will arise that he must leave his post.'[40]

When, on 26 July Tanner wrote in similar terms to J. K. Paasikivi, then the Finnish minister in Stockholm, he was bluntly and properly told by Paasikivi of Mannerheim's importance. 'Certainly Mannerheim himself would gladly leave. He is hard pressed by the responsibility on his shoulders. It is God's good fortune that Mannerheim still has the strength to direct the development of the defence forces. What other officers do we have? Absolutely nobody who would be capable of major tasks ... You say Mannerheim has lost his nerve. In all great issues Mannerheim has the same attitude as you and me ... In all important and major questions Mannerheim has been very moderate and in our opinion on the right side. Mannerheim certainly has his personal defects which are conspicuous – everyone has his faults. But the man whom you quote about Mannerheim is talking nonsense this time. One does not need to talk long to Mannerheim to observe how intelligent and experienced he is. It would be quite indefensible to remove Mannerheim now, when the country's foreign policy position has greatly worsened ... I think that as an old soldier Mannerheim is able to assess matters "more realistically" than "civilian politicians" such as you and me.'[41]

The 'great issues' referred to by Paasikivi were the fortification of the Åland islands and the lease of the small islands in the Gulf of Finland. Mannerheim's new proposals mentioned by Tanner included a massive plan to acquire from Sweden additional anti-tank and anti-aircraft guns together with equipment for four more divisions. This

---

[40] Tanner, *Kahden maailmansodan välissä*, p. 233.
[41] *Ibid.*, pp. 228–9.

would have raised the army's wartime strength to thirteen divisions. Sweden delayed its decision and sent the first anti-tank guns only in October 1939. In mid July Mannerheim sent the Defence Ministry an urgent programme for extensive fortification works on the Karelian isthmus. On 22 July he urged that the defence industries should work at full production capacity: nothing was done. He also wanted to obtain equipment from the United States, paid for by a loan, but this was opposed by Tanner. Though very expensive, Mannerheim's demands were not unreasonable given his appreciation of the international situation. The government, however, clung to its optimistic view.

The outbreak of the Second World War in September 1939 with the German invasion of Poland, closely followed by the Soviet occupation of the east of that country, confirmed Mannerheim's view of Finland's acutely dangerous situation. He had never liked the Nazis – to an old conservative of his type fascism was an inherently vulgar phenomenon, inimical to the established social order – although he did at first welcome their erection in Germany of a bulwark against communism. In 1934 he had noted the 'energy and many-sided capacity' in Germany which was 'now building up a new Reich' although 'the methods are often closely related to Moscow's.'[42] By February 1938, when Poland rejected German demands for the incorporation of Danzig in the Reich, he was glad that at last someone had the courage not as hitherto 'humbly to put up with all expressions of the Nazis' arrogance and insolence'.[43] After the German occupation of Czechoslovakia he wrote in a private letter: 'It seems quite simply to be the aim to change the people of Europe into white negroes in the service of the Third Reich'.[44] The destruction of Poland deeply upset him, not least because of the fate of his friends there. He expressed the hope that the British and French were as well equipped as their adversary 'otherwise we are all going towards slavery'.[45] Stalin and Hitler were 'two tyrants'. 'And whose turn is next, when the appetite of these gentlemen has managed to grow?'[46] Finland, as Mannerheim feared, was soon to find out.

[42] To Eva Sparre, 23 December 1934. Mannerheim, *Brev*, p. 249.
[43] To Eva Sparre, 27 February 1939. Mannerheim, *Brev*, p. 283.
[44] To Eva Sparre, undated, received 19 March 1939. Mannerheim, *Brev*, p. 285.
[45] To Palaemona Mannerheim, 14 September 1939. Mannerheim, *Brev*, p. 293.
[46] To Eva Sparre, September 1939. Mannerheim, *Brev*, p. 294.

CHAIRMAN OF THE DEFENCE COUNCIL
NEGOTIATIONS WITH THE SOVIET UNION CONTINUED

Immediately on the outbreak of the war Mannerheim had asked for powers to enable him to call up reservists. He did not get them, but the government did authorize the call-up of some for special training. By 11 September the navy and the coastal artillery were ready for war. Between 24 September and 1 October the Soviet Union 'invited' the Baltic states to conclude agreements allowing its forces to be established on their territory: all had done so by 11 October. Already on 5 October the Soviet Union had asked for a Finnish delegation to be sent to Moscow to discuss concrete political questions. In view of this, and fearing a Soviet attack before the Finnish army could be mobilized, Mannerheim proposed the concentration of troops on the Karelian isthmus. On 11 October he proposed full mobilization in the form of 'extraordinary reserve training', with the men called up on an individual basis, so as not to attract attention. The government agreed. This early mobilization beginning on 14 October, with the opportunity it gave for training and the strengthening of defensive positions, was to prove invaluable, although it also revealed the army's desperate deficiencies in equipment; it even lacked sufficient uniforms. Yet, because of the cost the government was prepared on 20 November to demobilize some 195,000 of the 295,000 men under arms. This time Niukkanen, the defence minister, threatened resignation in order to prevent this dangerous proposal from being carried out.

Mobilization brought up the question of the command of the defence forces. As chairman of the Defence Council, Mannerheim had no executive authority beyond matters of defence preparedness. Article 30 of the constitution permitted the president to transfer the supreme command to another person in time of war, but Finland was not at war and so the arrangement that Mannerheim should be appointed commander-in-chief in the event of war could not be implemented. Nor could he be appointed to the peacetime post of commander of the defence forces since he was over retirement age for service on the active list. The solution adopted was based on a decree of 17 October 1939 giving the president authority, in special circumstances, to appoint a commander of the defence forces and to prescribe his duties. On the same day Mannerheim was appointed to that post although his duties were not prescribed and the appointment was not made public. Orders were given on 18 November to create a headquarters for him by drawing together the general staff and some staff from the defence ministry who were subordinate to the army commander. Mannerheim's position was now virtually that of commander-in-chief. This strengthened his relationship with the government just as mobilization strengthened Finland's position in the negotiations with the Soviet Union.

Paasikivi was chosen to lead the Finnish negotiators who met Stalin and Molotov, the foreign minister, on 12 and 14 October. His instructions gave him no room to manoeuvre; only the small islands might be ceded in return for territory elsewhere. The Soviets' main concern was the security of Leningrad: they wanted the frontier on the isthmus moved further from the city and, as outer defences in the Gulf of Finland, wanted Hanko and an anchorage nearby, and in addition part of the Rybachii peninsula which belonged to the Petsamo region on the Arctic coast. The discussions made no progress. Paasikivi, like Mannerheim, favoured considerable concessions, but although it became clear that help was unlikely to come from Germany or Sweden, the government would only give way on the smallest points. Renewed negotiations, in which Tanner joined Paasikivi, took place on 23 October but were interrupted so that the Finns could obtain new instructions. A new round of negotiations on 3–4 and 9 November also made no progress although the Soviets were prepared to consider a base on islands near Hanko instead of at Hanko itself. The talks were broken off.

Mannerheim, who was involved in discussions with members of the government, was prepared to meet what he regarded as genuine Soviet security concerns with concessions on the Karelian isthmus, an island base near Hanko, and over the Rybachii peninsula. In November he even told a delegation from the Conservative Party – who noted from the empty picture frames on the walls of his house how seriously he took the threat of war – that relinquishing Hanko 'would be severe but he could not regard it as fatal for Finland'.[47] He emphasized to the government that the country was not sufficiently well equipped to fight a war. In his view the government did not have the army its foreign policy required. As he wrote to his friend G. A. Gripenberg, the Finnish minister in London, on 6 November, 'For

[47] Linkomies, *Vaikea aika*, p. 50.

us the Moscow negotiations and the threat of war come particularly inopportunely. We would have needed at least a year longer of intensive work to be anywhere near ready.'[48] Finland was too weak militarily to be able to resist foreign pressure backed by military force.

It remained Mannerheim's policy to make concessions in order to gain time. Niukkanen was against concessions, believing that the army could hold out for at least six months, and in their resistance to Soviet demands he and other members of the government insisted that Finland was neutral and was no threat to Leningrad. In this they represented the opinion of members of parliament and of public opinion generally: belief in the rightness of Finland's principled stand was widespread and suspicion of the Soviet Union deep. The government did not believe that the Soviet Union would resort to war – as was clear from its willingness for a partial demobilization – and expected negotiations to be resumed.

Instead, towards the end of November, the Soviet Union launched an anti-Finnish propaganda campaign. On 26 November the Red Army staged a frontier provocation near Mainila on the Karelian isthmus by firing seven artillery rounds against its own troops. Finland was accused of the incident which was used by Molotov as an excuse to denounce the Finno-Soviet non-aggression treaty, and on 29 November the Soviet Union broke off diplomatic relations. An attempt by the United States to mediate was accepted by Finland but rejected by the Soviet Union. Parallel with these events the Red Army and the Baltic Fleet were completing their preparations for war against Finland.

FROM RESIGNATION TO COMMANDER-IN-CHIEF

On 27 November, in the course of a meeting with Kallio, Mannerheim submitted his resignation. As he later wrote: 'the president in principle agreed to my retirement.'[49] During a conversation with Lieutenant-General Hugo Österman 'a few days before the outbreak of war', Mannerheim informed the general that he intended to transfer him to general headquarters to familiarize himself with the situation 'and after that to retire himself'. He did not tell Österman

[48] To G. A. Gripenberg, 6 November 1939. Mannerheim, *Brev*, p. 297.
[49] Mannerheim, *Memoirs*, p. 319.

that he had already resigned.[50] Österman was his most likely successor although the choice lay not with Mannerheim but with the president.

The events of 1939 had weighed heavily on Mannerheim, sapping his energy and deepening his pessimism and dissatisfaction with the government's handling of negotiations with the Soviet Union. He had served the two years from 1937 to which he considered himself committed. He felt he was of an age – seventy-two – at which he might reasonably be relieved of responsibility, particularly in view of his policy disagreements with the government and conviction that Finland's defence forces were inadequately equipped for war.

Bitterness pervaded the letter he sent the president on 27 November pointing out the deficiencies in the air force, in tanks, and in artillery, the lack of equipment, and failure to implement plans for the supply of ammunition. Bureaucracy and the long-drawn-out consideration of proposals had lost valuable time and the opportunity to obtain equipment. 'The army's spirit is the best possible and the people's morale is also high, but Finland's people trust that the government has provided for the country's defence preparedness, and the army does not doubt that it will stand equipped with the necessary weapons at the moment when it is called to a battle of life and death with the country's hereditary enemy.'[51]

This extensive indictment of the government's failure to provide adequately for the country's defence might be regarded as questioning the effectiveness of Mannerheim's own work as chairman of the Defence Council since 1931, a period he described in his *Memoirs* with hindsight as 'Eight years of racing the storm'.[52] In fact matters might have been much worse without his constant goading and the influence he exerted on opinion through press and politicians. He succeeded in getting increased sums allocated to defence as the economy recovered from the recession and in 1938, when the economic situation was good, he secured a major spending programme. Unfortunately, by the time more money had been made available for defence procurement in 1938–9, rearmament was in progress everywhere and orders, where they were accepted, could not be fulfilled quickly. He was right to blame the government for the situation.

[50] Österman, *Neljännesvuosisata elämästäni*, p. 197.
[51] Mannerheim, *Minnen*, II, p. 114.
[52] Mannerheim, *Memoirs*, p. 265.

(*Left*) 9. Seventieth birthday, 4 June 1937: flowers are strewn in Mannerheim's path as he leaves his home in Helsinki. (*Above*) 10. Seventieth birthday parade in Senate Square, Helsinki. (Both photos: Military Museum of Finland)

(*Above left*) 11. Kyösti Kallio (1873–1940), agrarian party politician, prime minister four times in the 1920s and 1930s, president 1937–40. (*Above*) 12. Juho Niukkanen (1888–1954), agrarian party politician, minister of defence 1931–2 and 1937–40. Opposed peace in March 1940. (*Left*) 13. Väinö Tanner (1881–1966), cooperative movement leader and social democrat politician, prime minister 1926–7, finance minister 1937–9, foreign minister 1939–40. Jailed in 1946–8 as one of those held responsible for the war with the Soviet Union. (All: Ministry of Foreign Affairs, Helsinki)

(*Left*) 14. Risto Ryti (1889–1956), progressive party politician, lawyer and banker, finance minister 1921–2 and 1922-4, prime minister 1939–40, president 1940–4. Jailed in 1946–9 as one of those held responsible for the war with the Soviet Union. (*Below*) 15. Erik Heinrichs (1890–1965), general, commander of the army on the Karelian isthmus 1940, chief of the general staff 1940–4 with interval as commander of the Karelian army 1941–2. Retired as defence forces commander, 1945. (Both photos: Ministry of Foreign Affairs, Helsinki)

(*Right*) 16. Rudolf Walden (1878–1946), general and industrialist, war minister 1918–19, member of the Defence Council from 1931, minsiter of defence 1940–4. (Ministry of Foreign Affairs, Helsinki) (*Below*) 17. The Winter War: Mannerheim at General Headquarters. (Hulton Getty Picture Collection)

They proposed defence expenditure to parliament, and both government and parliament were highly reluctant to ask the nation to fund the level of expenditure Mannerheim requested. His assessment of the likelihood of war was shared by very few politicians, most of whom regarded defence expenditure as only one among many demands on the public purse.

Mannerheim's careful advocacy of a Scandinavian policy, though influential in Finland, failed to arouse the response he hoped for from Sweden and in practice its results were restricted to some orders for defence equipment. These, of course, proved useful, but Sweden would not jeopardize its own neutrality by promising military support for the neutrality of Finland.

Mannerheim always believed that political influence on defence matters was pernicious. The habits of democracy irritated him, as was clear from his letter of 27 November 1939. In 1935 he had written with characteristic irony to G. A. Gripenberg: 'Whether one belongs in the political life, or like me occupies a peaceful function, which aims to prepare the nation for the possibility of being thrown at some time into the great mass slaughter, well equipped and with courage, one will be dragged along to take part in unproductive discussions, deliberations etc. Yes, God bless everything that is called democracy and the parliamentary system, I am too old to take it completely seriously.'[53]

Like it or not, political control was a characteristic of Finland's parliamentary system but Mannerheim's desire to limit its consequences for the country's defence lay behind his constant determination to strengthen his position as chairman of the Defence Council at the expense of the ministry of defence. Here he had some success, helped by his unique position as commander-in-chief during the War of Independence, a former head of state, and a field marshal. No other general would have secured the special position Mannerheim obtained for himself as chairman of the Defence Council, a position which was unsatisfactory organizationally in that it divided authority instead of concentrating it in the defence ministry. Mannerheim became widely trusted by Finns as their leading soldier and he himself contributed significantly to establishing that trust. He endeavoured to prepare not only the defence forces but also the nation for the test of war by emphasizing the need for unity.

[53] To G. A. Gripenberg, 6 February 1935. Mannerheim, *Brev*, pp. 250–1.

MANNERHEIM: THE FINNISH YEARS

On 30 November 1939 the Soviet Union invaded Finland. Mannerheim's resignation was now out of the question. He immediately reported to the minister of defence for duty as commander-in-chief and went on to see the president, who had formally to appoint him, to declare that he would not leave his post if the president and government required his services. The Council of State met at 1.30 p.m. and President Kallio declared the country at war and appointed Mannerheim commander-in-chief. A few days later Mannerheim wrote to his daughter Sophy: 'I had not wanted to undertake the responsibility as commander-in-chief – my age and health entitled me to that – but I have had to yield to appeals from the president of the republic and the government, and now I am at war for the fourth time.'[54] Finland's finest hour, the Winter War, had begun.

---

[54] To Sophy Mannerheim. Cited in Jägerskiöld, *Mannerheim mellan världskrigen*, p. 307.

CHAPTER V

THE WINTER WAR

'Soldiers! I have fought on many battlefields but never yet have I seen your equals as warriors.'[1]

AT WAR

Mannerheim had no illusions about the outcome of a war between Finland and the Soviet Union given their disparity in resources, the poor equipment of his country's armed forces and Finland's lack of allies. However, the pessimism with which he had regarded the country's situation before the Soviet invasion of 30 November 1939 was instantly overlaid by the responsibility of supreme command, and Mannerheim displayed an energy, determination and outward confidence which amazed those around him. Juho Niukkanen, the minister of defence, noted the huge amount of work which he did on the day he assumed command and thought that 'pessimism and even age' had been swept away.[2] Colonel Paavo Talvela, who had dinner with Mannerheim and General Rudolf Walden on 3 December just before the commander-in-chief left Helsinki for General Headquarters at Mikkeli in Eastern Finland, commented later: 'The atmosphere was astonishing and the Marshal was composed as God … The fate of Finland was in his hands.'[3]

The outbreak of war was followed by a change of government, prompted by Väinö Tanner and the social democrats who believed that a new government would stand more chance of getting negotiations with the Soviet Union restarted. The foreign minister, Eljas Erkko, and the prime minister, A. K. Cajander, were replaced and the coalition was broadened. Mannerheim felt no regret at Cajander's departure. On 29 November, when the Soviet Union broke off diplomatic relations with Finland, Lieutenant-General Oesch heard Mannerheim on the phone to Cajander, stating that there would now be war, and blaming the prime minister for neglecting the

[1] Order of the Day, no. 34, 14 March 1940. *Puhtain asein*, p. 76.
[2] Niukkanen, *Talvisodan puolustusministeri kertoo*, p. 117.
[3] Talvela, *Sotilaan elämä. Muistelmat*, I, p. 159.

equipment of the defence forces. 'He had never heard anyone berated as the Marshal berated Cajander.'[4] Risto Ryti, governor of the Bank of Finland, became prime minister and Tanner foreign minister. Mannerheim was content with Tanner in this post for reasons of domestic politics since he recognized the importance of retaining the full support of the social democrats for the war. He attended the meeting of the government's foreign affairs committee on 2 December at which the aim of reestablishing contact with Moscow was agreed. J. K. Paasikivi, a conservative whose realistic views on relations with the Soviet Union coincided in many ways with Mannerheim's own, joined the government as minister without portfolio. Niukkanen remained as minister of defence.

A significant development from Mannerheim's point of view arose from the proposal of General Walden on 5 December that he should act as the representative of GHQ with the government. Mannerheim 'fully agreed' and Walden transferred his existing duties as chairman of the military equipment council to the assistant minister of defence.[5] Henceforth Mannerheim had a trusted contact in Helsinki who could exert pressure on the ministry of defence whenever this was required and who often attended government or ministerial meetings at which he was able to give Mannerheim's views on the matters under consideration. Walden, in turn, kept Mannerheim informed of developments in the capital. The military situation made it impossible for Mannerheim to leave GHQ for Helsinki during the war, but members of the government travelled to Mikkeli to consult him when necessary.

Mannerheim's duties and authority as commander-in-chief were laid down by decree on 7 December. His powers extended well beyond the actual command of operations by the defence forces, their organization and training, and appointments and promotions. He was empowered to conclude an armistice. He was to ask the government for manpower reinforcements and propose the procurement of equipment. In addition he had the right 'to make proposals to the government on those foreign and internal policy measures which he regards as necessary for the defence of the state' and 'for the direction of economic life'. He was to act independently and be responsible for

---

[4] Talvela, *Sotilaan elämä. Muistelmat*, I, p. 156.
[5] Juva, Rudolf Walden, p. 466.

his actions to the president.[6] His authority was thus outside the control of the government as well as being extremely wide-ranging, which gave him a formal voice even in foreign policy. It was reasonable to conclude that another appointee as commander-in-chief would have been given more restricted powers. As it was, 'Mannerheim gained ... the possibility in his capacity as commander-in-chief to participate in the taking of important political decisions.'[7] Only the arrangements for the procurement of equipment proved unsatisfactory to him, and in August 1940 he was to secure the transfer of the procurement departments from the ministry of defence to GHQ, putting them firmly under his own control.

One of the prescribed duties of the commander-in-chief which Mannerheim in that capacity had no occasion to perform was the direction of the mobilization and concentration of the defence forces. Thanks to his initiative, that had already been accomplished well before he assumed supreme command. The army was in position to meet the Soviet invasion. The Isthmus Army, numbering 120,000 men, under Lieutenant-General Hugo Österman with headquarters at Imatra, comprised the covering troops (the bulk of the peacetime army), who were deployed between the frontier and the main defence position, and five divisions, three forming II Corps under Lieutenant-General Harald Öhquist on the west of the Karelian isthmus, and two forming III Corps, under Major-General Erik Heinrichs, on the east. The Isthmus Army's task was to prevent the enemy from penetrating into the country through the isthmus. The main defence position, which lacked depth, ran for some 87 miles (140 km.) across the isthmus from the Gulf of Finland to Lake Ladoga. It was strongest in the east, where the River Vuoksi constituted a natural barrier, and weakest in the west. There, and particularly between Summa and Lähde, were the most fixed defences. These comprised a number of reinforced concrete bunkers armed with machine-guns. Although they were usually too widely spaced to provide adequate mutually-supporting fire, they provided some valuable backbone for the field fortifications, anti-tank obstacles and barbed wire of the Finnish defence position which international journalists made famous as the 'Mannerheim Line'. In no way was it comparable with the Maginot Line. Mannerheim wrote of the Mannerheim Line: 'That it held was

[6] Jyränki, *Sotavoiman ylin päällikkyys*, pp. 321–2.
[7] Selén, *C. G.E. Mannerheim ja hänen puolustusneuvostonsa*, p. 351.

entirely due to the tenacity and courage of our soldiers, and not to the strength of the position'.[8]

On the north-eastern side of Lake Ladoga and north to Ilomantsi lay IV Corps (two divisions and some covering troops) comprising around 40,000 men. The long frontier from Ilomantsi to Petsamo on the Arctic Ocean was defended by the independent battalions (16,000 men) of the North Finland Group. The commander-in-chief had two divisions in reserve, one in the south near Luumäki and one – lacking artillery – in the north between Oulu and Kemi. The defence forces totalled some 295,000 men. Their deficiencies in artillery (field, anti-tank and anti-aircraft), in tanks and modem planes, as well as in stocks of ammunition, have already been mentioned. Moreover, a Finnish division numbered only 14,200 men compared with 17,500 in a Soviet division, which had in addition huge superiority in firepower and fifty-five tanks.

For the conquest of Finland the Red Army had concentrated four armies supported by up to 1,000 planes. The Baltic Fleet was to cut Finland off by sea from the west: in this it failed. On the Karelian isthmus some twelve divisions and five or six armoured brigades (200,000 men) were to break through the Finnish defences, capture Viipuri and advance west towards the River Kymi. Six divisions and an armoured brigade (130,000 men) were to advance north of Ladoga. Three divisions (75,000 men) were to advance from the eastern frontier across the 'waist' of Finland, cutting Finland off from Sweden. Two or three divisions (65,000 men) were to seize Petsamo, isolating Finland from the northern sea route. The invaders possessed massive superiority, and the concentration of so many troops along the eastern frontier came as a particularly unpleasant surprise to the Finns.

A further surprise was the immediate establishment by the Soviet Union of a puppet Finnish government in the Finnish border seaside resort of Terijoki. Its head was O. W. Kuusinen, one of the exiled communist leaders of the Finnish Red insurrection of 1918. His Finnish People's Government signed a treaty on 2 December with the Soviet Union ceding the territory required by the Moscow government. The creation of the Terijoki government left absolutely no doubt of the Soviet intention to occupy the whole of Finland and turn it into a communist state. This strengthened the Finns' determi-

[8] Mannerheim, *Memoirs*, p. 371.

nation to resist the invaders. The war really did appear, in the words of the order of the day Mannerheim issued to the army on 1 December, to be 'the continuation and final act of our War of Liberation' against 'the enemy over the centuries' as well as a fight 'for home, religion and fatherland'.[9] Although no country except the Soviet Union recognized the Terijoki government, it enabled the Soviet government to repudiate the existence of the 'Ryti-Tanner' government. No peace negotiations were therefore possible. Finland had no alternative but to fight, which won it a great deal of sympathy in the West.

The first days of the war were a particularly anxious time for Mannerheim as the scale of the Soviet invasion became apparent and the Finnish army's response to it was not yet clear. On the Karelian isthmus the role of the Finnish covering troops gave rise to a clash between the commander-in-chief and the commanders of the Isthmus Army and II Corps. The original task of the covering troops was to delay the enemy long enough for the field army to mobilize and deploy in the main defence position. Because that deployment had already taken place, General Österman wanted the covering troops to fall back to the main defence line, thereby minimizing their casualties. Öhquist favoured a more mobile defence. Mannerheim was aware from his own experience at the start of the First World War of how effectively small, well-led forces could disrupt an invading army. He wanted ground to be held and the active use of the covering troops, supported by units from the field army, to delay the enemy's approach to the main defence line, thereby giving more time for it to be strengthened.

Already on 1 December Mannerheim expressed to Österman his discontent at what he considered the insufficiently active use of the covering troops. On 3 December he ordered a counterattack at Vammelsuu but it was not carried out. On 4 December he went to Österman's headquarters to which Öhquist had also been summoned. Österman considered the meeting 'not at all dramatic' although Öhquist described how 'Österman, Oesch, Tapola [Österman's chief of staff] and Airo [head of the Operations Department at GHQ] sat deathly pale, deprived of sleep and with beads of cold sweat on their

---

[9] Order of the Day no. 1, 1 December 1939. *Puhtain asein*, p. 64. Some social democrats were unhappy with the reference to the War of Liberation. Ostrobothnian Social Democrats to Mannerheim, 2 December 1939. Mannerheim Archive, Box 434.

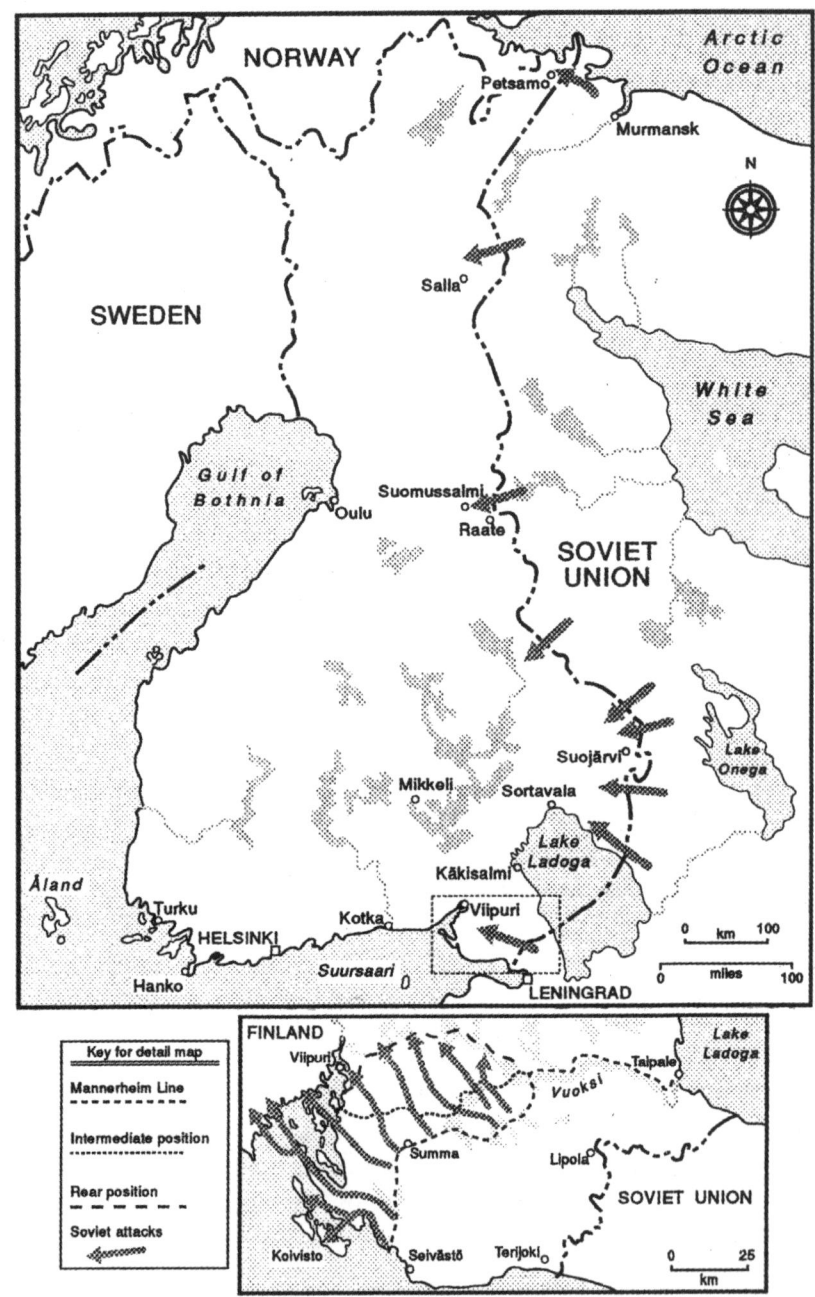

The Winter War

foreheads: the marshal was especially displeased.'[10] By the end of the meeting the atmosphere had improved and Öhquist believed Mannerheim had been convinced that reinforcing the covering troops would have served only to weaken the main position. This belief was wrong, to judge from Mannerheim's *Memoirs* where he wrote that 'the fighting was taken up by altogether insufficient forces which made long delaying actions impossible.'[11] Österman – privately – offered Mannerheim his resignation but it was refused. Mannerheim's expectations of the covering troops were probably unrealistic, but he remained irritated that greater delay and casualties had not been inflicted on the enemy. By 6 December the Red Army had reached the entire length of the Mannerheim Line. Attacks on it at Taipale on 6–7 and 15–17 December and in the area of Summa and Lähde on 17–21 December were repulsed after heavy fighting.

North-east of Lake Ladoga the situation was much more disturbing. Finnish troops were retreating rapidly and the important nodal point of Suojärvi was lost. Mannerheim ordered IV Corps to counterattack on 3 December, laying down the details of the operation and giving little time for its implementation in a controversial order that showed his lack of confidence in the Corps commander, Major-General Juho Heiskanen. The attack failed. Heiskanen was replaced by Major-General J. W. Hägglund: Mannerheim did not scruple to sack unsuccessful commanders. To stop an enemy breakthrough, he committed troops from his reserve and created a new command under Talvela – 'Group Talvela' – whose task was to restore the situation in the area of Tolvajärvi and Ilomantsi. The Group's successful attack on 12 December stopped the Soviet advance and gave the Finns the initiative.

Further north, the situation was equally threatening. More reserves were committed to the North Finland Group under Colonel Hjalmar Siilasvuo to push back the enemy who had reached Suomussalmi. By 9 December the situation there too had been stabilized, and a counterattack began two days later. The enemy advance towards Salla was checked by 20 December after a separate Lapland Group had been formed on 11 December. Petsamo was lost but by 19 December the enemy advancing from there had been stopped at Höyhenjärvi. By

[10] Österman, *Neljännesvuosisata elämästäni*, p. 208; Öhquist, *Vinterkriget 1939–40 ur min synvinkel*, p. 89.
[11] Mannerheim, *Memoirs*, pp. 326–7.

this time Mannerheim had committed half of his reserves to the defence of the eastern frontier despite the danger on the isthmus. This decision was justified because without it the strategic consequences for Finland could have been disastrous, with the country being cut in half and the overland link to Sweden severed. After three weeks of war the Soviet Union had not only failed to crush Finland but had lost the initiative. Mannerheim's initial fears that his army was not fighting had proved groundless. There was to be no rapid walkover by the enemy. Bombing raids had strengthened rather than destroyed civilian morale, which was further raised by awareness of sympathy for Finland abroad.

The deepening of what became an exceptionally cold winter proved at first to be advantageous to the Finns, especially along the eastern frontier, where the Soviet motorized divisions became tied to the roads while the lightly-armed Finns could move rapidly around and behind them on skis across the snowy country. The Finns pressed home these advantages during January and February 1940. A Soviet division was cut off, broken up and destroyed by IV Corps, which also prevented Soviet troops from breaking through at Kollaa and thus getting into central Finland and behind the front on the isthmus. Another Soviet division was destroyed by Group Talvela, and two more by Siilasvuo at Suomussalmi and Raate. Mannerheim liked to show his appreciation of success by the use of promotions and both Talvela and Siilasvuo became major-generals, the former in December 1939, the latter in April 1940. An enormous amount of booty fell into Finnish hands as the result of these spectacular victories which were widely reported abroad. Nevertheless, the Red Army continued to fight tenaciously along the eastern frontier, preventing Mannerheim from moving troops from there to the isthmus except at the end of February when a formation composed of Swedish volunteers assumed responsibility for the defence of the Salla sector.

On 4 January 1940 a Swedish officer who visited GHQ reported Mannerheim to be calm and confident.[12] Mannerheim was able to write with some satisfaction to his sister Eva on 21 January: 'In 3 days it will already be 8 weeks that we have held our own against the Bolshevik in spite of his superiority in numbers. The cold has given us a certain support in spite of our by no means being equipped for

---

[12] Carlgren, *Svensk utrikespolitik 1939–1945*, p. 92.

such a hard winter campaign.'[13] Stalin, on the other hand, was deeply disturbed by the failure of the Red Army to conquer Finland and the loss of prestige the Soviet Union was suffering internationally. The situation on the isthmus caused him particular concern.

Plans for a third Soviet offensive towards Viipuri had been disrupted by a Finnish counterattack on 23 December 1939. This counterattack was itself controversial. Österman, strongly pressed by Öhquist, had advocated a counterattack on 11 December but Mannerheim decided against it, wanting to await the first enemy assault on the main position. Österman did not expect Mannerheim to approve Öhquist's proposals on 20 December for a large-scale counterattack; this would involve the use of 6 Division which had just been transferred from the commander-in-chief's reserve to the Isthmus Army. However, Mannerheim did approve and the attack began as planned on 23 December between Kuolemajärvi and Muolaanjärvi, but already the same afternoon it was abandoned as a failure. Cooperation and communications between units and arms were poor, there was insufficient ammunition for proper artillery preparation, the troops were generally unprepared for an offensive operation, and even the aim was unclear. GHQ should have tightened up the plan. Even so, the Finnish counterattack had a disproportionate effect on the Red Army's operations. The planned offensive against Viipuri was replaced by an attack on the Taipale sector of the Mannerheim Line on 25–26 December: this was repulsed by the Finns. The situation on the isthmus then stabilized.

The Red Army on the Karelian isthmus paused, reorganized its command structure, developed tactics appropriate to the task of breaking through the Mannerheim Line and deployed twenty-three new divisions along the frontier with Finland, bringing the total to forty-five and the number of men to 600,000. Meanwhile Mannerheim and his staff struggled to find reinforcements, equipment and ammunition. Manpower was available although much of it was untrained. The trained men were used not as casualty replacements in existing formations but to constitute two new – and poorly-equipped – divisions which were deployed in the rear of III and IV Corps. Had they been deployed on the western isthmus they could have speeded up the construction of defence positions in the rear of the Mannerheim Line. The lack of casualty replacements meant that the divisions of

---

[13] To Eva Sparre, 21 January 1940. Mannerheim, *Brev*, p. 299.

the field army were rapidly ground down when the Soviet offensive was resumed. Mannerheim's use of his reserves is therefore open to criticism. His last reserves – fourteen battalions – were prepared for action in March 1940 although they had received little training and their combat value would have been slight.

The procurement of equipment and ammunition from abroad was pursued vigorously, if sometimes haphazardly. Domestic production, though increasing, was insufficient for the army's needs. Because of the lack of anti-tank guns, the soldiers had to resort to Molotov cocktails and explosive charges to destroy Soviet tanks. However, useful quantities of anti-tank, anti-aircraft and field guns were obtained quickly from Sweden as it became clear to the Swedes that Finland's successful resistance made the despatch of material worthwhile. Sweden refused to compromise its neutrality by sending troops to Finland although it allowed some recruitment of volunteers. Germany followed a strictly neutral line during the war and would not even allow the transit of arms to Finland, but Britain and France, both very sympathetic to Finland, were sources of arms which Mannerheim tried to tap. He was assisted in this by the expulsion of the Soviet Union from the League of Nations on 14 December 1939 because of its aggression against Finland. The League appealed for countries to provide Finland with both material and humanitarian aid.

Sir Walter Citrine, who headed a British Labour delegation to Finland in January 1940, recorded Mannerheim's flattering and appealing words to him: 'Your army is the best equipped in the world ... It doesn't matter where I have met them, I have always admired their equipment. That is why I hope that Great Britain can now spare some for little Finland.'[14] The problems over getting arms from Britain and France – and even more from the United States – were, first, the delays in obtaining decisions and, secondly, transit times. However, Britain sent some 100 aircraft and France thirty fighters, while field artillery, ammunition and other stores were also supplied. Some of the captured Soviet guns were brought into use by the Finns before the war ended. But despite all these efforts, the Finnish army remained under-equipped and short of ammunition throughout the war. Neglect of the procurement of equipment and leaving some men untrained meant, as Mannerheim pointed

---

[14] Citrine, *My Finnish Diary*, p. 107.

out, that, 'The economies achieved in time of peace had now to be paid for in blood.'[15]

WAR OR PEACE?

By the end of January 1940, thanks initially to private Finnish contacts with the Soviet minister in Stockholm, Mme Kollontai, it had become clear to the Finnish government that the Soviet Union was prepared, on its own terms, to open peace negotiations with it. Stalin abandoned the Terijoki government as the international situation became more complicated and the possibility of intervention in the war by the British and French began to seem more likely. The Finnish army had not fought in vain: the country's independence no longer appeared under threat. However, parallel Finnish contacts with the Soviet Union – through Swedish mediation – about peace and with Britain and France about Allied intervention took place against the background of a renewed Soviet offensive on the isthmus on 1 February. This ended the Finnish army's breathing space.

The first attacks were probes to test the efficacy of the Red Army's new tactics. Heavy artillery preparations and bombing preceded local combined arms assaults on Finnish strong points. Mannerheim afterwards thought that from the first week of February cooperation between Soviet artillery, tanks and aircraft was 'almost perfect'.[16] The Red Army had attained the state of efficiency which Mannerheim had mistakenly expected at the start of the war. The Finns were able to repair most of their defences but were worn down by the weight of enemy fire, the unremitting work and the lack of sleep. Mannerheim, surprisingly, had concentrated the bulk of his reserves not behind II Corps, where there was fierce fighting, but behind IV Corps, where they could be used either on the isthmus or north of Lake Ladoga. Thus when the main Soviet offensive on the Summa sector of the Mannerheim Line began on 11 February, reserves were rather distant from the most threatened area. By 13 February, when the Red Army had broken through near Lähde, he had decided to reinforce II Corps, but counterattacks that day and the next failed to restore the line.

On 14 February Mannerheim went to the headquarters of II Corps to discuss with Airo, Österman and Öhquist what had become an

[15] Mannerheim, *Memoirs*, p. 372.
[16] Foreign Office to Vereker, 8 April 1940. F.O.371/24795, N4094/1/56.

extremely grave situation. Military considerations pointed to the urgent need to withdraw from the western part of the Mannerheim Line, although the abandonment of territory was undesirable for reasons of foreign policy and morale. Österman favoured withdrawal not to the so-called intermediate position (running from Turkinsaari in the west via Näykkijärvi and Äyräpääjärvi to the Vuoksi) but to the rear position (from Viipuri via Tali to the Vuoksi). The intermediate position comprised very sparse field fortifications while the rear position was somewhat better prepared and ran through terrain more favourable to the defence. On 15 February Mannerheim ordered a withdrawal to the intermediate position: political considerations outweighed military ones. This difficult manoeuvre was carried out successfully and by 17 February the army was occupying the new line. Österman, who had become increasingly dissatisfied with Mannerheim's conduct of operations and felt under great strain, asked to be relieved of his command and was replaced by Erik Heinrichs on 19 February.

On 17 February Mannerheim issued a 'backs to the wall' order to the army on the isthmus: 'The enemy attack must again be halted by firm, steadfast action at the new defence line I have chosen', while officers were told in a separate order: 'The whole future of our people is now in the balance. Only our perseverance and faith can save it. I am convinced that every officer will do his duty.'[17] Nevertheless, the situation continued to deteriorate. The evacuation of Koivisto on the coast on 23 February, made necessary by the withdrawal, opened up a threat to the Finnish right flank by Soviet troops moving across the ice. The exceptionally cold winter had made the sea ice so strong that it would bear the weight of tanks. At this stage in the war the winter ceased to be the ally of the Finns: an early thaw would have made operations more difficult for their attackers.

The Soviet attack on the intermediate position began on 18 February, and a week later the Red Army broke through near Näykkijärvi. On 27 February Mannerheim had no alternative but to permit a withdrawal to the rear position. This was carried out in good order. There was a brief pause before the Soviet attacks resumed. At the beginning of March the Red Army attacked north-east of Viipuri at Tali and further east at Vuosalmi. Soviet troops also advanced across

---

[17] Cited in Vuorenmaa, 'Defensive strategy and basic operational decisions in the Finland-Soviet Winter War 1939–1940', pp. 88–9.

the ice of the Gulf of Viipuri and established a bridgehead on the western shore from which they moved forward to cut the road between Helsinki and Viipuri on 7 March. This serious threat to the troops on the isthmus was met by the creation of a Coastal Group under Lieutenant-General Oesch, Mannerheim's chief of the general staff, on 28 February and by moving troops from further east, from where they could ill be spared. There was an additional danger from Soviet troops advancing from Suursaari and other islands across the frozen Gulf of Finland towards Hamina and Kotka, but these were repulsed by the Finnish coastal artillery. The attacks at Vuosalmi threatened to cut off the Finnish troops on the eastern isthmus. The Finnish position was thus dangerously exposed. Mannerheim ordered Heinrichs to be 'mentally' prepared for a major withdrawal towards the line of the river Kymi but gave no permission for this operation to take place.[18] The commander-in-chief still tried to hold on to territory because peace negotiations were in progress.

Mannerheim only learned of Soviet readiness to consider a settlement with the 'Ryti-Tanner government' after the government had discussed that information on 30 January. Although the Finns were prepared to consider further concessions, the Soviet government stated on 5 February that these did not provide an acceptable basis for negotiations. Matters were complicated by the apparent willingness of France and Britain from mid January to intervene in the war by sending troops to assist Finland now that it had become clear that Finland would not be quickly overwhelmed by the Red Army. An initial, and totally unrealistic, scheme was to liberate Petsamo, which had been seized by Soviet forces, reopen Finland's port on the Arctic Ocean, and subsequently advance to cut the Murmansk railway. Mannerheim considered an Allied Arctic operation of potential value only if directed further east, to Archangel, where it would act as a diversion without the risk of drawing Finland into the European war. However, by 5 February the Allies had in effect abandoned the Petsamo scheme in favour of what, to them, was a more attractive plan to occupy Narvik and northern Sweden and thus stop the export of Swedish iron ore to Germany, thereby intensifying their economic blockade. Part of that expeditionary force would continue to Finland, thus responding to widespread anti-Soviet feeling in France and Britain.

[18] Vuorenmaa, 'Defensive strategy', p. 93.

Two Allied liaison officers, the British Brigadier C. G. Ling, who had visited Finland with General Sir Walter Kirke in 1939, and the French Lieutenant-Colonel Jean Ganéval, had arrived at Mannerheim's headquarters in January to assess the Finns' military needs. Mannerheim is said to have greeted Ganéval with the words, 'Have you only come to prolong our agony?'[19] Ling noted Mannerheim's desire for Allied help in the form of war materials and in the raising of volunteers. 'The Field Marshal smilingly referred to the precedent of the Italian and German non-intervention in Spain.'[20] Ling's report encouraged Britain to increase its material assistance, and in correspondence with senior British and French officers Mannerheim kept up the pressure for arms deliveries, particularly long-range heavy artillery.

On 5 February the Allied Supreme War Council decided to send troops to northern Norway and Sweden to prevent iron ore exports, more troops to central Norway and southern Sweden to guard against German countermeasures, and some to northern Finland to act against the Soviet Union. News of possible Allied intervention reached Finland on 7 February. Mannerheim wanted more information about Allied plans but was extremely cautious about them. He feared that intervention might prevent the vital transit of war material through Sweden. On 10 February Ryti and Tanner went to GHQ to discuss the situation with him. The commander-in-chief and the Defence Council, which met during a break in the discussions, agreed with Tanner's proposal that peace with the Soviet Union should be Finland's primary aim, with military aid (troops) from Sweden second and military assistance from the Allies in third place. Two days later Tanner learned that the Soviet peace terms included the cession of the Karelian isthmus and the eastern shore of Lake Ladoga as well as Hanko on the south coast, together with the conclusion of a treaty of friendship. Finland was not yet prepared to agree to such severe conditions for peace.

The government's second option – troops from Sweden – was ruled out publicly by the Swedish government on 17 February. This also had the effect of stiffening Soviet demands. The third option, Allied intervention, seemed more attractive when Ling and Ganéval returned to Finland and more information about Allied plans was

[19] Snow to Halifax, 10 January 1940. F.O.419/34, N712/1/56.
[20] Memorandum by Ling, January 1940. F.O.371/24796, N606/9/56. Ling saw Mannerheim on 8 January.

provided by the new British minister, Gordon Vereker, on 24 February. However, the attitude of Norway and Sweden to the transit of Allied troops remained unclear and even the size of the force to be sent to Finland and its date of arrival were the subjects of conflicting information: there might be 22,000 men in Finland by 15 April. Mannerheim said to Walden on 25 February, 'Are there men who have the courage to gamble? Too late 15.IV.'[21] A few days later it became clear that there would be only 12–13,000 men in Finland, and not until the end of April. Norway and Sweden were not prepared to grant transit rights. Mannerheim remained sceptical about aid from Western troops because this could draw Norway and Sweden into the European war and cut Finland off from the receipt of arms from Western Europe and the United States. However, he was in favour of exploiting the threat of Allied intervention to try to alleviate the Soviet peace terms and put pressure on Sweden. Against all probability, he did not abandon hope of getting troops from Sweden until early March.

When the government discussed the situation in session with the president on 28 February, Mannerheim could not be present as intended because of the critical situation at the front. Kallio was concerned to learn Mannerheim's opinion since he wanted a united front behind acceptance of the peace terms. Although several members of the government knew that Mannerheim considered acceptance of the Soviet conditions inevitable, Ryti with four of the ministers and General Walden travelled to consult the commander-in-chief. About the military situation he was quite pessimistic, and Western help was too uncertain to be relied upon. He did not state outright that the government should accept the Soviet terms, but that was the clear impression the members of the government received. On 29 February the government decided to open peace negotiations but deferred action because the Allies, on learning of this intention, increased pressure to accept intervention. Only after the Soviet Union threatened on 5 March to increase its demands did the Finnish government decide, on 6 March, to despatch a peace delegation to Moscow, where it arrived on 7 March. Next day the Finnish negotiators in Moscow, who included Mannerheim's confidant Walden, learned that the peace conditions were even harsher than they had anticipated.

---

[21] Cited in Jägerskiöld, *Fältmarskalken*, p. 133.

During the tense and difficult days of early March Mannerheim's opinions about the need to accept the peace terms changed with the military situation and the conflicting information received from the allies. On 4 March he 'rather heatedly' asked the British military attaché 'whether the allied governments seriously thought that two Brigades could save his country when he had had 200,000 Finns fighting day and night for weeks and yet barely, if at all, holding their own'.[22] His view the following day that Allied intervention forces were too few and would arrive too late influenced the government towards peace. The success of Soviet operations across the Gulf of Viipuri on 7 March made him fear that the Soviet government would seek to prolong negotiations. On 8 March, having heard about Allied plans from Colonel Aladár Paasonen who had returned to Finland from Paris, Mannerheim wondered whether an appeal could be kept as an option in parallel with the negotiations in Moscow, and that appeal actually made if no modifications were made to the Soviet peace terms. He was also anxious to expedite the despatch of the 100 bombers he had requested from the Allies on 7 March. Only on 9 March, when he became finally convinced that Allied troops could not arrive until it would be too late to save the situation at the front, did Mannerheim return to his original position of supporting peace. His scepticism about the Allied expedition was wholly justified. The troops had been prepared for despatch but their transit remained unsettled and the likelihood of men reaching Finland before Finnish resistance collapsed was remote.

The military situation, which had been bad on 7 March, was worsening all the time as the Finnish soldiers became increasingly exhausted by continuous fighting and casualties reduced units to small fractions of their war establishments. There were no trained reserves to replace losses. The shortage of artillery ammunition was also acute. Plugging gaps in the line demanded the desperate movement of battalions and even companies, and caused units to become seriously mixed up, complicating command and control. Mannerheim asked on 9 March that the government should take no decision about peace until it had received a report from him on the situation at the front. This report, which comprised a statement from Heinrichs about the condition of his Isthmus Army, became known, from Niukkanen's

---

[22] Points in conversation between Mannerheim and Lieutenant-Colonel King-Salter, 4 March 1940. F.0.371/24804, N2935/9/56.

characterization of it, as the 'pessimistic report'. It emphasized that 'the present state of the army is such that further military operations would lead to nothing but the continuing weakening of the situation and fresh losses of territory.'[23] Öhquist believed his part of the front 'could still hold for 4–6 days'.[24] Both generals were in fact too optimistic since the troops were already at breaking point. However, the advice was clear: peace should be made while there was still time.

The following day Mannerheim urged peace before Viipuri had to be abandoned and the front crumbled. There were members of the government who were opposed to peace – notably Niukkanen, who argued that the army had not been beaten. Some ministers were even prepared to leave the decision on peace to Mannerheim, which Tanner totally opposed since the decision was political. The suggestion was a measure of their desperation. A measure of Mannerheim's own desperation on 11 March was an idea he tried out on Tanner that Finland might offer to cede areas in the north to try to save Hanko and some territory in the south-east. On 11 March the delegation in Moscow received authority to sign the peace treaty. The government sought Mannerheim's advice early the next day about the time needed by the army for an armistice to take effect. There was no further need to consult him: the Moscow peace treaty was signed on 12 March 1940. Fighting ended on 13 March. The treaty was approved by parliament on 15 March and ratified five days later.

Although the Soviets dropped the demand for a treaty of friendship with Finland along the lines of those concluded with the Baltic states, the territorial cessions were severe. They included the Viipuri province, the islands in the Gulf of Finland, parts of Salla and Kuusamo and of the Arctic coast as well as the lease of the Hanko peninsula and nearby islands for thirty years. There was little time to evacuate the ceded areas but their population abandoned their homes and sought refuge in the remainder of Finland. The army had to abandon to the enemy territory which had never been conquered. The nation was shocked and in deep mourning; flags were flown at half mast. Over 25,000 Finns (out of a population of 3,600,000) had been killed in the war. Nevertheless, as Mannerheim was to write, 'Our unbroken resistance, above everything else, gave possibilities for terms which would ensure the independence of our country and

---

[23] Heinrichs, *Mannerheim Suomen kohtaloissa*, II, p. 469.
[24] Öhquist, *Vinterkriget*, p. 317.

save us from annihilation.'[25] 'The Finnish people, face to face with an apparently hopeless situation, were able to resist a feeling of despair and, instead, to grow in devotion and greatness. Such a nation has earned the right to live.'[26] Of General Walden at this time his biographer wrote: 'He expressed his joy that the Finnish people were now unanimous in fighting for their freedom and independence. He now saw the Finnish people like he had always hoped ... now he finally found the Finnish people.'[27] The same could be said of Mannerheim.

THE EXERCISE OF SUPREME COMMAND

On 16 December 1939 Mannerheim wrote to his nephew: 'Here I am sitting with my Headquarters in the same building as 21 years ago.'[28] Mikkeli was a suitable choice as the seat of GHQ because communications were good from there to army and corps headquarters. The various departments were distributed round the town, which was better for safety against enemy bombing than for efficiency. Mannerheim, the chief of the general staff and the operations section worked in the town's senior school while the commander-in-chief and his senior staff lived in Hotel Seurahuone until it was bombed on 5 January 1940. Mannerheim and some of his staff then moved to live and work first at an adult education college at Otava, some 7½ miles (12 km.) west of Mikkeli and from 5 March to the end of the war at Inkilä manor house in Juva, 12½ miles (20 km.) east of the town. Tanner, after his visit on 10 February, recorded: 'Generally speaking, headquarters lived extremely modestly. Lodging and food were very simple. For breakfast, for example, no hot food at all was served.'[29]

The pressure of work was intense. To his sister Mannerheim wrote on 21 January 1940: 'One day is like another in a headquarters – N.B. so long as no catastrophes occur – but the work goes on so that one scarcely notices how time is passing before one is far into the night hours.'[30] Somehow, in the midst of directing the war, Mannerheim

[25] Mannerheim, *Memoirs*, p. 365.
[26] *Ibid.*, p. 373.
[27] Juva, *Rudolf Walden*, p. 482.
[28] To Augustin Mannerheim, 16 December 1939. Mannerheim, *Brev*, p. 298.
[29] Tanner, *The Winter War*, p. 153.
[30] To Eva Sparre, 21 January 1940. Mannerheim, *Brev*, p. 299.

found time to sign the preface to the English translation of the diaries of the expedition he had undertaken in Sinkiang and North China in 1906–8 for the Russian general staff: it is dated 'General Headquarters of the Finnish Army, February 1940'.[31] Mannerheim made occasional visits to subordinate headquarters at critical moments, as to II Corps on 14 February – when he and his party, clad in white cloaks for camouflage against the snow, had to take cover under trees during a bombing raid – and to the Isthmus Army on 24 February. He received numerous visitors at GHQ but the press were kept away.

Basic to the routine of GHQ were the twice-daily situation reports made to Mannerheim at 09.00 and 21.00 by the quartermaster-general, who headed the operations department, Colonel (from January 1940 Major-General) A. F. Airo, who not only held a highly significant post but also enjoyed Mannerheim's confidence. The other heads of department – as well as the commanders of arms and services and the various inspectors – were like Airo in that they reported directly and separately to the commander-in-chief. The history of the Winter War compiled by the Finnish Military Science Institute noted that GHQ was 'noticeably centred on the commander-in-chief'. This was attributed to the organization of GHQ only when the army was mobilized and to the lack of time to prepare a proper distribution of work.[32] However, it was due above all to Mannerheim's personal preference.

His attitude to the organization of GHQ showed clearly in his relationship with the chief of the general staff. He later told General Heinrichs, before appointing him chief of the general staff in June 1940: 'I do not want to be the prisoner of *one* man … I must be able to consult with anyone whatsoever, whether he belongs to headquarters or not, and draw my own conclusions.'[33] The same applied during the Winter War. The chief of the general staff, Lennart Oesch, did not coordinate the work of the GHQ staff; Mannerheim did that himself. Oesch was more of an assistant to the commander-in-chief than a chief of staff in the conventional sense. Mannerheim kept him in post until 3 March 1940 when he transferred him to command the Coastal Group, a vital front-line appointment. Oesch returned briefly as chief of staff on 24 March. The absence of an immediate replacement showed the relative unimportance of his position at GHQ.

[31] Mannerheim, *Across Asia*, I, p. [4].
[32] *Talvisodan historia*, 4, p. 204.
[33] Heinrichs, *Mannerheim Suomen kohtaloissa*, II, p. 205.

Mannerheim's personal style of command also excluded large scale situation reports, conferences or briefings at which all key GHQ personnel were present. He sometimes arranged meetings at which he listened to the opinions of others and left without giving his own. He was generally slow to take major decisions – the order to IV Corps to attack on 3 December 1939 was an unhappy exception – and he took some convincing of the rightness of a course of action of which he had at first disapproved. This was the case over the withdrawal from the intermediate position on the isthmus in February 1940.

Mannerheim was by no means always easy to work with, and at times relations with his generals were difficult. Öhquist noted: 'The marshal ... in critical situations could be quite irritable and harsh towards his closest subordinates' but not invariably.[34] Total self-control could hardly be expected of a commander-in-chief under pressure and Mannerheim's outbursts were hardly surprising. They could be balanced by remarkable displays of courtesy. He was generous in his thanks for tasks well done – as his orders of the day show – and encouraged his commanders as well as goading them. The unsuccessful were likely to be promptly removed. His concern for detail frequently irritated his subordinates, and he undoubtedly let himself be caught up in too much detail – but, for example, his impatience at the lack of exact figures of his units' strengths during the Soviet February offensive was understandable given their importance to the endurance of the defence. Mannerheim's determination to hold on to territory as long as possible may not always have been tactically prudent, but it was based on his view that the position of the front line would influence the peace terms. This proved unfounded, but the assumption was reasonable and the abandonment of Viipuri, for example, would have had a bad effect on national morale.

Niukkanen noted how 'personnel questions were generally delicate matters in conversations with Mannerheim'.[35] The commander-in-chief nevertheless approved Niukkanen's suggestion at the end of January 1940 that Major-General Hanell be put in charge of fortification work. Generals usually knew if Mannerheim regarded them favourably. Talvela enjoyed the field marshal's regard. Oesch sensed that Mannerheim had become dissatisfied with him. Öhquist believed

---

[34] Öhquist, *Vinterkriget*, p. 201.
[35] Niukkanen, *Talvisodan puolustusministeri kertoo*, p. 228.

that Mannerheim disapproved of some of his qualities, while Österman objected to what he regarded as increasing interference in his command of the Isthmus Army in February 1940. He believed Mannerheim to be out of date in his thinking as a commander: 'The commander-in-chief had rather remained a typical great power cavalry general from the First World War whose ideas, for example, of methods of command and of the influence of the time factor never really fitted the command of the ill-equipped Finnish reserve formations. He was seemingly conscious of this himself deep inside and it is only regrettable that it often appeared in the form of groundless severe and sarcastic remarks to his subordinates, who had never before been subjected to such treatment'.[36] Österman asked to resign his command and Mannerheim politely recorded that he had been unable to stand the strain. Of Heinrichs, whom he chose to succeed Österman, Mannerheim wrote that he had 'shown himself to possess nerves which did not fail in the worst crisis'.[37] Unlike Österman, Airo rebutted any charge that the commander-in-chief had fallen behind more recent developments in military science or the military art. Nor, according to Airo, had he become fossilized as a commander because of his age: 'He had the ability to improvise and in his taking of decisions he could well perceive different solutions.'[38] Österman's judgement was undoubtedly too harsh, but the fact remains that Mannerheim's personal method of command did represent 'a lack of system'.[39]

Mannerheim's health suffered as the war drew towards its end. Tanner noted on 5 March that Walden had told him the Marshal was ill – 'he had a fever and was worn out – but [he] had nevertheless taken the phone.'[40] Colonel Paasonen found him on 8 March 'with a cold and in a poor shape'.[41] Airo believed that Mannerheim was by then 'tired and wanted to end the war even on harsh terms'.[42] Although Niukkanen commented that Mannerheim was 'changing

---

[36] Österman, *Neljännesvuosisata elämästäni*, p. 264.
[37] Mannerheim, *Memoirs*, p. 358.
[38] Turtola, *Aksel Fredrik Airo*, p. 170.
[39] Ibid., p. 173.
[40] Tanner, *The Winter War*, p. 211.
[41] Paasonen, *Marsalkan tiedustelupäällikkönä*, p. 101.
[42] Kuosa, *A. F. Airo*, p. 138.

his opinion from week to week' about the Russian peace terms,[43] the commander-in-chief was not alone in agonizing over whether to end the war or fight on. There were good reasons for indecision and changes of mind as the situation shifted. Weary as he was, Mannerheim held out, and it must be remembered that even if he looked to Citrine 'about sixty-four'[44] he was actually seventy-two – twenty or more years older than most of his generals. He fulfilled his own prescription that those in higher command required 'sure intuition, realistic imagination, and great strength of will' to overcome what could be the sometimes 'overwhelming strain' on 'the physical and mental forces'.[45]

General Heinrichs related some remarks by Mannerheim on a quiet evening after the Winter War had ended. The marshal wondered what was the most important quality of a commander. '"Courage? – Yes, both physical and moral courage. Conscientiousness in his duty and at the same time a sense of responsibility towards those entrusted to his command? – Quite so. Good judgement? – Quite so. Personal tenacity even in the most difficult situations? Now, I think, we are approaching the most important fact. Tenacity is required, that is the question, but not only physical tenacity but also mental – what we call fortitude. That, I believe, is the most important, the most fundamental of all: fortitude." The Winter War commander-in-chief had unconsciously listed precisely those qualities for which the officers and the army honoured him, and he had concluded with that quality, fortitude, which made the honoured commander much more than just a dominant man and a firm leader of operations.'[46]

And Mannerheim was an honoured commander. Despite his embittered criticism, Österman acknowledged that 'unreserved recognition' was due to Mannerheim's 'political and especially his military-political superior critical judgement', while he remained 'to the end a great unifying figure, around whom the Finnish nation tightly united in the hour of danger'.[47] The government, quite properly, took the decision to make peace, but Mannerheim's advice was

[43] Niukkanen, *Talvisodan puolustus ministeri kertoo*, p. 256.
[44] Citrine, *My Finnish Diary*, p. 108.
[45] Mannerheim, *Memoirs*, p. 358.
[46] Heinrichs, *Mannerheim Suomen kohtaloissa*, II, p. 185.
[47] Österman, *Neljännesvuosisata elämästäni*, pp. 264–5.

crucial. He had judged correctly the total unreliability of the Allied promises of military support.

Mannerheim possessed the ability to rise to the role expected of him. Nowhere was this clearer than in the order of the day he issued to the army on 14 March 1940. In it he thanked not only 'the soldiers of Finland's glorious army', of whom he was proud 'as if you were my own children'. He thanked all ranks and all branches of the services, but singled out for special praise the reserve officers, whose 'sacrifice in percentage terms was the highest of the war' – praise which those officers prized and never forgot. He remembered the Lottas – the women's auxiliaries – and the workers. He pointed out that the government had been compelled to make peace on harsh terms because the army was small and short of weapons and equipment. He noted the importance of the military aid received from abroad but added pointedly and bitterly: 'Unfortunately the significant promise of aid given by the Western powers could not be fulfilled because our neighbours, concerned for themselves, refused the right of passage to their troops.' He acknowledged that 'Our fate is hard when we are compelled to give up to a foreign race ... land which we have cultivated for centuries with sweat and toil.' Looking to the future, he accepted the duty 'to house those who have become homeless', while 'we must be ready as before to defend our diminished fatherland with the same determination and strength with which we have defended our undivided fatherland'.[48]

Paasikivi wrote: 'The order of the day of the commander-in-chief, Field Marshal Mannerheim, was impressive and beautiful, and one could not read it without elevation of the mind and without emotion. It breathed a deep patriotism, a martial spirit and at the same time humanity.'[49] In this great order of the day Mannerheim not only caught and responded to the mood of the nation, united in pride and sorrow, but sought to channel it towards facing the problems of the future. He was an exceptional commander-in-chief, and in spite of defeat, the war had enhanced his personal prestige and that of the defence forces.

---

[48] Order of the Day no. 34, 14 March 1940. *Puhtain asein*, pp. 76–80.
[49] Paasikivi, *Toimintani Moskovassa ja Suomessa 1939–41*, p. 200.

CHAPTER VI

THE 'ARMISTICE'

'The shadow the Russian colossus casts over our country looks as if it is darkening more and more.'[1]

PEACETIME COMMANDER-IN-CHIEF

In Finnish historiography the period between the Peace of Moscow in March 1940 and the resumption of hostilities with the Soviet Union in June 1941 is known as the Armistice or the Interim Peace (terms sometimes used at the time), while the new war is known as the Continuation War, to emphasize its connection with the Winter War of 1939–40. Of course in 1940–1 there was no idea that the Peace of Moscow might not be permanent. However much Finns resented its injustice and hoped that the end of the European war might lead to its revision, Finland at the time accepted the situation brought about by the Peace of Moscow. In particular prompt measures were taken to resettle the farmers displaced from Karelia and provide for the defence of the truncated country, a task made more difficult because the new frontier in the south-east was far less favourable strategically than the old one.

The broad coalition government was reconstructed after the peace and the departure of those ministers who had wanted to fight on with Allied support. Paasikivi also left on becoming minister in Moscow. Ryti remained as prime minister and Professor Rolf Witting became foreign minister. Both Ryti and Mannerheim, who always took a keen interest in the appointment of the foreign minister, would have preferred Mannerheim's friend G. A. Gripenberg, then minister in London, to Witting but he declined. Unlike Ryti and Mannerheim, who were considered pro-British, Witting was regarded as pro-German. Rudolf Walden became minister of defence, to the satisfaction of Ryti and Mannerheim, particularly the latter, who now

[1] To G. A. Gripenberg, [April 1941]. Mannerheim, *Brev*, p. 312.

THE 'ARMISTICE'

acquired a trusted friend in the government. This was to facilitate the development of defence policy and administration along the lines Mannerheim wanted. Walden was only prepared to serve as minister while Mannerheim remained commander-in-chief.

According to the Finnish constitution, the powers of commander-in-chief should have reverted to the president with the return of peace. However, Mannerheim remained commander-in-chief. The reasons for this formal breach of constitutional law are unclear: President Kallio may have wanted Mannerheim to continue[2] or, being in poor health, he was perhaps unable to press sufficiently strongly for the restitution of his authority as commander-in-chief – which may also have seemed undesirable to Ryti as prime minister, especially since the country's situation remained dangerous and the state of war, declared on 30 November 1939, was never revoked.[3] In these circumstances the continuation of Mannerheim as commander-in-chief was understandable and, with his high sense of duty, he was evidently willing to go on in that capacity; he might not have been if his authority had been reduced. In any case his remaining in the position of commander-in-chief was reassuring to the country. He wrote to his sister-in-law in July 1940: 'My age means, however, that I cannot expect for a longer period to bear the responsibility associated with the said position without running the risk of being called uncle, like ... Marshal Pétain.'[4]

Despite his age, Mannerheim threw himself energetically and successfully into the reorganization of the country's defences after the Peace of Moscow. During the 'Armistice' he secured the authority over defence matters for which he had striven since 1931, enjoying powers more or less equal to those he had possessed during the War of 1918. The defence minister was both compliant and supportive while parliament, whose influence had in any case declined due to the increase of executive power during the national emergency brought about by the Winter War and its aftermath, was kept from close scrutiny of defence matters by suggestions that Mannerheim, who was considered indispensable, might resign if members asked too many questions. The decree of 15 August 1940, which reduced the activity of the ministry of defence by transferring procurement to

[2] Turtola, 'Ryti ja Mannerheim', pp. 251–2.
[3] See Jokipii, 'Mannerheimin rooli 1939–1944', pp. 86–7.
[4] To Palaemona Mannerheim, 18 July 1940. Mannerheim, *Brev*, p. 305.

general headquarters under the commander-in-chief, was intended not only to improve arrangements for procurement but also to protect Mannerheim against a future defence minister of whom he disapproved.[5] Earlier changes had in fact strengthened the financial position of the defence ministry by permitting the Council of State to allow the ministry to exceed its budget and for parliament subsequently to cover the excess. In the circumstances of 1940–1 this practically gave Mannerheim a blank cheque for defence expenditure. He made the most of the opportunity and of the exceptional authority conferred by his position as commander-in-chief.

General Heinrichs left a vivid description of a meeting of senior officers with Mannerheim on 22 March 1940 to consider the siting of a newline of fortifications. 'The 72-year-old commander-in-chief, crawling on his knees beside a large map spread out on the floor, studied different alternatives, and after a long discussion he then announced to those present his decision that the line Klamila-Luumäki (nearest to the Gulf of Finland) was to be fortified without delay and as rapidly as possible.'[6] Though incomplete, a major defensive line had been constructed by June 1941 between the Gulf of Finland and Lake Saimaa in a massive and costly scheme involving at its peak almost 35,000 men. Fortifications were also built to block routes across the lake district, and there was a strong defensive line to cut off the Soviet base at Hanko from the interior of Finland. These defence lines often lacked depth but they would have provided valuable support for defending troops and raised the cost of a new Soviet invasion, which Mannerheim always regarded as a distinct possibility.

Fear of renewed hostilities was a key factor in keeping a large number of men under arms. In the summer of 1940 there were still 195,000 serving and in January 1941, 109,000. The period of compulsory service was raised from one to two years from the beginning of 1941, and extensive reserve training was held to familiarize men with equipment acquired since the war. The output of reserve officers and of new regular officers was greatly increased. The peacetime army was reorganized in June 1940 into thirteen infantry brigades, grouped along the frontier. Mobilization plans were altered to provide for an enlarged army of sixteen divisions. The arrival from abroad of much equipment ordered during the Winter War, together with

[5] Heinrichs, *Mannerheim Suomen kohtaloissa*, II, pp. 208–10.
[6] *Ibid.*, p. 193.

THE 'ARMISTICE'

home production and the repair of war booty, raised appreciably the number of field guns, anti-tank and anti-aircraft guns, mortars and aircraft, though the heterogeneity of equipment complicated training, maintenance and ammunition supply.

In a speech to senior officers on 17 December 1940 about the progress of the defence forces Mannerheim described the growth in artillery firepower and the rapid and extensive construction of fortifications, adding that he believed 'everyone will be at one with me in the view that gigantic work has been performed to strengthen the defence of the country'.[7] He had good reason to be proud of this achievement just as he was proud of the generals and colonels he addressed, 'a distinguished assembly of men, who all looked death in the whites of the eyes and bore responsibility great enough to frighten anyone.'[8]

As well as strengthening the defence forces Mannerheim was anxious to maintain the unity of the nation forged during the Winter War. It was his decision to abandon the customary celebration on 16 May, the anniversary of his victory parade in 1918. He prescribed instead an annual commemoration of the fallen and of unity, held in 1940 on 19 May. He also abandoned his original idea of extending the Association of Veterans of the War of Independence to include veterans of the Winter War. Instead he backed a new veterans' organization in order to maintain the unity engendered by the war. This forestalled the possible formation by the social democrats of their own veterans' organization. In August 1940 Mannerheim practically ordered General Talvela to become chairman of the new organization, which drew together the moderate right and left. The threat of communism, which was very real both externally from the Soviet Union and internally from vociferous and well-organized extreme leftists, undoubtedly played its part in inducing Mannerheim to make these concessions, which were not altogether popular with the right. Nevertheless, he also believed that in the changed circumstances after the Winter War the time for commemoration of the White victory in the Civil War had passed. He did, however, maintain the independence of the Defence Corps, although that organization lost much of its former character through becoming closely linked to the army as part of the home troops and through its new role in the machinery of mobilization.

[7] Jokipii, *Jatkosodan synty*, p. 99.
[8] To Eva Sparre, 17 December 1940. Mannerheim, *Brev*, p. 308.

MANNERHEIM: THE FINNISH YEARS

IN THE 'WAR CABINET'

Mannerheim's move back to Helsinki enabled him to participate more easily in the discussions of the so-called inner circle of the government, the unofficial 'war cabinet' comprising Ryti, Witting and Walden. After the resignation for health reasons of President Kallio in November 1940 and the election of Ryti as his successor in December, the new prime minister J. W. Rangell, a banker and non-party man of the right, joined the war cabinet. Because of the need to keep the social democrats on side, Tanner was also sometimes consulted, even after he left the government, due to Soviet hostility to him, in August 1940. The war cabinet was concerned above all with foreign policy. A determination to maintain secrecy meant that foreign affairs rarely came before the government for discussion and even more rarely before its foreign affairs committee. Mannerheim, despite his integration into the war cabinet, was careful to leave the responsibility for political decisions to the government, but his independent authority as commander-in-chief – which continued without being reconfirmed by Ryti on becoming president – and his expertise in foreign affairs gave his views weight even if his proposals did not invariably gain approval.

Until April 1941 the Soviet Union kept up relentless pressure on Finland, which completely precluded the normalization of relations following the Peace of Moscow. Mannerheim's expectation of a resumption of hostilities and his military measures have been already mentioned. He strongly supported plans for a defensive alliance with Sweden and Norway after the Winter War, but these plans were difficult to achieve in any case, and came to nothing when the Soviet Union opposed them as early as the latter part of March 1940. A subsequent plan, originating in Sweden, for a union between Sweden and Finland, which would have emphasized the two countries' common neutral foreign policy, was considered sympathetically by both governments in November 1940. Mannerheim supported the idea since it would have provided support for Finland's neutrality, but the Soviet Union made plain in November its hostility to any formal links between the two countries. Mannerheim sent General Talvela to Berlin in December 1940 to find out if Germany would back the union plan, but Germany was by then developing its own interest in the fate of Finland, and refused. The union scheme failed and Finland obtained no shelter from Sweden.

The successful German invasion of Denmark and Norway in April 1940 isolated Finland from Western Europe, and the defeat of France in June 1940, and the expulsion of British troops from the continent which followed it further emphasized Germany's military preeminence and dominance. Finland was now dependent on Germany as an export market and as the source of vital supplies of fuel and grain. At the same time as Germany was making conquests in the west, the Soviet Union was strengthening its western frontier by occupying the Baltic states, Bessarabia and Northern Bukovina. Finland felt dangerously isolated and exposed. It acceded to Soviet demands in June 1940 for the demilitarization of the Åland islands and eventually to transit by rail across Finland to the Soviet base at Hanko. The incorporation of the Baltic states into the Soviet Union in July 1940 presented a chilling threat to Finland; Mannerheim referred to 'Stalin's theatrically-carried out coup d'état tragedies'.[9] The disruptive activities in Finland of the Soviet-Finnish Friendship Society caused further alarm, although in the end the government took steps to curtail this trouble.

Mannerheim was so worried by the events of the summer of 1940 that he sent some personal papers to his sister-in-law in Sweden for safe keeping. He wrote to her in August to thank her 'for the hospitable reception afforded in the Grensholm archive to my two bags filled with papers ... Additionally I would like to put in some of the things kept since the beginning of our war in the Bank of Finland's vaults, which ought not to fall into the wrong hands ... There is nothing agreeable to relate from here. One lives in constant tension, which places almost too great a demand on a small, poor and severely tried people, not to mention that at my age it is too severe to carry a commander-in-chiefs responsibility under such conditions.'[10] Mannerheim's sense of strain was not alleviated when on 8 August 1940 the government rejected his advice that partial mobilization should be ordered because of threatening Soviet troop movements; it feared that such action would worsen the situation, and fortunately it transpired that the troop movements were not directed against Finland.

[9] To Eric von Rosen, 27 July 1940. Mannerheim, *Brev*, p. 307.
[10] To Palaemona Mannerheim, 11 August 1940. Grensholm Collection, VAY 5632.

The presidential election at the end of 1940 clearly demonstrated the extent of foreign interference in Finnish internal affairs. The most threatening messages came from the Soviet Union: the election of Tanner, Kivimäki, Mannerheim or Svinhufvud would be regarded as a sign that Finland did not intend to fulfil its obligations to the Soviet Union under the peace treaty. In Germany's view, on the other hand, both Svinhufvud and Kivimäki were suitable but where Finno-Soviet relations were concerned, Mannerheim's election would be a liability (in any case Mannerheim was not prepared to be a candidate). Risto Ryti, who had been acting president, and who was acceptable both within Finland and to the foreign powers, was elected by an overwhelming majority. Before the election Mannerheim arranged to let the Conservative Party, whose electors had doubts about voting for Ryti, know that he considered him the best candidate. Afterwards Mannerheim wrote: 'Personally I am satisfied with the outcome, for of all the candidates who were mentioned, I regard Ryti as the most fitted in these serious times to pilot the ship of state into calmer waters.'[11] Calmer waters were far away: the level of tension was in fact about to rise because of Soviet demands relating to the nickel mine in the Finnish district of Petsamo.

The concession to operate the nickel mine at Kolosjoki in Petsamo, which was expected to begin production by 1941, was held by an Anglo-Canadian company. By the spring of 1940 Germany was actively concerned to obtain nickel from Finland, and the Finnish government saw in this German economic interest a means of improving its relations with Germany and gaining support against the Soviet Union. In June 1940, however, the Soviet Union demanded that it be given the nickel concession or that a Finno-Soviet company be established instead. The international complications for all the parties involved were considerable and negotiations dragged on for the rest of 1940. The Finns were prepared to accept a joint Finno-Soviet company but not to permit Soviet control over it or over the area of the mine. This would have had implications both for Finland's sovereignty and for economic relations with Germany.

In January 1941 the Soviet Union put renewed pressure on Finland to accede to its demands in the nickel question. Troop movements and a nasty propaganda campaign added to the tension. On 23 January 1941 Mannerheim proposed to the war cabinet that two divisions

[11] To Palaemona Mannerheim, 19 December 1940. Mannerheim, *Brev*, p. 310.

THE 'ARMISTICE'

be mobilized as a precautionary measure. As in August 1940, the government rejected his advice, and for the same reason; they feared that military measures would irritate the Soviet Union and make negotiations more difficult. Nevertheless, the government decided against further concessions in the nickel question, their resolve stiffened by Mannerheim's own view that Finland could afford no more concessions. This was partly a matter of principle since he feared the erosion of Finland's sovereignty, but it was also because he considered the country's defences in better shape and he was more confident of German interest in, and likely support for, Finland.

Mannerheim had backed up his concern by asking to resign as commander-in-chief on 10 February 1941, at a moment when negotiations in Moscow over the nickel question were at a difficult point. He gave the reason for his resignation as 'because I have come to the conviction that our policy by extending concessions ever further from day to day is leading our state on a dangerous road, endangering also the preconditions for our military defence'.[12] Walden submitted his resignation on the same date in a clearly concerted move. Ryti persuaded Mannerheim not to go, and his resignation was withdrawn already on 11 February. Walden also continued in office. A harder Finnish line in the nickel negotiations resulted, to the dismay of Paasikivi, who was even prepared to exchange Petsamo to appease Soviet demands. Paasikivi was recalled from Moscow in March and resigned in May; his line favouring compliance had been rejected. The nickel negotiations became deadlocked. Ryti recorded that at a dinner on 24 February there had been 'much conversation about relations with Russia, Mannerheim [seemed] bold'.[13] The key to this apparently surprising change in Mannerheim's attitude – from depression to boldness – lay in Finnish contacts with the Germans.

FINLAND AND GERMAN PLANS

The Nazi-Soviet pact, by placing Finland in the Soviet sphere of influence, deprived it of any support from Germany during the Winter War and immediately afterwards. The conclusion of a trade treaty between Finland and Germany on 29 June 1940 gave the Finns some encouragement. However, the real change in Germany's attitude to

[12] Cited in Jokipii, *Jatkosodan synty*, p. 163.
[13] *Ibid.*, p. 172.

Finland occurred in August 1940 and Mannerheim related in his *Memoirs* the secretive and dramatic manner of that change. He received from the Finnish minister in Berlin on 17 August a request to receive an important letter from Berlin which would be delivered to him personally by a named Finn at Malmi (Helsinki) airport the following day. Mannerheim made the necessary arrangements and asked Lieutenant-General Heinrichs to be present. Walden and Witting had also been invited. 'After reading the letter, I informed the two Ministers of its contents. I had been requested to receive on the same day the German Lieut.-Colonel Veltjens, who had orders to present a communication from Marshal Göring. Lieut.-Colonel Veltjens reported to me in my home the same evening and conveyed greetings from Göring. I was asked if Finland, like Sweden, would permit the transit of materials and men on leave, and sick, to and from Kirkenes [in northern Norway], Veltjens further informed me that it would now be possible to obtain war material in Germany.'[14]

Mannerheim's reaction was to express satisfaction at the possibility of purchasing arms, but he said that the transit question was a matter for the government, and persisted in this view even when Veltjens objected he was not authorized to discuss the matter with anyone else. That evening Mannerheim phoned Ryti, who told him to agree to the transit request. Thus on 19 August Mannerheim gave Veltjens the affirmative answer which he wanted. Ryti subsequently denied that Mannerheim had asked for his consent to the German proposal, but the balance of probability, based on such contemporary sources as are available and on Mannerheim's respect for the responsibility of the government, suggests that Mannerheim's version of events was correct and that Ryti took the decision.[15]

Talvela and another officer were sent to Berlin to discuss arms purchases and the details of the transit agreement at the end of August. A simple memorandum between the military authorities concerning the transit of German troops and equipment through Finland was signed on 12 September and a brief 'political' agreement by diplomats in Berlin on 22 September. The number of Germans involved was not large, but large enough for their presence in Finland to upset both Britain and the Soviet Union, the latter subsequently increasing

[14] Mannerheim, *Memoirs*, p. 399.
[15] Jokipii, *Jatkosodan synty*, p. 117; Jägerskiöld, *Fältmarskalken*, pp. 231–2; Manninen, 'Ryti ja kauttakulkusopimus', p. 41.

THE 'ARMISTICE'

its pressure on Finland. However, the general reaction to the transit agreement in Finland was one of relief at evidence of some potential German counterpoise to Soviet pressure. The secret purchase of military equipment in Germany, including artillery and fighter aircraft, made a significant contribution to the rearmament of the Finnish defence forces.

With hindsight, the transit agreement can be seen as the fateful first step towards Finland's involvement in a new war with the Soviet Union because, unknown to the Finns, increasing German interest in their country, particularly Lapland, became connected with Hitler's decision on 31 July 1940 to order planning for an invasion of the Soviet Union. The Germans took for granted Finnish participation in a war against the Soviet Union, while their own military presence in Lapland, assured by the transit agreement, offered the opportunity to mount an attack on the Murmansk railway from Finnish territory. Hitler did not sign the plan to invade the Soviet Union (Operation Barbarossa) till 18 December 1940, and the plan as such was never revealed to the Finns. However, by October 1940 the Finns had been told that Hitler believed that sooner or later there would be war between Germany and the Soviet Union. This revelation came as part of a series of contacts, and eventually discussions, between Finnish and German officers in the course of which German intentions became progressively clearer. These military contacts, which were more important than diplomatic ones, were not undertaken by the Finnish side on Mannerheim's independent initiative although they placed him in a key position; he discussed the progress of contacts with the Germans with the war cabinet. He was also as careful to keep in the background of the discussions as he was to ensure that the officers involved understood their lack of authority to conclude any formal agreements with the Germans.

At first the Finns were concerned in their contacts with the Germans to discover whether they would receive help from them in the event of being attacked by the Soviet Union. Molotov's discussions with Hitler and Ribbentrop in Berlin in mid November 1940 caused great anxiety in Finland. The Soviet Union attempted to get the Germans to remove their troops from Finland so that the country could finally be brought under Soviet domination, but Hitler emphasized the economic importance of Finland to Germany and declared his opposition to a new war in the Baltic region. A little later it was made clear unofficially to Mannerheim and the Finnish leadership that Germany would not allow the prevailing peace in the north to be disturbed, but despite this reassurance, the Finns continued to fear that Germany might once more sell out Finland to the Soviet Union; these fears persisted right up to the moment when Operation Barbarossa began.

In October 1940, on behalf of the German army in Norway, the German military attaché in Helsinki asked for information about Finland's defence preparedness, terrain and communications. After discussions between Ryti, Mannerheim, Walden and Heinrichs, this information was supplied. Talvela's contacts in Berlin in December 1940 included a meeting with Colonel-General Franz Halder, the army's chief of the general staff, at which Halder asked how long the Finnish army needed to mobilize and concentrate for an attack in the south-east – a hint of Germany's intention to attack the Soviet Union. Talvela reported the question to Mannerheim and Ryti, and Mannerheim decided to send Heinrichs to Germany to meet Halder and answer his questions. He did so on 30 January 1941, and Halder revealed that war with the Soviet Union was possible and that if it occurred there would be German offensives against Leningrad and Kandalaksha, the latter from northern Finland. This striking information about Germany's aggressive intentions towards the Soviet Union may have strengthened Mannerheim's determination to force the government in February 1941 to halt its policy of concessions to the Soviets.

The information the Finns had received about German intentions was insufficiently precise to allay their anxiety about those of the Soviet Union. Mannerheim's own concerns about Soviet pressure were apparent in a letter to his sister-in-law in February 1941, just days after he had withdrawn his resignation. 'The winter has been unpleasant like last year's, not only through cold weather but also as regards Moscow's insolence. One asks oneself with alarm what these bandits are really planning. It is not easy to carry a heavy responsibility on old, worn-out shoulders.'[16] In early April he suffered a bad attack of influenza and felt so weak that he decided to go to the sanatorium at Ulricehamn in Sweden to convalesce, handing over the supreme command temporarily to Heinrichs on 15 April. The 'radiation treatment, massage, baths, walks and mealtimes… look like

[16] To Palaemona Mannerheim, 14 February 1941. Grensholm Collection, VAY 5632.

doing me a lot of good. I already feel much better and hope that it will not be long before strength returns'.[17] He was well enough to leave on 3 May and after a busy visit to Stockholm, where he had lunch with the Crown Prince and a meeting with the commander-in-chief, was back in Finland on 7 May.

Mannerheim's health had improved but his anxieties persisted. He wrote to G. A. Gripenberg: 'With feverish zeal and without counting the cost we have been trying to build up a new and stronger defence. The foreign policy leadership and the Moscow legation have not had the strength which is needed to stand up against unjustified demands and threats from the east and I am afraid that it would have gone far worse had not the surprise the German transit traffic gave the gentlemen in Moscow made them lower the pressure somewhat.'[18]

It was thus as the result of Soviet hostility to Finland that Mannerheim and the war cabinet were induced to clutch at the straw of German support. Mannerheim had gradually abandoned his customary desire to obtain support from Sweden after the demonstrable failure of that policy with the collapse of the union plan. He and the war cabinet then began to move closer to Germany and to plan to participate in the German attack on the Soviet Union. It was a fundamental and fateful decision.

TOWARDS WAR

It has been rightly held that the decisive events leading to Finland's entry into the Continuation War were the agreement by President Ryti on 20 May 1941 to hold military discussions with Germany, Finland's despatch to Germany on 30 May of information about what it hoped to gain from a war with the Soviet Union, and Finnish agreement in the course of military discussions in Helsinki on 3–6 June to German plans relating to Lapland and other cooperation. The war aims and the military discussions were decided by the war cabinet. The approval of military cooperation with the Germans was based on the expert knowledge and recommendations of Mannerheim as commander-in-chief and his staff. Thus Mannerheim's part in involving Finland in the war was crucial since he carried the

---

[17] To Palaemona Mannerheim, [April 1941]. Grensholm Collection, VAY 5632.
[18] To G. A. Gripenberg, [April 1941]. Mannerheim, *Brev*, p. 312.

responsibility for military decisions.[19] Had he opposed military collaboration with Germany it would not have happened, a point Paasikivi subsequently confided to his diary.[20] In this sense it is true to say that Mannerheim 'had something like a right of veto in foreign policy questions'.[21]

Mannerheim was normally cautious in matters of policy, and his admiration for German order and efficiency was counter-balanced by his known lack of sympathy for German policy in general and the Nazi regime in particular. Why, therefore, was he prepared to throw in Finland's lot with the German invasion of the Soviet Union? Paasikivi recorded on 4 October 1944 that he had said 'he thought that Germany would defeat Russia but ... he added that by going to war we put everything on one card, German victory.'[22] Mannerheim was undoubtedly impressed by Germany's succession of victories, and in that he was not alone. He believed that the German armed forces, unlike those of the Soviet Union, were well led. There appeared a strong probability that Germany would defeat Soviet Russia. Even Ryti, who believed that Germany would ultimately lose the war, hoped that it would defeat Russia before doing so.[23]

The German plans reawoke the old anti-Bolshevik ideal in Mannerheim. In May 1941 he told his sister in a letter: 'You will understand what a blow it would be to me if I were not to join in when the Soviet Union is going to be crushed.'[24] Though 'most friendly', he 'adopted a somewhat bellicose and intransigent attitude' to the hope expressed by the British minister in Helsinki on 14 June 1940 that Finland would 'avoid becoming embroiled in general hostilities in this part of the world'. Mannerheim then declared that 'it would be the best act ever done by "that terrible Hitler" if he could destroy Bolshevism once and for all', and added that 'the Bolsheviks were an element of unrest in the world which he would gladly see eliminated'.[25] Later, in 1942, he was concerned that his Russian friends and comrades should not believe that he had drawn

[19] Jokipii, *Jatkosodan synty*, pp. 622–3.
[20] Paasikivi, *J. K. Paasikiven päiväkirjat 1944–1956*, II, col. 339.
[21] Manninen, *Suur-Suomen ääriviivat*, p. 8.
[22] Paasikivi, *op. cit.*, I, col. 50.
[23] Turtola, *Risto Ryti*, p. 257.
[24] Cited in Paasivirta, *Suomi ja Eurooppa 1939–1956*, p. 152.
[25] Vereker's report, 15 June 1941. F.O.371/29363, N2829/202/56.

his sword against the country where he had served for more than thirty years without recognizing that 'the gigantic struggle in which we also have our modest part is the last chance to put an end to Bolshevism … this scourge of humanity'.[26] In addition, he saw the opportunity to seize the moment for Finnish national preservation. As he wrote to his sister in July 1941, he hoped the war would 'save us from "being wiped from the face of the earth" which otherwise, knowing the Bolsheviks' methods, would quite certainly have taken place in the near future'.[27]

Rational calculation also played its part. Mannerheim believed that the Soviet Union would attack Finland if it were attacked by Germany. By joining in German plans he anticipated such an attack and secured for Finland a powerful helper. It must be admitted that allowing the concentration of German troops in Lapland, a consequence of the transit agreement of September 1940, made a Soviet attack on Finnish territory seem almost inevitable. Yet in the circumstances of 1940–1, fearful as it was of Soviet intentions, Finland was in no position to resist German aims in Lapland although it did not have to foster them as it actually did. Finland went to war with the Soviet Union in June 1941 on its own initiative, although the war cabinet was careful to allow hostilities to be begun by the Soviet Union: Finland's war was therefore ostensibly defensive and a 'continuation' of the Winter War.[28]

A German initiative which was taken up in the spring of 1941 by certain pro-German circles in Finland was the voluntary recruitment of a Finnish battalion of the Waffen-SS. Mannerheim later claimed to have opposed its formation, but in fact was at first quite positive towards it to encourage German interest in Finland. Shortly before the war in the east began, however, he wanted the men back for service in the Finnish army. He accomplished this aim only in the summer of 1943 when the men's term of enlistment ended. To the annoyance of the Germans, he refused to allow its renewal and the battalion was disbanded.[29]

[26] To [Prince Paul] Demidoff, 2 July 1942. Mannerheim Archive, Box 502.
[27] To Eva Sparre, [July, 1941]. Mannerheim, *Brev*, p. 314.
[28] Jokipii, *Jatkosodan synty*, pp. 620, 624.
[29] Mannerheim, *Memoirs*, p. 466; Ueberschär, *Hitler und Finnland*, p. 307; Jokipii, *Jatkosodan synty*, p. 207.

MANNERHEIM: THE FINNISH YEARS

During the first half of 1941 the Germans prepared for war with the Soviet Union. In February they continued to seek information about circumstances in Finland of relevance to their plans in the north, with visits to Finland by General von Seidel for the air force and Colonel Erich Buschenhagen from the army in Norway. Mannerheim met both of them but took no part in the discussions, which were cautious on both sides. Only a few weeks before the planned start of Operation Barbarossa did Hitler seek more active cooperation from Finland. On 20 May he sent Ryti a special envoy, Karl Schnurre, who mentioned the possibility of war between the Soviet Union and Germany and asked for a military delegation to be sent to Germany to coordinate operations in case war should break out. Ryti, who told Schnurre that Finland would welcome German support if it were attacked, discussed the proposal with Mannerheim, Rangell, Walden and Witting. All agreed to it, and Mannerheim promptly sent a delegation to Germany, led by Heinrichs.

On 25 May in Salzburg Heinrichs met Field Marshal Wilhelm Keitel and Colonel-General Alfred Jodl from the Supreme Command of the German Armed Forces (OKW), and went on to meet Colonel-General Franz Halder of the Army Command (OKH) at Berlin (Zossen) on 26 May. The Finns were told of the German plans of attack and of what was hoped for from themselves, and in reply stated that they had no authority to make any commitments – Mannerheim had been explicit on that point. However, useful preliminary discussions took place, which were continued in Helsinki between 3 and 6 June. By then the Finnish war cabinet had agreed to meet the Germans' wishes, although the political aspects of cooperation still had to be made clear. The Finns were insistent that their forces should not attack across the frontier until the Soviets had attacked them; nor were the Germans to begin operations from Finnish territory. Any appearance of a war of aggression by Finland was to be avoided.

At the military discussions in Helsinki between the German Colonels Kinzel and Buschenhagen and the Finns led by Heinrichs (and at parallel naval discussions in Kiel) arrangements were agreed for the arrival of German troops, ships and aircraft in Finland and for the use of certain Finnish airfields. A border was settled between German troops in the north of Finland and Finnish troops in the south; Finnish troops in the north were to be put under German command. The timing of Finnish mobilization was agreed: on 15 June in the north,

THE 'ARMISTICE'

and on or after 16 June elsewhere. Mobilization and concentration would take twelve days. Operational tasks were made clear though details were not precise. The Finns were to attack on their southeastern frontier to immobilize Soviet troops in the area of Lake Ladoga; they were also to occupy the Åland islands and blockade Hanko. Halder, on receiving Kinzel's report of the discussions, commented: 'The Finnish military leadership has adapted itself to our proposal and apparently enters into the tasks under full sail.'[30] Buschenhagen reported: 'Finland is now ready for full cooperation within the framework of the conversations of Salzburg and Berlin'.[31] Heinrichs had kept in close touch with Mannerheim during the discussions and there is no doubt that their outcome represented Mannerheim's views, even to a warning to the Germans not to attempt to set up any kind of Quisling government in Finland since this would paralyse any further cooperation with Germany. It is reasonable to interpret this warning as 'more … evidence that although Mannerheim had resolved to co-operate with Germany if she did attack the USSR … he was equally resolved … not to allow Finland to be used as a mere pawn in Germany's game.'[32]

Despite the agreement between the Finns and Germans over military action, there was no formal written accord or any alliance between them. This was further evidence of the determination of Mannerheim and the war cabinet not to bind themselves to fight as Germany's ally in spite of taking advantage of its war with the Soviet Union to acquire a powerful cobelligerent against a common enemy. Mannerheim was also careful not to discuss the question of the supreme command of all forces in Finland. He did not want that position since it would have made him subordinate to the German high command, and declined it when the Germans offered it to him in July 1944. He remained an independent national commander-in-chief throughout the war. Although a German general, Waldemar Erfurth, was appointed German representative at the Finnish GHQ, he was only a liaison officer, and Mannerheim sent a Finnish general to German army headquarters in order to emphasize the principle of reciprocity. The absence of a single command in Finland caused problems in the direction of the war but they were more irksome for

---

[30] Halder, *Kriegstagebuch*, II, p. 447.
[31] *Documents on German Foreign Policy*, Series D, XII, p. 963.
[32] Upton, *Finland in Crisis*, p. 267.

the Germans than for the Finns, for whom they were preferable to German strategic direction.

In response to a request from the Germans, Finland presented on 31 May 1941 a statement of what it hoped to achieve from a peace agreement between Germany and the Soviet Union. These aims, which had been discussed by the war cabinet, included a German guarantee of Finland's independence, the restoration of the 1939 frontiers, and possible territorial compensation, proposals for which were drawn up by Airo at Mannerheim's instigation. They varied in extent according to the degree of collapse of the Soviet Union but at their maximum they included the whole of Eastern Karelia. Mannerheim was personally against the annexation by Finland of Eastern Karelia and by Germany of the Kola Peninsula, which was also mooted. He believed that as a great power, Russia could not be deprived of areas which historically belonged to it, even if it were defeated.

The Germans were careful not to reveal to the Finns prematurely the date for the invasion of the Soviet Union. However, following a request by the Finnish general staff, Field Marshal Keitel informed them on 15 June that the preconditions for Finnish mobilization could be counted on. The order was given on 15 June to mobilize III Corps, but only on 17 June was full mobilization ordered, in the guise of general reserve training, to begin the following day. Ryti and Witting wanted to delay mobilization until after the German invasion had begun, but Mannerheim's advocacy of earlier mobilization prevailed. German troops in Finland moved towards the frontier on 18 June. The full government, the chairmen of parliamentary party groups and the parliamentary foreign affairs committee were informed in mid June of the general development of the situation but not of the extent of Finland's commitment to Germany. On 21 June Finnish GHQ was told of the date of Operation Barbarossa. Lingering doubts about German intentions were over; the invasion began on 22 June 1941.

CHAPTER VII

THE CONTINUATION WAR

'As you will understand, it is difficult to bear the trust [of] a people who are fighting for the right to live in the land their forefathers built with sweat and toil and where the church bells daily toll their sons into eternal rest, and which shows me its trust and recognition in such an overwhelming manner.'[1]

SUCCESSFUL FINNISH OFFENSIVES BUT NO GERMAN VICTORY

In his speech to mark the invasion of the Soviet Union Hitler said: 'In alliance with their Finnish comrades, the victors of Narvik stand on the shore of the Arctic Ocean. German divisions, led by the conqueror of Norway, along with Finnish liberation fighters under their Marshal, protect Finland's territory.'[2] Although no formal alliance existed between Finland and Germany, it was disingenuous of Mannerheim to suggest in his *Memoirs* that Hitler intended in his speech to 'face Finland with a *fait accompli* which would lead to a Russian attack'.[3] Finland did indeed stand alongside the Germans. Finnish troops in northern Finland were placed by Mannerheim under German command on 15 June. From the time of mobilization, before the start of Barbarossa and during Finland's brief period of neutrality, the Finnish GHQ had been issuing directives for possible offensive operations. Finland had assisted German minelaying operations in the Gulf of Finland and in providing refuelling facilities for German aircraft which bombed Leningrad. There was no reason for Hitler to suppose that Finnish cooperation would not continue as had been discussed on 3–6 June.

---

[1] To Eva Sparre, 25 July 1942, referring to his seventy-fifth birthday celebrations. Mannerheim, *Brev*, p. 321.

[2] Cited in Upton, *Finland in Crisis*, p. 282.

[3] Mannerheim, *Memoirs*, p. 412.

However, Hitler's speech did cause difficulties for Finland both abroad and at home since it apparently contradicted the declaration of neutrality issued by the Finnish government on 23 June. For political reasons Finland could not appear as an aggressor. However, as Mannerheim had expected, the Soviet military proved unable to disregard the threat posed by the presence of German troops in Finland. On 25 June Soviet aircraft bombed Finnish airfields in raids which also caused civilian casualties in several towns. Ryti and Rangell were thus able to claim that Finland had been attacked by the Soviet Union and was therefore at war. Parliament gave the government a vote of confidence. Mannerheim admitted to Gripenberg later that 'he was pleased when the Russians attacked because then we too could take up arms without having made ourselves guilty of an attack on Russia.'[4] The Continuation War had begun, with Finland ostensibly the injured party.

By July 1941 Finland had mobilized 475,000 men in the armed forces, and the total number of men and women in service, including civil defence personnel, was 630,000 or a little over 16 per cent of the population. This was a prodigious effort which was unsustainable for more than a short period. Mannerheim exhorted his soldiers to a 'holy war' and to 'follow me one last time'.[5] He did not decide for a few more days in what direction they were to follow him.

Despite their cooperation with the Germans, the Finnish war cabinet were determined that Finland's war with the Soviet Union should be seen as separate from Germany's. Finland was not an ally of Germany but a co-belligerent. This was important in trying to avoid being drawn into the World War. Mannerheim's independent position as Finnish commander-in-chief emphasized this separateness, and all his planning was informed by it. He did not take orders from the German high command but pursued Finnish interests. However, he was willing to undertake an offensive in Karelia, in agreement with the Germans. Although the Finns looked forward to the early reconquest of ceded Karelia, Mannerheim decided to attack first in Ladoga Karelia, east of the lake. A successful offensive there would not only cut off Soviet troops on the Karelian isthmus from those north of Lake Ladoga but would also fit in with German plans for an eventual junction with the Finns on the River Svir. The

[4] Cited in Jägerskiöld, *Marskalken av Finland*, p. 41.
[5] Order of the Day no. 1, June 1941. *Puhtain asein*, p. 116.

plan had the additional merit of not threatening Leningrad when German forces were still far from the city. Mannerheim was determined throughout the war not to attack Leningrad, despite the obvious military importance of such an operation, because he believed it was an action for which no government in Russia would ever forgive the Finns. This was a clear indication of his pursuit of Finnish objectives. The war was for Mannerheim a crusade against Bolshevism but he did not fight it without regard to Finland's long-term relations with Russia.

Mannerheim's GHQ moved from Helsinki to Mikkeli on 25 June but he only arrived there two days later after visiting various corps headquarters to explain his plans. He was described on arrival by Major-General Tuompo, who served at GHQ, as 'tanned and vigorous looking'.[6] Mannerheim formed the Karelian Army under General Heinrichs to attack towards the northern shore of Lake Ladoga, then to continue along the north-east shore to Olonets and the River Svir. The offensive began on 10 July, with a considerable Finnish superiority in numbers and firepower. By 16 July the Finns had reached Lake Ladoga and on 24 July the River Tuulosjoki. There was then a pause while the northern flank was cleared.

The Finnish offensive on the Karelian isthmus, which the Germans had urged in order to tie down Soviet forces north of Leningrad, began on 21 August. Viipuri was seized on 29 August. By 2 September the rest of the Karelian isthmus had been cleared and the troops were halted on or just over the old frontier. In the north the progress of the German and Finnish offensives was less satisfactory. The Germans failed to advance from Petsamo to Murmansk or to cut the northern part of the Murmansk railway. In October and November Mannerheim refused German requests to allow Finnish troops to be used in operations towards Kandalaksha and Belomorsk. Despite German wishes the Finns did no more at Hanko than contain the Soviet forces until, on 2 December, the Soviets evacuated their base there.

Operations in Karelia to the north-east of Lake Ladoga resumed on 4 September and the Svir was reached on 7 September. The Murmansk railway was cut in the south the following day but this lacked strategic significance since another branch, running east from Belomorsk, remained open. The Finns then cleared the isthmus

---

[6] Tuompo, *Päiväkirjani päämajasta,* p. 17.

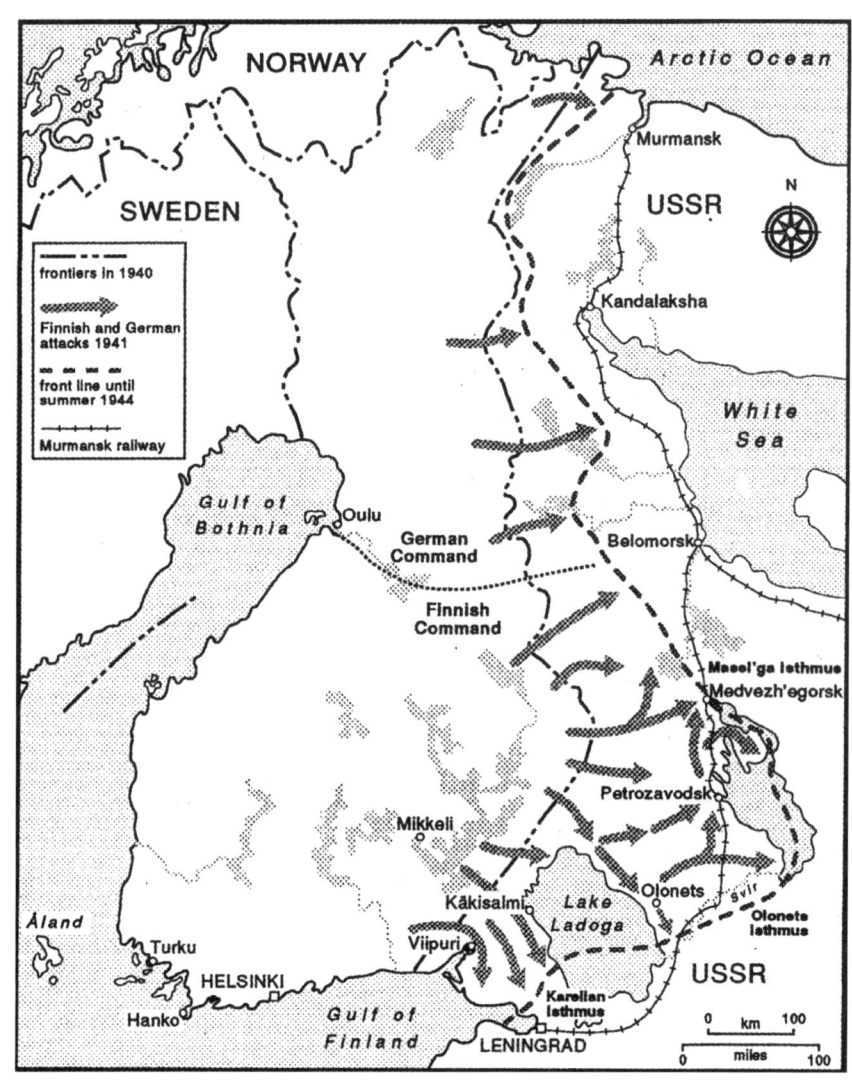

The Continuation War

between Lakes Ladoga and Onega, with Petrozavodsk, the capital of Eastern Karelia, falling to them on 1 October. A bridgehead was established south of the Svir in early October, making a better defensive line. Similar strategic defensive considerations led Mannerheim to continue to attack north of Petrozavodsk, where operations went on until 6 December when Poventsa was occupied. The Finns then went over to the defensive along the Karelian, Olonets and Masel'ga (*Finnish* Maaselkä) isthmuses.

Already in August 1941 Mannerheim had written to his sister: 'Here everything is going its appointed way … However, the battles are incredibly hard, even harder than last winter … The Bolsheviks fight with a tenacity and bitterness which borders on the incredible, especially because it is constant. However pleasure in the successes won is darkened by the daily reports of killed and wounded – whose figures show how many brave Finnish boys will never again see the homes they took the field to defend.'[7] He had evidently underestimated the patriotism of the Russians, even when suffering under an oppressive regime. The casualties of the offensives were considerable – some 25,000 killed – and some troops had been reluctant to cross the old frontier into Eastern Karelia. Furthermore, by the end of the campaign a degree of war-weariness had begun to affect morale. Yet the Finnish offensives had been extremely successful. The territory in Karelia lost in 1940 had been recovered (and was reincorporated into the country by decision of parliament on 6 December 1941), part of Soviet Eastern Karelia had been occupied, considerable Soviet forces had been eliminated and much booty captured.

However, operations in Eastern Karelia had caused serious problems both at home and abroad. On 10 July 1941 Mannerheim issued an order of the day to encourage his troops as they began their offensive into Karelia. The draft had been prepared at GHQ about a week beforehand. As was his practice with orders of the day, he had made substantial amendments to the draft in his own hand; the order thus represented his views and was neither sanctioned nor authorized by the government. Mannerheim, who was normally sensitive to political considerations, failed in this case to anticipate the surprise and storm this order was to cause among the government and politicians and, despite censorship, the comment it provoked in the press which was often favourable and at times even enthusiastic. This was because

---

[7] To Eva Sparre, 7 August 1941. Mannerheim, *Brev*, p. 314.

the order apparently raised the delicate question of Finland's war aims. In it Mannerheim recalled his promise from 1918 not to 'sheathe his sword ... until the last of Lenin's soldiers and hooligans is driven out of Finland and Eastern Karelia as well'.[8] Now he wrote: 'For twenty-three years Eastern Karelia and Olonets have awaited the fulfilment of that promise; for a year and a half after our glorious Winter War Finnish Karelia has desolately awaited the dawn ... A new day has dawned! Karelia is rising ... The freedom of Karelia and a great Finland gleam before us in the mighty avalanche of the events of world history. May the providence that guides the destinies of nations allow the Finnish army to fulfil the promise I made to the people of Karelia. Soldiers ... Your victories will liberate Karelia, your deeds will create a great, auspicious future for Finland.'[9]

This became known as Mannerheim's 'scabbard order' and it was interpreted as setting out an annexationist war aim which conflicted with the government's statement that the war was purely defensive. The elevated language of the order went over the heads of the troops, although there were many officers – in the field as well as at GHQ – who welcomed the opportunity to create a Great Finland which would incorporate Eastern Karelia into Finland as it had existed in 1939. Ryti was sympathetic to this aim as were many politicians of the right and centre. On the other hand the Swedish People's Party and the Social Democrats were against expansionist war aims, and wanted to fight only to safeguard Finland's independence. On learning of the order, the social democrat ministers threatened to resign from the government since they objected to a war of aggression beyond the old frontier, but the coalition managed to hold together, and regaining the territory lost in 1940 was stated to be the government's official war aim. Despite its displeasure the government could not repudiate Mannerheim's order; his position as commander-in-chief was too independent and too strong.

In practice the creation of a Great Finland also remained on the agenda, and policy towards the occupied territory of Eastern Karelia was based on the assumption of its annexation. Russians there were treated more harshly than Karelians who were destined to become Finnish citizens. Mannerheim nevertheless acted as a restraining

---

[8] Ignatius, *Carl Gustaf Mannerheim*, p. 41.
[9] Order of the Day no. 3, [10] July 1941. *Puhtain asein*, p. 120.

influence.[10] He was displeased by some of the measures adopted in Eastern Karelia; for example, he was concerned to maintain the Orthodox faith of the Karelians and objected to their baptism by Finnish Lutheran military chaplains.

Paasikivi believed in the latter part of 1941 that Mannerheim was making policy in Finland.[11] This was going too far. It is curious that Mannerheim, who did not personally favour the permanent annexation of Eastern Karelia, should have written as he did.[12] His use of the term 'great Finland' (Finnish: *suuri Suomi*) instead of 'Great Finland' (*Suursuomi*) may or may not have been significant: he later claimed it was. As far as his war aims were concerned, the principal one was to have the Bolsheviks crushed by the Germans. His aims in Eastern Karelia were strategic and not annexationist. He wanted to secure for Finland a buffer zone behind strategically-desirable defensive borders (the Olonets and Masel'ga isthmuses) so that the Soviets would not be able to prepare an attack on the country in fixture. At the same time he was aware of the strong current of opinion that supported an invasion of Eastern Karelia as a prelude to annexation. When Ryti had earlier asked him why the Finns were going into Eastern Karelia – a somewhat odd question to be asked by the president – Mannerheim had not elaborated on the military considerations involved but said: 'Is it not the wish of our people?'[13] The encouraging words of his 'scabbard order' reflected important contemporary opinions and expectations. The government was right to point this out to foreign diplomats as part of its damage limitation exercise in the aftermath of the order's publication.

The sharp reaction to the order caused Mannerheim to recognize the existence of strong political opposition to the Eastern Karelia operation. He immediately became more cautious in his direction of the offensive, an approach to which the visit of Ryti and Rangell to him at GHQ on 23 July may have contributed. In future he was to consult the president more over politically-sensitive plans; he had learned a lesson from his 'scabbard order' but had not compromised his position as commander-in-chief. The government accepted that Mannerheim's conduct of operations in Eastern Karelia should be

[10] Manninen, *Suur-Suomen ääriviivat*, pp. 187–8.
[11] Paasikivi, *Jatkosodan päiväkirjat*, p. 130.
[12] Heinrichs, *Mannerheim Suomen kohtaloissa*, II, p. 276.
[13] Cited in Jokipii, *Jatkosodan synty*, p. 444.

dictated by military considerations. In practice it was he who decided which strategic questions were sufficiently political in character to be discussed with the president.[14] But discuss them he did. Ryti occasionally expressed his doubts about operational plans discussed with Mannerheim but in March 1942 stated: 'The Field Marshal has naturally complete freedom to decide the matter according to his own judgement.'[15] A less independent-minded commander-in-chief might have found the lack of clear political direction a disadvantage. Tanner tried to draw a firm boundary between the respective responsibilities of the commander-in-chief in Mikkeli and the government in Helsinki. He failed and what was perceived as the dualism between the two foci of authority persisted although Mannerheim did not exceed his powers as commander-in-chief by taking decisions which were the responsibility of the government, with which he kept in regular contact. Nevertheless, Finland did not fight the war with a unified civil and military command structure until Mannerheim became president in August 1944.

The most serious difficulties for Mannerheim and the government towards the end of 1941 were caused by deteriorating relations with Britain and the United States and by German pressure for further Finnish offensives. The 'scabbard order' upset western countries (including Sweden), which considered that Finland was now participating in Germany's war of aggression. The British, under pressure from the Soviet Union, attempted to persuade Finland to halt its offensive. There was an exchange of letters between Churchill and Mannerheim in which the British prime minister on 29 November urged Finland to 'leave off fighting and cease military operations ... and make a *de facto* exit from the war'. Mannerheim replied on 2 December that it was 'impossible for me to halt the military operations at present being carried out before the troops have reached the positions which in my opinion will provide us with the necessary security'.[16] Britain declared war on Finland on 6 December 1941 — ironically it was the day on which the Finnish offensive ended. Mannerheim had proposed a reduction in the British legation's staff to limit their intelligence-gathering activity, but he had opposed a break with Britain and was subsequently incensed by Witting's claim that he had wanted

[14] Jyränki, *Sotavoiman ylin päällikkyys*, p. 142.
[15] From Risto Ryti, 25 March 1942. Mannerheim Archive, Box 129.
[16] Mannerheim, *Memoirs*, pp. 435–6.

THE CONTINUATION WAR

it. He also opposed Finland's adherence to the Anti-Comintern Pact in November 1941. Despite its protestations about fighting a separate war, Finland was becoming involved in the general war and, because of its dependence on Germany for grain and munitions, was vulnerable to German pressure. It was a measure of Mannerheim's determination and diplomatic skill that he was able to resist German proposals that Finland should join in the blockade of Leningrad and in new offensives against the Murmansk railway. Finnish participation in the latter would have had serious adverse effects on relations with the United States because of the importance of the railway as a supply route into Russia for the Allies.

By the end of 1941 it had become clear that the war would not be over quickly. Mannerheim wrote to his sister-in-law: 'Yes, it would be splendid to know that the end of this bloody drama is near, but above all it matters that we obtain a favourable outcome because for us what is at stake is simply the Finnish people's opportunity to live. If the Bolsheviks remain in power they will undoubtedly carry out their threat to wipe our people from the face of the earth.'[17] The failure of the Germans to win rapid success disturbed Mannerheim greatly. Ryti, who met him at GHQ on 21 January 1942, commented: 'The Marshal was very pessimistic regarding the Germans' situation in Russia. He thought it was very worrying and could simply lead to a catastrophe.'[18]

The German blockade of Leningrad eased the situation on the Karelian isthmus and enabled Mannerheim, albeit reluctantly, to agree to the release of many older men from the army by the middle of 1942, to be partly replaced by new conscription classes. The Finnish army was reorganized into three defensive groups on the three isthmuses: a period of static warfare began. The Germans had not achieved their expected quick victory and Mannerheim believed that, with a long war in prospect, they would be defeated.

WARTIME GHQ

The central part of the GHQ at Mikkeli was housed, as during the Winter War, in the senior school while Mannerheim lived at first outside the town and then in the town centre. He moved 3 miles

[17] To Palaemona Mannerheim, 28 December 1941. Mannerheim, *Brev*, p. 316.
[18] Cited in Jägerskiöld, *Marskalken av Finland*, p. 230.

(5 km.) out to the Sairila manor house in early 1944 when it was expected that Mikkeli would be bombed. He told his sister-in-law: 'Life in the same confined surroundings and society would be unconscionably monotonous if one were not so severely occupied from morning till night that one does not notice how the weeks hasten by.'[19] His routine at normal times was precise. 'He rides almost every morning from 7 to 8. Arrives here [GHQ] at 9 and, with the exception of taking lunch from 12.30–14 and dinner from 19.30–21, sits until 23.30–24 at night or until the evening reports have been considered.'[20] Mannerheim's habit of going riding with only one or two officers as companions and his practice of walking in town between GHQ and the Mikkeli Club where he had lunch and dinner astonished the Germans who perceived a security risk. The small group of security men detailed to guard him had a difficult time. Mannerheim resented their presence and on occasion took a boyish delight in shaking them off. Only exceptionally on tours of inspection did he carry a pistol; he normally carried nothing more offensive than a cane or walking stick.

Much – too much – has been made of the elegance of Mannerheim's 'court' at Mikkeli, which centred on the lunches and dinners attended regularly by his most senior generals and his ADCs as well as occasional guests. 'Two rooms are reserved for me and a dozen senior officers in the town's "most fashionable" club while the numerous other personnel from GHQ eat in a large restaurant connected with the same club. There is one kitchen for both dining rooms and it is run in a particularly creditable way by the lady who owns the restaurant and a hotel in the same building. People who arrive here to meet me on duty or other business are usually invited to my table, where they bring with them a little change for us and perhaps for themselves.'[21]

Except when there were guests, the food and drink were modest though sometimes the menu was improved by gifts sent to Mannerheim, for example venison from his sister-in-law in Sweden or the salmon sent from Rovaniemi each midsummer by the Kemi Company. The German General Erfurth, whom Mannerheim liked, noted Mannerheim's attentiveness towards his guests and the 'good form'

[19] To Palaemona Mannerheim, 28 October 1941. Mannerheim, *Brev*, p. 315.
[20] Tuompo, *Päiväkirjani päämajasta*, p. 31.
[21] To Palaemona Mannerheim, 28 October 1941. Mannerheim, *Brev*, p. 315.

that was characteristic of Finnish GHQ.[22] The conversation at table kept off military and political matters; Mannerheim was a fine raconteur and often spoke of his travels, hunting or his experiences in Russia. Even during the crisis of August 1944 G. A. Gripenberg noted of the conversation at table that 'a stranger would have found the mood light, almost gay ... We told anecdotes and amusing stories.'[23] Meals, though formal, were a period of relief from the strain of work though the pressure of responsibility remained, and manifested itself in various ways. As Mannerheim wrote to his nephew, 'One can exercise command over more than several hundred thousand men but not be able to dispose of one's own time.'[24]

Mannerheim's time was taken up by an unending stream of officers reporting to him. The quartermaster-general reported on the operational situation morning and evening, and there was at least one daily intelligence report and an evening report on the supply situation and casualties. Mannerheim usually decided matters at the time when they were submitted to him. Some reports concerned questions which could well have been decided by one of his subordinates had he been more capable of delegating and less fond of detail. He read and annotated a mass of documents and tried also to keep up with the press, paying particular attention to the foreign policy articles in the *Journal de Genève*. He sometimes spoke by telephone to General Walden, the defence minister, several times in the course of one day and often to the president.[25]

The routine was varied by occasional visits by the president and members of the government and by foreign diplomats, generals and other dignitaries. Mannerheim also travelled regularly to inspect different parts of the front, and a special train – which also carried his car – was always at his disposal. He found these tours of inspection a refreshing break from the routine of GHQ. He visited Helsinki occasionally though not always when the government asked him; he certainly did not go there on leave. The staff at GHQ had cause to complain that Mannerheim, who had no family and took no leave himself, was unreceptive to suggestions that they might like an occasional break to see their families.

[22] Cited in Jägerskiöld, *Marskalken av Finland*, pp. 65–6.
[23] Gripenberg, *Finland and the Great Powers*, p. 342.
[24] To Augustin Mannerheim, 5 November 1943. Grensholm Collection, VAY 5632.
[25] Paasonen, *Marsalkan tiedustelupäällikkönä*, pp. 115–16; Tanner, *Suomen tie rauhaan*, p. 14.

Mannerheim's intensely personal exercise of command, which disregarded the concept of the collective responsibility of the general staff, involved a determination to obtain the views of junior as well as senior staff officers. This caused hurt and practical problems for the generals immediately subordinate to him. Heinrichs, as chief of the general staff, complained that he succeeded no better than his predecessor during the War of Independence in 'bringing about a strictly logical division of work and cooperation between the different staffs, departments and sections of the commander-in-chief's general headquarters'.[26] In his unpublished comments Heinrichs was even more critical, particularly of Mannerheim's 'system without a system' and his 'unhealthy' suspicion of intrigue on the part of those around him.[27]

In his personal relations with his staff and other senior officers Mannerheim had pronounced likes and dislikes which affected the appointments he made. He had no time for yes-men. Tuompo was right when he wrote of Mannerheim's excellent judgement of character[28] but there was an element of prejudice in his long memory of personal failings. He kept his distance from even his closest subordinates. He valued Heinrichs, Airo (the quartermaster-general) and Tuompo, although they felt his occasional displeasure as well as sometimes receiving charming demonstrations of his regard. Tuompo, after being invited to sauna with Mannerheim, noted: 'The Marshal was extremely courteous, as only he can be (when he is).'[29] On another occasion he wrote that Mannerheim's 'speech is outspoken and aggressive when he wants to "flog" someone'.[30] Headquarters staff in person and field commanders on the telephone could experience his sharpness; Talvela recorded in June – July 1944 how he 'abruptly demanded that I must do my duty' and was at times 'cool and irritable', 'snappy' and 'exasperated'.[31] Heinrichs was quick to observe Mannerheim's reaction to people and noted immediately that Mannerheim 'obviously liked Diet [German commander in Lapland from 1942 to 1944] – it showed in his eyes'.[32]

[26] Heinrichs, *Mannerheim Suomen kohtaloissa*, II, p. 314.
[27] On Heinrichs's view of Mannerheim see Turtola, *Erik Heinrichs*, pp. 167–80.
[28] Tuompo, *Päiväkirjani päämajasta*, p. 27.
[29] Ibid., p. 204.
[30] Ibid., p. 152.
[31] *Talvela, Sotilaan elämä*, II, p. 373, 400, 440, 451.
[32] Heinrichs, *Mannerheim Suomen kohtaloissa*, II, p. 301.

(*Above*) 18. The Continuation War. At Lipola on the Karelian isthmus, 8 October 1943. *Front* (*left to right*): President Ryti, Colonel Niilo Hersalo, Mannerheim, J.W. Rangell (prime minister) and General Walden (defence minister). (*Left*) 19. Seventy-fifth birthday, 4 June 1942: Mannerheim greeted by his old friend General Walden. On the right is General Heinrichs, chief of the general staff, and on the steps Lt.-Col. Ragnar Grönvall, senior ADC. (Both photos: SA-Kuva)

(*Right*) 20. Adolf Hitler invited himself at the last minute to Mannerheim's seventy-fifth birthday. Here the Marshal bids farewell to his guest. (SA-Kuva) (*Below*) 21. Mannerheim on a tour of inspection in Eastern Karelia in the summer of 1943. (Military Museum of Finland)

THE CONTINUATION WAR

Mannerheim was more relaxed with junior officers, soldiers and women of the Lotta Svärd auxiliary service; he found talking to them easy and they responded to his manner. In June 1942 Gripenberg accompanied him on a visit to his military tailor in Helsinki. A crowd gathered outside. 'Some young officers, one an invalid, had come into the entrance of the building to get a closer look at the legendary, popular and aloof Supreme Commander ... the officers stood rigidly at attention. The Marshal stopped, shook hands, and exchanged a few friendly words with the invalid and his comrades.'[33] Mannerheim was always concerned about the wounded. An officer in a front-line unit he visited near Poventsa in June 1942 was hit by a splinter from an anti-tank shell that exploded only 20 metres from them. Mannerheim, who was unhurt and had been unperturbed by the shelling, went to the dressing station to see how the officer was, and promoted him from captain to major.[34] His concern for Soviet prisoners-of-war, many of whom died from malnutrition, prompted him to arrange food parcels for them through the International Red Cross. He acknowledged and encouraged the role of industrial workers in the war effort by visits to factories and the award of medals.

Numerous soldiers and civilians wrote to him about their particular concerns. Mannerheim was 'almost touched'[35] by the suggestion of Ensign Toivo Jussila in 1942 that he might honour the mothers of Finland on Mother's Day by conferring on them collectively the Cross of Liberty as a mark of the country's and the army's thanks. He acknowledged this 'warm-hearted and fine proposal'[36] and carried it out on 10 May 1942 with a suitably-worded order of the day. In an imaginative gesture that originated with General Tuompo, each church in the country received the Cross and the accompanying order of the day. They are still to be seen.

Mannerheim's wish to reward bravery and exceptional merit, without regard to rank, had caused him in December 1940 to instigate the creation of two new classes in the Order of the Cross of Liberty: the Mannerheim Cross, 1st and 2nd class. These could be awarded irrespective of rank, and carried the title 'Knight of the Mannerheim Cross'. The Knights were carefully and sparingly

---

[33] Gripenberg, *Finland and the Great Powers*, p. 238.
[34] Paulaharju, 'Vierailu tulenjohtopaikalla', p. 295.
[35] Tuompo, *Päiväkirjani päämajasta*, p. 131.
[36] To Toivo Jussila, 22 January 1942. Mannerheim, *Brev*, p. 317.

appointed and the honour carried great prestige. On 7 July 1941, at the request of all the then holders of the Mannerheim Cross, President Ryti asked Mannerheim himself to accept both classes of the decoration in recognition of his unique qualities as commander-in-chief.

Further honour came to Mannerheim on the occasion of his seventy-fifth birthday on 4 June 1942. He had not wanted to celebrate the day. 'Merry-making at headquarters while men and officers are roughing it and sometimes seeing their comrades carried away would simply be an instance of bad taste.'[37] However, the president had other ideas and insisted on coming to greet Mannerheim accompanied by members of the government, the speaker and deputy speakers of parliament and a delegation of trade unionists. Mannerheim gave way on condition that all troops were given special rations accompanied by beer and a dram of spirits. What was to have been a lunch for some fifty guests in the president's train at a picturesque location beside Lake Saimaa (near the airfield at Immola) swelled to a major international occasion with over seventy guests when Hitler announced at the last minute that he would come in person to offer Mannerheim his congratulations. This was a remarkable gesture, and in Mannerheim's words the Führer 'won the liking of many through his simplicity and the natural manner which he displayed all the time'.[38] Finnish fears that Hitler's visit and Mannerheim's obligatory but reluctant return visit to Hitler at his headquarters in East Prussia three weeks later might have political or military implications proved groundless.

Mannerheim was greatly touched by the government's address and Ryti's speech. He told his sister 'how overwhelmed I was, and quite simply crushed by all the good will, appreciation and gratitude ... but of course it is an occasion when people are always prone to go to extremes when celebrating an anniversary, and perhaps more than usual if it is likely to be the last'.[39] A special mark of recognition was the conferment by the Council of State of the title and rank of Marshal of Finland – this time Mannerheim did not have to pay stamp duty. His birthday was also designated Defence Forces' Day, which it remains. Parliament decided to purchase for him the house he rented

---

[37] To Eva Sparre, 13 May 1942. Mannerheim, *Brev*, p. 318.
[38] To Eva Sparre, 25 July 1942. Mannerheim, *Brev*, p. 320.
[39] *Ibid.*

in Helsinki. In addition his National Fund was greatly increased by a new collection, strongly supported by industry and three large banks, amounting to nearly 18 million marks. Several towns, including Helsinki, named one of their principal thoroughfares after him. The anniversary was a highlight for the nation amid the grim reality of a protracted war, with its accompanying uncertainty, shortages and suffering. More than ever he stood out as a symbol of national unity and resolve: it was no wonder that he found the confidence placed in him personally and as a symbol so 'hard to bear'.[40]

HEALTH

For a man of his age, subject to the stress of high command, Mannerheim bore up very well. He normally worked twelve hours a day with only half an hour's rest after lunch in the unupholstered armchair in his modestly-furnished office in which maps showing the military situation were prominent. During crises he worked even longer hours.[41] His health, mental alertness and mood were regularly commented on by his staff and by visitors. In May 1942 G. A. Gripenberg 'found him calm, collected and kind, as always. He seemed to be in excellent health, his movements were quick and easy, he had a good complexion, and his somewhat nasal speech was just as clear and strong as ever.'[42] Talvela thought he looked 'worn out' at the end of Hitler's visit and he had a high temperature for a few days afterwards.[43] Mannerheim had a tendency to develop congestive lung infections, and usually suffered in winter from a bad bout of influenza, accompanied by a high temperature which was difficult to get down. He also had occasional painful attacks of gout and some dental trouble. Hardening of the arteries caused problems. Eczema on his hands was probably as much a reaction to stress as to their long-standing 'particular sensitivity to cold and on the whole to violent changes of temperature from warm to cold', as he wrote to his sister thanking her for some ointment.[44]

[40] Ibid., Mannerheim, Brev, p. 321.
[41] Paasonen, Marsalkan tiedustelupäällikkönä, pp. 114–15; Tanner, Suomen tie rauhaan, p. 14.
[42] Gripenberg, Finland and the Great Powers, p. 236.
[43] Talvela, Sotilaan elämä, II, p. 155.
[44] To Eva Sparre, [March 1944]. Mannerheim, Brev, p. 327.

In early April 1943 he had a dangerous stomach and lung infection which led to pneumonia and a temperature of 39.6°. Mannerheim thought he was going to die and wanted to change his will, but pulled through with the help of his doctor, Lauri Kalaja. With some difficulty, he was persuaded to go to Switzerland for three weeks' convalescence, and Heinrichs acted as commander-in-chief in his absence. The authorities were informed of Mannerheim's identity but he travelled incognito as Baron Marheim. Accompanied by Kalaja and an ADC, he flew via Berlin to Zürich. Talvela reported to him at an airfield near Berlin, and Kalaja told him that Mannerheim's condition was so weak that he had plied him with cognac throughout the flight and that the Marshal's display of bad temper to Talvela could be attributed to the amount of alcohol he had drunk.[45] From Zürich Mannerheim continued by train to Lugano. 'It was like a dream to find myself thirty hours after my departure from Helsinki in an earthly paradise with a display of flowers such as I had never set eyes on before and whose fragrance filled the air amidst cheerful and friendly people.'[46]

His convalescence did him good and his health was much better for several months after his return to Finland. The United States *chargé d'affaires*, who saw him in May 1943, commented on his 'vitality', while 'his mind was clear as a bell'.[47] However, Mannerheim was severely ill with a lung infection at the turn of 1943–4, and it was perhaps this illness which prompted him to send a third packet of papers to his sister-in-law in Sweden for safekeeping. These were papers 'which I could find useful if after the end of the war I hit on the bizarre idea of writing my memoirs ... Also I should be grateful if Palla, in case anything happens to me before the war comes to an end, will hand over all three packets to my daughters without ceremony.'[48] Despite Mannerheim's anxieties about his health, Tuompo thought in July 1944 that the Marshal was 'almost as before, only his back (perhaps) a little bent (sometimes).'[49] Gripenberg described how, in the difficult days of August 1944, Mannerheim, 'Tall, straight and

---

[45] Talvela, *Sotilaan elämä*, II, p. 244.
[46] To Eva Sparre, 3 June 1943. Mannerheim, *Brev*, p. 325.
[47] McClintock to Secretary of State, 11 May 1943, no. 664. *Foreign Relations of the United States, 1943*, III, p. 276.
[48] To Palaemona Mannerheim, 19 January 1944. Grensholm Collection, VAY 5632.
[49] Tuompo, *Päiväkirjani päämajasta*, p. 286.

THE CONTINUATION WAR

slender ... strode into the room; he had a healthy complexion, and his voice, as always, was clear and strong. He gave the impression of health, buoyancy and balance.'[50] However, Heinrichs recalled that the 'many boxes of pills' on the bookshelf in Mannerheim's office 'did not suggest health and balance'.[51]

Edwin Linkomies, who became prime minister in March 1943, commented later on the difficulty Mannerheim found in taking decisions but added: 'In spite of his age he had preserved a rare flexibility in his thinking.' Linkomies also acknowledged 'the feeling of security' he gained from 'the Marshal's long experience and unique statesmanship in our affairs'.[52] Heinrichs recorded that although Mannerheim readily interfered in details, 'at the same time his experienced eye watched the main lines. He constantly observed and kept a watchful eye on the political background and its fluctuations, which a commander-in-chief by no means always does and most professional soldiers only do rarely.'[53] The commander-in-chief was indeed a very politically-minded general. Though sometimes referred to by staff officers as 'the old man', Mannerheim was no elderly figurehead at GHQ. Even when weary of responsibility, he possessed the inner strength and determination to undertake his duties – in his own idiosyncratic and often inefficient way. He was in every respect the commander-in-chief.

ATTEMPTS TO LEAVE THE WAR

Apart from Soviet attacks south of the Svir, on the Masel'ga front and at Kestenga in April 1942, all of which were repulsed, the Finnish front was quiet throughout 1942 and 1943. Soviet forces nevertheless outnumbered the Finns whose casualties of over 7,000 killed and wounded in 1942 and over 3,500 in 1943 were a constant source of concern to Mannerheim. He was a humane commander. Casualties, which he was concerned to avoid where possible, often touched him personally and when he knew the family of a man who had been killed he sent a message of sympathy. His readiness to reduce the sentences given to soldiers who refused to obey orders was severely

---

[50] Gripenberg, *Finland and the Great Powers*, p. 341.
[51] Heinrichs, *Mannerheim Suomen kohtaloissa*, II, p. 398.
[52] Linkomies, *Vaikea aika*, p. 177.
[53] Heinrichs, *Mannerheim Suomen kohtaloissa*, II, p. 316.

criticized by Talvela in 1941.[54] Both the fear of losses and political considerations were arguments against further Finnish operations. In mid 1942 the Germans again pressed for a Finnish attack on the Murmansk railway, and in August Mannerheim hinted that he would agree to it but carefully laid down conditions, including the German capture of Leningrad, which were never fulfilled. The Germans abandoned the Murmansk railway plan in early September.

Mannerheim could genuinely plead lack of troops for the operation. General Heinrichs, who returned to GHQ as chief of the general staff in January 1942, noted that during the war's defensive phase Mannerheim's efforts were directed particularly towards strengthening the front on the three isthmuses and to creating the commander-in-chief's reserve.[55] The reduction in the army's size, made necessary by the demands of the home front, meant that only a few formations could be placed at the commander-in-chief's disposal and even their availability was largely at the expense of troops at the front. The decision to reduce divisions from three to two regiments proved tactically wrong. The construction of fortified rear positions on each of the three isthmuses was ordered in early 1942 but serious work on them began only at the beginning of 1943. The front-line defences lacked depth and the rear positions were too far in the rear to create an effective defensive zone.

Although some new equipment was brought into use and an armoured division created, the long period of static warfare was marked by a decline in the army's standard of training and fighting capability. Erfurth thought at the end of 1943 that 'the war of position has assumed such a dead character that one can scarcely call it war'.[56] Mannerheim acknowledged in his *Memoirs*: 'Our men had to some extent lost the habit of war.'[57] He had tried to counter this: for example, in his order of 17 April 1944 he drew the attention of commanders to the danger of a weakening of the fighting spirit inherent in a war of position, and urged them to keep troops healthily active and not to leave them a long time in the same sector.[58] Nevertheless, a certain slackness set in at the front. In the early summer of 1944 Colonel

---

[54] Talvela, *Sotilaan elämä*, II, p. 76.
[55] Heinrichs, *Mannerheim Suomen kohtaloissa*, II, p. 309.
[56] Erfurth, *Krigsdagbok*, p. 39.
[57] Mannerheim, *Memoirs*, p. 489.
[58] Cited in *Kansakunta sodassa*, 2, p. 38.

Valo Nihtilä from the operations section of GHQ found in the sector of one division 'about a thousand men, but not one of them working, instead they were sunbathing everywhere.'[59]
Few war games or field exercises were arranged to prepare officers for operational contingencies.[60] Little heed was paid to German experiences of Soviet operations at a time when the Soviet armed forces had been radically reformed and restructured although Mannerheim had listened attentively to a lecture at Finnish GHQ in January 1944 by a German colonel about Soviet offensive tactics and subsequently ordered Öhquist and another general to attend a repeat of it.[61] There were failures in command and Mannerheim undoubtedly bore ultimate responsibility for the decline in the army's condition.

President Ryti's term of office (in fact the end of Kallio's mandate) ran out early in 1943. There was a move by politicians from the Agrarian and Swedish People's Parties and some conservatives to elect Mannerheim as president. This was thought likely to improve Finland's relations with the western allies and the possibility of peace. He was acceptable to both supporters and opponents of peace. Niukkanen noted that the Marshal was 'greatly interested in the office of president',[62] but he only agreed to be a candidate if soundings showed that his election was assured by a large majority. That could not be guaranteed; the social democrats were against the union in one man of civil and military authority and some still thought him unsuitable. Therefore he refused to allow his name to go forward, and Ryti was reelected on 15 February 1943 by an overwhelming majority. A new coalition government was formed soon afterwards under the conservative Edwin Linkomies. The foreign minister was Henrik Ramsay, with whom Mannerheim got on well, and who kept him informed of foreign policy developments. The pro-German Witting, for whom Mannerheim had not a good word, was dropped. Walden remained as defence minister. The war cabinet aimed to extricate Finland from the war but proceeded cautiously. This was an advance on the failure of Witting and Ryti in the autumn of 1942 to follow up an indirect approach by a Soviet diplomat

---

[59] Kilkki, *Valo Nihtilä*, p. 120.
[60] Paasonen, *Marsalkan tiedustelupäällikkönä*, pp. 119–20 says none were arranged but Seppälä, *Karl Lennart Oesch*, p. 148, mentions a war game in February–March 1944 ordered by GHQ.
[61] Erfurth, *Krigsdagbok*, p. 45.
[62] Sorvali, *Niukkasesta Kekkoseen*, p. 162.

in Stockholm about the possibility of peace. Neither Walden nor Mannerheim had been informed of this approach, to their intense annoyance.

Making peace presented serious difficulties. What terms would the Soviet Union offer? How acceptable would they be to parliament and people? How would Germany react? There was a general reluctance in Finland to consider peace on any basis other than the 1939 frontiers, although the war cabinet was prepared to negotiate on the frontier question. However, even Mannerheim, who was anxious not to reject an opportunity for peace, commented in August 1943. 'It is tragic that an army which has won such victories should be forced to give up all or nearly all of what it has won.'[63] Germany's reaction would be crucial. Quite apart from Finland's dependence on Germany for grain and as a trading partner, there was the acute risk of military action against Finland by German forces in Lapland and the Baltic region because a Finnish peace would cause a dangerous gap in the eastern front.

The German surrender at Stalingrad in February 1943 and defeat at Kursk in August 1943 were clear indications that Germany had been, at best, forced strategically on to the defensive. Finland's defensive position worsened appreciably when German troops were forced back from Leningrad to Narva in January 1944: the blockade of Leningrad had already been lifted a year earlier, and by early 1944 the tide had clearly turned in favour of the Red Army. A 'peace party' in Finland began to grow, and Mannerheim had contacts with it for almost the entire war and 'listened sincerely' to its opinions, as one of them subsequently recorded.[64] When Paasikivi, who had excellent contacts with politicians of the 'peace party', remarked to Mannerheim in September 1943 'We must get out of this war', the Marshal replied: 'I have thought about that for months, but have not found a way.'[65] Indeed, the briefing and discussion he had arranged for the president and war cabinet on 3 February 1943 marked, in Tanner's words, 'an important turning point' towards peace.[66]

Peace feelers early in 1943 came to nothing. Towards the end of March 1943 the Finnish government accepted an offer by the United

---

[63] Gripenberg, *Finland and the Great Powers*, p. 273.
[64] Wirtanen, *Poliittiset muistelmat*, p. 103.
[65] Paasikivi *Jatkosodan päiväkirjat*, p. 289.
[66] Tanner, *Suomen tie rauhaan*, p. 17.

States of its good offices for bringing about peace between Finland and the Soviet Union. Concern to act correctly towards the Germans caused the war cabinet to decide to send Ramsay to Berlin to inform Ribbentrop of Finland's desire for peace; this provoked anger in Germany, and a demand for Finland to conclude an alliance with Germany which would exclude the possibility of a separate peace. Finland managed to resist this demand although relations with Germany worsened, affecting trade. No progress was made as the result of the American initiative because the United States provided no information about Soviet peace terms. Mannerheim, who had been involved in the war cabinet's discussions, had supported sending Ramsay to Berlin although he later wrote in his *Memoirs* that he thought the move 'inadvisable'.[67] Like Ryti and the government, he strongly opposed a treaty with Germany which would remove Finland's freedom of action.

Although he expected to be consulted, Mannerheim took the view that peace was a matter for decision by the politicians and not by him. In August 1943 he told Gripenberg, whom he had been pleased to see appointed to the key post of Finnish minister in Stockholm: 'The political leaders ought naturally to request Supreme Headquarters' views on the military situation, but then they should draw their own conclusions.' Gripenberg noted this reiteration of Mannerheim's 'firm resolve ... not to get involved in political decision-making'.[68] Even his orders of the day kept strictly to military matters. Linkomies acknowledged that Mannerheim wanted to avoid giving his opinion officially on political matters but added: 'His word was often of decisive significance.'[69]

In the summer of 1943, following contacts in Stockholm between a Soviet diplomat and the Belgian minister, further peace soundings took place but they proved unfruitful because of the Soviet demand for the 1940 frontiers. By the autumn, despite his cautious determination to support peace attempts, Mannerheim was becoming worried about the conduct of Finnish foreign policy, which he considered unnecessarily irritating to the great powers. He was also anxious about the effect on the army's morale of uninformed public speculation about the possibility of peace, and tried to dampen it down. Any

---

[67] Tanner, *Suomen tie rauhaan*, p. 53; Mannerheim, *Memoirs*, p. 463.
[68] Gripenberg, *Finland and the Great Powers*, p. 273.
[69] Linkomies, *Vaikea aika*, pp. 313–14.

chance of peace seemingly disappeared in early November 1943 with the apparent Allied demand that Finland, like Germany and its allies, should surrender unconditionally: that was totally unacceptable to Finland. However, later in November Mme Kollontai, the Soviet minister in Stockholm, informed the secretary-general of the Swedish foreign ministry that the Soviet Union was willing to receive a Finnish peace delegation; in Stalin's view, she said, it was important that Mannerheim should back the peace to ensure that its conditions would be fulfilled. The Finnish government wanted to continue the peace contacts that had opened up through Sweden but unwillingness to surrender Viipuri brought progress to a halt at the beginning of 1944. Mannerheim, with an eye to the Soviet Union's sensitivity to its prestige as a great power, had played a part in formulating a more moderate reply to the Soviet Union than the government had originally drafted.

At the end of January 1944 the United States publicly urged Finland to begin peace negotiations. In consequence Ryti arranged a meeting with Mannerheim on 8 February to discover his opinion of the general situation. Both men acknowledged that Finland would have to make peace on the basis of the 1940 frontiers – Mannerheim believed that nothing better could be expected. He also said that the army would not be able to hold out for long if subjected to a major Soviet offensive. Peace would then have to be made quickly. To find out the Soviet conditions for peace, the war cabinet sent Paasikivi to Stockholm in mid February for discussions with Mme Kollontai. Soviet peace terms included the internment of German troops in Finland, a return to the 1940 frontiers and discussion of reparations.

Linkomies was convinced that the only way the country and the armed forces would accept such harsh conditions was if Mannerheim took responsibility for them. He wanted the Marshal to become prime minister and then, after Ryti's immediate resignation, president. Tanner opposed the concentration of power in Mannerheim as undemocratic, but in any case nothing came of the scheme because Mannerheim rejected it, pleading that he had enough burdens as commander-in-chief. However, he was increasingly aware that he was regarded as the man who could get Finland out of the war and make the people accept the inevitably hard conditions that peace would involve. Paasikivi wrote to him on 4 March 1944 urging him to inform members of parliament of the danger of Finland's situation:

'The only man whom the Finnish people trusts is you.'[70] Nevertheless, Mannerheim remained unwilling to intervene directly in political matters since he believed that it would diminish his influence in the army. Some months of crisis passed before he could be persuaded to accept the presidency.

The government sent Paasikivi and Carl Enckell, a former foreign minister, to Moscow on 26 March to learn more details of the Soviet peace terms. Mannerheim had been asked beforehand for his opinion of the military situation and given it in what Tanner, with some frustration, described as an 'oracular statement': 'If the Soviet Union is able and willing to drive into Finland, it is also capable of doing so.'[71] Paasikivi and Enckell returned on 1 April. The government was horrified by the demands for massive reparations (to the value of 600 million US dollars), rapid internment of German troops and speedy demobilization of the Finnish army. Mannerheim was alarmed at the need to demobilize while the European war continued. He also believed the internment timetable to be impossible but was not prepared to sacrifice the possibility of peace because of that condition. He was prepared, if necessary, to fight the Germans. However, it was above all the reparations which caused the government to reject the Soviet terms, which it did, with the support of parliament, on 15 April. The failure of the peace talks was made public by both Finland and the Soviet Union, and in retaliation Hitler stopped arms and food exports to Finland. In May Mannerheim attempted in vain to assure Hitler that German weapons would not fall into the wrong hands, but the embargo remained.

NEAR DISASTER

After the collapse of the peace negotiations Mannerheim called his front-line commanders to Mikkeli and warned the army to expect Soviet action. He also ordered defensive positions to be improved.[72] On the Karelian isthmus, in addition to the main position which was well forward (its strength was seriously overestimated), there was a prepared position further back between Vammelsuu and Taipale (the 'VT position') and even further in the rear a position was under con-

[70] Paasikivi, *Jatkosodan päiväkirjat*, p. 347.
[71] Tanner, *Suomen tie rauhaan*, p. 207.
[72] Turtola, *Aksel Fredrik Airo*, p. 277.

struction between Viipuri, Kuparsaari and Taipale (the VKT position'). Airo and Tuompo commented on 17 May on Mannerheim's 'pessimism and excessive caution. He is sure that the Russians will attack and reserves and other troops have been moved round quite a lot.'[73]

With justice, Mannerheim has been severely criticized for not concentrating sufficient troops on the Karelian isthmus, the area which proved in the summer of 1944, as in December 1939, to be the main point of the Soviet offensive. Unquestionably his determination to hold Eastern Karelia as a buffer zone and as a possible bargaining counter in peace negotiations influenced his dispositions. Holding Eastern Karelia required troops, even if the six divisions and two brigades in the front line there held sectors twice as long as those of the three divisions and one brigade in the front line on the Karelian isthmus. Nevertheless, 3 Division was ordered to move from Eastern Karelia to the Karelian isthmus to add to the Armoured Division and the Cavalry Brigade which had earlier been placed there as reserves. Despite Mannerheim's warnings of an attack, when none came in April or May the army returned to what has fairly been described as a mood of 'semi war'.[74]

Preparations for the Soviet offensive in June 1944 were carefully concealed, but Finnish intelligence did obtain information of the enemy build-up though not of the timing of the attack, and General Heinrichs blamed the failure to act on the information received at Finnish GHQ on Mannerheim. According to him, this information had all been available to Mannerheim but his defective system of command prevented the various threads from being drawn together and the Marshal from coming to the right conclusion: 'The trees hid the wood from the old observer, who wanted to see everything himself.'[75] The result was that when the offensive began not only were there fewer Finnish troops on the Karelian isthmus than there could have been, but also that the Red Army achieved tactical surprise.

Of course, troop dispositions were not everything. General Talvela thought that the long period of static warfare and the extraordinarily powerful enemy firepower were what caused the bad fighting morale

---

[73] Tuompo, *Päiväkirjani päämajasta*, p. 266.
[74] Turtola, *Risto Ryti*, p. 289.
[75] Turtola, *Erik Heinrichs*, pp. 176, 179.

THE CONTINUATION WAR

of the Finnish troops when the Soviet offensive began.[76] General Oesch reasonably argued: 'The long war had obviously caused mental tiredness ... The orders and directives of the higher authorities no longer managed to restore alertness.'[77] However, this problem, just like the failure to take more action in anticipation of the Soviet offensive on the Karelian isthmus, leads back to Mannerheim as commander-in-chief. His own genuine and well-founded anxieties did not translate into effective action. He did not succeed in maintaining the army at the necessary level of efficiency and preparedness.

In all, the Soviets concentrated against the Finns 450,000 men and over half of the Red Army's artillery. On the Karelian isthmus, where the aim was to capture Viipuri, there were two Soviet armies comprising 300,000 men. Their offensive began on 9 June 1944, with a bombardment that could be heard as far away as Mikkeli and Helsinki, and probing attacks so strong that the Finns mistook them for the main thrust. This followed on 10 June at Valkeasaari where Soviet superiority of twenty to one in firepower and six to one in men forced a breakthrough. There followed a rapid Finnish retreat first to the VT line and then, after a further Soviet breakthrough at Kuuterselkä on 14 June, to the VKT position between 19 and 20 June. Finnish casualties were heavy and although no formations were lost there were alarming instances of panic. Between 12 and 16 June Mannerheim ordered the transfer of more and more formations from Eastern Karelia; these were thrown into the battle as they arrived, their journey luckily unimpeded by enemy action. His direct command of the two corps on the isthmus proved unsustainable and on 14 June he transferred it to Lieutenant-General Oesch. This proved an excellent appointment. On 15 June the Marshal was pessimistic about the situation and believed that the Finnish army was beaten; he still thought the situation grave on 17 June but was more optimistic the next day.[78] However, Viipuri fell on 20 June, and this came as a major blow to morale in Finland. The situation on the Karelian isthmus nevertheless stabilized as the Soviet offensive paused.

The transfer of troops from Eastern Karelia to the Karelian isthmus compelled Mannerheim on 16 June to order withdrawal from that area. This began between 17 and 19 June before the Soviet offensive

[76] Talvela, *Sotilaan elämä*, II, pp. 352–3.
[77] Oesch, *Suomen kohtalon ratkaisu*, p. 126.
[78] Tanner, *Suomen tie rauhaan*, pp. 262, 269, 273.

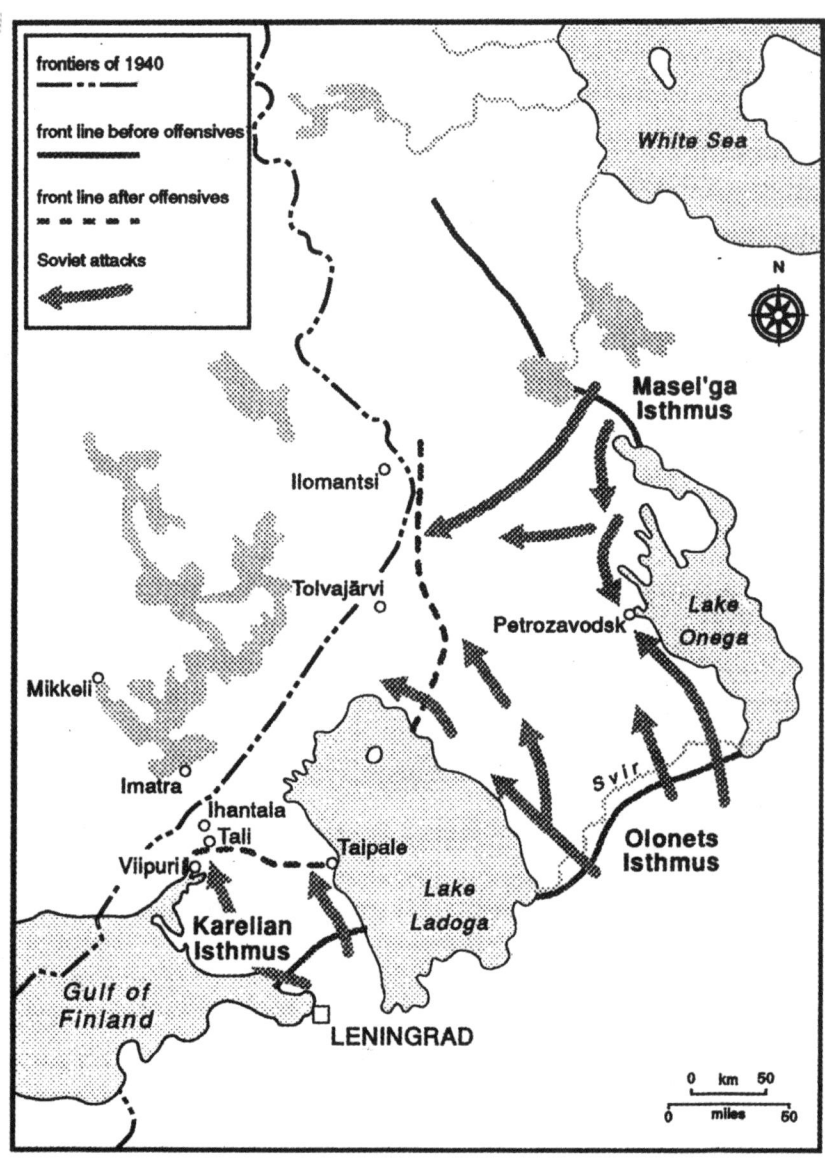

The Soviet offensives, June 1944

THE CONTINUATION WAR

there started on 20 June. Despite difficulties, the Finns withdrew successfully to the 1939 frontier, where their resistance stiffened. Eastern Karelia in the end proved useless as a bargaining counter in peace negotiations.

The urgent need to stop Finland from being defeated in the field made German assistance one of Mannerheim's immediate concerns. Hitler lifted the arms embargo on 12 June and grain shipments were also resumed. Mannerheim's request for air support led to the arrival of seventy German dive-bombers and fighter bombers. The Germans also sent numerous hand-held anti-tank rocket weapons which – with some already in Finland but inexplicably not yet issued to the troops – contributed greatly to strengthening the Finns' hitherto weak anti-tank defence and helped raise the troops' morale. Mannerheim's view of the situation was so pessimistic that he also wanted German troops and secured Ryti's permission to request as many as six divisions. On 20 June the Germans agreed to help but sent only a battalion-strength unit of self-propelled assault guns (Sturmgeschütz-Brigade 303) and one infantry division, the latter for only a short time.

Ryti's reaction to the Soviet offensive was to consider a change of government to facilitate the reopening of peace talks. He offered Mannerheim the post of prime minister on 14 June but the Marshal, completely occupied with the military situation, refused, stating that he was a soldier not a politician. Tanner and Ramsay then proposed to Ryti that he should be replaced as president by Mannerheim, thus uniting civil and military authority at a time of crisis. Ryti travelled to GHQ on 16 June to offer the presidency to Mannerheim but he again met with a refusal. Mannerheim did, however, want a new government. Ramsay agreed to form a government but on 20 June Mannerheim turned against the idea. He now wanted to take advantage of the improving military situation as the army's resistance increased. Two days later, when the chance of peace talks opened up through Stockholm, he again favoured the formation of a new government but evidence of Soviet opposition to Ramsay as premier put a final end to the attempt. News on 23 June that the Soviet Union required the surrender of Finland finally ruled out the pursuit of peace talks.

Matters were complicated further when Ribbentrop arrived in Helsinki on 22 June seeking to exploit Finland's plight in order to extract a formal public commitment to Germany as the price of military aid. Faced with the stark choice between surrender to the Soviet Union or a commitment to Germany, which would help ensure effective military resistance, Mannerheim strongly backed the commitment to Germany. Discussions with Ribbentrop on the form of that commitment took place against the renewal of the Soviet offensive east of Viipuri on 21 June. This caused Mannerheim to intensify his pressure on Ryti and the government to conclude an agreement. Finally, on 26 June, Ryti signed a personal commitment to Hitler that neither he nor any government he had appointed would start peace negotiations with the Soviet Union except with Germany's agreement. Mannerheim subsequently recorded his regard for Ryti's action as a 'meritorious civic act'.[79] However, it almost caused the social democrats to leave the government. It made the United States break off diplomatic relations and it upset the Swedes. Still, Mannerheim and the war cabinet had succeeded in their intention to make the commitment to Germany in the Ryti-Ribbentrop agreement as loose as possible; in their opinion, Ryti's departure from office would make it invalid. Ryti's days as president were thereby numbered since the war cabinet continued to aim to make peace with the Soviet Union as soon as the military situation and Soviet terms permitted.

At first the military situation looked very threatening. The new Soviet offensive intended to advance first to the line Virojoki – Lappeenranta – Imatra, then to Kouvola – Kotka, and finally to halt on the eastern bank of the river Kymi. After penetrating the Finnish front at Tali, the Soviet assault force of some twelve divisions was halted at Ihantala by five Finnish divisions, with strong artillery support, in the biggest battle fought in northern Europe. The battle of Tali-Ihantala between 25 June and 10 July was a decisive defensive victory for the Finns – with some German support – and after attacks on the Vuoksi and in Viipuri bay had also failed, the Soviet high command acknowledged failure even to reach the first of its objectives. On 12 July 1944 the offensive was abandoned and the assault forces were moved away to be used against the Germans on what was the main Soviet front. Having failed to defeat Finland, the Soviet leadership was now prepared for a peace settlement which, because troops were not available, would not involve the occupation of the

[79] Mannerheim, *Memoirs*, p. 483.

THE CONTINUATION WAR

country. The Finnish army was back approximately on the 1940 frontier but it was intact and fighting well – even attacking and destroying two Soviet divisions at Ilomantsi in August 1944. Above all, the Finnish army was undefeated. It had been a near thing but, as Mannerheim wrote, 'The armed forces did not fail. They provided diplomacy with its opportunity.'[80]

The commander-in-chief, too, had not failed. Tuompo described him on 18 June as 'calm but very serious'. Only on 25 June, after many days of exceptionally long working hours, did he note that Mannerheim looked tired.[81] Erfurth commented on 10 July that Mannerheim 'had discharged his command steadfastly and vigorously and intervened strongly when it seemed necessary to him. (Example: the relief of one commanding general, two divisional commanders and the commander of the cavalry brigade). Even if the Marshal has noticeably aged during the last four weeks, he takes his supreme command at all events with the highest degree of seriousness.'[82] Heinrichs, who was closer to Mannerheim during those testing days, noted his weariness and his 'care-worn features'.[83] Despite his age, Mannerheim had endured both Soviet military and Finnish political pressure – the former with perhaps greater equilibrium than the latter. With the end of the Soviet offensive the pressure on Mannerheim to become president in order to lead his country towards peace would become irresistible.

---

[80] *Ibid.*, p. 490.
[81] Tuompo, *Päiväkirjani päämajasta*, pp. 269, 276.
[82] Erfurth, *Krigsdagbok*, p. 229.
[83] Heinrichs, *Mannerheim Suomen kohtaloissa*, II, p. 371.

CHAPTER VIII

PRESIDENT

'Trusting in the Almighty, I hope and I believe that, supported by parliament and government, with a united nation behind us, we will succeed in safeguarding our independence and our national existence.'[1]

PRESIDENT FOR PEACE

In early July 1944 the Finnish leadership learned indirectly that the Soviet Union was willing to discuss peace with a new Finnish government that excluded Ryti and Tanner and that had taken the initiative to open negotiations. The demand for unconditional surrender was dropped. A change of government was thus essential to meet the Soviet precondition for negotiations, and Ryti's resignation was in any case needed to free Finland from the undertaking he had given Hitler not to make a separate peace without German consent. Finland now had the opportunity to make peace, helped by the stability of the front and the deteriorating position of the Germans in the Baltic which reduced the possibility that they would intervene militarily if Finland left the war. Tanner was somewhat surprised that Mannerheim – who had been waiting for this opportunity – agreed with him on 22 July, albeit cautiously, that peace was now essential. Mannerheim also made plain to the politicians that a renewed Soviet offensive could not be stopped.

Both Linkomies and Tanner recognized the need for a change of government. Tanner, who by now had accepted that Mannerheim's authority was required to extricate Finland from the war, tried to persuade him to become prime minister but the Marshal prudently refused on the grounds that he was too old and unacquainted with the technique of government. Linkomies wanted him to become president. Walden had been working on him to become head of state as regent and by 26 July thought that he could be persuaded to agree.

[1] Speech to Parliament, 4 August 1944. *Suomen presidentit puhuvat*, p. 89.

PRESIDENT

Mannerheim's concern was that matters should be done in the proper order; Ryti should resign before he could give his answer. Ryti was not prepared to resign until he knew that Mannerheim was prepared to take over as head of state. Linkomies, Tanner and Walden nevertheless worked out a timetable according to which Ryti would resign on 31 July and a law electing Mannerheim regent would be passed by parliament the next day. The title of regent was considered appropriate as emphasizing the exceptional character of his election. In the evening of 28 July Ryti and Tanner discussed the matter with him at GHQ. Mannerheim wanted to be certain of his election by parliament and Tanner was able to give him that assurance; Tanner then arranged a 'gentlemen's agreement' (he used the English term) between Ryti and Mannerheim whereby Ryti stated that he would resign and Mannerheim promised to become head of state as regent.

On 29 July Ryti submitted his resignation, giving as his reasons both the need to concentrate civil and military authority in one person at a critical moment and the state of his health. In the midst of the government's discussion on 31 July of the consequences of Ryti's resignation, Mannerheim telephoned Linkomies to say that he now preferred to be elected president to avoid any misconceptions about his assumption of the office. The Council of State formally accepted Ryti's resignation on 1 August and approved a draft law appointing Mannerheim president for the normal period of six years. A period of two or four years had been originally suggested but Mannerheim wanted the normal period – although he did not expect to hold office that long – to mitigate the exceptional character of his election. The law passed rapidly through parliament – unanimously at its third reading – and was confirmed on 4 August. That afternoon Mannerheim attended parliament and took the oath of office. An old monarchist, he was now president of the republic as well as commander-in-chief.

To some extent Mannerheim's election as president in 1944, which signalled the inability of Finland's politicians (those who had not been ruled out by the Soviet Union) to lead the country towards peace, represented a compensation for his defeat in the presidential election of twenty-five years before but the circumstances were totally different. In 1919 he had been in the prime of life and eager for office; in 1944 he accepted the presidency out of a sense of duty and with a heavy heart. 'Ill as I was, and worn out by the burden and heavy responsibility I had carried for so many years, it was with great reluctance that I accepted a new responsible task, and I did so only after members of the government and other prominent politicians had repeatedly appealed to me.'[2]

During the discussions leading up to his resignation, Ryti had sharply criticized Mannerheim as being 'at such an age that his moods changed from day to day and this caused his sudden changes of opinion. Mannerheim thinks too much of his own obituary and of the light in which he will appear to posterity.'[3] But the new president's conduct during his first months in office did not justify Ryti's harsh words. Gripenberg described him on 20 August. 'He is in excellent condition; not for a long time, perhaps a year, have I seen him so vigorous, healthy, active and energetic as now. He has acquired just as strong a grip on political questions as he has in the military field; he has thought about these problems a long time, he is familiar with the details. His memory is just as good as ever; he is precise, observant, and in fighting trim ... He dominates the political scene and ... is his own prime minister and foreign minister. But of course he keeps his own counsel.'[4] This was the view of a friend.

Walden, another friend, commented to Gripenberg: 'Yes, now we have again a real man in charge of things, who in every sense of the word resolutely symbolizes our country's will to independence.'[5] Mannerheim's acceptability to all shades of opinion in parliament and among the people testified to his position as a trusted national leader at that moment. Opponents of the war, the so-called 'peace opposition', looked to him to extricate Finland from the war while the right and the army believed he would ensure that peace was made on acceptable terms. Mannerheim's election as president raised national morale as it was generally recognized that he would end the war. Since June 1944 there had been widespread popular recognition of the inevitability of peace on hard terms.

The harsh political reality of the presidency became clear to Mannerheim immediately when he had great difficulty in appointing a new government in place of that led by Linkomies which had resigned. Nobody wanted to be prime minister, prompting Mannerheim to threaten to resign since no one was willing to help him. Eventually

---

[2] Mannerheim, *Memoirs*, p. 491.
[3] Tanner, *Suomen tie rauhaan*, p. 331.
[4] Gripenberg, *Finland and the Great Powers*, p. 346.
[5] *Ibid.*

PRESIDENT

Antti Hackzell, a conservative, agreed to form a government and Carl Enckell became foreign minister. To their dismay, no leaders of the 'peace opposition' were included in the new government. Tanner was left out. While Gripenberg should not be taken literally in saying that Mannerheim was his own prime minister and foreign minister, the burden of responsibility fell on the president since Hackzell and Enckell took no initiatives themselves, believing that 'Mannerheim will naturally find the right way'.[6]

At first Mannerheim moved slowly, causing the keen advocates of peace to doubt his willingness to act, and national morale to weaken because there was no news of peace. Mannerheim was worried about making the break with the Germans. On 17 August Field Marshal Keitel came on a visit to congratulate him on the presidency and Mannerheim took the opportunity to inform him that Finland was no longer bound by Ryti's undertaking to Hitler. He then waited for possible German reprisals, but none came and supplies of grain and munitions continued up to the beginning of September. The first weeks of Mannerheim's presidency were also used to establish that Sweden would be willing to provide a supply of grain for six months if Finland broke off its relations with Germany. Finally, at a meeting with Hackzell, Walden, Tanner and Gripenberg in his train to the east of Helsinki in the evening of 24 August, Mannerheim decided to approach the Soviet Union about peace. When the tension died down, 'The Marshal insisted that we all take a glass of his good whisky and smoke one of his strong Havana cigars.'[7] Next day Gripenberg flew to Stockholm with a letter from Enckell to Mme Kollontai, who was to be contacted through the Swedish foreign ministry. Events then moved very fast.

The Finnish government received the Soviet preconditions for peace negotiations on 29 August. Relations with Germany had to be broken off before a delegation could be received in Moscow. German troops who had not left Finland by 15 September must be disarmed and taken prisoner. In the evening of 30 August Mannerheim summoned a council at the presidential official residence of Tamminiemi outside Helsinki, which in addition to members of the government –

[6] Gripenberg's diary, 12 August 1944, cited by Jägerskiöld, *Från krig till fred*, p. 30.
[7] Gripenberg, *Finland and the Great Powers*, p. 347. The American translator wrote 'whiskey' but in his diary Gripenberg used 'whisky'. Cited by Jägerskiöld, *Från krig till fred*, p. 40. Mannerheim was evidently a drinker of Scotch.

Hackzell, Enckell and Walden – also consisted of Ryti, Linkomies, Tanner and General Heinrichs, chief of the general staff. Grave doubts were expressed about taking what Mannerheim described as 'a leap into the unknown',[8] and particularly over what would be the reaction of the Germans to the demand to remove their troops (there were 220,000 in Lapland) and over putting the country at the mercy of the Soviet Union after a breach with Germany, but no other way seemed possible.

In an attempt to overcome the problems with the Germans, Mannerheim on his own initiative proposed to Stalin via Sweden on 1 September that a truce should come into effect before the peace negotiations began. Finland could take care of the Germans south of a line between the river Oulu and Sotkamo and could defend that line against attack from the north provided troops were released from elsewhere, by which he meant the Soviet front. He also proposed the withdrawal of Finnish troops behind the 1940 frontier after the truce had come into effect. Finland could meet the Soviet preconditions if a speedy end to hostilities were agreed. News of the Soviet acceptance of this proposal was received late on 3 September. Before that the Soviet Union had hastened a Finnish decision by imposing the evening of 2 September as their deadline for the acceptance of its preconditions. Mannerheim took the leap into the unknown. On 2 September a hastily-summoned parliament approved acceptance of the Soviet preconditions, some of the doubters swayed by the prime minister's reference to the opinion of the supreme military command (in other words Mannerheim) that to continue the war would result in final defeat and bring about the destruction of the nation. Hackzell broadcast to the nation the decision that peace negotiations were to begin. He omitted to mention the breach of relations with Germany, as required by the Soviet Union, and in consequence the truce was begun by the Finns on 4 September while the Soviet Union continued hostilities for another twenty-four hours.

Also on 2 September, Enckell announced the breach of relations with Germany to the German minister in Helsinki. The reaction was bitter but the minister knew that with the popular and authoritative Mannerheim as president there was no hope of finding and installing a pro-German régime. Anxious to be correct in his relations with Germany, Mannerheim wrote to Hitler on 2 September setting out

---

[8] Tanner, *Suomen tie rauhaan*, p. 371.

PRESIDENT

the reasons of national self-preservation which lay behind Finland's decision to make peace. On 4 September he gave a farewell lunch for General Erfurth, the German liaison officer at his headquarters. The two men had a great respect for each other, and their parting was difficult. Left to them, the break in relations would be handled as tactfully as possible.

Finland's peace delegation left for Moscow on 7 September, crossing the front line near Ihantala and then continuing by air. The delegation comprised Hackzell, Walden, Heinrichs and Lieutenant-General Oscar Enckell together with four experts. Mannerheim had opposed Paasikivi's inclusion, fearing that he would be too prone to make concessions. The delegation was kept waiting in Moscow for a week and Hackzell had a stroke just before the first meeting on 14 September. The draft armistice terms presented to the Finns by Molotov in threatening terms included the nasty surprise of the lease of a base at Porkkala, much nearer to Helsinki than Hanko which had been leased to the Soviet Union in the 1940 peace treaty. The other terms were similar to those presented in the spring of 1944 – the 1940 frontiers but without Petsamo – though the reparations were halved to 300 million US dollars. The Germans were to be disarmed and the Finnish army rapidly demobilized. 'Hitlerite' (fascist) organizations were to be disbanded, war criminals put on trial and politically discriminatory (i.e. anti-communist) laws rescinded. An Allied Control Commission was to oversee the implementation of the armistice.

News of the terms were received by Mannerheim and the government with horror. Mannerheim told Tanner on 18 September that militarily they were frightful. Finland could now hardly avoid bolshevization. On the other hand, further military resistance would need a miracle which was not to be expected. Acceptance was inevitable. Carl Enckell, who was sent to take charge of the delegation (Ramsay refused to go), was given no chance for proper negotiations. The terms were dictated by the Soviet Union in agreement with Britain. Molotov even referred to the 'bloody and criminal' Finnish government.[9] Parliament was informed of the terms on 18 September and accepted them the following day. Enckell, faced with a Soviet ultimatum, had already signed the agreement on 19 September 1944 before receiving authorization from Helsinki.

[9] Polvinen, *Between East and West*, p. 35.

Colonel-General A. A. Zhdanov, notorious in Finland as the sovietizer of Estonia, signed on behalf of the Allies. The war against the Soviet Union had ended in terrible defeat. Moreover, a new war had already begun against the Germans, who had attacked Finnish troops on Suursaari in the Gulf of Finland on 15 September.

How deeply Mannerheim felt about Finland's situation was revealed in different ways to his niece on 19 September and to Paasikivi on 6 October. Mannerheim invited his niece Evo Weckman, his brother Johan's eldest daughter, to lunch at Tamminiemi on 19 September. She remarked on the beauty of the view. 'Yes, our country is beautiful, said the Marshal – the words came slowly and quietly, like a reflection – and our people are a good people. A good people whom I can no longer help ... And all the white crosses ... His otherwise so self-controlled voice broke and tears glistened in his strained eyes. He made no attempt to hide them.'[10] The personal responsibility for defeat was hard to bear.

Paasikivi was invited, with Walden, to dinner with Mannerheim at Tamminiemi on 6 October, and recorded that Mannerheim had said: 'The armistice is hard, we are in the hands of the Russians. The agreement does not speak of a capitulation but in truth the armistice is a capitulation. We cannot defend ourselves.' He even spoke of resigning as president but Paasikivi said that it was impossible. As Mannerheim acknowledged, 'We must carry out the armistice agreement exactly. That is the inevitable precondition so that we can in general think of life.'[11] He had spoken to his niece with the human voice of emotion, but to Paasikivi with the statesman's voice of realism.

UNDER THE CONTROL COMMISSION

The Soviet grip on Finland was felt even before the Control Commission arrived in Helsinki on 5 October. The Finnish delegation in Moscow had been asked searching questions about the progress of the internment of German troops in Finland, to which the Soviet Union attached great importance. Already at the beginning of September Mannerheim had taken precautions by arranging for the movement of Finnish formations northwards and later by evacuating

---

[10] Mannerheim-Weckman, *Laivalamppu ja muuta muistelua*, p. 176.
[11] Paasikivi, *Päiväkirjat 1944–1956*, I, col. 50.

Finnish civilians from Lapland to Sweden, but hopes remained of avoiding hostilities. Mannerheim's desire to move troops to Kemi and Tornio prompted a sharp exchange with Airo who was planning with the Germans what were called 'autumn manoeuvres' during which a gradual German withdrawal northwards would be followed up by the Finns. Significantly, Mannerheim's Order of the Day to the army on 22 September 1944 — a message of thanks which concluded with a reference to turning the country towards 'sincere and friendly relations with our neighbouring countries' — mentioned that, 'The situation in Lapland still remains unclear at the present moment, and the same sense of duty and determination is required of our troops as they have shown throughout the entire war.'[12]

The Soviet Union was determined that the Finnish army should fight against its former comrades-in-arms, a change of sides that was made easier by the German attack on Suursaari on 15 September. Mannerheim's recognition of the need to bow to Soviet pressure to fight the Germans made the 'autumn manoeuvres' impracticable. Plans for an offensive in Lapland were hastily drawn up at GHQ in response to threatening Soviet demands for action by 1 October. Lieutenant-General Hjalmar Siilasvuo, whom Mannerheim had appointed commander in northern Finland on 22 September, landed troops at Tornio just in time, and hostilities against the Germans began. However, the Germans managed repeatedly to avoid encirclement and capture, to the annoyance of the Soviets who hoped that the Finns would facilitate their attack on Petsamo by tying down more German troops. The continuation of operations in Lapland — where the Germans pursued a scorched earth policy — was complicated by the requirement in the armistice that the Finnish army should be demobilized; no concessions were made on this point. Nevertheless, most of Lapland had been cleared by the end of November 1944 although the Germans only left their final positions in the far north on 25 April 1945. The war against the Germans cost the Finnish army 774 dead to add to the 52,102 killed or died of wounds in the Continuation War. This was part of the price of compliance with the armistice.

Because Hackzell's stroke left him incapable of continuing as prime minister, a reconstruction of the government was essential. The implementation of the armistice was the unstated aim of the

---

[12] Order of the Day no. 132, 22 September 1944. *Puhtain asein*, p. 180.

new government formed by Urho Castrén, president of the supreme administrative court, on 21 September 1944. As in August, it had not been easy for Mannerheim to find a prime minister, but Castrén as a lawyer was thought suitable because of the legal aspects of the armistice. However, he was inexperienced in politics and knew no Russian, which was a handicap in dealing with the Control Commission. Enckell and Walden continued in their appointments but two of the 'peace opposition' social democrats, Karl-August Fagerholm and Eero Wuori, entered the government although two prominent non-socialist opposition figures, J. K. Paasikivi and Urho Kekkonen, remained outside it.

Abused by the Control Commission on the one side and pressed by the rising left-wing tide at home on the other as the national unity of the war years came to an end and social and economic discontent surfaced, the Castrén government lost authority and, to Mannerheim's dismay, proved short-lived. It was difficult for the president to grasp the consequences of the rapid return to politics of the hitherto proscribed extreme left. Mannerheim was subjected to considerable pressure from Finnish politicians to accept Paasikivi as prime minister. He regarded Paasikivi as an old friend but believed him to be a talker who got nothing done and was therefore unwilling to appoint him. However, Paasikivi's acceptability to the left, his good standing with the Soviet Union and his clear conception of the political consequences of Finland's fresh start in relations with the Soviet Union made him the unavoidable choice despite Mannerheim's reservations and his being aged nearly seventy-four. The appointment of Paasikivi's government on 17 November 1944, in which Mannerheim had been gradually and reluctantly forced by the new prime minister to accept some communist and extreme left-wing ministers as well as the dissident Agrarian Kekkonen, marked the beginning of a serious decline in the president's influence. He no longer actively led the government as he had done when the armistice was concluded and his inexperience of domestic politics and lack of a party political power base made their influence felt.

As president and active commander-in-chief Mannerheim possessed large powers and, in the absence of capable and effective subordinates, he remained the strong man of government until the appointment of the formidable Paasikivi as prime minister. The burden of the combined tasks of president and active commander-in-chief

PRESIDENT

had been recognized at the time of Mannerheim's election as president. To alleviate it a decree delegated some of his presidential authority to the prime minister, including the issuing of decrees, the power to grant pardons, dispensations, naturalization and nominations to lower offices. This was a sensible arrangement in 1944 while Mannerheim remained in active command of the defence forces. Perhaps because of his health he rarely exercised his right under the decree to decide for himself any of the matters delegated to the prime minister. The effect of the decree thus increasingly emphasized his separation from the routine work of government, cut off much of the flow of information he would otherwise have received about detailed internal political matters, and so increased his isolation.

Up to the end of 1944 the war in Lapland and other military matters required Mannerheim's regular attention and he spent about a third of his time at GHQ, travelling regularly back and forth to Helsinki in his special train. Only on 13 December did he bring part of his possessions back to Helsinki as a preparation to putting his house in order. On 31 December 1944 he formally relinquished what he described as 'the active direction' of the defence forces,[13] of which he appointed General Heinrichs commander while of course retaining the normal presidential powers as commander-in-chief.

Zhdanov was appointed head of the Control Commission and at Tamminiemi on 7 October 1944 Mannerheim received him together with his deputy Lieutenant-General G. M. Savonenkov and a considerable retinue. Thanks to Mannerheim's dignity and amiability the meeting passed off well, and he did not meet Zhdanov again until 1945 although he received several unwelcome communications from him in the meantime. The Control Commission was determined to assert its authority at the outset, causing Mannerheim to complain to Paasikivi: 'The Russians are making difficulties everywhere – they interpret the armistice agreement to our disadvantage and take no notice of our proposals and our points of view.'[14] According to Paasikivi, Mannerheim acknowledged that 'he understood the tsarist Russians, but these he does not understand. Mannerheim said also that the Russians do not of course like him because he has just fought against the Russians. Perhaps in the future they will arrest and shoot him.' Paasikivi replied, with reason, that the Russians 'tolerate

---
[13] Order of the Day no. 137, 31 December 1944. *Puhtain asein*, p. 184.
[14] Paasikivi, *Päiväkirjat 1944–1946*, I, col. 62.

him because they understand that he is now essential in Finland'.[15]

Mannerheim was certainly not optimistic about the future of Finland at this time, which is hardly surprising since it was now at the mercy of the men who, as he had believed, wanted to wipe the Finnish people off the face of the earth. On 27 October 1944 he sent a sealed packet of documents to his sister-in-law in Sweden for safekeeping. These documents were intended for his possible personal use, but not for the use of any politician, journalist or biographer. If he did not use them, they could be handed over after fifty years 'for example to the National Archives of an *independent* Finland as material for future historians. On the other hand should bolshevism gain influence in the government of the country and independence be no more than a shadow, these papers should remain in Sweden and be transferred to a suitable historical research institute, or even burned'.[16]

The Control Commission was nominally an allied organization with British as well as Soviet members, but any hopes among the Finns that the British might exert a moderating influence were quickly dashed. Appeasement of the Soviet Union remained British policy and the Foreign Office was anxious that its political representative in Finland, Francis Shepherd, should not be placed in a delicate position by Finnish criticism of Britain's Soviet ally. Shepherd was received by Mannerheim at Tamminiemi on 20 October 1944. 'The Marshal was in uniform, and his erect and commanding figure in the sunny and rather stagey setting of an old-rose carpeted salon looking out on the water and the autumnal birches gave the scene a strong flavour of royalty of the pre-Great-War age: an impression which the Marshal's demeanour was not calculated to dispel.' Mannerheim welcomed the British representative to Finland and expressed his regret that circumstances had placed the countries on opposing sides in the war. He stressed the difficulties of carrying out the military articles of the armistice agreement – the expulsion of the Germans at the same time as the demobilization of the army. He also expressed suspicion of the Porkkala base, which he thought unnecessary for the protection of Leningrad. Mannerheim referred to the Russians as 'Bolshies', to Shepherd's slight embarrassment, but 'Marshal Mannerheim, who speaks extremely careful and correct English, phrased his remarks so

[15] Paasikivi, *Päiväkirjat 1944–1946*, I, col. 51.
[16] A facsimile of the letter is reproduced in Kuusanmäki & Labart, 'Mannerheimiana', *Historisk Tidskrift för Finland*, 79, 1994, p. 789.

as to give no ground for demurring.' Mannerheim's lack of faith in the future and extremely low view of Soviet intentions were noted by the Foreign Office.[17]

Despite his pessimism, Mannerheim worked hard to carry out Finland's obligations under the armistice. Nevertheless, Soviet criticism was sharp and continuing, whether of the alleged slowness of mine clearance as the army withdrew to the new frontier or lack of action against the Germans. The demobilization of the armed forces prompted a dispute over their future peacetime strength; the Finns wanted the 1941 level but were forced to accept the smaller 1939 numbers. Demobilization was completed within the specified time although this had an adverse effect on the war in Lapland. Soviet hostility to the Defence Corps on ideological as well as military grounds prompted the demand for its disbandment: sadly Mannerheim had to accept this. The Defence Corps was disbanded on 7 November and the Lotta Svärd women's auxiliary organization on 23 November.

Numerous fascist organizations, mostly connected with the IKL (Patriotic People's Movement) were dissolved in September 1944 but the demand in January 1945 for the dissolution of the Veterans' Association as a fascist-type organization shocked the Finns. Mannerheim wanted to resist this since the association was humanitarian and not political, but he had no option but to comply. The punishment of 'war criminals' proved a serious and continuing problem. He was particularly alarmed when the names of two prominent generals appeared on a Soviet list of those alleged to fall into this category, and as a result of his protests the Control Commission later stated that it had no charges against them. Mannerheim had less to do with economic questions arising from the armistice agreement where there were unpleasant surprises such as the demand for reparations payments at 1938 price levels. The Finns managed to negotiate minor improvements in the reparations treaty signed on 17 December 1944.

The Control Commission's demand in December 1944 for the removal of large-calibre guns from the Finnish coastal artillery batteries could not be construed as part of the armistice agreement, and Mannerheim decided to protest about it in a constructive way by pointing out the importance to the Soviet Union of good artillery on the Finnish coast west of Porkkala, especially since the war with

[17] Shepherd's report, 21 October 1944. F.O. 371/43203, N6825/6290/56.

Germany had not ended. Zhdanov refused to allow guns of over 120-mm. calibre, but extended the deadline for the removal of the larger-calibre weapons. Mannerheim pressed the case for some heavier guns to be retained – with eventual success – but in a discussion with Zhdanov on 18 January 1945 he moved on to consider possible Finno-Soviet cooperation over defence. Zhdanov sent him the texts of the defence and mutual assistance treaties concluded by the Soviet Union with France and Czechoslovakia. After studying these and discussing the matter with Heinrichs at GHQ, Mannerheim drafted in Russian in his own hand a similar treaty between Finland and the Soviet Union which provided for mutual defence assistance in the northern Baltic and the Gulf of Finland, for non-intervention by each state in the other's internal affairs, and for an undertaking by each state not to conclude alliances directed against the other. This draft was discussed on 22 January with Zhdanov, who thought it was a beacon towards which they could strive but made no practical response. He brought up the question of a treaty with Paasikivi in May 1945 although the Soviet Union then decided that no agreement could be concluded with Finland before signing of the peace treaty.

Mannerheim attempted to initiate discussions starting 'from the basic premise that Finland and the Soviet Union have a common interest in respect of the defence of the northern Baltic and particularly the waters of the western Gulf of Finland, in which Finland wishes and is able, as an independent nation, sincerely and effectively to participate',[18] and this showed not only a clear recognition of the reality of Finland's situation *vis-à-vis* the Soviet Union but also represented a shrewd bid to secure both stability and equality in Finno-Soviet relations. Mannerheim's contacts with Zhdanov were recalled by Paasikivi in 1948 when, at Soviet instigation and in unpropitious circumstances, Finland did conclude the Treaty of Friendship, Cooperation and Mutual Assistance which was to govern the two countries' relations until the collapse of the Soviet Union. The draft treaty of January 1945 demonstrated that Mannerheim's grasp of foreign relations was undiminished.

It was clear from Mannerheim's contacts with Zhdanov and Shepherd that he had not lost his touch as a dignified head of state. He was

---

[18] Mannerheim to Zhdanov, 8 January 1945, cited in Polvinen, *Between East and West*, p. 117.

acutely conscious of the dignity of the presidency. After discussion with his staff of a letter to the German commander in Lapland in early October 1944, Mannerheim refused to sign it himself: 'The president of Finland sends no reply to a German army commander.'[19] Mannerheim objected strongly when Paasikivi, as an old friend, spoke to him on official business using the familiar form of the second person singular, pointedly addressing him in reply as 'prime minister'. In the spring of 1945, when taxed with not giving public support to Paasikivi, Mannerheim replied that although he approved of the prime minister's policy, 'he did not consider, having regard to his position as head of state, that he could publicly appear to do so.'[20] In this Mannerheim was undoubtedly constitutionally correct. Heinrichs wrote: 'For Mannerheim the head of state was like some third person, a symbolic person, to whom he himself rendered great respect and to whom he demanded the same respect from other citizens as well.'[21] And yet Gripenberg was astonished on one occasion to find the president filling out his own application form for a ration card; it did not seem to have occurred to him that this could have been done for him.

Mannerheim lived modestly at Tamminiemi, preferring it to the presidential palace which he had always disliked. He carried out a limited number of public engagements. One, on 6 December 1944, was attending a memorial service at the Helsinki synagogue for Jewish soldiers killed in the war, and it made a deep impression on him. Another, on 28 January 1945, involved going to a national celebration of President Ståhlberg's eightieth birthday. This was stated to be the first personal contact between the two men for over a quarter of a century.[22]

On 5 March 1945 Paasikivi recorded: 'Mannerheim seemed somewhat depressed and was fairly tired. But his intelligence is working. However, he no longer seems able to follow current developments.'[23] There were numerous arguments between the president and the prime minister. Paasikivi disagreed with Mannerheim's approach to relations with the Control Commission. Mannerheim was

---

[19] Cited in Jäagerskiöld, *Från krig till fred*, p. 128.
[20] Paasikivi, *Päiväkirjat 1944–1956*, I, col. 244.
[21] Heinrichs, *Mannerheim Suomen kohtaloissa*, II, p. 400.
[22] Blomstedt, *K.J. Ståhlberg*, p. 503.
[23] Paasikivi, *Päiväkirjat 1944–1956*, I, col. 202.

prepared, as over the coastal artillery, to protest to the Soviets when he considered their demands unjustifiable under the armistice agreement. Paasikivi believed that Mannerheim's policy of 'getting on our high horse' would only harm Finland's relations with the Soviet Union while an eventual climb-down could not be avoided.[24] Paasikivi also criticized his judgement over domestic politics and politicians, and Mannerheim certainly lacked contacts with influential politicians in Finland's new circumstances and was unwilling to make the compromises with the left which Paasikivi regarded as unavoidable and necessary. The election held on 17–18 March 1945, which was considered a vital testimony to Finland's democratic credentials, produced a very different parliament from the old one and marked a watershed in Mannerheim's presidency.

POWER SLIPS AWAY

Mannerheim wrote to his sister that the election in March 1945 'went rather better than many had expected, but the communists' electoral offensive was not of the most pleasant description. It was a battle with unequal weapons, where one side attacked with heavy artillery and tanks while the other had to weigh every word so as not to bring greater forces into the game.'[25] The new parliament contained 101 non-socialists to 99 socialists, but the decision of the Agrarians to cooperate with the Social Democrats and the new People's Democrats (most of whom were communists) ensured the pursuit of a radical left-wing programme. There were also many new members of parliament since Paasikivi, despite Mannerheim's disapproval, had exerted considerable pressure on former members not to stand again.

The president opened the new parliament on 7 April, wearing for the occasion a new uniform, the last he was to order. He gave a brave speech, telling the members: 'Your task will be to create the conditions for the continuation of life in freedom under the law in which all citizens have equal rights and equal security. It will also, above all, be the role of this parliament, jointly with the government, to direct the entire strength and unanimous will of the people to the fulfilment of our promises and our duties towards our eastern neighbour to create lasting friendly relations … with the Soviet Union …

[24] Paasikivi, *Päiväkirjat 1944–1956*, I, col. 143.
[25] To Eva Sparre, [spring 1945]. Mannerheim, *Brev*, p. 330.

PRESIDENT

In addition there will be the work of reconstruction … It is clear that this will involve new sacrifices but … we must be able to look with confidence towards a brightening future.'[26] The People's Democrat members of parliament, ostentatiously wearing flowers tied with red ribbons in their buttonholes, were a visible indication to Mannerheim of the difficulty and unpleasantness of the months ahead.

On 9 April Mannerheim congratulated Paasikivi on his success in winning confidence both abroad and at home, and asked him to form a new government. Paasikivi hesitated and Mannerheim renewed his request on 11 April, having in the meantime obtained the backing of the speaker of parliament and the chairmen of the party parliamentary groups. Paasikivi emphasized the difficult matters ahead, notably the questions of war guilt and war criminals. He asked if the president would support him but Mannerheim would only agree to consider each matter individually. It was to become a standing complaint by Paasikivi that Mannerheim did not back him up publicly over unpleasant matters. Over the next few days there followed a number of difficult conversations between the two about the composition of the government, a coalition which reflected the new strength of the extreme left in parliament.

Particularly annoying to Mannerheim was the determination of the politicians to appoint a civilian, Mauno Pekkala, as minister of defence. He wanted a soldier to hold the post. His old friend, General Rudolf Walden, had suffered a stroke on 27 November 1944 and been replaced as minister of defence by Lieutenant-General Väinö Valve. Now Mannerheim wanted Lieutenant-General Einar Mäkinen to become minister but he had to give way and eventually approved Pekkala's appointment 'with a depressed voice'.[27] Paasikivi's new government was appointed on 17 April 1945. Carl Enckell remained foreign minister and Urho Kekkonen minister of justice; Yrjö Leino, a communist, became minister of the interior.

Walden's complete incapacity deprived Mannerheim of one of his few close friends and confidants and increased his isolation. Helsinki too was not the same. He wrote to his sister in the spring of 1945: 'I have myself been away from Helsinki since the end of '39 with the exception of a few visits of 1 or 2 days. Many have died, life has changed and I scarcely manage to see anyone except on official

[26] *Suomen presidentit puhuvat*, pp. 100–1.
[27] Paasikivi, *Päiväkirjat 1944–1956*, I, col. 250.

business.'[28] Gripenberg, who was not often in Helsinki, was one of the few people to whom Mannerheim could talk and vent his indignation at Paasikivi's unreliability and his concessions to the left. Mannerheim was prepared to implement the political changes required by the armistice but he opposed other concessions. The duties of office and the difficulty of going abroad as president meant that he could not travel to his sister's seventy-fifth birthday celebrations in Sweden, writing to her with regret: 'My wings are clipped.'[29] He enjoyed the fine summer weather of 1945 and the opportunity to go for walks and swim in the sea near his official residence. Politically, however, the summer was anything but fine. A major problem during 1945 was how Finland was to fulfil its obligation under article 13 of the armistice agreement 'to collaborate with the Allied powers in the apprehension of persons accused of war crimes and in their trial'. This question became acute that summer.

Another matter which became acute at the same time was what became known as the arms concealment or arms dump affair. This affair, which caused Mannerheim great anxiety, originated in the determination of two officers in the operations section of GHQ, Lieutenant-Colonel Usko Sakari Haahti and Colonel Valo Nihtilä, in the immediate aftermath of the armistice, to make provision for guerilla operations in Finland if the Soviet Union were to occupy the country. To that end they arranged secret dumps of weapons and stores sufficient to arm 34,000 men (one battalion in each Defence Corps district). By the spring of 1945 the immediate danger of occupation seemed past and it was planned to return the concealed weapons to army stores. But already before then some weapons had been found and in April 1945 an informer alerted the state police – by then under communist control – to the existence of further caches. The Control Commission investigated these discoveries and reacted strongly to what it regarded as a breach of the armistice agreement – and one, furthermore, that had been organized from GHQ. In May the minister of defence wrote to Heinrichs demanding the return of the weapons and the punishment of those responsible and in early June Zhdanov wrote sharply to Paasikivi demanding the investigation of the affair and the punishment of those involved. Haahti and Nihtilä were arrested on 9 June. Soon afterwards the Control Commission suggested

[28] To Eva Sparre, [spring 1945]. Mannerheim, *Brev*, p. 331.
[29] To Eva Sparre, [mid-1945]. Mannerheim, *Brev*, p. 329.

that influential military figures were trying to impede the investigation and punishment of the fascist conspirators who had been concerned in the concealment of weapons. The government were faced by a threatening situation.

Haahti and Nihtilä had deliberately concealed the details of their operation from more senior officers because of its political sensitivity. However, Nihtilä had drawn the attention of Airo to the scheme at the end of September 1944, and Airo approved of it. Nihtilä later recalled: 'Perhaps it was the following day that Airo mentioned to me that he had spoken about the matter to Mannerheim in case it should be brought to his knowledge through other channels, and he would surely not think that action had been taken behind his back. M, according to Airo, had only warned of the danger of detection and urged the greatest caution.'[30] Thus Mannerheim not only knew of the scheme – though not its details – but took no action to prevent it although he clearly recognized the risks involved. Airo also knew no details, but left the work to Haahti and Nihtilä.

The arrest of the two officers principally concerned sent a shock through the army and the government. However, the state police made little progress with their enquiries because the two would not talk. The government's foreign affairs committee, meeting on 26 June, believed that GHQ had organized the arms concealment despite Mannerheim's assertion to it that 'There is nothing to prove that the army commander and chief of staff had any responsibility for the arms dumps'.[31] The president expressed no further opinion but evidently decided to take action, however unpalatable. He sent a message to Haahti telling him to volunteer information about the affair, and the officer replied on 29 June, explaining his patriotic motives and involvement and asking if he should keep silent or tell what he knew if the latter were in the national interest. Mannerheim, visibly moved, felt that he had no option but to convey to Haahti the need to tell the state police everything. He even showed Haahti's letter to Leino, the minister of the interior; he recognized that there was no hope of the investigation being conducted by the army, and was keen to limit the inevitable damage to its position.

Soon afterwards Leino and the far left unleashed a savage and concerted attack on the military as reactionary conspirators. Pressure

[30] Kilkki, *Valo Nihtilä*, p. 165.
[31] Paasikivi, *Päiväkirjat 1944–1956*, I, col. 290.

from the minister of defence forced Heinrichs to resign. Mannerheim was outraged that the government was prepared to allow the state police to arrest Airo but, as usual, was forced to submit; he entertained Airo to lunch before sending him to Paasikivi who told him he was to be arrested. Airo was one of some 2,000 people arrested during a searching and lengthy investigation. With that investigation so obviously under way, the Control Commission took no further direct action in the affair. Thanks to Nihtilä's and Airo's denials, no connection was established between Mannerheim and the concealment of arms, but the enforced changes to the army's senior appointments had left him very exposed. The eventual trials of the numerous 'conspirators' took place on the basis of a retroactive law passed in January 1947 — after Mannerheim's presidency had ended — and did not finally end till March 1950. Airo was acquitted but Haahti and Nihtilä were jailed.

In addition to implementing the armistice agreement, the government was concerned with other consequences of the end of the war. One of the most important of these was the provision of land for the farmers from the ceded areas. The land acquisition law took land mostly by compulsory purchase for the benefit of the evacuees, war disabled, war veterans, and war widows and orphans. It proved controversial, and both Mannerheim and Paasikivi were disturbed by the extent to which the proposed law interfered with private property rights. Paasikivi eventually went along with the proposals of the majority in the government, but Mannerheim remained unconvinced.

Most of the land taken for redistribution was owned by the state, local authorities, corporate bodies and foundations, but a high proportion of arable land was taken from farmers who worked their own farms, and larger farms were particularly hard hit. Mannerheim recognized the political advisability of providing land quickly for the evacuees and other groups so that they would not become an alienated element in society, but he feared that the law would reduce food production and even lead to famine because it took land from efficient larger farms and created numerous very small ones. Mannerheim was persuaded by Paasikivi to accept the will of the majority, but he dictated his objections into the minutes of the Council of State on 29 January 1945. He did so 'in the hope that in the continuing constitutional consideration of the proposal account

22. Mannerheim speaks as president at the opening of parliament, 7 April 1945. (Military Museum of Finland)

(*Left*) 23. Mannerheim as president attending the installation of Archbishop Aleksi Lehtonen in Turku Cathedral, 10 June 1945. J.K. Paasikivi, the prime minister, is behind him. (Military Museum of Finland) (*Above*) 24. J.K. Paasikivi (1870–1956), conservative politician, banker, prime minister 1918 and 1944–6, president 1946–56, who led Finland into a new relationship with the Soviet Union after the Second World War. (Ministry of Foreign Affairs, Helsinki)

PRESIDENT

will be taken of all opportunities to attain complete unanimity in the present difficulties'.[32] The land acquisition law, with its profound social and economic consequences, was promulgated on 5 May 1945.

Mannerheim continued to be involved in major foreign and domestic policy questions about which Paasikivi saw him frequently but, as the land acquisition law showed, he had by 1945 virtually no opportunity to assert his personal authority as president. He could not take decisions independently of the will of his forceful prime minister who had the backing of a government with powerful support in parliament. A study of the role of the president in Finland has shown that Mannerheim's personal decisions were limited to nominating two members of the supreme court against the vote of the Council of State.[33] Another scholar, who emphasized the symbolic character of Mannerheim's presidency, suggested that, 'Mannerheim's position was loftily distant. It was also parliamentary because he kept himself apart from government policy'.[34] This separation resulted from policy differences rather than from a vision on Mannerheim's part of a 'parliamentary' presidency. However, it was no wonder that the presidency became such a burden to a man who was both old and, increasingly, ill. The extent of his ageing was apparent from his physical appearance at public engagements, such as the installation of the new archbishop in Turku Cathedral on 10 June 1945 and the reception at the presidential palace on 7 October 1945 to mark the twenty-fifth anniversary of General Mannerheim's Child Welfare Association.

HEALTH DETERIORATES

As early as November 1944 Mannerheim's doctor gave as his opinion that 'it has to be considered as uncertain whether because of his illness the Marshal of Finland is able to continue in future to carry out the duties of President of the Republic.'[35] Congestive lung infections continued to threaten. Gripenberg noted in February 1945 that Mannerheim 'looks quite dreadful'.[36] The eczema which afflicted him

---

[32] Cited in Virkkunen, *Mannerheim. Marsalkka ja presidentti*, pp. 423–4.
[33] Jyränki, *Presidentti*, p. 141.
[34] Tiihonen, *Hallitusvalta*, p. 172.
[35] Medical certificate, 4 November 1944. Mannerheim Archive, Box 129.
[36] Gripenberg's diary, 25 February 1945, cited by Jägerskiöld, *Från krig till fred*, p. 193.

particularly at times of strain had then spread from his hands to his head and face. On 5 March he informed Paasikivi that illness prevented him from carrying out his presidential duties. Paasikivi had proposed this action so that Mannerheim would not have to approve what for him was the thoroughly objectionable law granting compensation to wartime Finnish political detainees, including some convicted of treason. But in spite of its being politically expedient, the illness was genuine. He was living at that time in his house in Kaivopuisto to which he tended to move from Tamminemi when he was ill, although that did not necessarily stop him from receiving official visitors there. Despite his circulation problems, the summer of 1945 seems to have been a period of better health and mental vigour when he carried out his duties, but at the end of August his condition showed a marked change for the worse.

Mannerheim had invited his friends Henrik Ramsay and Henry Hackman to stay for a couple of days at his hunting lodge in Loppi, some 44 miles (70 km.) from Helsinki. The lodge was a reconstruction of the handsome log structure in Eastern Karelia built for him in 1942 as a birthday gift by Major-General Erkki Raappana and men of 14 Division. In April 1945 Mannerheim bought a lakeside plot in Loppi and paid for the rebuilding of the hunting lodge which he described as the only house he actually owned. He already had a cold when travelling there on 26 August and cut short the trip to return to Helsinki the following day when he began to suffer stomach pains. On 12 September he informed Paasikivi that he had not been out for several days because of illness and that he was prevented from undertaking his duties as president. At his request the prime minister and acting president visited him on 29 September and noted: 'Mannerheim was very passive, he just does not follow matters at all.'[37] On 2 October Mannerheim's doctor, Lauri Kalaja, brought Paasikivi – with Mannerheim's knowledge – a medical certificate stating that for health reasons the president ought to spend four weeks in the south, in Portugal.

The British diplomat Francis Shepherd had a meeting with Mannerheim on 5 October, and thought him 'still deeply suspicious of Russia' and 'most anxious to procure a Peace Treaty ... as quickly as possible, as a successful culmination of his tenure as president'. Shepherd thought that Mannerheim looked 'a good deal thinner and

[37] Paasikivi, *Päiväkirjat 1944–1956*, I, col. 416.

PRESIDENT

older than when I saw him last year but his mind, though evidently rather inelastic, is still clear and precise.'[38] Gripenberg found him on 28 October bowed down by his responsibility and exhibiting a rare nervousness. He was anxiously awaiting the diagnosis of his stomach pains, and towards the end of October was able to give his sister relatively comforting news: 'By means of a thorough x-ray examination at the Red Cross Hospital it has been stated absolutely plainly that my spasmodic pains are not caused by cancer, which I feared, but only by an inconsiderable small stomach ulcer.'[39] Paasikivi, who visited him in hospital, told his secretary: 'President Mannerheim said that he is suffering from an ulcer, but it is striking that he smokes cigars and that a glass of cognac stood on his table. With an ulcer one should neither drink nor smoke.'[40] Smoking and drinking over many years could have aggravated Mannerheim's ulcer, but old habits died hard. The diagnosis evidently raised Mannerheim's morale but his ulcer turned out to be far more serious than had originally been supposed. The last months of his presidency, which were politically difficult and personally threatening, were also to be overshadowed by illness.

THE WAR RESPONSIBILITY CASE

The thirteenth article of the armistice agreement, with its requirement that war criminals should be apprehended and tried, proved one of the most difficult and controversial to put into effect. The problem lay in the Soviet understanding of what constituted a war crime. On 8 July 1945 Paasikivi accurately summarized the Soviet position. 'The Russians consider Finland's war crime and guilt to be that Finland waged war alongside Germany against the Soviet Union, and those Finns who led Finland into the war bear war guilt. (That our war was "lawful" in that the president, government and parliament were involved in it does not affect the matter ... The president, government and parliament and all who influenced the matter are war guilty.) In the Russians' opinion just as Hitler and his men must be punished for starting the world war, so must the Finns who were guilty of starting the war be punished.' Neither national

[38] Shepherd's report, 10 October 1945. F.O.371/47370, N14043/33/56.
[39] To Eva Sparre, 29 October 1945. Mannerheim, *Brev*, p. 333.
[40] Heikkilä, *Paasikivi peräsimessä*, p. 136.

interest nor the desire to take back what the Russians had seized by attacking Finland in 1939 was an acceptable defence.[41] The matter was made worse by the very fact that the war was legal for the Finns meant that under the constitution no crime had been committed with which the wartime leadership could be charged.

The government deferred action by appointing on 5 February 1945 a committee to look into the course of events that led to the outbreak of war in 1941. It reported on 17 July but produced insufficient evidence, in the government's view, to initiate legal proceedings. The Allied decision in August 1945 that planning, initiating and waging aggressive war constituted a crime against peace brought matters to a head. The Control Commission demanded action, threatening that otherwise it would take matters out of the Finns' hands: only by means of a retroactive law could the Finns comply with the armistice agreement. Paasikivi accepted the necessity of this as did Kekkonen, the minister of justice, who played a major part in the practical arrangements. Of course, the extreme left had long demanded the condign punishment of the 'war guilty'.

A retroactive law to punish the 'war guilty' was objectionable to Mannerheim although he had to accept it. He tried 'to introduce a few alterations which made the proposed stipulations slightly less repugnant'.[42] These included limiting the law to the prosecution only of members of the government, the possibility of punishment by imprisonment as well as by penal servitude, and a provision for the presidential power of pardon to apply to those convicted. Mannerheim also objected to the original composition of the proposed special court, which would have comprised only one lawyer to twelve lay members elected by parliament. Some of his proposals survived into the final law but not the limitation of prosecution to members of the government. Illness conveniently saved Mannerheim from the disagreeable task of attending the Council of State on 12 September 1945 at which the law was confirmed. Paasikivi, who did the job for the president, wrote in his diary: 'Fate does not spare me.'[43]

After the law was enacted, the Council of State set up an inquiry commission, chaired by the lawyer Onni Petäys (chosen by Kekkonen),

---

[41] Paasikivi, *Päiväkirjat 1944–1956*,1, cols. 297–8.
[42] Mannerheim, *Memoirs*, p. 508.
[43] Paasikivi, *Päiväkirjat 1944–1956*,1, col. 395.

to determine who had exercised a decisive influence on Finland's going to war in 1941 and who had prevented the conclusion of peace. Petäys and his colleagues questioned forty-nine people, concentrating on the origin of the transit agreement with the Germans in September 1940 and the Ribbentrop agreement of June 1944. On 29 September 1945, as Kekkonen informed Paasikivi, Petäys had asked him when he could question Mannerheim 'because there were certain circumstances which could not be made clear without him'.[44] Mannerheim wrote to Petäys on 14 October that he was willing to see him but was ill and had been urged by his doctor to go abroad.[45] However, on 18 October Petäys interviewed Mannerheim at his home in Kaivopuisto for five and a half hours. The notes of the interview made by Mannerheim's ADC, Colonel Ragnar Grönvall, were subsequently amended, retitled as the record of an interrogation, and incorporated in the evidence to the war guilt court.[46]

On the matters about which Petäys's inquiry concentrated, Mannerheim said that Ryti had authorized the acceptance of Veltjens's proposal for the transit of German troops and the beginning of military operations. He also stated boldly that he regarded Ryti's signature of the Ribbentrop agreement as an act of 'civic heroism'. There were various questions to which Mannerheim replied that he had no knowledge or recollection, but in general he emphasized the government's responsibility for political matters. He had often made this last point to Paasikivi: that he had taken no decision during the war which had not been agreed with the political leadership.[47] Earlier, in August or September, he had taken the precaution of going with his doctors to see General Walden who, despite his serious illness and minimal powers of speech, had confirmed Mannerheim's recollection of contacting Ryti about Veltjens's proposal.

Opinions differ over whether Mannerheim had advance warning of Petäys's questions.[48] It would not be surprising if he had, but it is

[44] *Ibid.*, col. 417.
[45] To Onni Petäys, 14 October 1945. Mannerheim Archive, Box 425.
[46] Jägerskiöld, *Från krig till fred*, p. 172.
[47] Heikkilä, *Paasikivi peräsimessä*, p. 138.
[48] Jägerskiöld, *Från krig till fred*, p. 170, denied the advance warning claims made by Tarkka, *13. artikla*, pp. 163–6. Suomi, *Vonkamies*, pp. 225–6, accepted the case for the advance warning but commented that it was dependent on the testimony of Kustaa Vilkuna, a friend of Kekkonen.

more significant that the preliminary report of the inquiry commission had been drawn up on 11 October, a week before Petäys interviewed Mannerheim, and that the president told Paasikivi on 18 October that he had read it 'and had noticed that it wanted to lay the guilt on the shoulders of the commander-in-chief of the defence forces'.[49] The preliminary report was highly incriminatory of Mannerheim since it showed the powerful influence of GHQ in internal and foreign policy in 1941. This, of course, was the truth, but it raised the highly sensitive question of whether Mannerheim should be prosecuted as one of the 'war guilty'. Kekkonen pointed out to Paasikivi on 12 October that because of the nature of Petäys's questions Mannerheim would be compromised and have to resign. It is also arguable that if it was the intention to spare Mannerheim from prosecution, Petäys's questions could have been intended to show that there was no justification for indicting him.[50]

On 6 October Paasikivi recorded Kekkonen's opinion that it would be difficult for Mannerheim to remain as president after the war guilt accusations had been made public. 'Petäys had said that in his opinion Ryti is war guilty No. 1 and Mannerheim No. 1a.'[51] The question of Mannerheim's culpability thus became linked with attempts to get him to resign. It must be asked why he was not prosecuted as one of the war guilty – he bore a considerable share of responsibility for Finland's involvement in the war and recognized this himself. There was no legal obstacle to prosecuting the president in his former capacity as commander-in-chief, and the special law, from which the restriction of indictment to government members had been removed, also gave him no protection. Yet on 6 November 1945 the Council of State decided to prosecute Ryti, the wartime president, the former prime ministers Rangell and Linkomies, the former ministers Ramsay, Tanner, Kukkonen and Reinikka, and the former Finnish minister in Berlin, Kivimäki. Once more Paasikivi had presided at the session because of Mannerheim's absence on sick leave, a matter also closely connected with the war guilt case. Neither Mannerheim nor any other soldier was indicted. With the exception of Kivimäki, a civil servant, all those charged had carried political responsibility, particularly for foreign relations.

[49] Paasikivi, *Päiväkirjat 1944–1956*, I, col. 438.
[50] Tarkka, *13. artikla*, p. 166.
[51] Paasikivi, *op. cit.*, col. 426.

PRESIDENT

There is no single explanation of why Mannerheim was spared from being publicly blamed and punished for Finland's involvement in the war in 1941. If the Soviet Union had wanted him to be tried, nothing could have saved him. For example, the Soviets were determined to convict Tanner, who was anathema to them as an anticommunist social democrat, and they succeeded despite the weakness of the 'war guilt' case against him. A pretext could have been found, if one had been wanted, to dishonour the assurance given to Sweden as a condition for its mediation during the war that the Soviet Union would not interfere with Mannerheim's position.[52] Zhdanov had initially wanted revenge on those directing Finnish policy during the war and stated that Mannerheim's responsibility for Finland entering the war on Germany's side in 1941 was so evident that if anyone were brought to trial on that account 'the first one would be Mannerheim'.[53] The communist 'Freedom Radio', which broadcast from Petrozavodsk, attacked Mannerheim as a war criminal in November 1944. However, on 22 August 1945, when speaking to Paasikivi about the war guilt issue, Zhdanov listed Ryti, Tanner, Rangell, Linkomies and Kivimäki as men who should be tried, and Mannerheim's name was conspicuously absent.

To say that Mannerheim was not tried because the Soviet Union did not want it raises the question of what were the reasons behind the Soviet attitude to the president of Finland. There is some force in the argument that Moscow acted towards Mannerheim in the same way that Washington did towards the Emperor of Japan and for the same reasons: there would have been no practical advantages to putting them on trial, and doing so would have increased the difficulties of the victorious power.[54] Mannerheim, who had the merit of concluding the armistice, was seen by the Soviets as having an important role in fulfilling its terms; particularly in the early stages of the armistice, his authority ensured that Finland carried out its obligations. It was in the Soviet interest to have Mannerheim as president because he helped to hold Finnish society together and on the new course. His trial would have outraged large sections of public opinion and might have caused internal unrest – resulting possibly in an interruption to the reparations deliveries, which were extremely important

---

[52] Manninen, 'Mannerheim ja sotaansyyllisyys', pp. 343–4; Boheman, *På vakt*, p. 251.
[53] Cited in Nevakivi, 'The Soviet Union and Finland after the War, 1944–53', p. 93.
[54] Tarkka, *13. artikla*, p. 241.

to the Soviet Union. However, it was clear to the Soviets by early 1945 that Paasikivi would be more effective than Mannerheim in holding Finland to its new political course and, as will be seen below, they encouraged him to resign by stating unequivocally that he would not have to face trial even if he ceased to be head of state.

One of the remarkable aspects of the war guilt issue was the extent to which the Control Commission left its settlement to the Finns, although it did intervene during the trial and over the verdicts. In discussing the issue with the Control Commission, both Paasikivi and Kekkonen often robustly defended Finnish principles and sometimes gained their point. It is noteworthy that in this they followed the line for dealing with the Control Commission that had earlier been unsuccessfully advocated to Paasikivi by Mannerheim. The role of the Finnish government in the war guilt issue, which included deciding who should be prosecuted, made its attitude to Mannerheim's possible indictment crucial.

Members of the government were just as aware as the Control Commission of the unpopularity that would have resulted from putting Mannerheim on trial. Their position became bad enough with regard to the politicians accused, since most Finns looked on these men as innocent victims of the country's defeat. Even the communists were reluctant to press for Mannerheim being charged in the absence of a clear lead from the Control Commission. Leino had told Paasikivi as early as 1 April 1945 that Mannerheim had gained such credit from taking Finland out of the war that he should be left entirely aside – and he still maintained this opinion in October. For motives that were possibly as much personally and calculatingly political as patriotic, Paasikivi (who wanted to succeed Mannerheim as president) and Kekkonen (who wanted to be prime minister) were determined to save Mannerheim from a prosecution which might have turned out to be political suicide for them.

Kekkonen is reported to have said that one of the wartime leaders must be saved and that one had to be Mannerheim.[55] His archives contain a document setting out four points relating to Mannerheim. These were that the final report of the inquiry commission should not touch on him, that no military persons should be indicted, that the prosecutor should not allude to Mannerheim in court, and that the president of the court should not allow Mannerheim's views to

[55] Suomi, *Vonkamies*, p. 224.

PRESIDENT

be pleaded as a defence by the defendants.[56] These were the lines generally followed before and during the trial, and they helped to lessen potentially damaging conflicts of opinion in court. However, Kekkonen was keen to use the war guilt issue to force Mannerheim's resignation, and at the beginning of October 1945 the problem of his health, his position over the war guilt question and his possible resignation all came together.

RESIGNATION

The advice of Mannerheim's doctor on 2 October that he needed to travel to Portugal for four weeks for the sake of his health was discussed by Paasikivi with Leino, Kekkonen and members of the government, all of whom wanted Mannerheim to resign. Moreover, Kekkonen believed that Mannerheim should go abroad and remain there until the end of the year. 'Then the war guilt question has been decided because the decision has to be made during this year'[57] (this referred to the provision in the special law that charges had to be brought before the end of 1945). Paasikivi informed Mannerheim that it would be good if he went abroad as soon as possible and stayed away in order to keep him apart from the war guilt case. At first Mannerheim was prepared to go, but after reading the preliminary report of the Petäys commission he told Paasikivi on 18 October that he could not 'because that could be regarded as flight. He wants to remain here to defend himself against accusations.'[58] Nevertheless Paasikivi believed that Mannerheim should regard the doctors' opinion as decisive; he himself could act as president while Mannerheim was away.

Word of Mannerheim's intended journey became an open secret in political circles where there was some hostile talk of flight. News then got into the press. This prompted the Soviet minister in Helsinki to ask why Mannerheim wanted to go to Portugal and not to the Crimea or the Caucasus. Mannerheim told Paasikivi it was too late to arrange that. Zhdanov then intervened on 3 November, the day before Mannerheim was due to travel. Paasikivi was told in no uncertain terms that the president's absence from the country was a serious

[56] Suomi, *Vonkamies*, pp. 224, 228.
[57] Paasikivi, *Päiväkirjat 1944–1956*, I, col. 426.
[58] *Ibid.*, col. 438.

political question and not a purely personal matter. The journey should be deferred until the Soviet authorities had come to a decision about it. Paasikivi explained in vain that there was no lawful obstacle to the journey and that he, as prime minister, would attend to the president's duties in his absence. Mannerheim now had no option but to delay his departure. However, by the time Paasikivi had returned to Zhdanov to say this had been done but that Mannerheim hoped to go soon, Zhdanov had received permission from Moscow to allow Mannerheim to travel. Paasikivi went back to the president. 'Mannerheim was pleased and phoned his ADC ordering the cancellation to be cancelled.'[59]

So on 4 November 1945 Mannerheim set out for Portugal accompanied by his ADC, Colonel Grönvall, and Dr Kalaja, and arrived at the place chosen by Kalaja, the small seaside resort of Praia de Rocha in the Algarve, six days later. The journey 'was most tiring in spite of all the kindness shown me in the form of cars, railway carriages, meals and all possible and impossible help from the authorities in France, Spain and here in Portugal. However, I have now had time to rest and enjoy the warmth, the Atlantic and the wonderful steep precipitous coasts ... My lungs seem to be as good as cured and even my stomach ulcer is on the way to improvement.'[60] Although Mannerheim had diplomatically avoided a meeting with General Franco, believing that it might exacerbate Finno-Soviet relations, he did meet the president of Portugal and the prime minister, Dr Salazar, in spite of his visit being unofficial.

Mannerheim's stay in Portugal – marred only by a worrying absence of mail from Finland – stretched to six weeks and his return journey from Lisbon began on 20 December. He thought he had recovered, but fell ill again while travelling through Spain; his ulcer had reopened, and he had to go into hospital in Paris. From there he went on by plane to Stockholm on 29 December 1945 and reached Helsinki on 2 January 1946. By then he was so ill that he almost immediately had to go into the Red Cross Hospital, where he stayed for several weeks.

The war guilt trial began while Mannerheim was away but had not ended when he returned although the period for charging the 'guilty' had run out two days previously. This did not necessarily

[59] *Ibid.*, col. 449.
[60] To Palaemona Mannerheim, 23 November 1945. Grensholm Collection, VAY 5633.

mean that he was out of danger. Despite the government's precautions, the trial had revealed Mannerheim's part in events and disclosed the difference between his and Ryti's accounts of the origin of the transit agreement. Particularly damaging to him was the release by the Soviet authorities on 8 January of the testimony of General Erich Buschenhagen, then their prisoner of war, about Mannerheim's alleged role in the discussions of plans for aggressive war with the Germans in December 1940 and the early months of 1941. Buschenhagen subsequently admitted that this evidence had been false and obtained under duress. Mannerheim immediately denied its truth. However, the Buschenhagen evidence led to the left increasing their pressure for Mannerheim's resignation, a matter that had already been under intense discussion in political circles before and during his absence in Portugal.

The discussion by politicians of Mannerheim's resignation was nothing new – Paasikivi recorded such comments from the spring of 1945 onwards – and Mannerheim himself had said on 9 April: 'I too believe that I ought to go.' Paasikivi added: 'He would certainly be glad to go but if he could be of use in stabilizing the country's position, then would not refuse to stay on. He received letters every day urging him to remain in his post.'[61] In the autumn, when calls for Mannerheim's resignation intensified, Paasikivi was concerned that it should be handled in such a way that the people would not think Mannerheim had been driven out by a government intrigue: he had to take the decision himself. In this Paasikivi accurately reflected Mannerheim's own position. As late as 28 February 1946 the president stressed 'that he wants to take his decision freely without it being said that he did it under pressure'.[62] Hints to Mannerheim from Paasikivi and from Fagerholm, the speaker of parliament, that he should resign apparently fell on deaf ears. Moreover, some members of the Agrarian Party, unlike Kekkonen, remained firm defenders of his presidency: Niukkanen wanted him to remain as president until the peace treaty was concluded.

Dr Kalaja told Paasikivi on 4 January 1946: 'Mannerheim's powers of judgement and discernment have fallen so low that he cannot evaluate affairs. In consequence he should give up the appointment

[61] Paasikivi, *op. cit., col. 238.*
[62] *Ibid.*, col. 535.

of president.'⁶³ A little later Kalaja commented that Mannerheim's health 'is such that if he begins something which can cause anxiety his illness worsens'.⁶⁴ Mannerheim was well aware of this. Paasikivi had by now become thoroughly annoyed with the uncertainty and the burden of undertaking presidential duties as well as his own, and in the presence of Gripenberg exclaimed: '[I have] no support from Mannerheim. He says nothing, only watches his own popularity. He does nothing either. He does not even resign. Must one really march to the hospital and drag him off the president's chair?'⁶⁵ This outburst may have been relayed to Mannerheim.

By the beginning of February 1946 he had made up his mind to go. He wrote to his sister: 'I am thinking of shortly laying down my appointment not because of the newspapers' importunate exhortations but because *my* health has recently begun to give ever clearer signs of its frailty. The present constellation with a compact majority bloc under the leadership of the communists in government and parliament (150 to 50 partly uncertain [of the 200 members of parliament]) makes my exercise of the powers of head of state illusory. Nobody can really ask me to remain as a mere figurehead in such circumstances, when I have already accomplished significantly more than I was asked to do when I allowed myself to be persuaded by numerous members of the then government and parliament to accept the presidency.'⁶⁶

Mannerheim decided to resign after the announcement of the verdicts of the war guilt court, and after Savonenkov, Zhdanov's deputy, went to see him in hospital on 26 January and gave an assurance that the Soviet Union had no intention of prosecuting him for war crimes whether or not he remained president. The original message drafted by Zhdanov ran: 'If Mannerheim is obliged to resign, he may take into consideration that Russia will allow nobody to arrest him, since he has concluded the peace between Finland and the Soviet Union.'⁶⁷ Mannerheim regarded this as pressure, 'but it was in a pleasant form.'⁶⁸

---

⁶³ *Ibid.*, col. 506.
⁶⁴ *Ibid.*, col. 517.
⁶⁵ Gripenberg's diary, 19 February 1946, cited in Jägerskiöld, *Från krig till fred*, p. 215.
⁶⁶ To Eva Sparre, 1 February 1946. Mannerheim, *Brev*, pp. 336–7.
⁶⁷ Cited in Nevakivi, 'The Soviet Union and Finland after the War, 1944–53', pp. 98–9. Nevakivi thought that the use of the word Russia was intended to have an effect on Mannerheim as a former Russian officer.
⁶⁸ Paasikivi, *Päiväkirjat 1944–1956*, I, col. 521.

The assurance had a calming effect, but it was a deliberate attempt to encourage him to resign and may have been instigated by Kekkonen, Leino, Kalaja and others although his resignation also conformed to Soviet interests.[69] The war guilt verdicts, made more severe as the result of the Control Commission's demands, were announced on 21 February. It was obviously disagreeable to Mannerheim to see his wartime colleagues jailed for terms of up to ten years and he urged Paasikivi to ensure that they received all possible privileges.

Mannerheim formally resumed the duties of president on 3 March. He had been infuriated by an action of Lieutenant-General Lundqvist, the acting commander of the defence forces whom he had reluctantly appointed (believing him to be pro-Allied) after Heinrichs was forced out. Lundqvist had tried, for political reasons, to press a number of officers to resign, which in Mannerheim's view usurped his prerogative as commander-in-chief. Now, accordingly he took the opportunity to deliver a stinging rebuke to Lundqvist who, in consequence of failing to get his way, resigned in May. The appointment in his place of General Aarne Sihvo, Mannerheim's former rival from 1918, who had been sidelined by GHQ during the war, marked how significantly the army leadership had changed in the post-war era.

Mannerheim's letter of resignation had been carefully prepared with the help of General Heinrichs on 2 March, and on 4 March 1945 he submitted it, with a medical certificate, to the Council of State. 'I announced my intention of resigning my office because of the deterioration of my health. I added that I considered that the task which had induced me to accept the position of Head of State had, so far as concerned me, been accomplished, as now even the trial of those accused of responsibility for the war had ended. As to the conditions of the Armistice Agreement, those remaining would require several years to carry out. I had decided to inform the government of this in order that it could take the necessary measures.'[70]

Paasikivi broadcast that evening to the nation. 'The name of President Mannerheim is deeply engraved in the history of our country ... Under his leadership and under the protection of his authority our country disengaged itself from the war. Nobody else

[69] Suomi, *Vonkamies*, p. 233; Nevakivi, 'The Soviet Union and Finland after the War, 1944–53', pp. 98–99.
[70] Mannerheim, *Memoirs*, p. 512.

could have carried out this task, because nobody else enjoyed as he did the confidence of the great majority of the people … Now that owing to poor health he feels compelled to resign from the office of President, the gratitude of our people should find public expression. President Mannerheim can retire to a well-earned rest in the consciousness that the people of Finland will not forget the exceptional services he has rendered the fatherland.'[71]

The presidency was an unhappy period in Mannerheim's life. Given the harshness of the armistice terms and the presence in Finland of the Control Commission, the first years of peace were inevitably difficult. What made them so much more threatening to Mannerheim was the activity of the Finnish far left. The realism he brought to the consideration of public affairs helped him to adjust to Finland's compulsory change in the direction of its foreign policy, but it would hardly allow him to adjust similarly to the shift to the left in domestic politics. As president he was alarmed and depressed by the apparently irresistible demands of the far left which systematically undermined those aspects of state and society which he held in the greatest respect. He had always been an outsider where party politics were concerned, but he was deprived of even the limited influence over politicians which he had been able to build up during the 1930s and '40s. His political isolation was increased by the deterioration of his health which necessitated lengthy periods of sick leave when he was unable to perform his presidential duties. He was constantly worried that he might be prosecuted as one of those responsible for the war. Only his sense of duty and consciousness of continuing public regard sustained him.

The Control Commission, so dominant during Mannerheim's time as president, did not leave until September 1947 after the ratification of the Treaty of Peace between Finland and the Allies which was signed in Paris on 10 February 1947. Soviet influence remained strong even after its departure and the danger of Finland becoming a people's democracy was not over. Yet Mannerheim's presidency, wretched as it had been for him and degenerating into a purely symbolic role, played its part in preserving Finland from a communist take-over. It proved important that the armistice with the Soviet Union had been concluded by him and the established Finnish government. There

[71] *Ibid.*, pp. 512–13.

PRESIDENT

had been no Finnish resistance or liberation movement which the Soviet Union could exploit to its advantage.

More significant than Finland's avoidance of a Soviet military occupation was the preservation intact of its social and legal system, and to a great extent its army and police. It was the case that 'These formed a firm obstacle to infiltration and the use of salami tactics.'[72] Mass purges of 'class enemies' could not be implemented in a country where civil servants enjoyed security of tenure. Leino often complained to Zhdanov that in many ways the old president was hindering the 'democratization' of the administration.[73] The Finnish communists thought that his popularity as president with the majority of the people hampered the attainment of their aims.[74] The parliamentary system functioned vigorously and Paasikivi was not afraid to assert that parliament represented the will of the people, not mass demonstrations whipped up by the communists. Even the communist ministers had no option but to work within the parliamentary and legal framework. The president was an important part of that framework. By his presence in office Mannerheim – even at his most ineffective – gave a crumb of comfort to those who had lost most from the change in political direction and who feared for the future. He also represented the continuity and strength of Finland's democratic constitution and tradition and the rule of law.

On 9 March Paasikivi – another old monarchist – was elected president of the republic by a special law. Two days later he paid an official call on Mannerheim, which the ex-president returned. Paasikivi recorded that Mannerheim 'was in a good mood'.[75]

---

[72] Jussila, *Suomen tie 1944–1948*, p. 254.
[73] Nevakivi, 'The Soviet Union and Finland after the War, 1944–53', p. 98.
[74] Hirvikallio, *Tasavallan presidentin vaalit*, pp. 136–7.
[75] Paasikivi, *Päiväkirjat 1944–1956*, I, col. 538.

CHAPTER IX

TESTAMENT

'Was it not my duty, now that the West seemed to have forgotten the gallant Finnish people, to communicate to all our friends near and far what I knew about its indomitable battle for all that a nation holds sacred, and had not my countrymen a right to hear my interpretation of the causes that had led to the position where Finland now stood?'[1]

RETIREMENT

By early April 1946 Mannerheim had settled the final matters relating to his presidency and now had 'to make such convenient arrangements as possible in the new circumstances in which I want to begin the simplified life, as it seems to me, of a recluse. The future will show whether this idea corresponds to reality or not.'[2] His retirement was certainly to be simpler than his years in office.' It has its points to be liberated from many heavy responsibilities, indeed it is fine at last to be free, but I too often miss secretaries and ADCs.'[3] His former ADCs, Colonel Grönvall and Major Bäckman, took service with the new president. However, he requested and was allowed by the government the services of an ADC, and Major Carl Olof Lindeman of the Uusimaa Dragoons reported to him as such for the first time on 10 May 1946. Lindeman came to act as Mannerheim's trusted man of affairs. Much adjustment was needed to the practical side of life 'Now I have to start to keep house as a private individual with my ration book and, if it seems possible, now and then with the help of the 'black' market. I am reluctant to have recourse to the latter.'[4] He asked his sister in Sweden to send him unrationed food from there.

[1] Mannerheim, *Memoirs*, p. xi.
[2] To Palaemona Mannerheim, 2 April 1946. Grensholm Collection, VAY 5633.
[3] To Palaemona Mannerheim, 17 August 1946. Grensholm Collection, VAY 5633.
[4] To Eva Sparre, 8 March 1946. Mannerheim, *Brev*, p. 339.

TESTAMENT

The severe inflation in Finland sharply reduced the value of the income from his National Fund which had not even doubled between 1939 and 1947 whereas the cost of living had grown nearly six-times over. The purchasing power of his pensions was also reduced by inflation. However, income from his estate and, above all, bank loans freed him from the need to economize. He retained his pre-war life style, and his expenses remained considerable. They included the wages of his domestic staff, the rent for his house in Helsinki, the generous allowances he paid to his daughters, their medical expenses and his own, travel and, later, financing the writing of his memoirs.

Mannerheim's life in retirement was not to be that of a recluse although bouts of serious illness kept him out of circulation for long periods. At other times he continued to travel and occupied himself with the country estate he had bought in 1945 and, from 1948, with the writing of the *Memoirs*. However, death was inescapably and, constantly narrowing the circle of his friends and acquaintances, and his life became more lonely. Already before retiring he had remarked: 'At my age one no longer replaces' the friends who die[5] and 'I begin to see only graves around me.'[6] His friend Rudolf Walden died in October 1946 after a long illness when Mannerheim was in hospital in Stockholm. He wrote to Anni Walden, the general's widow, of 'his faithful friendship. It bound us together from the moment when our ways joined in the darkest days of the War of Liberation. Not the smallest cloud darkened it.'[7] Anni Walden, on the other hand, thought that her husband and Mannerheim 'were certainly very good acquaintances but for all that hardly friends with each other in the deepest sense of the word.'[8] Palaemona Mannerheim, described by the Marshal as 'the dearest of my sisters-in-law', died in 1948.[9]

Mannerheim's sister Eva, with whom his relationship was close, and his half-sister Marguerite survived him. Contact with his daughters, Anastasie in London and Sophy in Paris, became easier after the war but was generally confined to correspondence although in the summer of 1947 they both came to stay with him in the country

---

[5] To A. Conte, 12 March 1943. Mannerheim Archive, Box 502.
[6] Fagerholm, *Puhemiehen ääni*, p. 206.
[7] Cited in Juva, *Rudolf Walden*, p. 624.
[8] Cited in Lehmus, *Tuntematon Mannerheim*, pp. 221–2.
[9] To Augustin Mannerheim, 4 April 1948. Grensholm Collection, VAY 5633.

in Finland and Anastasie visited him again in the summer of 1949. They were dependent on his monthly allowances to them, which he contrived to arrange even during the war. Mannerheim remained in regular contact with G. A. Gripenberg, in whom he could confide, and with Erik Heinrichs, although there was always a certain distance between them because of the general's consciousness that Mannerheim was his former commander-in-chief. A new friend, and an enlivening and cheering influence in Mannerheim's life, was Countess Gertrud Arco-Valley, a friend of his daughter Sophy, whom he met in Stockholm in September 1946 when she was aged fifty-one. She was divorced the following year. Gripenberg wrote of him with understandable astonishment: 'A remarkable man in truth, 79 years old, a stomach ulcer, and still so full of life, of interest in young ladies.'[10] Countess Arco accompanied Mannerheim on some of his travels in Switzerland, Italy and France and also stayed with him in Finland.

Mannerheim's house in Helsinki survived the war undamaged, though with potatoes growing in the rose beds, but the shortage of accommodation in the capital was so acute that Walden warned Mannerheim of the risk of tenants being forced on him. He recommended anticipating the problem by taking as tenant part of the War Casualty Archives, whose pleasant female staff would cause no difficulties. Mannerheim therefore rearranged the house so that he could live on the first floor while the ground floor was let, as Walden had suggested, from 22 January 1945 at a rent of 4,250 marks a month, which he passed on to the landlord.[11] It remained let until late 1950 and probably until his death. He retained his housekeepers.

More troublesome than the need to take a tenant was the question of the ownership of the house. In 1942 parliament had promised to buy it for him as a seventy-fifth birthday present but because the owner wanted to exchange the property for a plot of land elsewhere, and a suitable one could not be found, nothing was done. Mannerheim consequently stopped paying the rent, but was angry to learn in 1944 not only did he not own any house but that he was also in debt to the landlord. He paid off the debt, for which parliament reimbursed him, and on 5 March 1945 turned to Paasikivi for help over the promised house. 'He said that he has no property worth mentioning but he has two daughters. I promised to find out about the matter and try to get

[10] Gripenberg's diary, 19 September 1946, cited in Jägerskiöld, *Från krig till fred*, p. 234.
[11] Virkkunen, *Mannerheim*, p. 393.

TESTAMENT

the present parliament to arrange it.'[12] The speaker of the house, who was responsible for the blunder, offered money, and despite initial reluctance because of the rate of inflation, Mannerheim decided to accept the offered 12 million marks, which parliament on 5 April agreed to pay him for the purchase of a property. He received the money in June 1945.

When he failed to find anything suitable in Helsinki, Mannerheim began to look for a country estate, helped by his friends Henrik Ramsay and Petter Forsström. The choice eventually fell on Kirkniemi (in Swedish Gerknäs) in the parish of Lohja some 37 miles (60 km.) west of Helsinki. It dated back to the fifteenth century and no fewer than six marshals or field marshals had owned it – Mannerheim became the seventh. The manor house, containing fifteen rooms, was a handsome two-storey wooden building, rebuilt at the beginning of the nineteenth century in the classical style. There was a large garden with an attractive view of the nearby lake. The estate itself comprised about 1,500 hectares (3,700 acres) of which 305 hectares (754 acres) were cultivated land. The purchase was completed on 9 August 1945, about half of the cost coming from what parliament had provided and the rest from the sale of shares owned by General Mannerheim's National Fund. It was an elegant property worthy of its new owner.

Fears that he might be drawn into the war guilt case prompted Mannerheim to organize his private affairs; he made a new will on 16 August 1945 and changed his National Fund into a foundation, the regulations for which were approved by the end of that month.[13] He transferred the ownership of Kirkniemi to what subsequently became the Mannerheim Foundation. This did not affect his ability to restore the house or run the estate, but it had the serious consequence of causing the land to fell under the severest terms of the land acquisition law. He spoke to Paasikivi in March 1946 about his concern for the estate, and in May 1946 wrote to his sister that it was unclear 'who will be the ultimate owner of Kirkniemi, I or evacuated Karelians'.[14]

The possibility of exempting Kirkniemi from the law was discussed by the government and the political parties in July 1946, but in the face of opposition from the communists Mannerheim decided that it

[12] Paasikivi, *Päiväkirjat 1944–1956*,1, col. 202.
[13] Öhman, 'Stiftelsen "General Mannerheims Nationalfond"', pp. 157–8.
[14] Cited in Jägerskiöld, *Från krig till fred*, p. 222.

would be inappropriate to seek a privilege which was not unanimously supported by parliament. To his annoyance, therefore, the estate was reduced by over half to 709 hectares (1,750 acres) with a reduction of 60 per cent of the cultivated land to 124 hectares (306 acres). But the land around the house remained unaffected and there was sufficient forest left from which timber felling helped to pay the costs of work on the house and the remaining land.

It was a disappointment to Mannerheim that the previous owner of Kirkniemi, Uno Donner, could not leave the house until 1 May 1946. Mannerheim was eager to take possession and put the place in order, although he wrote that with each of its rooms heated by stoves 'it will never be a winter home ... During the summer it will not of course need much heating and then one can be happy at Kirkniemi, but in winter it is a matter of putting up with a few rooms and coming for a weekend, for a few days' hunting or to rest and be alone for a little while.'[15] He was able to live there for a time in the summer of 1946. In August 1947 he wrote from there that 'the rationalization of the farming is in full swing but I have lacked the necessary courage for a restoration of the main building, at any rate so far.'[16] He took a keen interest in the farm – for which he employed a manager – and in improving the garden and gradually the house itself.

He enjoyed receiving visitors at Kirkniemi and walking through the forest and bathing in the lake. General Heinrichs, himself a guest, recorded Mannerheim's contented reaction to the view of the manor house from the opposite shore of the lake: 'It really makes quite a stately impression.'[17] Kirkniemi brought Mannerheim something to occupy him, a means of relaxation, and pride of possession.

On 2 June 1946 he left Kirkniemi to spend his seventy-ninth birthday quietly at Rafael von Frenckell's estate of Anola near Pori. From there he intended to stay with a former ADC, Major-General Heikki Kekoni, at Pietarsaari but was taken ill on the way with what proved to be a perforated ulcer. A life-saving operation was carried out at Pietarsaari hospital where he stayed until 23 June. His health then improved until the autumn when in the course of a visit to Sweden he suffered severe stomach pains. He was admitted in October to the Karolinska Hospital in Stockholm where a duodenal ulcer

[15] To Eva Sparre, 8 March 1946. Mannerheim, *Brev*, p. 339.
[16] To Palaemona Mannerheim, 2 August 1947. Grensholm Collection, VAY 5633.
[17] Heinrichs, *Mannerheim Suomen kohtaloissa*, II, p. 445.

was diagnosed, and remained there till 4 December 1946. At the hospital he came under the care of Professor Nanna Svartz, one of Sweden's leading gastro-enterologists, who recorded that 'periodically for around 15 years' Mannerheim had suffered from 'the symptoms of stomach ulcers'.[18] He developed a relationship of trust and friendship with Nanna Svartz, and it was she who found out about the Val-Mont Clinic at Glion near Montreux in Switzerland which was to become his base during the writing of the *Memoirs* from autumn of 1948 until his death.

In February 1947 Mannerheim was back in hospital in Stockholm for a week but then set out for Switzerland with its favourable climate. There, in March, he made his first acquaintance with Val-Mont, 'a hotel in the mountains with doctors, masseurs and everything to do with the care of the sick'.[19] In April he informed Colonel Grönvall: 'I have ... eaten with an appetite, slept well, gone for walks, kept to a strict diet, been massaged and feel myself healthy.'[20] Before returning to Finland he intended to visit Lausanne to see an ear specialist about his reduced hearing and also see his dentist. He enjoyed being in Switzerland, which was such a contrast to the war-torn parts of Europe through which he had travelled. He wrote to a friend: 'If on this earth there is a place to be found which is dedicated to forgetting, calm and rest, it is Switzerland, with all the convenience which makes life easy, hotels, communications, order, food and the beauty of the landscape, but above all the mountains, the Alps which give the impression of being somewhere in the atmosphere, above the clouds between earth and sky.'[21] Mannerheim spent the summer of 1947 in Finland. Nanna Svartz congratulated him in June on a heart and vascular system corresponding to that of a fifty or sixty-year-old and on a healthy central nervous system.[22] Later he noted: 'I have pains and am very tired but my condition is much better ... The summer, too, has done me good.'[23] But he was ill again in November with a severe haemorrhage from

---

[18] 'Exposé résumé sur la maladie du Maréchal de Finlande, 7 février 1947'. Mannerheim Archive, Box 2.
[19] To Evo Weckman, 12 December 1948. Mannerheim Archive, Box 904.
[20] To Ragnar Grönvall, 13 April 1947. Mannerheim, *Brev*, p. 343.
[21] To Andreé von Nottbeck, 19 May 1947, cited in Jägerskiöld, *Från krig till fred*, p. 245.
[22] From Nanna Svartz, 1 June 1947. Mannerheim Archives, Box 2.
[23] To Palaemona Mannerheim, 11 September 1947. Grensholm Collection, VAY 5633.

his ulcer leading to persistent severe anaemia. His doctors in Helsinki sent him in an air force plane to Stockholm for urgent treatment. There on 18 December he had a major operation on his duodenal ulcer and returned to Finland in mid February 1948 after a rapid recovery. In the spring of 1948, following Nanna Svartz's advice to spend a lot of time in the sunshine and open air, he was back in Switzerland at Lausanne and Lugano. In May he went to Milan and the French Riviera. On his way back to Finland to vote in the parliamentary elections in July ('to set an example')[24] he arranged to meet General Erfurth in Tübingen. Later in July, he was back in the Karolinska Hospital suffering from kidney stones and haemorrhages but was fit enough to return to Switzerland in the autumn. With the exception of a late summer visit to Finland, he spent 1949 at Val-Mont working on the *Memoirs*.

The presidential election in January 1950 brought him back to Finland to vote, and his subsequent stay at Val-Mont was interrupted by visits to Nice and Monte Carlo in April. Summer in Finland was followed in October by illness – severe influenza, inflammation of the mouth and some hypertension – which took him again to hospital in Stockholm followed by convalescence there. Gripenberg had 'never seen him looking so bad' as on his arrival.[25] Paasikivi, in Stockholm in November for the funeral of King Gustav V, found that 'Mannerheim is quite weak, cannot eat and has therefore become thin.'[26] His weight (between 70 and 80 kilos in 1946–8) had dropped during the illness to 57.5. However, he was able to leave hospital in mid December and be back in Switzerland to spend Christmas 1950 – his last – in Lugano with Countess Arco-Valley.

Neither Mannerheim's retirement nor his constant sickness and long periods abroad diminished his concern for the future of Finland. He remained extremely pessimistic about the intentions of the Soviet Union and the danger of the Finnish extreme left. At the time of the communist take-over in Czechoslovakia he ordered Major Lindeman to burn some of his papers, and personally supervised the operation. Some papers relating to cooperation with the Germans had already been burned before he moved from Mikkeli to Helsinki at the end of 1944. Now he feared Finland would go the way of Czechoslovakia,

[24] To Nanna Svartz, 1 July 1948. Mannerheim Archive, Box 950.
[25] Gripenberg's diary, October 1950. cited in Jägerskiöld, *Från krig till fred*, p. 283.
[26] Paasikivi, *Päiväkirjat 1944–1956*, II, col. 290.

and in February 1948, he told Paasikivi, with whom he remained in regular personal contact, 'that there is no doubt about the Russians intentions ... when one takes account of their conduct in other countries'. He also believed that Finland, whose right to arm itself was restricted, should avoid a military alliance with the Soviet Union.[27] This was a change of mind since his discussions with Zhdanov in January 1945. Mannerheim told Count Folke Bernadotte in early March 1948 that he believed the treaty proposed by the Soviet Union would lead to a Soviet take-over of Finland.[28]

Despite initial grave misgivings about the political and military implications, Finland concluded the Treaty of Friendship, Cooperation and Mutual Assistance with the Soviet Union in April 1948. Mannerheim's journey to Stockholm the previous month at a time of international tension led to rumours that he had gone into voluntary exile or had left to form a government-in-exile; these rumours upset the government in Helsinki and he strenuously denied them. Later in April American diplomats even thought of encouraging him to return to Finland in the belief that his presence would have a bracing effect on public opinion. Of course Mannerheim, who was well informed of events in Finland, knew that his comings and goings attracted attention, hence his scrupulousness in returning home to vote.

Paasikivi became fed up with Mannerheim's constant pessimism. On 1 July 1948 he wrote in his diary of a discussion with his predecessor whose 'attitude is totally sterile and quite pessimistic about the future of Finland. In his opinion the Russians have evil thoughts towards Finland. The Russians are able to wait, it is an illusion to think well of them.' Mannerheim was unable to answer Paasikivi when he asked what Finland should do. The president said that 'if one adopts his line, then there was nothing to be done but go into the forest and fire a bullet into one's forehead.'[29] However, at the end of August 1948 Paasikivi recorded: 'Mannerheim is not so pessimistic as before.'[30] In October 1949 Mannerheim even admitted 'that the president and government have had much success' and that 'People

---

[27] *Ibid.*, I, col. 1069.
[28] Ylitalo, *Salasanomia Helsingistä Washingtoniin*, p. 224.
[29] Paasikivi, *Päiväkirjat 1944–1956*, 1, col. 1215.
[30] *Ibid.*, II, col. 50.

are optimistic here, in his opinion more than can really be justified'.[31] Political change in Finland can in fact be dated from 1948 when the elections reduced the representation of the extreme left. Its exclusion from the government followed.

The reaction of the Western powers to the Berlin blockade heartened Mannerheim. He wrote to Carl Enckell on 11 November 1948: 'My greatest interest ... has been in the "poker game" in Berlin and the struggle of gigantic dimensions for which little Truman had the courage and capacity to get America and Europe, and even the whole world, to prepare themselves. It is at the eleventh hour, [one hopes] it may not be too late. Only think if, instead of trying to lull the nations into an unjustified sense of security, one had already consciously striven thirty years ago to open people's eyes to the deadly danger which the spread of Bolshevism must bring about!'[32] Mannerheim never relaxed his fear of Soviet aggression or changed his view of the dangers of communism.

THE *MEMOIRS*

In the 1930s Mannerheim had resisted calls to write his memoirs, and despite renewed interest in the idea after the Winter War nothing came of it: he was 'not fond of writing'.[33] As already mentioned, he thought in January 1944 that he might turn to that 'bizarre idea' after the war.[34] However, he only began the project in the spring of 1948, impelled by his fear that Finland was at that time particularly threatened by the Soviet Union: a defence of its position would be timely. Thus he began to collect material – paradoxically this was soon after he had destroyed some of his papers – and to consider who might help him in the task. There was no question of his undertaking it alone. His choice fell on Colonel Aladár Paasonen who had been head of intelligence at GHQ for most of the Continuation War and had moved abroad, at Mannerheim's urging, in May 1945.

In mid April 1948 Mannerheim asked Paasonen if he would be willing to help, writing that 'Moscow's aggressive policy in Finland,

[31] *Ibid.*, col. 70.
[32] Cited in Enckell, 'Några minnen från mitt samarbete med Gustaf Mannerheim', pp. 43–4.
[33] Telegram to Peggy Gripenberg, [1940]. Mannerheim Archive, Box 110.
[34] To Palaemona Mannerheim, 19 January 1944. Grensholm Collection, VAY 5632.

TESTAMENT

which ever more plainly points to complete bolshevization as its immediate goal', had led him 'to ask myself if it were not my duty to set out to the political and politically-concerned world my recollections of the relevant years that we have all experienced and of Finnish policy from the War of Liberation onwards but with special emphasis on both its pre-war and wartime policy'.[35] Paasonen agreed to the proposal and, under the alias of Dr Bartha, worked with Mannerheim in Switzerland on the memoirs right up to the Marshal's death. He drew up an outline for the work which remained essentially unchanged. Paasonen induced Mannerheim to extend the book to include his service in Russia, but not to include personal details or anecdotes. He was also extremely restrained in his comments on individuals, having long thought such comments improper.[36] The memoirs were to be his political testament, dignified and devoid of inappropriate human interest or sensation. The focus was to be on Finland, its struggle to become and remain independent, and Mannerheim's own part in that struggle. The work was intended above all to set out Finland's case for non-Finnish readers.

Mannerheim obtained also the help of General Heinrichs but only until the autumn of 1948. Paasonen thus had to draft much more of the work than had originally been intended. G. A. Gripenberg helped to find a secretary, Mrs Sargit Avellan, who was appointed in December 1948 and, like Paasonen, continued until Mannerheim's death. The operation was discreetly run from the clinic at Val-Mont, where Mannerheim took an extra room to serve as an office, and the cost was considerable. It was funded partly by Mannerheim himself and partly by advances from his eventual publishers. Sometimes it was necessary, at that time of strict exchange controls, to resort to ingenious means of getting money to Switzerland. The devaluation of the Finnish mark in 1949 greatly increased the cost for him of living abroad.

The fact that he was writing his memoirs away from public attention in Switzerland was kept secret in Finland as long as possible, but it had become known early in 1949. Surprisingly, Mannerheim did not use as sources the material he had sent to Sweden for safekeeping during the war. He did dictate some reminiscences, although

---

[35] Paasonen, *Marsalkan tiedustelupäällikkönä*, p. 158.
[36] To Michael Gripenberg, 22 September 1934. Mannerheim Archive, Box 906.

he worried about his failing memory, and made numerous alterations of style and fact to the drafts submitted to him. Several outside contributors were involved: for example, Emerik Olsoni wrote the chapter on Mannerheim's Asian expedition based on his diary, and Erik Mandelin wrote on his humanitarian work. The contributors made use of published material as well as some documentation from the Finnish Military Archives, although that source dried up in February 1949 due to political pressure from the extreme left, which had learned of Paasonen's visits to the Marshal.

Mannerheim worked on the *Memoirs* assiduously, and the task gave his last years a somewhat exhausting but urgent sense of purpose. He informed his sister in November 1948 that 'the work has been in full swing here for 2 whole months and quite a lot has been done ... but the more things begin to become clear the more is needed'.[37] In June 1949 he told her: 'I am surrounded from morning to night with loose papers, files and suchlike. Sometimes it can be interesting to concern oneself with and live afresh among people who are long gone and in the memory of events which unfortunately are seldom as one had wished them, but it takes up the whole of one's time.'[38] A little later he informed Nanna Svartz that his legs were tired. 'Perhaps this has its origin in insufficient exercise caused by the daily work which ties me to my desk. However, I am glad to have the opportunity to work here, for nowhere else would I find the same quiet working conditions.'[39]

Although he had originally intended the book to be for foreign readers, the Finnish market was soon seen to be important. Arrangements were made for Schildts to publish the original Swedish-language version and for Otava to publish the Finnish translation. Despite negotiations, no English-language publisher had been arranged when Mannerheim died, although some of the text had been available in English translation since late 1949. As the work neared completion Mannerheim sought advice on particular aspects of it. He ran into the problem of self-censorship. He had realized from the beginning that 'the subject is politically so very sensitive that what could really interest each thinking person should probably

---

[37] To Eva Sparre, 20 November 1948. Mannerheim, *Brev*, p. 345.
[38] To Eva Sparre, 20 June 1949. Mannerheim, *Brev*, p. 348.
[39] To Nanna Svartz, [July 1949]. Mannerheim Archive, Box 950.

be struck out by way of caution and then what remains will be so commonplace that nobody will take the trouble to read the book to the end.'[40]

G. A. Gripenberg, whom he consulted, wanted him to make his criticism of Sweden less direct and, supported also by the urging of Paasikivi and Enckell, to tone down the anti-bolshevik line of his preface. They feared an adverse reaction from the Soviet Union and thought that publication should be deferred. Mannerheim defended himself to Gripenberg in February 1949. 'If I ... wish before my death to elucidate *my* attitude to these historical facts and the decisions to which they led, then the responsibility for this can surely not fall upon the country where I served ... My outlook ever since the Bolshevik Revolution contains nothing new which the Soviet would not know – perhaps even better than my own countrymen.'[41] Mannerheim told Paasikivi in October 1949 that he naturally did not want to harm Finland's interests and promised to consider what to do, but he added: 'I must tell the truth.'[42]

The *Memoirs* were still not ready for publication when Mannerheim died, but their completion and publication were not long delayed. Posthumous publication reduced the likelihood of controversy, and some of the contentious parts of the preface survived in an afterword. On 31 October 1951 the Finnish publishers brought Paasikivi the first copies. The president thought that the *Memoirs* made a disagreeable impression, seeking to show that Mannerheim was always right and praising himself. Paasikivi thought that in this respect they portrayed their author very well.[43]

The *Memoirs* naturally represented Mannerheim's view of events and his role in them, expressed as clearly as he believed possible in the difficult political circumstances of the late 1940s and early '50s. As such they will always be important even if they are often very general in character and contain little that was new. The way in which the *Memoirs* were written meant that many factual errors remained uncorrected. Mannerheim's opposition to bolshevism was clear, although his warning of the continuing danger from the east was watered down. His account of relations with Germany in 1940–1

[40] To Eva Sparre, 20 November 1948. Mannerheim, *Brev*, p. 345.
[41] To G. A. Gripenberg, 18 February 1949. Mannerheim, *Brev*, p. 346.
[42] Paasikivi, *Päiväkirjat 1944–1956*, II, col. 71.
[43] *Ibid.*, col. 477.

was disingenuous and an American scholar suggested furthermore that it was not always truthful.[44] Memoirs as a genre are inevitably *parti pris*, and Mannerheim was not writing objective history despite his protestation that he had to tell the truth. But with their praise for Finland's defence of its freedom and their appeal to the values which underpin that freedom – 'the faith of our fathers, the love of our country, and the determination to defend ourselves resolutely and unselfishly'[45] – the book achieved its aim. It constituted 'a last solemn greeting' from the Marshal 'in the midst of the grey, humdrum present moment and its historical and patriotic depression'.[46] The *Memoirs* attracted, and continue to attract, attention both in Finland and abroad where the abridged versions remain commonly-cited sources for the history of modem Finland. Mannerheim wrote an effective testament.

DEATH

Early in January 1951 Mannerheim, now aged eighty-three, was back at Val-Mont. 'Merely this insignificant journey from Stockholm to Lausanne exhausted me so much that I changed my plans and did not continue directly to Val-Mont but decided to travel to Lugano to seek for strength by complete rest. In this way only around ten days after my arrival in Switzerland did I become familiar with everything that had been gathering at Val-Mont during my four months' absence!'[47] He continued to work on the *Memoirs*. On 19 January he became ill with stomach pains, but on 21 and 22 January was again at work on the publication schedule and arrangements for publication rights outside Finland and Scandinavia.

On 22 January his abdomen became very swollen and on the next day his local doctor sent him to the Cantonal Hospital in Lausanne. On 24 January a major operation on a blocked intestine was performed there, and this gave him a chance of survival although he told his doctor that he expected to 'lose this battle, the last'.[48] Despite this

---

[44] Lundin, *Finland in the Second World War*, p. 255.
[45] Mannerheim, *Memoirs*, p. 519.
[46] Jaakkola, 'Suomen marsalkan muistelmat', p. 261.
[47] To Andreé von Nottbeck, 16 January 1951. Mannerheim, *Kirjeitä*, p. 363. This refers to material for the *Memoirs* which had not been forwarded to him.
[48] Cited in Jägerskiöld, *Från krig till fred*, p. 285.

TESTAMENT

premonition, he felt better on 25 January and even phoned his secretary at Val-Mont to ask what she was doing. Only in the afternoon of 27 January 1951 did his condition become dramatically worse. Professor Nanna Svartz, sent earlier from Stockholm by Paasikivi at the Finnish government's expense, arrived to find him in a very poor state. His heart and breathing were no longer functioning properly and his pulse rate fell sharply. He knew that death was near and bade farewell to those around him. From late evening he was unconscious and at 11.30 p.m. Central European Time he died peacefully and apparently without pain. In Finland it was already 28 January, the anniversary of the start of the War of 1918 when he had stepped into Finnish history.

Paasikivi broadcast a tribute later on 28 January. Many buildings flew the Finnish flag at half mast. The president reflected two days later that 'Mannerheim's death has been the subject of great and handsome attention in the press and in other non-communist circles ... It will awaken the nation and raise the patriotic mood and patriotic spirit. That we need.'[49] The Marshal was to be given a state funeral, arranged by the army, on 4 February 1951 but because he had left no instructions about where he was to be buried, the Council of State decided that it should be in the section of Hietaniemi Cemetery in Helsinki dedicated to the war dead. Paasikivi praised this decision because the grave would become a 'place of pilgrimage' and would 'thus always remind our people of a time of heroism and have an influence on the maintenance of a patriotic mood'.[50] This prophesy has been proved correct.

Mannerheim's body was brought by air with military honours first from Switzerland to Sweden and then on to Finland on 1 February. In accordance with his wishes, his body was dressed in marshal's uniform – it was photographed before the coffin was sealed. His body lay in state in the Lutheran Cathedral in Helsinki from 2 February until only five hours before the funeral on 4 February. The time allowed for the lying-in-state was extended again and again because of the tens of thousands of people who wished to pay their respects. It is estimated that some 60,000 did so, patiently queuing three or four deep in the cold for up to six hours.

[49] Paasikivi, *Päiväkirjat 1944–1956*, II, cols 337–8.
[50] *Ibid.*, col. 342.

The funeral service began at noon in the cathedral. Mannerheim's daughters were present. Paasikivi noted in his diary: 'In every way the ceremony was dignified and fine. The communists have written lamentably and insolently about Mannerheim and the funeral. The communists are even more isolated from their own people. The weather was fine but cold. Fagerholm [the speaker of parliament] gave a good speech, which really overshot the mark, but that is common on such occasions.'[51] Despite these strictures, Fagerholm's speech, which had not been an easy task for a social democrat, struck the right note. He praised 'a great warrior, a great statesman, a great citizen' who left his countrymen 'a precious heritage ... the country's freedom and independence, the lodestones of his life'.[52] Paasikivi, deeply moved, laid a wreath.

Fear of adverse Soviet reaction to a Finnish patriotic occasion had caused the government cravenly to vote to stay away from the funeral but two ministers, Kekkonen being one of them, did attend. There was no question of the people staying away. Over 100,000 watched silently as the coffin made the long journey from the cathedral to the cemetery. Many wept. The route was lined by university students and scouts as well as some 6,000 reserve officers in uniform with decorations: these men had not forgotten their commander-in-chief's unstinting praise. The coffin was placed on a horse-drawn gun carriage for the journey to the cemetery, and six officers carried his decorations. Representative contingents from the defence forces made up an impressive procession. Mannerheim's last charger, Kate, was in foal but a punctilious cavalry officer made sure that she took her rightful place in the procession for a short distance.

At Hietaniemi the coffin was lowered into the earth to the sound of two distant nineteen gun salutes. All who witnessed the funeral, attended services in other parts of the country or listened to it on the radio were conscious not only of the passing of a great man but also of an era in Finnish history.

THE MAN

At the time of his death Mannerheim's name was well known to all Finns, but few knew him personally and very few could have claimed

[51] *Ibid.*, col. 344.
[52] Cited in Jägerskiöld, *Från krig till fred*, p. 290–92.

(*Left*) 25. Mannerheim at Montreux in Switzerland towards the end of his life. (*Below*) 26. His funeral, 4 February 1951: the last moments before the lowering of the coffin. (Both photos: Military Museum of Finland)

(*Left*) 27. Mannerheim's death mask. (Military Museum of Finland) (*Below*) 28. Letter of thanks to Laurence Collier, head of the Northern Department at the Foreign Office, following Mannerheim's official visit to Britain in 1936. (Public Record Office. F.O. 371/20328, f. 78, r. & v.)

even a close acquaintance, much less friendship. General Heinrichs, one of the few who were close to Mannerheim, wrote that there was in him, 'more than in others, something which distinguished him in every way from ordinary people, something hard and rare.' Heinrichs defined it as 'unapproachability'.[53] Undoubtedly this quality – the distance he kept from other people – increases the difficulty of assessing Mannerheim's complex character.

Before Mannerheim's official visit to Britain in 1936 the British legation in Helsinki prepared a note describing his appearance, character, interests and influence: 'Mannerheim is over 65, but looks much younger. He is a tall, strongly built, vigorous man, still in the prime of his forces, a hard worker, a good shot and a keen horseman ... he is fond of golf, although he would perhaps not claim to be an accomplished golfer ... But the Marshal is more than a keen sportsman and a distinguished soldier ... He is also an enthusiastic social worker ... The Marshal, who is an accomplished linguist ... is a great lover of music and in Finland known as an eloquent speaker. He has also several literary accomplishments to his credit.' A separate note in the same file stated: 'He is proud of his noble birth and his military achievements, and is somewhat susceptible to flattery.'[54] A few months earlier the legation had noted: 'He is accustomed to be treated with excessive deference and is vain (this is a weak side of his character).'[55] Gripenberg, the Finnish minister in London, informed the Foreign Office that Mannerheim 'particularly dislikes being referred to as "von", since his ancestors were Dutch and came from a village in Holland called Marheim!'[56]

Mannerheim's striking appearance was commented upon by many observers. He was tall – six feet and two inches (187 cm.) – handsome, and even in old age was erect, and his movements, demeanour and dress had a studied elegance. He was aware of the value to a general or a national leader of a commanding presence and exploited the advantages which nature and nurture had given him. He took great care of his health, appearance and dress, and was fastidious over

---

[53] Heinrichs, *Mannerheim Suomen kohtaloissa*, II, p. 463.
[54] Note on career and personality of Field Marshal Mannerheim. F.O.371/20327, N656/52/56.
[55] Grant Watson to Collier, 16 January 1936. F.O.371/20327, N345/52/56.
[56] Note of conversation of Finnish Minister with Vereker, 5 August 1936. F.O.371/20328, N3967/52/56.

such details as the correct trim of his moustache, the daily ritual of cleaning his teeth by spraying them with water, the precise manner of shining his boots, and the food and drink served to his guests. His uniforms, decorations and civilian clothes had to be exactly appropriate to the occasion and perfectly made, although he allowed himself some divergence from regulations over the style of his uniform caps and summer tunics. His salute was distinctive, with the hand slightly curved. He was often pictured with one hand on his hip but this could have been to ease pain from a riding accident rather than to strike a pose. During the Continuation War he refused to allow the publication of photographs which showed him looking tired or less than immaculate. In all this there was of course an element of vanity but there was also recognition of the importance of maintaining the image appropriate to his public role. Even the furnishing of his homes reflected the good taste and elegance which were not just part of his character but also formed part of his public persona.

It was correct to describe Mannerheim as a hard worker. He craved activity and when he was without an official position he sought it in humanitarian work. He found relaxation chiefly through physical activity such as riding, hunting, golf and travel, although he also liked listening to music. He enjoyed good food and drink and fine cigars. He had an extensive library in which travel, history, biography and literature were well represented. Books on politics and biographies were prominent among his favourite reading in old age. He was an accomplished raconteur and possessed a fine Swedish literary style with a gift for the telling or descriptive phrase, whether in his private letters and diaries or in his public speeches. His handwriting was exceptionally clear although he wrote slowly and with difficulty because he had broken the index finger on his right hand. His knowledge of foreign languages enabled him to open up international contacts, and he acquired and maintained a wide circle of acquaintances and friends abroad. He was a loyal friend and felt a particularly close bond with his colleagues from GHQ during the War of Independence. His loyalty to the Russian imperial family and to his regimental comrades from before the Revolution endured to the end of his life. Emigré Russian officers remembered the fiftieth anniversary of Mannerheim's first commission in the imperial army, an occasion he marked by a luncheon party in Helsinki on 23 August 1939.[57]

[57] Grensholm Collection, VAY 5639.

TESTAMENT

Mannerheim was a shrewd judge of people and a good listener. He had no time for small talk or gossip but could only tolerate serious conversation, from which he expected to glean accurate information. He often paused to think carefully before a reply, but his rejoinders could also be quick and sharp. Those around him might then find themselves the butt of his irony. Gripenberg commented on Mannerheim's 'somewhat nasal speech'.[58] Karin Ramsay knew of nothing 'which could express so many nuances as the Marshal's harmonious voice. It could be ice-cold when he was displeased, reserved when he was uninterested, often obligingly polite; mostly it was kind, but there was an altogether particular warm tone in it when he spoke about something which gave him pleasure.'[59]

Mannerheim said that he was 'always uneasy about the fate of my daughters',[60] but was formal and distant in his dealings with them. He was plainly very fond of his sisters Sophie and Eva, of his brother Johan and of his sister-in-law Palaemona. He nevertheless liked to live an independent life free from the demands of others. This was part of his unapproachability. For all that, he was a hospitable host and an immediate focus of attention in any company. He enjoyed the friendship of his relations and the companionship of his friends, with whom he was sociable rather than intimate. To his closest relations he opened his more intimate thoughts and it is his correspondence with them that reveals an inner humility – despite all the adulation he received. Although he made effective use of the press to advance his public policies, he objected to intrusion into his private life, rejected proposals for publications about him which he thought would smack of self-advertisement, and was very critical of some biographies. However, he thought that Kai Donner's biography, published in 1934, 'contains so much undeserved flattering recognition that I have difficulty in sending it to anyone'.[61] Characteristically, he sent it to his sister-in-law just the same.

Professor Nanna Svartz commented on Mannerheim's 'lightning understanding'.[62] As an intelligent, determined and strong-willed leader, he was supremely confident of his abilities, including the

[58] Gripenberg, *Finland and the Great Powers*, p. 236.
[59] Ramsay, 'Mannerheim och Finlands Röda Kors', p. 114.
[60] To Andrée von Nottbeck, 8 September 1943. Mannerheim Archive, Box 505.
[61] To Palaemona Mannerheim, 24 November 1934. Grensholm Collection, VAY 5631.
[62] Svartz, *Steg för steg*, p. 177.

ability to bear responsibility. However, especially in old age, he was not free from anxiety at critical moments: he was no superhuman hero. He believed in the rightness of the courses of action he advocated and remarked when writing his *Memoirs* how often he had been proved right. This tendency in him was, of course, profoundly irritating to others. Mannerheim was sometimes impatient, dour, distant, demanding and given to outbursts of temper and strong language, and he could be extraordinarily touchy if he thought his honour, veracity or status had been impugned.[63] But he could also be generous, chivalrous and courteous. His sense of justice impelled him to restore good relations with anyone he felt he had treated unfairly. However, he also had a long memory for real or imagined injuries, as he also had for acts of kindness.

The British legation's characterization of Mannerheim missed what most impressed many people who met him. Gripenberg described this as 'the magnetism which radiated from his person, which aroused regard, trust and devotion, and which can perhaps best be indicated by the French word "*autorité*"'.[64] General Sir Walter Kirke wrote to Mannerheim in 1949: 'I have met most of the world leaders during the last 30 years, but there is none whom I rate so high as yourself and to me you will always be the beau ideal of soldier, diplomat and gentleman.'[65] However, not all were susceptible to Mannerheim's magnetism; some regarded him as a prima donna or thought he was acting a part. In the words of Paasikivi, 'Mannerheim, contrary to what many think, was very ambitious and egoistical and egocentric. He never in any way wanted to initiate anything unpopular. He greatly needed popularity.'[66]

Mannerheim knew very well that he was a big fish in a small pond. He was acutely conscious and even jealous of his position as national hero, ex-regent and, eventually, president and ex-president. He purposefully inquired of a French diplomat in 1925 what were the marks of respect accorded to a French ex-president.[67] It was natural that he, who held such an elevated concept of the status of a head of state,

[63] See, for example, the correspondence with Ernst von Born and A. L. Hjelmman in Mannerheim Archive, Box 301, and with Heikki Renvall, Box 305.
[64] Gripenberg, 'Försök till en karakteristik av Marskalk Mannerheim', p. 58.
[65] From Kirke, 11 January 1949. Mannerheim Archive, Box 504.
[66] Paasikivi, *Päiväkirjat 1944–1956*, II, col. 340.
[67] From J. L. Chauffault, 6 October 1925. Mannerheim Archive, Box 814.

TESTAMENT

should expect deference and also receive it. He was not above enjoying flattery but he could deflate those who carried sycophancy too far. The vast number of anecdotes about him were mostly affectionate or expressed general approval. Mannerheim had a positive public image, but it owed nothing to playing a part, and he did not want to jeopardise it. On occasions, as in 1930–2, he sat on the fence instead of coming out openly in favour of a particular course of action. But ambition for power in 1918–19 had given way to dutiful acceptance of it in 1944, and in 1939 he was quite prepared to put before the people the need for unpopular territorial concessions to the Soviet Union. Paasikivi overstated his case. When Mannerheim looked back over his life, as in the addresses he made on his seventieth and seventy-fifth birthdays, he stated that the recognition bestowed on him was undeserved, how grateful he was to providence for being able to serve his country, and how little he had really achieved. Mannerheim found the popularity expressed in the manifest trust of the Finnish people both touching and humbling. As a realist, he also recognized its political significance.

Mannerheim, who lived life to the full, had reflected on death. He thought it was hard to believe that everything came to an end with death but that it was difficult to envisage in what form it could continue.[68] This prompts the question: was he a religious man? As a soldier he was a fatalist, with a conviction that 'higher powers' controlled man's destiny.[69] He was also superstitious. Yet at an audience with the archbishop on returning to Finland as regent, he knelt to receive a blessing, clearly wanting to be consecrated, albeit privately, for his service as head of state. He was registered as a member of the Lutheran church, and as a public figure he attended many religious services. For him as for his contemporaries, the forms and expressions of religion constituted part of his background and way of thinking. He was certainly made aware that 'the religiously-awakened people of Finland pray earnestly and diligently for the Field Marshal'.[70] Not surprisingly, Mannerheim's speeches frequently invoked the aid of the Almighty. In his letters he made occasional reference to phrases from Russian Orthodox formularies which had obviously impressed

---

[68] Heinrichs, *Mannerheim Suomen kohtaloissa*, II, p. 458.
[69] Jägerskiöld, *Gustaf Mannerheim 1906–1917*, pp. 271–2.
[70] From Anni Walden, 20 April 1942. Mannerheim Archive, Box 429.

him. He prayed in an Orthodox church in Helsinki when his divorced wife died. He wore a cross around his neck but his innermost beliefs remained private.

It was natural that Mannerheim should have been proud of his military achievements both in the imperial Russian army and in Finland in 1918 and of having commanded the Finnish army from 1939 to 1944, 'this army incomparable in its valour',[71] but he was careful both in 1918 and during the Winter and Continuation Wars to acknowledge that the honours heaped on him were also honours for the men he had commanded. His admiration for the Finnish soldier was profound, as was his devotion to the war veterans and disabled ex-servicemen.

Much has been made of Mannerheim's aristocratic background and its influence on his character and opinions. The motto he chose in 1922 – *Candida pro causa ense candido* (With a shining sword for a shining cause) – was redolent of chivalrous ideals. He had good reason to be proud of his family (for a man with a passion for precision it was annoying when he was erroneously referred to as von Mannerheim – an error which occurs in many modern reference books). However, the Dutch origin of his family, which he so confidently asserted, is probable rather than certain. But if his noble origin had one important consequence it must have been the sense of *noblesse oblige* which permeated his life. Mannerheim was above all a man to whom duty was an imperative, and with a strong sense of civilized values, justice and responsibility. In April 1944 he expressed to General Erfurth his regret to be living at a time when 'all spiritual, ethical and cultural values are deliberately spoiled'.[72] In a speech in 1933 he said that he raised his glass to 'the man who takes responsibility and is able to carry it'.[73]

Mannerheim derived little advantage from his apparently privileged background. The Finnish aristocracy was modest in status and wealth and in any case he began his Russian career as a poor man whose family had lost its fortune, and who had to make his own way in the glittering world of the rich Russian upper class. He had to struggle to get on and his success in doing so made his achievements all the sweeter – and their nullification by the Revolution all the more bitter. He

---

[71] Speech to the President, 4 June 1942. *Kesäkuun neljäs päivä 1942*, p. 84.
[72] Erfurth, *Krigsdagbok*, p. 139.
[73] Cited in Borenius, *Field-Marshal Mannerheim*, p. 249.

acquired in Russia the ability to mix easily in exalted circles, where he quickly learned good form and to appreciate the thought-processes of the élite of a great power. He took these abilities with him into the modest circumstances of independent Finland where he inevitably stood out because his background was so totally different from that of the leaders of the democratic republic. He found this background, with Swedish as his mother tongue and his long service in Russia, more of a handicap than a help when he returned to Finland.

His frequent disenchantment with the workings of Finnish democracy need not have had any connection with his aristocratic origin or supposed aristocratic way of thinking. It might have owed something to his military background; some soldiers are impatient of democracy, and he objected to political influence and interference in military command as inimical to efficiency. But these determinist explanations fail to acknowledge Mannerheim's evident capacity to draw his own conclusions about democracy based on his own experience of it, particularly what he regarded as the disastrous outcome in 1917–19 of Finland's constitutional reforms of 1906–7 which introduced universal suffrage and increased the importance of political parties.

His service to the country resulted not from his character or background and certainly not from his personal involvement in electoral and party politics, which he eschewed as diminishing the responsibility of the individual and favouring the commonplace. Significant though it was, his popularity could not be a substitute for a party-political power base. His influence was based on his personal connections. As a senior professional soldier he could not be politically neutral if he were to do his job properly, and his connections helped him in this respect. There were times when the state had need of his ability and experience, and it was a matter of chance or luck when and how he was called on to serve. The luck accrued both to Mannerheim and to Finland.

The involvement of military men in the politics of European countries was not uncommon in the twentieth century, particularly between the World Wars, but the permanence of Mannerheim's legacy as a 'general in politics' was exceptional. The failure or incapacity of politicians to deal with major national crises led some countries to have recourse to the leadership of a prominent soldier who – as a political outsider, seemingly above politics – became a symbol around whom the nation could rally. This was certainly true of Mannerheim in 1944, and arguably true of General de Gaulle in 1958 (by which time he had long been a political figure). But military men also became involved in politics for ideological reasons, some seizing power to save the nation from a political course (typically socialist) of which they disapproved, from instability or anarchy. Others acted as the result of personal ambition or as part of a struggle for power within the armed forces. After gaining power, some generals abandoned their military past for a purely political career. There are significant differences between Mannerheim and those types of 'generals in politics'.

Mannerheim was not alone in displaying staunch anti-communism – the Russian White generals did so too – or in suppressing a left-wing *coup* at home; Admiral Horthy took credit for crushing the communist regime in Hungary in 1919. The Russian Whites were beaten, but Mannerheim defeated Russian revolutionary troops in Finland. However, Mannerheim's approach to power was different from Horthy's and also from that of General Piłsudski, who repulsed the Soviet invasion of Poland in 1919–20. It differed, too, from that of General Franco who later suppressed a left-wing government in Spain. Mannerheim did not retain the position of head of state like Horthy and Franco, nor did he seize power by *coup d'état* like Piłsudski in 1926 or General Metaxas in Greece in 1936. The reasons were partly personal: Mannerheim did not want power at any price and was imbued, like most Finns, with a sense of legality. They were also partly connected with the nature of Finnish government and society. Even before its declaration of independence, Finland possessed many of the characteristics of a state: established borders and traditions of autonomous government and a democratically-elected parliament. This gave it significant advantages over most of the new countries founded after the First World War. Finland's evident political maturity – despite the Civil War and the troubles of the early 1930s – diminished the opportunity for a 'strong man' to carry out a successful *coup*. Mannerheim recognized in July 1919 the practical political obstacles to his seizing power. He surely did so again in 1930 and 1932 when his personal position – he was no longer commander-in-chief or even serving in the army – was significantly less favourable to intervention. A further brake on his actions in 1918–19 resulted from suspicion of

TESTAMENT

his long service in the army of Russia, which his fellow-countrymen widely considered as their oppressor.

Yet if Mannerheim was deterred from carrying out a *coup* by the practical difficulties, allied with his sense of legality, he also recognized – over the course of time – the need to adjust his approach to politics and society to the realities of Finnish conditions. This adjustment was not accompanied by his entry into politics, about which his sense of honour as a soldier would have made him feel strong reservations. However, his acceptance of Finland as it was, together with the change in the political climate in the early 1930s, facilitated his return to public service and opened the way to the supreme command and the presidency during the Second World War. Mannerheim thus differed from many 'generals in politics'. He was capable of reining in his ambitions and of relinquishing power. He recognized when military intervention in politics was impossible or when its price in division and bitterness would be too high for the nation. He paid for this recognition in frustration at the course of politics in Finland, but over time he was rewarded by the trust of the majority of Finns, not merely his original White supporters. Although he never shared the Finns' devotion to democratic and particularly party politics, his respect in practice for Finland's Western-style democracy, vigorous defence of its interests and devotion to Western civilized values enhanced his reputation, while his actions as a soldier and statesman, which were directed to securing and maintaining Finland's independence, left a lasting legacy.

THE LEGACY

Mannerheim's historic role had its origin in the event he most hated: the Russian Revolution. The Revolution transformed him from a successful and contented professional officer in the imperial Russian army into a man with a mission to fight Bolshevism. His military experience, his qualities of leadership and above all his determination first to stop and then to defeat the Bolshevik Revolution made him the man of the hour in Finland in January 1918. His subsequent involvement in the country's history stemmed from his success as commander-in-chief of the White Army in 1918. He saw himself as an instrument of destiny, telling Carl Enckell in February 1919 of his understanding that 'regard is not directed at me personally but is evidence that providence has embodied in me what the Finnish people need at this moment.'[74]

As the White General of 1918, Mannerheim attained a high level of prestige and popularity with the ordinary people whose way of life he had safeguarded. The politicians regarded him with less enthusiasm, sensing that his popularity no less than his opinions presented a potential threat to their own positions and perhaps even to the normal processes of politics. For the defeated Left, Mannerheim was the symbol of their oppression. Only as the Social Democrats were drawn into government and as Mannerheim himself recognized them as an unalterable factor in politics did left-wing opinion towards him become more conciliatory. By the time the Winter War broke out, the White General had become a national figure, and by the time it ended he was an international figure and his position as commander-in-chief was unassailable. Although formally he left political decisions to the politicians, he wielded immense influence as a soldier who was actually aware that preparation for war and the conduct of war had an essentially political character. The value of this political awareness must be held to offset the sometimes deleterious effects of the highly personal and unsystematic methods by which he exercised supreme command in the 1940s.

Mannerheim's ambition to crush Bolshevism and to promote intervention in Russia in 1919 failed, and so far was it from being crushed that by the time of his death it was triumphant in Eastern and Central Europe as well as in Russia, and was to make further gains in other continents. Viewed in that light his life could be seen as a tragic failure. His hopes for an independent Finland were also unfulfilled. Instead of being militarily strong and linked in a defensive alliance to Scandinavia which he hoped to create, the country after the Second World War was militarily weak and linked by a security treaty to the Soviet Union, the very country Mannerheim regarded as its enemy, and it seems ironic that the basis for Finland's new relationship with the Soviet Union was laid during his presidency. Yet his attitude to the Soviet Union was moulded by a recognition of political reality. Just as he had hoped in 1918–19 for Finland to live peacefully alongside a reconstituted White Russia, so in 1939 he accepted the need for territorial concessions to satisfy what he acknowledged to be the security interests of Finland's great power neighbour.

[74] Enckell, *Poliittiset muistelmani*, II, p. 10.

TESTAMENT

Of course Mannerheim might not have been so inclined to make concessions to the Soviet Union if his policy of creating a strong national defence and a defensive alliance with Sweden had succeeded. He told Paasikivi in March 1945 that his life's work had meant the strengthening of Finland's defence, and in that he considered he had achieved something,[75] but this work foundered first on the rock of domestic politics, the reality of which he came increasingly to realize, and secondly on military defeat in 1944. The idea of an alliance with Sweden got nowhere because of the Swedes' determination not to compromise its neutrality through a commitment to defend Finland. It was remarkable that Mannerheim's sense of reality never quite made him lose faith in Sweden.

His characteristic caution was overcome in 1941 by his belief that Germany would defeat the Soviet Union and thus provide Finland with a more secure existence. He quickly realized his mistake and understood that Finland, despite the risk to its social and political structure, would have to come to an accommodation with the Soviet Union, and accordingly he was able to make the leap into the unknown which this portended in 1944. For a man whose belief that the Soviets intended to wipe the Finns off the face of the earth was well known, and who had good reason to fear for his personal safety, this was a terrible decision. Yet the extent to which Mannerheim, however reluctantly, adjusted to Finland's new circumstances – a total change of direction in foreign policy – can be seen in his discussions with Zhdanov about a security treaty between their two countries as being in the interests of both.

To Mannerheim the emergence after the Second World War of a powerful extreme left in Finland was a further cause of anxiety. He had learned to live with the Social Democrats and admire the patriotism of their leader Väinö Tanner, but he was understandably suspicious of the motives of the Finnish Communist Party and the left socialists. Even while president he was powerless to prevent the abolition of the Defence Corps, that prop of the Right from the 1920s and '30s, and the purge from the defence forces of officers whom he admired. Social and economic change brought about by the war and by post-war austerity affected the nature of Finnish society quite apart from changes resulting from the 'democratization' of politics. Yet, despite his gloom there were signs before his death

---

[75] Paasikivi, *Päiväkirjat 1944–1956*, I, col. 202.

of recovery at home, while the weakness of the Finnish communists, the strength of the political system and the constitution, and fact that the country did not have to endure Soviet occupation prevented it from sliding into a people's democracy. Finland remained not only independent but also a Western-style democracy.

It is on its independence that Mannerheim's legacy to Finland is focused. He first established it in the War of 1918, and his victory then prevented the possible absorption of a socialist Finland into Soviet Russia. Secondly, he restored Finland's relations with the victorious Western powers in 1919, ensuring the recognition of independence. Thirdly, he helped to maintain Finland's independence at the time of the Winter War in 1939–40. He was not prepared to gamble on Allied promises of aid but recommended peace before the weakened Finnish army collapsed. Fourthly, he extricated Finland from the Continuation War in 1944, again preserving its independence. He had, of course, also played a key role in getting Finland into the war but he had prudently fought it separately from the war being waged by the Germans, as was clear from his refusal to attack Leningrad or the Murmansk railway. It was generally accepted in Finland that he alone commanded the authority in the country and over the army to make a harsh peace with the Soviet Union acceptable to the nation, a peace which even involved war against the Germans, the country's former co-belligerents. The Armistice of 1944 proved the basis for Finland's future peaceful coexistence with the Soviet Union as an independent state.

Mannerheim was unusual in Finland in acknowledging the primacy of foreign policy. He told Paasikivi in February 1944 that – regrettably in his view – all matters in Finland were seen in terms of domestic politics, whereas foreign policy should come first because everything else depended on it.[76] Mannerheim's achievements in foreign affairs were remarkable but so was his role in preventing or avoiding revolutionary social and political change in 1918–19 and 1944–6. His 'Finnish years' left him with less happy memories than his 'years of preparation' in Russia. In spite of bringing him a wealth of admiration and trust, which he felt to be beyond his deserts, they also brought much bitterness and frustration. These were especially pronounced in the 1920s when he held no public office, but they were present too in an acute form during his presidency. There were

---

[76] Paasikivi, *Jatkosodan päiväkirjat*, p. 340.

also many years of heavy responsibility, and even at an advanced age he was subjected to a heavy regime of work. His all-pervading sense of duty made this unavoidable.

Mannerheim was idolized by many, a controversial figure to others and hated by some. He was well aware of his place in Finnish history, and it is secure although he looms too large for its precise position ever to be finally settled. What is certain is that he can never be disregarded. During the radical and iconoclastic period from the late 1960s to the early 1980s a derogatory attitude to him and to other great men was fashionable in Finland; still a great number of Finns remained unshakeable in their loyalty to his memory and admiration for his achievements. However, his reputation has risen again in the new, frank climate of opinion that followed the end of Urho Kekkonen's long presidency in 1982 and the collapse of the Soviet Union in 1991. His qualities can be re-interpreted to suit the time. In the present period of internationalization it can be said that he combined Finnish patriotism with European cosmopolitanism.[77]

Mannerheim not only towered over his generation, but the lives of his compatriots in an independent and democratic Finland continue to be influenced by his decisive actions as a military commander, conservative statesman and patriot.

---

[77] On changes to Mannerheim's reputation see Kolbe, 'Marski – ihminen'.

BIBLIOGRAPHY

The letters å, ä and ö come at the end of the alphabet

UNPUBLISHED MATERIAL

Churchill Archives Centre, Churchill College, Cambridge
Churchill Papers
Char 8
Char 16
Char 20
Major-General Sir Edward Louis Spears Papers
SPRS 1/224
Ministry of Foreign Affairs Archives (Ulkoasiainministeriön arkisto), Helsinki Diplomatic correspondence, 1918–19
1.P.k
2.C.c.2
3.B
National Archives of Finland (Kansallisarkisto), Helsinki
C. G. E. Mannerheim Archive
Grensholm Collection
Public Record Office, Kew
F.O. 371. Foreign Office. Political Departments. General Correspondence
F.O. 372. Foreign Office. Treaty Department and Successors. General Correspondence
F.O. 419. Foreign Office. Confidential Print. Scandinavia and the Baltic States
F.O. 490. Foreign Office. Confidential Print. Northern Affairs
F.O. 608. Foreign Office. Peace Conference of 1919–1920. Correspondence
Åbo Akademi University Library, Manuscripts Department (Åbo Akademis bibliotek. Handskriftsavdelningen), Turku
Bertel Gripenberg's letter collection, X
Leo Ehrnrooth's collection. Letters to Ehrnooth, II
J. W. Reuter's letter collection, XII
R. A. Wrede's collection. Letters from Finnish correspondents, K-M

PUBLISHED MATERIAL

Ahti, Martti. *Kaappaus? Suojeluskuntaselkkaus 1921. Fascismin aave 1927. Mäntsälän kapina 1932.* Helsinki, 1990.

———. *Salaliiton ääriviivat. Oikeistoradikalismi ja hyökkäävä idänpo/itiikka 1918-1919.* Espoo, 1987.

Alanen, Aulis J. *Santeri Alkio.* Porvoo, 1976.

BIBLIOGRAPHY

Arimo, R. *Suomen puolustussuunnitelmat 1918–1939*. Helsinki, 1986–7. 3 vols. (Sotatieteen laitoksen julkaisuja, XXIII)
Bennett, Geoffrey. *Cowan's War: the Story of British Naval Operations in the Baltic, 1918–1920*. London, 1964.
Blomstedt, Yrjö. *K.J. Ståhlberg: valtiomieselämäkerta*. Helsinki, 1969.
Boheman, Erik. *På vakt. Kabinettssekreterare under Andra Världskriget*. Stockholm, 1964.
Borenius, Tancred. *Field-Marshal Mannerheim*. London, 1940.
C. G. Mannerheim. 2nd edn. Edited by H. Kekoni and H. J. Viherjuuri. Helsinki, 1938.
C. G. Mannerheim. Suomen Marsalkka. Editors Markus Palokangas *[et al.]*. [Helsinki], 1967.
Carlgren, Wilhelm M. *Svensk utrikespolitik 1939–1945*. Stockholm, 1973.
Citrine, Walter. *My Finnish Diary*. Harmondsworth, 1940.
Cooper, Diana. *The Light of Common Day*. London, 1959.
Documents on British Foreign Policy, 1919–1939. Edited by E. L. Woodward and Rohan Butler. 1st series, vol. III. *1919*. London, 1949.
Documents on British Foreign Policy, 1919–1939. Edited by E. L. Woodward and Rohan Butler, assisted by Anne Orde. 3rd series, vol. VI. *1939*. London, 1953.
Documents on German Foreign Policy 1918–1945. Series D 1937–1945), vol. XII: *The War Years February 1-June 22, 1941*. Washington, DC, 1962.
Donner, Kai. *Sotamarsalkka vapaaherra Mannerheim*. Porvoo, 1934.
Douglas, W. A. *Kriget i Finland 1918: till 10-årsminnet*. Stockholm, 1928.
Edelfelt, Berta. *Sophie Mannerheim: en levnadsteckning*. Helsingfors, 1932.
Enckell, Carl. 'Några minnen från mitt samarbete med Gustaf Mannerheim' in *Marskalken av Finland friherre Gustaf Mannerheim: krigaren – statsmannen – människan*. Helsingfors, 1953, pp. 31–44.
Enckell, Carl. *Poliittiset muistelmani*. Porvoo, 1956. 2 vols.
Engman, Max, and Jerker A. Eriksson. *Mannen i kolboxen. John Reed och Finland*. Helsingfors, 1979. (Skrifter utgivna av Svenska litteratursällskapet i Finland, 485)
Erfurth, Waldemar. *Krigsdagbok november 1943-september 1944*. Translated from the author's manuscript by Birgit Selin. Helsingfors, 1954.
Erich, R. 'Finlands riksföreståndares ställning och befogenheter', *Tidskrift utgiven av Juridiska föreningen i Finland*, 59, 1923, pp. 21–38.
Fagerholm, K-A. *Puhemiehen ääni*. Helsinki, 1977.
Finlands frihetskrig skildrat av deltagare, edited by Kai Donner, Th. Svedlin, Heikki Nurmio. Helsingfors, 1921–8. 8 vols.
Finlands frihetskrig år 1918, published by the Komittén för Frihetskrigets historia, Gösta Theslöf *[et al]*. Helsingfors, 1921–5. 6 vols.
Foreign Relations of the United States. Diplomatic Papers 1943, vol. III: *The British Commonwealth, Eastern Europe, The Far East*. Washington, DC, 1963.
Gallen-Kallela & Mannerheim: tutkimusmatkailijat, ystävät, vaikuttajat; forskningsresande, vänner, påverkare. Editors: Kerttu Karvonen-Kannas, Tuija Möttönen. [Helsinki, 1992].
Gripenberg, G. A. *Finland and the Great Powers: Memoirs of a Diplomat*. Trans-

BIBLIOGRAPHY

lated from the Swedish with an introduction by Albin T. Anderson. Lincoln, Nebraska, 1965.

———. 'Försök till en karakteristik av Marskalk Mannerheim', in *Marskalken av Finland friherre Gustaf Mannerheim: krigaren – statsmannen – människan*. Helsingfors, 1953, pp. 57–65.

Halder, F. *Kriegstagebuch*. Ed. by Hans-Adolf Jacobson. Stuttgart, 1962–4. 3 vols.

Hannula, J. O. *Finland's War of Independence*. London, 1939.

Heikkilä, Toivo. *Paasikivi peräsimessä: pääministerin sihteerin muistelmat 1944–1948*. Helsinki, 1965.

Heinrichs, Erik. *Mannerheim Suomen kohtaloissa*. Helsinki, 1957–9. 2 vols.

Heiskanen, Raimo. *Talvisodan operaatioiden johtaminen ja edellytysten luominen sodankäynnille Päämajan operatiivisen osaston näkökulmasta*. [Helsinki], 1996. (Maanpuolustuskorkeakoulun historian laitoksen julkaisuja, 1)

Hillgruber, Andreas. *Hitlers Strategie. Politik und Kriegführung 1940–1941*. Frankfurt am Main, 1965.

Hirvikallio, Paavo. *Tasavallan presidentin vaalit Suomessa 1919–1950*. Helsinki, 1958.

Hovi, Kalervo. 'Mitä Mannerheim teki Varsovassa syksyllä 1919?', *Faravid. Pohjois-Suomen historiallisen yhdistyksen vuosikirja*, 3, 1979, pp. 131–47.

Ignatius, Hannes. *Carl Gustaf Mannerheim. Biografi – tal – telegram*. Helsingfors, 1918.

———. *Från ofärdsår till självständighet*. Helsingfors, 1927.

Ikonen, Kimmo. *J. K. Paasikiven poliittinen toiminta Suomen itsenäistymisen murrosvaiheessa*. Helsinki, 1990 (Historiallisia Tutkimuksia, 158).

Itsenäistymisen vuodet 1917–1920. Helsinki, 1992–3. 3 vols.

Jaakkola, Jalmari. 'Marskin muistelmien loppuosa', *Historiallinen aikakauskirja*, 50,1952, pp. 225–9.

———. 'Suomen marsalkan muistelmat', *Historiallinen aikakauskirja*, 49, 1951, pp. 261–5.

Jakobson, Max. *Finland Survived: an Account of the Finnish-Soviet Winter War, 1939–1940*. 2nd enlarged edn. Helsinki, 1984.

Jokipii, Mauno. *Jatkosodan synty. Tutkimuksia Saksan ja Suomen sotilaallisesta yhteistyöstä 1940–41*. Helsinki, 1987.

———. 'Mannerheimin rooli 1939–1944', in *Asein, aattein, opein*. Oulu, 1996 (Acta Societatis Historicae Ouluensis, XXII), pp. 84–105.

Juottonen, Jorma. *Millainen materiaalinen puolustuskyky?* Riihimäki, 1997.

Jussila, Osmo. *Suomen tie 1944–1948. Miksi siitä ei tullut kansandemokratiaa*. Porvoo, 1990.

Jussila, Osmo., Seppo Hentilä and Jukka Nevakivi. *Suomen poliittinen historia 1809–1995*. Porvoo, 1996.

Juva, Einar W. *P. E. Svinhufvud*. II: *1917–1944*. Porvoo, 1961.

———. *Rudolf Walden 1878–1946*. Porvoo, 1957.

Jyränki, Antero. *Presidentti. Tutkimus valtionpäämiehen asemasta Suomessa v. 1919–1976*. [Helsinki], 1978. (Suomalaisen Lakimiesyhdistyksen julkaisuja, A-sarja, 123).

———. *Sotavoiman ylin päällikkyys. Tutkimus tasavallan presidentille HM 30§ nojalla kuuluvasta toimivallasta ja sen käyttämisestä*. [Helsinki], 1967. (Suomalaisen Lakimiesyhdistyksen julkaisuja, A-sarja, 76)

BIBLIOGRAPHY

Jägerskiöld, Stig. *Mannerheim: Marshal of Finland*. London, 1986.

———. *Den unge Mannerheim*. Helsingfors, 1964.

———. *Gustaf Mannerheim 1906–1917*. Helsingfors, 1965.

———. *Gustaf Mannerheim 1918*. Helsingfors, 1967.

———. *Riksföreståndaren. Gustaf Mannerheim 1919*. Helsingfors, 1969.

———. *Mannerheim mellan världskrigen*. Helsingfors, 1972.

———. *Fältmarskalken. Gustaf Mannerheim 1939–1941*. Helsingfors, 1975.

———. *Marskalken av Finland. Gustaf Mannerheim 1941–1944*. Helsingfors, 1979.

———. *Från krig till fred. Gustaf Mannerheim 1944–1951*. Helsingfors, 1981.

———. 'Marshal Gustaf Mannerheim of Finland in the Light of History' in *Otium et negotium: Studies in Onomatology and Library Science presented to Olof von Feilitzen*. Stockholm, 1973, pp. 160–9.

Kansakunta sodassa. Helsinki, 1989–92. 3 vols.

Kesäkuun neljäs päivä 1942. Suomen Marsalkan, vapaaherra C. G. Mannerheimin 75-vuotispäivän juhlallisuudet. Edited by W. E. Tuompo [*et al.*]. Helsinki, 1942.

Kilkki, Pertti. *Valo Nihtilä – päämajan eversti*. Porvoo, 1994.

Killinen, Kullervo. *Miekka tuppeen: poliittisen ja sotilaallisen johdon dualismi Suomessa sodissa 1939–1944*. Porvoo, 1983.

Klinge, Matti. *Mannerheim: kuvaelämäkerta*. Helsinki, 1968.

———. *Mesimarja, myytti, Mannerheim: tutkielmia ja puheenvuoroja*. Helsinki, 1994.

Kolbe, Laura.'Marski – ihminen', in *Mannerheim: sotilas ja ihminen*. Helsinki, 1992, pp. 89–107.

'Kolchak i Finliandiia', *Krasnyi arkhiv. Istoricheskii zhurnal*, 33. Moscow, 1939.

Korhonen, Markus H.,'Marsalkan vaatehuoneessa', *Kaltio*, 52, 1996, pp. 128–9.

Korppi-Tommola, Aura. *Tervelapsi – kansanhuomen. Mannerheimin Lastensuojeluliitto yhteiskunnan rakentajana 1920–1990*. Helsinki, 1990.

Kuosa, Tauno. *A. F. Airo: legenda jo eläessään. Päämajoitusmestari kenraaliluutnantti A. F. Airo operaatioiden johtajana 1939–1945*. Porvoo, 1979.

Kuusanmäki, Jussi and Niklas Labart. 'Mannerheimiana', *Historisk Tidskrift för Finland*, 79,1994, pp. 783–92.

Kähkölä, Paavo,Toivo Pihlajaniemi and Sauli Pyyluoma. *Toinen tasavalta*. Helsinki, 1976.

Könönen, Elsa. *Vuosikymmen Mannerheimin sihteerinä Suomen Punaisessa Rististä 1928–38*. Porvoo, 1966.

Labart, Niklas.'Kahvilanpitäjänä Hankoniemellä', in *Mannerheim: tuttu ja tuntematon*. Helsinki, 1997, pp. 130–2.

Lehmus, Kalle. *Tuntematon Mannerheim. Katkelmia sodan ja politiikan poluilta*. Helsinki, 1967.

Lenin,V. I. *Polnoe sobranie sochinenii*. 39. Moscow, 1963.

Linder, Ernst. *Från Finlands Frihetskrig*. Stockholm, 1920.

Lindman, Sven.'Eduskunnan aseman muuttuminen 1917–1919. II. Vuoden 1919 hallitusmuodon synty' in *Suomen kansanedustuslaitoksen historia*. VI. Helsinki, 1968.

Linkomies, Edwin.'Mannerheim valtiomiehenä' in Edwin Linkomies, *Ihmishengen tie.Valikoima puheita*. Helsinki, 1954, pp. 170–85.

BIBLIOGRAPHY

———. *Vaikea aika. Suomen pääministerinä sotavuosina 1943–44*. Helsinki, 1970.
Lubomirska, Maria. *Pamiętnik księżnej Marii Zdisxawowej Lubomirskiej 1914–1918*. Edited by Janusz Pajewski. Poznan, 1997.
Lukkari, Matti. *Asekätkentä*. Helsinki, 1984.
Lundin, C. Leonard. *Finland in the Second World War*. Bloomington, 1957.
Mannerheim, C. G. E. *Across Asia from West to East in 1906–1908*. Helsinki, 2 vols.
———. *Brev från sju årtionden*. Compiled by Stig Jägerskiöld. Helsingfors, 1984.
———. *Kirjeitä seitsemän vuosikymmenen ajalta*. Compiled by Stig Jägerskiöld. Helsinki, 1983.
———. *The Memoirs of Marshal Mannerheim*. Translated by Count Eric Lewenhaupt. London, 1953.
———. *Minnen*. 2nd edn. Helsingfors, 1952. 2 vols.
Mannerheim: sotilas ja ihminen. Helsinki, 1992.
Mannerheim: Suomen vapauttaja ja valtionhoitaja. Mitä hän on sanonut ja mitä hänestä sanottu. Edited by Yrjö Koskelainen. Helsinki, 1919.
Mannerheim: tuttu ja tuntematon. Toimitusneuvoston puheenjohtaja Martti Sinerma. Helsinki, 1997.
Mannerheim-Weckman, Evo. *Laivalamppu ja muuta muistelua*. Translated by Sirkka Rapola. Helsinki, 1953.
Manninen, Ohto. "'Kansan äänen ilmauksia'". Mannerheimin srjgäyttämisajatus maalis-huhtikuussa 1918', *Historiallinen aikakauskirja*, 71, 1973, pp. 257–86.
———. *Kansannoususta armeijaksi: asevelvollisuuden toimeenpano ja siihen suhtautuminen valkoisessa Suomessa kevättalvella 1918*. Helsinki, 1974. (Historiallisia tutkimuksia, 95)
———. 'Mannerheim ja punavangit', *Historiallinen aikakauskirja*, 79, 1981, pp. 195–206.
———. 'Mannerheim ja sotaansyyllisyys', in *Mannerheim: tuttu ja tuntematon*. Helsinki, 1997, pp. 341–4.
———. 'Mannerheimin ero toukokuussa 1918', *Sotahistoriallinen Seura ja Sotamuseo. Vuosikirja*, IX, 1976, pp. 5–49.
———. 'Mannerheims linje i maj 1918', *Historisk Tidskrift för Finland*, 68, pp. 145–51.
———. 'Murhayritys Mannerheimia vastaan ja muita uutisia', *Sotilasaikakauslehti*, 9/1998, pp. 66–8.
———. 'Ryti ja kauttakulkusopimus', *Historiallinen aikakauskirja*, 77, 1979, pp. 40–43.
———. *Suur-Suomen ääriviivat*. Helsinki, 1980.
Marskalken av Finland friherre Gustaf Mannerheim: krigaren – statsmannen – människan. Helsingfors, 1953. (Skrifter utgivna av Finlands Adelsförbund, IX)
Marski läheltä ja kaukaa. Edited by Ea Rahikainen, Tauno Majuri, Reino Juhonen. Helsinki, 1964.
Meinander, Henrik. 'Mannerheim and the war guilt trials', *Finnish Institute Yearbook*, 1994, pp. 20–7.
Meri, Veijo. *C. G. Mannerheim, Suomen marsalkka*. Porvoo, 1988.
Mikander, Kaj. 'Några bidrag till C. G. Mannerheims brevväxling hösten 1919', *Historisk Tidskrift för Finland*, 47, 1962, pp. 58–60.

BIBLIOGRAPHY

Morembert, T de. 'Hériot (Virginie)' in *Dictionnaire de biographie française*. Vol. 17. Paris, 1989, cols 1065–6.
Nevakivi, Jukka. *The Appeal that was never made: the Allies, Scandinavia and the Finnish Winter War, 1939–1940*. London, 1976.
———.'Mannerheim ja muukalaislegioona', *Suomen Kuvalehti*, 13/1989, pp. 10–13.
———. 'The Soviet Union and Finland after the War, 1944–53' in *The Soviet Union and Europe in the Cold War, 1943–53*. Edited by Francesca Gori and Silvio Pons. Basingstoke, 1996, pp. 89–105.
Niiniluoto, Yrjö. *Suuri rooli: Suomen marsalkan, vapaaherra Carl Gustaf Emil Mannerheimin kirjallisen muotokuvan yritelmä*. 2nd imp. Helsinki, 1962.
Niukkanen, Juho. *Talvisodan puolustusministeri kertoo*. Porvoo, 1951.
Nurmio, Yrjö. *Suomen itsenäistyminen ja Saksa*. Porvoo, 1957.
Oesch, K. L. *Suomen kohtalon ratkaisu Kannaksella v. 1944*. Helsinki, 1956.
Paasikiven hirmuiset vuodet: Suomi 1944–48. Helsinki, 1986.
Paasikivi, J. K. *Jatkosodan päiväkirjat 11.3.1941–27.6.1944*. Edited by Kauko I. Rumpunen. Porvoo, 1991.
———. *J. K. Paasikiven päiväkirjat 1944–1956*. Edited by Yrjö Blomstedt, Matti Klinge. Porvoo, 1985–86. 2 vols.
———. *Toimintani Moskovassa ja Suomessa 1939–41*. Porvoo, 1979.
Paasivirta, Juhani. *Finland and Europe: the Early Years of Independence 1917–1939*. Edited and translated by Peter Herring. Helsinki, 1988 (Studia Historica, 29).
———. *Suomi ja Eurooppa 1939–1956. Sotien ja murrosten ajanjakso*. Helsinki, 1992.
———. *Suomi vuonna 1918*. Porvoo, 1957.
———. *The Victors in World War I and Finland*. Helsinki, 1965 (Studia Historica, 7).
Paasonen, Aladár. *Marsalkan tiedustelupäällikkönä ja hallituksen asiamiehenä*. Helsinki, 1974.
Paavolainen, Jaakko. *Poliittiset väkivaltaisuudet Suomessa 1918*. Helsinki, 1966–7. 2 vols.
———. *Väinö Tanner. 3. Sillanrakentaja. Elämäkerta vuosilta 1924–1936*. Helsinki, 1984.
Paulaharju, Jyri. 'Vierailu tulenjohtopaikalla' in *Mannerheim: tuttuja tuntematon*. Helsinki, 1997, pp. 292–5.
Peltonen, Ulla-Maija. *Punakapinan muistot. Tutkimus työväen muistelukerronnan muotoutumisesta vuoden 1918 jälkeen*. Helsinki, 1996 (Suomen Kirjallisuuden Seuran toimituksia, 657).
Peltonen, Ulla-Maija. 'The Return of the Narrator' in *Historical Perspectives on Memory*, ed. by Anne Ollila. Helsinki, 1999 (Studia Historica, 61), pp. 115–37.
Polvinen, Tuomo. *Between East and West: Finland in International Politics, 1944–1947*. Edited and translated by D. G. Kirby and Peter Herring. Minneapolis, 1986.
———. *Venäjän vallankumous ja Suomi 1917–1920*. Porvoo, 1967–71. 2 vols.
Puhtain asein. Suomen Marsalkan päiväkäskyjä vuosilta 1918–44. Edited by Einari Kaskimies. Helsinki, 1970.
Ramsay, Henrik. *Sommar och segel*. Stockholm, 1946.
Ramsay, Karin. 'Mannerheim och Finlands Röda Kors: några personliga minnen' in *Marskalken av Finland friherre Gustaf Mannerheim: krigaren – statsmanne – människan*. Helsingfors, 1953, pp. 113–19.

273

BIBLIOGRAPHY

Relander, Lauri Kristian. *Presidentin päiväkirja.* Edited by Eino Jutikkala. Helsinki, 1967–8. 2 vols.
Ries, Tomas. *Cold Will: the Defence of Finland.* London, 1988.
Rintala, Marvin. *Four Finns: Political Profiles.* Berkeley, CA, 1969.
Rosén, Gunnar. *Sata sodan ja rauhan vuotta. Suomen Punainen Risti 1877–1977.* Helsinki, 1977.
Rumpunen, Kauko I. 'Erään isoisän ansioluettelosta', *Sotilasaikakauslehti*, 11/1998, pp. 69–71.
Saarikoski, Vesa. *Keskustajääkäri Aarne Sihvo. Näkökulma aseellisen voiman ja yhteiskunnan vuorovaikutukseen itsenäistymisen murroksesta paasikiviläiseen toiseen tasavaltaan.* Helsinki, 1997 (Bibliotheca Historica, 25).
Schauman, Georg. *Valtiomuototaistelu Suomessa 1918. Tosiasioita, mietelmiä ja muistoja.* Porvoo, 1924.
Screen, J. E. O. *Mannerheim: the Years of Preparation.* London, 1970; 2nd imp. 1993.
Selén, Kari. *C. G. E. Mannerheim ja hänen puolustusneuvostonsa 1931–1939.* Helsinki, 1980.
———. 'Mannerheimin toinen tuleminen', *Valvoja*, 2/1967, pp. 73–7.
Seppälä, Helge. *Itsenäisen Suomen puolustuspolitiikka ja strategia.* Porvoo, 1974.
———. *Karl Lennart Oesch. Suomen pelastaja.* Jyväskylä, 1998.
Shilder, M. K. *Imperator Aleksandr Pervy, ego zhizn' i tsarstvovanie.* III. St Petersburg, 1897.
Shtein, B. E. *Russkii vopros na Parizhskoi mirnoi konferentsii (1919–1920 gg).* Moscow, 1949.
Sihvo, Aarne. *Muistelmani.* Helsinki, 1954–6. 2 vols.
Siltala, Juha. *Lapuan Liike ja kyyditykset 1930.* Helsinki, 1985.
Soikkanen, Mauri. *C. G. E. Mannerheim: suurriistan metsästäjä.* Jyväskylä, 1997.
Soikkanen, Timo. *Kansallinen eheytyminen – myytti vai todellisuus? Ulko- ja sisäpolitiikan linjat ja vuorovaikutus Suomessa vuosina 1933–1939.* Turku, 1983. (Turun yliopiston julkaisuja, C 37).
Sorvali, Pentti. *Niukkasesta Kekkoseen.* Helsinki, 1975.
Stenvall, Taru. *Marski ja hänen "hovinsa".* 2nd imp. Porvoo, 1955.
Ståhlberg, Ester. *Ester Ståhlbergin kauniit, katkerat vuodet. Presidentin rouvan päiväkirja 1920–25.* Edited by Hilkka and Olli Vitikka. Porvoo, 1985.
———. *Ester Ståhlbergin voittojen ja tappioiden vuodet. Päiväkirja 1926–1934.* Edited by Hilkka and Olli Vitikka. Porvoo, 1986.
———. *Ester Ståhlbergin sodan ja rauhan vuodet. Päiväkirja 1935–1947.* Edited by Hilkka and Olli Vitikka. Porvoo, 1987.
Suomen asetuskokoelma 1919, 1944, 1945.
Suomen historia. 7. *Kansankulttuurin murros. Nuoren tasavallan taide ja tiede. Tasavalta hakee suuntaa. Suomi toisessa maailmansodassa.* Espoo, 1987.
Suomen historia. 8. *Paasikiven aika. Kekkosen aika. Taloudellinen kasvu ja yhteiskuntamurros. Massakulttuurin maihinnousu. Taistelut kulttuurista.* Espoo, 1988.
Suomen kansanedustuslaitoksen historia. VI. Helsinki, 1968.
Suomen presidentit puhuvat. Edited by Eero Saarenheimo. Helsinki, 1964.
Suomen sota 1941–1945. Edited by the Military History Dept. of the Research

BIBLIOGRAPHY

Institute for Military History. 1. [Helsinki], 1965 (Sotahistoriallisen tutkimuslaitoksen Sotahistoriallisen toimiston julkaisuja, IX: 1).
Suomi, Juhani. *Vonkamies: Urho Kekkonen 1944–1950.* Helsinki, [1988].
Sutela, Erkki. 'Sotamarsalkka ja Suomen marsalkka olivat sotilasarvoja', *Sotilasaikakauslehti*, 3/1998, pp. 31–3.
Svartz, Nanna. *Steg för steg: en självbiografi.* Stockholm, 1968.
Taajamaa, Bruno. *Mannerheim: lempeäkatseinen legenda.* [Klaukkala], 1996.
Talas, Onni. *Suomen itsenäistyminen ja Mannerheimin muistelmat.* Hämeenlinna, 1953.
Talvela, Paavo. *Sotilaan elämä. Muistelmat.* Jyväskylä, 1976–77. 2 vols.
Talvisodan historia. 1–4. Porvoo, 1977–9 (Sotatieteen laitoksen julkaisuja, XVI: 1–4).
Talvisodasta Jatkosotaan. Edited by Jarl Kronlund. Helsinki, 1991.
Tanner, Väinö. *Kahden maailmansodan välissä. Muistelmia 20-ja 30-luvuilta.* Helsinki, 1966.
———. *Suomen tie rauhaan 1943–44.* Helsinki, 1952.
———. *The Winter War: Finland against Russia 1939–1940.* Stanford, 1957.
Tarkka, Jukka. *13. artikla. Suomen sotasyyllisyyskysymys ja liittoutuneiden sotarikospolitiikka vuosina 1944–1946.* Helsinki, 1977.
———. 'Vastuun ja totuuden taakka: sotasyyllisyyskysymys Paasikiven päiväkirjassa 16.1.1968' in *Paasikiven hirmuiset vuodet: Suomi 1944–48*, Helsinki, 1986, pp. 71–84.
Tervasmäki, Vilho. *Mannerheim – valtiomies ja sotapäällikkö talvi ja jatkosotien käännekohdissa.* Helsinki, 1987.
Terä, Martti V. 'Marsalkan eronpyyntö vuonna 1939', *Peitsi*, 1/1964, pp. 10–15.
———. and Vilho Tervasmäki. *Puolustushallinnon perustamis- ja rakentamisvuodet 1918–1939.* Helsinki, 1973 (Puolustusministeriön historia, I. Sotatieteen laitoksen julkaisuja, XIII).
Thesleff, Wilhelm. *Upplevelser under krigsåren 1914–1918.* Helsingfors, 1919.
Tiihonen, Seppo. *Hallitusvalta. Valtioneuvosto itsenäisen Suomen toimeenpanovallan käyttäjänä.* Helsinki, 1990 (Hallintohistoriallisia tutkimuksia, 3).
Tuntematon talvisota. Suomi 1939–1940. Helsinki, 1989.
Tuompo, W. E. *Päiväkirjani päämajasta 1941–1944.* Edited by Tauno Kuosa. Porvoo, 1969.
Turtola, Martti. *Aksel Fredrik Airo. Taipumaton kenraali.* Helsinki, 1997.
———. *Erik Heinrichs – Mannerheimin ja Paasikiven kenraali.* Helsinki, 1989.
———. 'Erimielisyydet sodan johdossa' in *Tuntematon talvisota.* Helsinki, 1989, pp. 51–64.
———. *Risto Ryti. Elämä isänmaan puolesta.* Helsinki, 1994.
———. 'Ryti ja Mannerheim' in *Mannerheim: tuttu ja tuntematon.* Helsinki, 1997, p. 250–53.
———. *Tasavallan presidentit. Sodan ja rauhan miehet 1940–1956. Ryti. Mannerheim. Paasikivi.* [Espoo], 1993.
———. *Tornionjoelta Rajajoelle. Suomen ja Ruotsin salainen yhteistoiminta Neuvostoliiton hyökkäyksen varalle vuosina 1923–1940: puolustuspoliittinen vaihtoehto.* Porvoo, 1984.
Ueberschaer, Gerd R. 'Guerre de coalition ou guerre séparée. Conception et struc-

BIBLIOGRAPHY

tures de la stratégie germano-finlandaise dans la guerre contre l'URSS (1941–1944)', *Revue d'histoire de la deuxième guerre mondiale*, 30 (118), 1980, pp. 27–68.

Ueberschär, Gerd R. *Hitler und Finnland 1939–1941. Die deutsch-finnische Beziehungen während des Hitler-Stalin-Paktes.* Wiesbaden, 1978 (Frankfurter historische Abhandlungen, 16).

Upton, Anthony F. 'Finland' in *Fascism in Europe*, edited by S. J. Woolf. London, 1981, p. 191–222.

———. *Finland in Crisis, 1940–1941: a Study in Small-Power Politics.* London, 1964.

———. *Finland, 1939–1940.* London, 1974.

———. *The Finnish Revolution, 1917–1918.* Minneapolis, 1980.

Valtioneuvoston historia 1917–1966. II. Helsinki, 1977.

Valtiopäivät 1945. Asiakirjat I-II. Helsinki, 1946.

Van Dyke, Carl. *The Soviet Invasion of Finland 1939–1940.* London, 1997.

Vares, Vesa. '"Anderssonilla" ratsastaen. Martti Ahdin metodista, lähteistä ja oikeistokuvasta', *Historiallinen aikakauskirja*, 89, 1991, pp. 257–67.

Vares, Vesa. *"Kansakunnan kaapinpäällä – mutta mieluiten vain siellä". Porvarillisen eliitin Mannerheim-kuva sisällissodasta 1920-luvun alkuun.* Turku, [1990], (Turun yliopisto. Poliittinen historia, C:27).

———. *Konservatiivi ja murrosvuodet. Lauri Ingman ja hänen poliittinen toimintansa vuoteen 1922.* Helsinki, 1993 (Historiallisia Tutkimuksia, 174).

———. *Kuninkaan tekijät. Suomalainen monarkia 1917–1919. Myytti ja todellisuus.* Porvoo, 1998.

Vesikansa, Osmo. *Suomen partioliike 1910–1960.* Porvoo, 1960.

Virkkunen, Sakari. *Mannerheim: marsalkka ja presidentti.* Helsinki, 1989.

———. *Mannerheimin kääntöpuoli.* Helsinki, 1992.

Voionmaa, Väinö. *Kuriiripostia 1941–1946.* Edited by Markku Reimaa. Helsinki, 1971.

Voipio, Anni. *Lehtimatka. Sattumia kahdelta vuosikymmeneltä.* Porvoo, 1966.

———. *Suomen marsalkka: elämäkerta.* 3rd rev. and enlarged edn. Porvoo, 1951.

Vuorenmaa, Anssi. 'Defensive strategy and basic operational decisions in the Finland-Soviet Winter War, 1939–1940', *Revue Internationale d'Histoire Militaire*, 62, 1985, p. 74–96.

Westerlund, Lars. 'Bruno Jalander – vastaanhangoitteleva maaherra ja sotaministeri aktivistien Suomessa', *Historiallinen aikakauskirja*, 90, 1992, pp. 99–107.

———. *Polle. Generallöjtnanten Paul von Gerich 1873–1951.* Helsingfors, 1997. 2 vols.

Wirtanen, Atos. *Poliittiset muistelmat.* Helsinki, 1972.

Ylikangas, Heikki. *Tie Tampereelle. Dokumentoitu kuvaus Tampereen antautumiseen johtaneista sotatapahtumista Suomen sisällissodassa 1918.* Porvoo, 1993.

Ylitalo, J. Raymond. *Salasanomia Helsingistä Washingtoniin: muistelmia ja dokumentteja vuosilta 1946–48.* Translated and edited by Lauri Toivainen. Helsinki, 1978.

Öhman, C. A. 'Stiftelsen "General Mannerheims Nationalfond"' in *Marskalken av Finland friherre Gustaf Mannerheim: krigaren – statsmannen – människan.* Helsingfors, 1953, pp. 152–60.

Öhquist, Harald. *Vinterkriget 1939–40 ur min synvinkel.* Helsingfors, 1949.

Österman, Hugo. *Neljännesvuosisata elämästäni.* Porvoo, 1966.

BIBLIOGRAPHY

NEWSPAPERS

Dagens Nyheter, Helsingin Sanomat, Hufvudstadsbladet, Suomen Sosialidemokraatti, The Times, Uusi Suomi

UNPUBLISHED DISSERTATION

Eeva, Jouko Johannes. 'Vaiettu ja vaiennettu avioliitto. Tutkielma sairaanhoitaja, paronitar Anastasia Nikolajevna Arapovan ja valtionhoitaja, ratsuväenkenraali, vapaaherra Carl Gustaf Emil Mannerheimin avioliitosta ja sen taustoista.' Uncompleted pro-gradu diss., Finnish History Dept, University of Turku, May 1995.

INTERVIEWS

Mrs A.-M. Borenius, 25 September 1965.
Colonel O. R. Bäckman, 26 July 1962.
Baroness Isa Gripenberg, 2 November 1999.
Baroness Anastasie Mannerheim, 8 December 1962 and 11 July 1970.

INDEX

CGEM = Carl Gustaf Emil Mannerheim
The letters å, ä and ö appear after the other letters of the alphabet.

AAGE, *Prince*, of Denmark, 57, 102
Aberdeen, 47
Activist Committee (Finnish), 6–8
Activists, Finnish, 51, 61, 63–4, 80
Adenauer, Konrad, 102
Africa, East, 88
Africa, North, 92
Airo, Aksel Fredrik, Lieutenant-General, 111, 141, 147, 155, 157, 176, 188, 200, 213, 222–4
Alaska, 125
Alexander I, *Emperor of Russia*, 38
Alexandria, 91
Algeria, 92
Alkio, Santeri, 56, 57, 66, 71, 83
Allied (Soviet) Control Commission, 211, 212, 214–20, 222, 224, 228, 232, 236–7, 238
Anola, 244
Anti-Comintern Pact, 185
Arapova, Anastasia Nikolaevna, *see* Mannerheim, *Baroness* Anastasia
Archangel, 149
Arco-Valley, *Countess* Gertrud, *née* Wallenberg, 88, 242, 246
Armistice, between Allies and Finland (September 1944), 211–12, 266
Ausfeld, Eduard, Colonel, 26, 34, 35
Austria, 125
Avellan, Sargit, 249

BAD WILDUNGEN, 93
Baden-Powell, *Lady*, 96
Baden-Powell, *Lord*, 96
Bailey, F.M., 91–92
Balfour, A.J., 49–50

Baltic Sea region, 51, 62, 25, 27, 69, 96, 206, 218
Baltic states, 121, 165
Banabassa, 92
Barbarossa, Operation, 169, 170, 176, 177
Basra, 91
Belauri, 92
Belgium, 43
Belomorsk, 179
Berg, K. E., Major-General, 22, 98
Bergen, 47
Berlin, 90, 168, 174, 175, 192, 197, 230, 248
Bernadotte, *Count* Folke, 247
Bessarabia, 165
Bofors Company, 114, 123
Bombay, 91, 92
Bordeaux, 88
Brabourne, *Lord*, 92
Bracken, Brendan, 89
Brandenstein, Otto von, Colonel, 35
Brest-Litovsk, Peace of (March 1918), 28
Bukovina, 165
Burma, 90–91
Buschenhagen, Erich, Major-General, 174, 235
Bäckman, O. R., Colonel, 240

CAIRO, 91
Cajander, A. K., 115, 127–8, 137–8
Calcutta, 91
Carton de Wiart, *Sir* Adrian, Major-General, 79
Castrén, Arthur, 9

INDEX

Castrén, Jalmar, 34
Castrén, Kaarlo, 57, 58, 61, 69, 70–2
Castrén, Urho, 214
Caucasus, 233
Cecil, *Lord* Robert, 48–9
Ceylon, 92
Charpentier, Claes, Lieutenant-General, 8
Christian X, *King of Denmark*, 57, 100
Churchill, *Sir* Winston, 62, 75, 79,102,184
Citrine, *Sir* Walter, 146, 158
Clemenceau, Georges, 76, 119
Continuation War (1941–4): 160, 171, 177–212, 256, 260; diplomatic aspects, 177–8, 181–5, 195–9, 203–4, 206, 209–12; military operations, 177–81, 193–5, 199–205
Control Commission, *see* Allied (Soviet) Control Commission
Cooper, *Lady* Diana, 84, 89
Cooper, Duff, 84
Copenhagen, 54, 55, 94
Cowan, Sir Walter, Admiral, 67
Crimea, 81, 233
Curzon, *Marquess*, 75, 80
Czechoslovakia, 125, 130, 218, 246

DAGENS NYHETER, newspaper, 19
Danzig, 29, 130
Delhi, 91
Denikin, A. I., General, 76–7, 80
Denmark, 74, 165
Dietl, Eduard, Colonel-General, 188
Donner, Kai, 63–4, 105, 257
Donner, Uno, 244
Douglas, *Count* Wilhelm Archibald, Lieutenant-General, 22–23

EDEN, *Sir* Anthony, 124
Edward VIII, *King of Great Britain*, 124
Ehrnrooth, Leo, 61
Elisenvaara, 14
Enckell, Carl, 55, 57, 81–2, 86, 89, 199, 209, 210, 211, 214, 221, 248, 251, 263–4

Enckell, Oskar, Lieutenant-General, 99, 211
Erfurth, Waldemar, General, 175, 194, 205, 211, 246, 260
Erkko, Eljas, 123, 137
Essen, Georg Didrik, Colonel, 97–98
Estonia, 51, 54, 62, 76, 77, 80, 127, 212

FAGERHOLM, Karl-August, 214, 235, 254
Faltin, Richard, 96
Farmers' March, 105–6
Fazer, Karl, 84, 90
Finland
    air force, 113–14, 134, 169, 246
    army, (1918) 11, 16, 23, 24–6, 30, 35–7, 40–1, 50; (1919–39) 51, 52–3, 61, 67, 71–72, 98–9, 107, 112–15, 131, 134; (1939–45) 139–49, 152–3, 162–3, 169–76, 178–81, 189–90, 193–5, 199–205, 213, 216, 217–18, 230, 260; conscription, 24, 52, 113; GHQ (1918) 10, 18, 21–3, 27, 33, 34, 37; GHQ (1939–45) 137–9, 144–5, 150, 154–6, 161–2, 177, 183, 185–90, 195, 200, 213, 215, 222–3; regiments: Uusimaa Dragoons, 24, 89, 240
    Civil War (1918) 12–35, 262–3; Whites' organization and planning 10–13, 16, 21–6; Whites' strategy, 27–31; military operations, 13–14, 31–5; Whites' victory, 35–7; Reds' *coup d'état*, 12–13; Reds' strategy, 27; Red prisoners, 18–20; anniversaries, 67, 90, 99, 100, 111–12, 118, 163
    constitution, 37, 51, 52, 57–9, 63–5, 161, 239
    Defence Corps, 7, 10–13, 14, 17, 18, 23, 24, 31, 50, 52, 55, 61, 67, 68, 70–71, 97–8, 99, 101, 106–7, 112–13, 163, 217, 222, 265
    Defence Council, 99, 108–10, 127–8, 150

INDEX

Diet, 6
elections, 2, 53, 55–6, 68–9, 101, 105, 106, 108, 115, 123, 166, 195, 207, 220, 239, 246
foreign relations: recognition of independence, 2, 48–50, 53, 59; with Allies (Great Britain and France), 46–50, 53, 59, 127, 146, 149–52, 168, 195, 198, 211–12, 216–17, 226–7; with Baltic states and Poland, 121; with Germany, 17, 28–29, 40–41, 126, 166, 167–76, 177–9, 184–5, 196–7, 206, 209–13; with Soviet Union (Soviet Russia), 81, 121, 125–7, 131–3, 137–8, 147–53, 164, 166–7, 168, 172–3, 178, 179, 196–9, 203, 206–20, 222, 224, 227–8, 231–9; with Sweden, 17, 54–5, 121–4, 164; war aims (1941), 176
governments, 1, 2, 12, 16–17, 18, 24, 27, 28–9, 34, 36–7, 40–2, 44–5, 46, 53, 56–7, 58, 61, 71, 76, 90, 93, 105, 115, 118, 123, 125, 126, 134, 137–8, 160, 164, 176, 178, 184, 190, 195, 196, 199, 203, 206–7, 208–10, 211, 213–14, 215, 221, 225, 228, 230, 232–3, 235, 236, 253–4
independence, 1, 2
navy, 114–15, 131
parliament, 1, 2, 37, 46, 55–6, 61, 68–9, 105, 113, 114, 190, 195, 196, 199, 207, 210–11, 220–1, 225, 236, 239
political parties: non-socialist: 2, 7, 46, 48, 51, 55–56, 57,182; Agrarian Party, 39, 48, 55–6, 59, 68, 99, 113, 115, 123, 195, 214, 220, 235; Coalition (conservative) Party, 53, 55–6, 64, 68–9, 77, 132, 166; Patriotic People's Movement (IKL), 107, 217; Progressive Party (liberals), 39, 46, 55–6, 68, 112, 115, 123; Swedish People's Party, 46, 55–6, 68–9, 71, 101, 182, 195; socialist: 2, 7, 12–13, 55–6; Communist Party 51, 104, 106, 220–1, 239, 244, 265, 266; People's Democrats, 220–1, 265; Social Democrat Party, 46, 51, 55–6, 59, 61, 68, 106, 111, 115, 117–18, 123, 138, 163, 182, 195, 220, 264, 265
russification measures, 1
socialist *coup d'état* (1918), 12–13
War of Independence, *see* Finland: Civil War
War of Liberation, *see* Finland: Civil War
war responsibility (1944–6), 211, 227–33, 235, 236–7
Finland, Gulf of, 126, 129, 132, 139, 153, 162, 177, 212, 218
Finnish Cadet Corps, 3, 6, 39, 53
Finnish language, 119–20
Finnish nationalism, 1, 119
Finnish Red Cross, 96–7
Finnish Scouting Association, 96
First World War, *see* World War I
Foch, Ferdinand, Marshal, 76
Forsström, Petter, 90, 104–5, 243
France, 2, 29, 46, 47, 59, 62, 73, 76, 86, 88, 121, 125, 127, 146, 147, 149–52, 165, 218, 234, 242, 246
Franco, Francisco, General, 262
French Foreign Legion, 102
Frenckell, Rafael von, 244
Frey, Alexander, 16, 34, 41
Friedrich Karl, *Prince* of Hesse-Kassel, 46,49

GALLEN-KALLELA, Akseli, 66, 84, 99
Ganéval, Jean, Lieutenant-Colonel, 150
Gaulle, Charles de, General, 102, 262
General Mannerheim's Child Welfare Association, 85, 95–6, 225
George V, *King of Great Britain*, 124
George VI, *King of Great Britain*, 124–5

INDEX

Gerich, Paul von, Major-General, 10, 97–98

Gerknäs, *see* Kirkniemi

Germany: 2, 6, 7, 9, 23, 28, 34, 46, 114, 121, 125–7, 130, 132, 146, 149, 165, 166, 227; intervention in Finland (1918), 17, 21, 26, 27–9, 32–3, 38–9, 40–1, 51; operations in Finland (1941–5), 167–76, 177–9, 184–5, 194–6, 203–4, 206, 209–13, 265

Glion, 245

Goltz, *Count* Rüdiger von der, Major-General, 29, 33, 40

Göring, Hermann, Reichsmarschall, 90,168

Gough, *Sir* Hubert, Lieutenant-General, 61–2

Granfelt, Hanna, 87

Great Britain: 29, 46, 47, 51, 54, 59, 61–2, 76, 80, 114, 121, 124–5, 127, 146, 147, 149–52, 165, 168, 184, 211, 216, 255; Foreign Office, 45, 48–50, 75, 80, 124–5, 216–17, 255

Greece, 262

Grenfell, Harold, Captain, R.N., 60

Grensholm, 43, 85, 165

Gripenberg, *Baron* Bertel, 90

Gripenberg, Georg Achates, 89, 116, 132, 135,160, 171, 178, 187, 191–3, 197, 208–9, 219, 222, 225, 227, 236, 242, 249, 251, 255, 257, 258

Gripenberg, Marguerite (Olga Sofia Margareta) (Kissi) (1882–1970) (half-sister of CGEM), 5, 241

Gripenberg, Michael (Frans Michael), Lieutenant-Colonel (1882–1941) (brother-in-law of CGEM), 5, 17, 47, 93

Grönvall, Ragnar, Major-General, 229, 240, 245

Gustav V, *King of Sweden*, 43, 54–5, 246

Gustav VI Adolf, *King of Sweden*, 111, 171

Gustavus Adolphus, *King of Sweden*, 111

HAAPAMÄKI, 14, 28, 31

Hackman, Henry, 226

Hackzell, Antti, 122, 123, 209, 210–11, 213

Hahti, Usko Sakari, Lieutenant-Colonel, 222–4

Halder, Franz, Colonel-General, 170, 174–5

Hallberg, Aimo, captain, 10

Hamina, 149

Hanell, Edvard Fritjof, Lieutenant-General, 156

Hanko, 29, 85, 132, 150, 153, 162, 165, 175, 179, 211

Hardinge of Penshurst, *Lord*, 75

Harrow, 86

Heinrichs, Erik, General, 31, 139, 148, 149, 152–3, 155, 157, 158, 162, 170, 174–5, 179, 188, 193, 194, 200, 205, 210–11, 215, 219, 222, 224, 237, 242, 244, 249, 255

Heiskanen, Juho, Major-General, 143

Helsingfors Aktiebank, 82

Helsinki, 5, 6, 11, 12, 33, 34, 35–6, 42, 43, 45, 47, 49, 50–1, 69, 70, 73, 74, 81, 83–4, 85, 92, 102, 105, 126, 137, 138, 149, 164, 168, 170, 171, 172, 174, 179, 184, 187, 189, 192, 201, 203, 209, 210, 211, 212, 215, 221, 222, 226, 233, 242, 243, 246, 253–4, 255, 260

Helsinki, University of, 67, 119, 120

Hendon Air Show, 114

Hériot, Virginie, 85, 87–8

Hietaniemi Cemetery, Helsinki, 253–4

Himalayas, 91

Hindenburg, Paul von, Field Marshal, 29,111

Hirohito, *Emperor of Japan*, 231

Hitler, Adolf, 125, 130, 169,172,174, 177–8, 190, 191, 199, 206, 209, 210, 227

Hjelt, Edvard, 28–9, 38

Holland, 255, 260

Holsti, Rudolf, 47, 57, 61, 72,74,115, 123, 124

INDEX

Horthy, Miklós, Admiral, 262
Howard, *Sir* Esmé, 44, 45, 49
Hufvudstadsbladet, newspaper, 6
Hultin, Tekla, 66, 81
Hungary, 262
Hägglund, Woldemar, Lieutenant-General, 11, 143
Häme, 23, 31
Hämeenlinna, 31, 67
Höyhenjärvi, 143

IGNATIUS, Hannes, Lieutenant-General, 8, 10, 21, 29, 52, 77, 85, 100, 107, 120
Ihantala, 204, 211
Iisalmi, 69
Ilmajoki, 13
Ilomantsi, 140, 143, 205
Imatra, 139, 204
Immola, 190
India, 88, 90–2
Ingman, Lauri, 48, 49, 53, 54, 56, 57, 64, 76–7
Ingria, 51
Inkilä, 154
Ino, 35
International Red Cross, 96–7, 189
Italy, 125, 242

JODL, Alfred, Colonel-General, 174
Journal de Genève, newspaper, 187
Julin, Albert (John Albert Edvard) von (1846–1906) (uncle of CGEM), 39
Jussila, Toivo, 189
Jyväskylä, 14, 114
Jäger Battalion, 27th Royal Prussian, 7, 9, 11, 21, 25–6, 28, 30, 31
Järnefelt, Eero, 100

KALAJA, Lauri, 192, 225–6, 233–4, 235–6, 237
Kallio, Kyösti, president, 99, 115, 127–8, 129, 133–4, 136, 151, 161, 164, 195
Kandalaksha, 170, 179

Karelia (Eastern; Russian), 38, 40, 44, 51, 54, 60–1, 80, 126, 176, 178, 181–3, 200, 201–02
Karelia (Finnish), 7, 11, 12, 13, 14, 22, 23, 27, 28, 32, 34, 36, 67, 160, 178, 181–2
Karelian isthmus, 113, 114, 130, 131–3, 139–45, 147–50, 152–3, 178, 179, 181, 185, 199, 200, 201
Karlovy Vary, *see* Karlsbad
Karlsbad, 93
Karolinska Hospital, Stockholm, 241, 246
Katmandu, 92
Kauhajoki, 30–1
Keitel, Wilhelm, Field Marshal, 174, 176, 209
Kekkonen, Urho, President, 214, 221, 228–30, 232–3, 235, 237, 254, 267
Kekoni, Heikki, Major-General, 244
Kemi, 213
Kemi Company, 186
Kennard, *Sir* Coleridge, 74–75
Kestenga, 193
Kiel, 174
Kinzel, Eberhard, Colonel, 174
Kirke, *Sir* Walter, General, 90–1, 99, 150, 258
Kirkenes, 168
Kirkniemi, 243–4
Kivimäki, T.M., 107, 117, 122, 123, 166, 230–1
Klamila, 162
Klampenborg, 94
Koivisto, 148
Kokkola, 14, 114
Kola Peninsula, 176
Kolchak, A. V., Admiral, 59, 61–3, 76–7, 125
Kollaa, 144
Kollontai, Aleksandra, 147, 198, 209
Kolosjoki, 166
Kotka, 126, 149, 204
Kouvola, 27, 204
Kristiina, 24
Kronstadt, 35

INDEX

Kukkonen, Antti, 230
Kuolemajärvi, 145
Kursk, 196
Kuusamo, 153
Kuusinen, O. W., 140
Kuuterselkä, 201
Kymi, river, 33, 35, 140, 149, 204
Könönen, Elsa, 97, 120

LADOGA, Lake, 139–40, 143, 147, 150, 175, 178, 179, 181
Lahti, 35
Lapland, 143, 169, 171, 173, 196, 210, 213, 219
Lapland War (1944–5), 213, 215, 217
Lappeenranta, 204
Lapua, 13, 104
Lapua Movement, 104–7, 108
Latvia, 80, 127
Lausanne, 93, 245, 246, 252–3
League of Nations, 62, 119, 121–2, 146
Leino, Yrjö, 221, 223–4, 232, 233, 239
Lempäälä, 31
Lenin, V. I., 38, 78, 182
Leningrad, 126, 132–3, 170, 177, 179, 185, 194, 196, 216; see also Petrograd
Lindeman, Carl Olof, Major-General, 240, 246
Linder, Ernst, General, 22, 32, 35, 36, 85, 93–4
Linder, Hjalmar, 45
Linder, Kitty (Catharina Eugénie Marguerite), 45, 66, 87
Ling, C. G., Brigadier, 150
Linkomies, Edwin, 193, 195, 197, 206–7, 208, 210, 230–1
Lohja, 243
London, 39, 43, 47–50, 73, 78, 80, 91, 92, 93, 125, 241, 255
Loppi, 226
Lotta Svärd (women's auxiliary organization), 159, 189, 217
Lovén, Hanna (Elisabet Johanna Emilia), *née* von Julin (1843–1941) (aunt of CGEM), 30, 117

Loviisa, 35
Lubomirska, *Princess* Marie, 69, 70, 88, 89
Lucknow, 91
Ludendorff, Erich, General, 29
Lugano, 192, 246, 252
Lundqvist, Jarl, Lieutenant-General, 114, 237
Lützen, 111, 112
Luumäki, 162
Lyautey, Hubert, Marshal, 102
Lyse Fjord, 45
Lähde, 139, 143, 147
Löfström, Ernst, Major-General, 13, 33–34, 99

McCLINTOCK, Robert, 192
Madras, 92
Maginot Line, 139
Mainila, 133
Malmberg, Lauri, Lieutenant-General, 98, 106
Manchester, 43
Manchuria, 4, 96
Mandelin, Erik, 95, 250
Mannerheim, *Baroness* Anastasia, *née* Arapova (1872–1936) (wife of CGEM), 3, 43, 66, 86
Mannerheim, *Baroness* Anastasie (Stasie) (1893–1978) (daughter of CGEM), 3, 43, 86, 241–2, 257
Mannerheim, *Baron* Augustin (Carl Gustaf Lars Augustin) (nephew of CGEM), 154
Mannerheim, *Count* Carl Erik Johan (1865–1915) (brother of CGEM), 3
Mannerheim, *Baron* Gustaf (Carl Gustaf Emil), Marshal of Finland (1867–1951)
  chief events of life: ancestry, 3, 255, 260; birth, 3; marriage, 3, 43; children, 3, 43–44, 86, 241–2; separation, 3; divorce, 45, 66, 86; hope of second marriage, 45, 66, 87; seventieth birthday, 116–18;

INDEX

seventy-fifth birthday, 190–1; death, 253; funeral, 253–4
principal appointments: commander-in-chief (1918), 9–41; regent (1919), 48–69; chairman of the Defence Council, 108–35; commander-in-chief (1939–44), 136–215; president (1944–6), 207–39
character and characteristics: ability, 257–8; ambition, 258–9; appearance, 5, 36, 67, 225, 255–6; bravery, 4, 32, 189; character, 3, 5, 22–3, 66, 82, 186–7, 251, 255–8, 260; charm, 66–7, 88–9, 258; commander, qualities as, 22–3, 32, 35, 137, 155–9, 186–90, 193, 200–1, 205, 264; cosmopolitanism, 94, 267; courtesy, 156; determination, 5; dignity, 67, 219; diplomatic skill, 44–5, 50, 216–17; duty, sense of, 260, 267; epicureanism, 84–85, 256; favouritism, 188; flattery, susceptibility to, 255; friendships, 85–88, 94, 240, 256–7; homes and residences, 45, 65, 83–4, 85, 89, 209, 212, 215, 216, 219, 222, 226, 229, 242–4, 256; honour, 258, 263; horses and riding, 3, 36, 89, 186, 254; Jews, attitude to: negative, 93; positive, 219; language divide in Finland, attitude to, 38–9, 101; languages, knowledge of: 255–6; English, 39; Finnish, 39, 56, 120–1; French, 39; German, 39; Russian, 39; Swedish, 119–20, 256; life, concern to spare, 193; pessimism, 81–2, 122, 247; religion, 85,183, 259–60; sarcasm, 257; social life, 66–7, 84–5, 186–7, 256–7; smoking, 89, 227, 256; speeches, 36–7, 39, 67, 111–12, 117, 118, 256; sports and pastimes, 45, 84, 89, 90–2, 255–6; staff, personal and domestic, 11, 65–66, 89, 240–1; superstition, 259; temper, 156, 188; voice, 257; women, attitude to and relations with, 66, 87–9
education, 3
finances, 3, 42, 82–3, 241, 242–3, 249
foreign relations: 17, 21, 28, 29, 32, 266; intervention in Russia, 38–9, 40–1, 44, 47, 49, 54, 56–7, 59–64, 69, 71, 74–81, 172, 179, 264; with Allies (Great Britain and France), 44–5, 47–50, 146, 147–52, 159, 184, 197, 216–17, 226–7, 248; with Germany, 17, 21, 28–31, 32, 35, 38–9, 41, 45, 130, 164, 168–76, 177–9, 184–5, 196–7, 204, 209–11, 213, 219, 265; with Sweden, 17, 21, 50, 54–5, 119, 121–4, 135, 151, 164, 209, 265; with the Soviet Union, 81, 119, 121–2, 126–7, 130, 131–3, 137–8, 149–53, 172–3, 178, 179, 196–9, 204, 207, 209–20, 227–8, 231–2, 233–7, 246–8, 264–5
health, 22, 45, 55, 92–93, 125, 157, 170–1, 191–3, 225–7, 233–4, 235–6, 237, 244–6, 252–3
honours: Order of St George, 4th Class, 4; general of cavalry, 30; Cross of Liberty, 4th class, 32; Grand Cross of the Order of the Sword, 43; doctor of philosophy, *honoris causa*, University of Helsinki, 67; honorary commander-in-chief, Defence Corps, 70; honorary colonel, Uusimaa Dragoons, 89; scouting, 96; field marshal, 100, 110–11; Knight Grand Cross of the Order of the British Empire, 124; Knight of the Mannerheim Cross, 190; marshal of Finland, 190; state funeral, 253–4
Memoirs, 241, 246, 248–52
military service: in Russia, 3–5;

INDEX

joins Military Committee, 7–9; forms headquarters, 9–10; Civil War (1918), 12–35; victory parade (1918), 35–7; resignation (1918), 40–2; appointments declined (1918–19), 40–2, 71–2; supreme command as regent (1919), 52–3, 69; failure to obtain appointments (1920s), 98–9; desire to serve in French Foreign Legion (1925), 102; chairman of the Defence Council (1931): 90, 91, 102; resignation, 127–8, 133–6; commander-in-chief: in Winter War (1939–40), 132, 136, 137–59; powers as, 138–9; during the 'Armistice' (1940–1), 160–76; powers as, 161–2; threatened resignation (February 1941), 167; in Continuation War (1941–4), 177–213
National Fund, 83, 191, 241, 243
orders of the day, 33, 69, 141, 159, 178, 181–3, 213
political activity: in 1918–19, 36–7, 44–6, 47–48, 262–3, 266; as regent, 48, 69, 266; in 1919 and 1920s, 76–7, 101; Lapua Movement, 104–07, 262–3; in 1930s, 111–13; in 1940s, 166, 195, 206–7, 266; as president, 207–39, 265–7
political opinions: 3, 4–5, 6, 17, 33, 35, 36–7, 40–41, 50–1, 56–9, 64–5, 67, 81, 90, 101, 107–8, 111–12, 117–18, 134–5, 138, 172–3, 196, 197, 198–9, 203, 206, 207–8, 212, 214–15, 220–2, 224–5, 235, 236–7, 238, 246, 247–8, 260–3, 264–6; anti-socialism and anti-communism: 3, 5, 33, 36–7, 59, 64, 76, 81, 101, 107–8, 117–18, 172–3, 214, 236, 238, 265; Red prisoners, attitude to: 19–20, 101; monarchism: 5, 37, 57–8

reputation, 20, 48, 77, 159, 267
social policy, 69–70, 85, 95–7
travel: 88, 89–94; to Sinkiang and North China (1906–8), 4, 90, 155, 250; in 1919, 73; in Europe (1920s-30s), 90, 93–4, 124; to India, Burma and Nepal, 90–92; in retirement, 242, 246, 247, 252
Mannerheim, *Baron* Johan (Carl Fridolf Johan) (1868–1934) (brother of CGEM), 16, 21, 36, 39, 40, 43, 82, 83, 85, 95, 212, 257
Mannerheim, *Baroness* Marguerite (Olga Sofia Margareta), *see* Gripenberg, Marguerite
Mannerheim, *Baroness* Palaemona (Sophia Palaemona) (Palla), *née* Treschow (1878–1948) (wife of Johan Mannerheim; sister-in-law of CGEM), 43, 85–6, 165, 186, 192, 216, 241, 257
Mannerheim, *Baroness* Sophie (Eva Charlotta Lovisa Sophie) (1863–1928) (sister of CGEM), 5, 43, 69, 76, 85, 95, 144, 257
Mannerheim, *Baroness* Sophie (Sophy) (1895–1963) (daughter of CGEM), 3, 43–4, 66, 73, 81, 86, 125, 136, 241–2, 257
Mannerheim Badge, 96
Mannerheim Cross, 189–90
Mannerheim Foundation, 243
Mannerheim Line, 139–40, 143, 145, 147, 148
Mannerheim Museum, 84
Mannerheim Sparre, *Countess* Eva Hedvig Wilhelmina Johanna, *née* Mannerheim (1870–1958) (sister of CGEM), 44, 85, 116, 222, 240, 241
Maria Fedorovna, *Empress of Russia*, 94
Marseilles, 90
Masel'ga isthmus, 181, 183, 193
Mengden, *Countess* Sofia (Sonia), *née* Arapova (sister-in-law of CGEM), 86
Metaxas, Ioannis, General, 262

INDEX

Mikkeli, 21, 34, 137, 138, 154, 179, 184, 185–6, 199, 201, 246
Milan, 246
Military Committee (Finnish), 7–10
Molotov, V. M., 133, 169, 211
Monte Carlo, 246
Montecatini, 93
Montreux, 245
Mooltan, S.S., 91
Morocco, 92, 102
Morris, Ira, 44
Moscow, 76, 130, 151, 167, 199, 209, 211, 212
Moscow, Peace of (1940), 153, 60, 61, 64
Munich, 87
Munich Agreement (September 1938), 125
Muolaanjärvi, 145
Murmansk, 54, 179
Murmansk Legion, 54, 69, 72
Murmansk railway, 149, 169, 179, 185, 194
Mäkinen, Einar, Lieutenant-General, 221
Mäntsälä revolt, 106–07
Mäntyharju, 18

NARVA, 196
Narvik, 149, 177
Nazi-Soviet Pact (August 1939), 127, 167
Nepal, 91–92
Nepal, *Maharajah of*, 92
Nice, 246
Nihtilä, Valo, Lieutenant-Colonel, 194–5, 222–4
Nikolai Nikolaevich, *Grand Duke*, of Russia, 94
Niukkanen, Juho, 115, 131, 137, 138, 152–3, 156, 157–8, 195, 235
Nobel, Emanuel, 93
Nordenskiöld, Erland, 46
Northcliffe, *Lord*, 75
Norway, 45–6, 102, 126, 150–1, 164, 165, 170, 177

Näykkijärvi, 148

ODESSA, 5
Oesch, Karl Lennart, Lieutenant-General, 137–8, 141, 149, 155, 156–7, 201
Olonets, 54, 61, 63, 179, 181–3
Olsoni, Emerik, 250
Onega, Lake, 181
Opera, Finnish, 67
Orel, 76
Orivesi, 27, 31, 32
Oslo, 54–5
Ostrobothnia, 7, 8–9, 11, 12, 13, 14, 21, 23, 24, 67, 104
Otava, 154
Otava Publishing Company, 250
Oulu, 14
Oulu, river, 210

PAASIKIVI Juho Kusti, President, 37, 122, 129, 132, 138, 159, 160, 167, 172, 196, 198, 199, 211, 212, 214, 215, 216, 218, 219–22, 224–39, 242–3, 246–8, 251, 253–4, 258–9, 265
Paasonen, Aladár, Colonel, 152, 157, 248–50
Palestine, 88
Paris, 43, 45, 48–9, 73, 76, 78, 80, 81, 86, 93, 94, 125, 152, 241
Paris, Peace of (1947), 238
Peace Conference, Paris (1919), 55, 62
Pekkala, Mauno, 221
Pétain, Philippe, Marshal, 161
Petrograd, 1, 5, 11, 12, 27, 38–9, 41, 47, 53, 54, 56, 60–4, 69, 71, 74–80; *see also* Leningrad
Petrozavodsk, 181, 231
Petsamo, 44, 60, 62, 132, 140, 143, 149, 166–7, 179, 211, 213
Petäys, Onni, 228–30, 233
Pichon, Stephen, 49
Pieksämäki, 14
Pietarsaari, 244
Pitsudski, Jozef, Marshal, 80, 262

286

INDEX

Plymouth, *Earl of*, 118, 124
Poland, 4, 59, 79–80, 81, 121, 130, 262
Pori, 31, 244
Porkkala, 211, 216, 217
Portugal, 233–4
Poventsa, 181, 189
Praia de Rocha, 234
Press, Finnish, 40, 104, 111, 113, 117, 118, 122, 136
Procopé, Hjalmar J., 87, 100
Procopé, Mary, 87
Prussia, East, 90, 190
Pulkovo, 76

RAAPPANA, Erkki, Major-General, 226
Raate, 144
Ramsay, Henrik, 85, 87,195, 203, 211, 226, 230, 243
Ramsay, Karin, 257
Rangell, J. W., 164, 174, 178, 183, 230–1
Rawalpindi, S.S., 90
Red Army, 140–9, 179, 196, 200–5
Red Cross Hospital, Helsinki, 97, 227
Red Guards, Finnish, 7, 12–13, 14, 27–8, 31–5
Red prisoners (1918), 18–20
Rehausen, Adolf von, Colonel, 10
Reinikka, Tykö, 230
Relander, Lauri Kristian, President, 99,100–1, 105, 108
Rennie, *Sir* Ernest, 100
Renvall, Heikki, 16, 25, 26, 34
Ribbentrop, Joachim von, 169, 203–4, 229
Ritavuori, Heikki, 58
Rovaniemi, 186
Runni, 69, 70
Russia
army: in Finland (1917–18), 1–2, 7, 9, 11, 12–13, 14, 18, 23, 27–8; regiments: Chevalier Guards, 3, 94
Provisional Government (1917), 2

Revolutions (1917), 1, 4–5, 6–7
Bolshevik (Soviet) government, 2, 12, 13, 27, 28, 35, 51, 59–61, 74–81; *see also* Red Army *and* Soviet Union White Russians, 38–9, 47, 51, 54, 59–63, 75–81, 262
Russian Political Conference, 76
Rybachii Peninsula, 132
Ryti, Risto, President, 112, 129, 138, 149, 150, 151, 160, 161, 164, 166, 167, 168, 170, 171, 172, 174, 176, 178, 182, 183, 185, 187, 190, 195, 197, 198, 203, 204, 206–8, 229–31

SAASTAMOINEN, Armas, 94, 109–10
Safeguard Finland Association, 101
Saimaa, Lake, 162, 190
St Petersburg, *see* Petrograd *and* Leningrad
Sairila, 186
Salla, 143, 144, 153
Salverte, *Countess* Jeanne de, 87, 91
Salzburg, 174, 175
Satakunta, 22, 23
Savo, 23, 27, 28, 67
Savonenkov, G. M., Lieutenant-General, 215, 236
Savonlinna, 14
Sazonov, S. D., 78–79
Schauman, Georg, 37, 48
Schildts, publishers, 250
Schnurre, Karl, 174
Second World War, *see* World War II
Seidel, Hans Georg von, General, 174
Seinäjoki, 13, 21, 26
Seoni, 91
Shebeko, N. N., 79
Shepherd, Francis, 216–17, 218, 226–7
Siberia, 76
Sihvo, Aarne, General, 11, 34, 35, 99, 106, 110, 237
Siilasvuo, Hjalmar, Lieutenant-General, 143, 144, 213
Sikkim, 91

287

INDEX

Sivén, V. O., 40
Soininen, Mikael, 56
Sotkamo, 210
Soviet-Finnish Friendship Society, 165
Soviet-Finnish War, 1939–40, *see* Winter War
Soviet-Finnish War, 1941–4, *see* Continuation War
Soviet Union, 112, 113, 121–4, 125–7, 130, 131–3, 136, 137–53, 163, 164–6, 169–71, 173, 174, 176, 177–81, 184–5, 193, 196–205, 206–7, 209–20, 222, 227–8, 231–7, 238–9, 264–5, 267; *see also* Red Army *and* Russia: Bolshevik (Soviet) government
Spain, 150, 234, 262
Sparre, *Countess* Eva, *see* Mannerheim Sparre, *Countess* Eva
Sparre, *Count* Louis Per (1863–1964) (brother-in-law of CGEM), 92
Spears, *Sir* Edward Louis, Major-General, 79
Stalin, J. V., 130, 145, 147, 165, 198, 210
Stalingrad, 196
State Aircraft Factory (Finnish), 114
State Artillery Factory (Finnish), 114
Stavanger, 45
Stenroth, Otto, 47
Stockholm, 14, 17, 42, 43–6, 47, 50, 54–5, 73, 93, 125, 129, 147, 171, 196, 197, 198, 203, 209, 241, 242, 244, 245, 246, 247, 252, 253
Stockholm Plan (1939), 123–4
Ståhlberg, Ester, 88–9, 95–6
Ståhlberg, Kaarlo Juho, President, 56, 58, 59, 68–9, 71, 76, 97, 98, 99, 106, 108, 115, 117, 219
Sudan, 88
Summa, 139, 143, 147
Sunila, Juho, 100
Suojärvi, 143
Suomussalmi, 143, 144
Suursaari, 126, 149, 212, 213
Svartz, Nanna, 245, 246, 250, 253, 257

Svechnikov, M. S., Colonel, 28
Svinhufvud, Pehr Evind, President, 2, 8–9, 12–13, 29, 34, 40, 42, 48, 83, 98, 105–8, 109, 115, 166
Svir, river, 178, 179, 181, 193
Sweden, 2, 9, 13, 14, 17, 21, 34, 42, 50, 51, 54–5, 73, 74, 119, 121–4, 126–7, 129–30, 132, 135, 144, 146, 147, 149, 150–1, 164, 165, 170–1, 186, 192, 198, 204, 209, 210, 213, 216, 240, 244–5, 253, 265
Swedish language, in Finland, 6, 119–20
Swedish volunteers, in Finland, 21–2, 30, 31, 43, 144
Switzerland, 43, 88, 93, 192, 242, 245, 246, 249, 252, 253
Söderblom, Nathan, 56

TAIPALE, 143, 145, 199–200
Tali, 148, 204
Tallinn, 33, 34
Talvela, Paavo, General, 108, 122, 137, 143, 144, 163, 164, 168, 170, 188, 191–2, 194, 200
Tamminiemi, 209, 212, 215, 216, 219, 222, 226
Tampere, 9, 14, 19–20, 23, 27, 28, 30, 31–3, 39, 67, 101, 114
Tanner, Väinö, 115, 117–18, 129, 132, 137, 138, 149, 150, 153, 154, 157, 164, 166, 184, 196, 198, 199, 203, 206–7, 209, 210, 211, 230, 231,265
Tapola, Kustaa Anders, Lieutenant-General, 141
Tartu, Peace of (1920), 81
Tegnér, Esias, 67
'Terijoki government', 140–1, 147
Thesleff, Wilhelm, Major-General, 25, 32, 40
Theslöf, Gösta, Major-General, 22
Thiébaut, Eugène, 44
Times, The, newspaper, 75
Tolvajärvi, 143
Tornio, 14, 66, 213
Treaty of Friendship, Cooperation and

INDEX

Mutual Assistance (Soviet-Finnish, 1948), 218, 247
Trepov, A. F., 47
Truman, Harry S., 248
Tübingen, 246
Tula, 76
Tuompo, W. E., Lieutenant-General, 179, 188, 189, 200, 205
Turku, 42, 50, 81, 225
Tuulosjoki, river, 179
Tyrol, 90
Törngren, Gösta (Gustaf Mauritz), Major-General, 22, 29

ULRICEHAMN, 170
Union Bank, 82
United States of America, 29, 47, 59, 130, 146, 151, 184, 185, 192, 196–7, 198, 204, 231, 247, 248
USSR, see Soviet Union
Uusi Suomi, newspaper, 128

VAASA, 9, 12, 13, 28, 34
Val-Mont Clinic, 245, 246, 249–50, 252–3
Valkeasaari, 201
Valve, Väinö, Lieutenant-General, 221
Vammelsuu, 141, 199
Veltjens, Joseph, Lieutenant-Colonel, 168, 229
Venice, 91
Vennola, J. H., 71, 108
Vereker, Gordon, 151, 172
Veterans' organizations (Finnish), 163, 217
Vichy, 93
Vienna, 45
Viipuri, 11, 33, 34–5, 67, 140, 145, 148, 149, 153, 156, 179, 198, 201, 204
Viipuri, Gulf of, 149, 152
Vilkuna, Kustaa, 121, 229
Vilppula, 14, 22, 28
Virojoki, 204
Voionmaa, Väinö, 118
Vuoksi, river, 14, 139, 148, 204
Vuosalmi, 148, 149

Vöyri, 25

WAFFEN-SS, Finnish battalion, 173
Walden, Anni, 241
Walden, Rudolf, General, 49, 57, 61, 71, 85, 105, 107, 120, 137, 138, 151, 154, 157, 160–1, 164, 167, 168, 170, 187, 195–6, 206–8, 209, 210–11, 212, 214, 221, 229, 241, 242
Wallenberg, Jacob, 88
Wallenberg, Marcus, 88
Wallenius, Kurt Martti, Major-General, 107
Warsaw, 4, 45, 79–81, 84, 88
Weckman, Evo (Eva Sofia Helena), née Mannerheim (niece of CGEM), 212
Wetzer, Martin, General, 10, 22, 31, 33
White Rose, Order of the, 55
Wilhelm II, German Emperor, 29, 39
Wilkman, afterwards Vilkama, Karl Fredrik, General, 34, 98–99
Winter War (1939–40): 136, 137–59, 161, 167, 173, 182, 260, 264; diplomatic aspects: 138, 147, 149–53; military operations, 139–46, 147–9, 152–3
Witting, Rolf, 160, 164, 168, 176, 184, 195
World War I, 1, 4, 46, 69, 88, 141, 157, 262
World War II, 130, 178, 263
Wuolijoki, Wäinö, 111
Wuori, Eero, 214

YARTSEV, Boris, 125–6
Ylihärmä, 13
Ylistaro, 13
Ylppö, Arvo, 95
Yudenich, N. N., General, 62–3, 76–8, 80

ZHDANOV, A. A., Colonel-General, 212, 215, 218, 222, 231, 233–4, 236, 239, 247, 265
Zürich, 192

INDEX

ÅLAND ISLANDS, 17, 28, 29, 50, 54–5, 119, 121, 123–4, 125, 126–7, 129, 165, 175

ÄYRÄPÄÄJÄRVI, 148

ÖHQUIST, Harald, Lieutenant-General, 138, 141, 143, 145, 147, 153, 156, 195

Österman, Hugo, Lieutenant-General, 108, 110, 133–4, 139, 141, 143, 145, 147–8, 157, 158